Roswell D. Hitchcock

Hymns and Songs for Social and Sabbath Worship

Roswell D. Hitchcock

Hymns and Songs for Social and Sabbath Worship

ISBN/EAN: 9783337286194

Printed in Europe, USA, Canada, Australia, Japan

Cover: Foto ©Lupo / pixelio.de

More available books at **www.hansebooks.com**

HYMNS AND SONGS,

FOR

SOCIAL AND SABBATH WORSHIP,

May be had direct of the Publishers, or may be ordered of

W. G. HOLMES,
                79 Madison Street Chicago.

M. H. SARGENT,
                Congregational House, Beacon Street, Boston.

FOR

SOCIAL AND SABBATH WORSHIP.

EDITED BY

ROSWELL D. HITCHCOCK, ZACHARY EDDY,
PHILIP SCHAFF.

NEW YORK:
ANSON D. F. RANDOLPH & COMPANY,
770 BROADWAY.

Entered according to Act of Congress in the year 1875, by
ANSON D. F. RANDOLPH & COMPANY,
In the Office of the Librarian of Congress, at Washington, D. C.

Electrotyped by
SMITH & McDOUGAL,
82 & 84 Beekman St.,
NEW YORK.

Printed by
EDWARD O. JENKINS,
20 North William St.,
NEW YORK.

Bound by
ROBERT RUTTER,
82 & 84 Beekman St.,
NEW YORK.

PREFACE

THIS Book is not a mere abridgment of HYMNS AND SONGS OF PRAISE. It omits a great deal; but it also contains a considerable amount of material not found in the larger collection. As in that Book, so in this, along with much that is fresh and new, most of the Hymns, and most of the Tunes, are the old favorites. Our aim has been, first of all, to meet the requirements of social worship. What may be called Prayer-meeting Hymns are the most prominent. But we have had also in mind the many Sabbath congregations which, for one reason or another, have been wanting a smaller book. Provision has accordingly been made for all the ordinary occasions of Church life.

In abridging Hymns, which we have chosen to do rather than reduce their number, great pains have been taken not to mutilate them. The text is commonly that of the authors themselves. The alterations adopted are such as have been advisedly made, and almost universally approved. In any case, each Hymn is so edited as to tell its own story. The dates in parentheses, which are never repeated at the same opening, are of the author's birth and death, if ascertained. The date that follows is either of composition (if certainly known), or of publication. A second or third date indicates revision by the author himself.

The musical adaptations have been carefully studied. Many of them are simply traditional, and consequently beyond, if not always above, debate. Some had to be nicely weighed in the balance with rival candidates; and some, it is hoped, will be thought none the less of for being new.

Thanks are due to Messrs. BIGLOW & MAIN for the use of their large musical library; also to Mr. HUBERT P. MAIN for valuable assistance in editing both Hymns and Tunes. But we are under special obligations to the Rev. LEWIS W. MUDGE, who has made several of the Indexes, and read all the proof; whose varied experience, good judgment, and rare critical acumen have been of great service to us.

ROSWELL D. HITCHCOCK,
ZACHARY EDDY,
PHILIP SCHAFF.

NEW YORK, April 15, 1875.

CONTENTS.

	HYMNS.	PAGES.
PREFACE		iii
OPENING CHANT		vi
OPENING AND CLOSING OF SERVICE	1— 74	1— 32
SABBATH PRAISE	75—125	33— 55
GOD'S WORD	126—134	56— 59
THE GREAT SALVATION	135—146	59— 63
CHRIST	147—223	64— 99
SALVATION OFFERED	224—257	100—115
SALVATION SOUGHT AND FOUND	258—345	116—155
PILGRIM SONGS	346—405	156—183
CHRISTIAN LIFE	406—483	184—217
BAPTISM	484—489	218, 219
CONFESSION OF FAITH	490—494	220, 221
LORD'S SUPPER	495—505	222—225
COMMUNION OF SAINTS	506—516	226—231
CHURCH DEDICATION	517—521	232, 233
FOR THOSE AT SEA	522—525	234, 235
THE KINGDOM OF GOD	526—555	236—247
CHRISTIAN WORK	556—580	248—257
LIFE AND DEATH	581—603	258—267
CHRIST'S COMING	604—611	268—271
HEAVEN	612—636	272—285
TIMES AND SEASONS	637—660	286—296
DOXOLOGIES		297, 298
CHANTS		299—317
ALPHABETICAL INDEX OF TUNES		318, 319
METRICAL INDEX OF TUNES		320, 321
INDEX OF SCRIPTURE TEXTS		322—324
INDEX OF SUBJECTS		325—339
INDEX OF FIRST LINES		340—347
INDEX TO CHANTS		348
INDEX OF AUTHORS		349—351
INDEX OF COMPOSERS		352, 353

OPENING CHANT.

OUR FATHER. Thomas Tallis. (c. 1529—1585.) 1575.

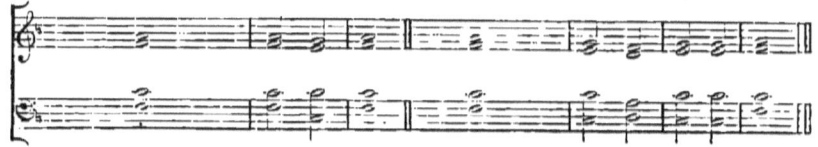

The Lord's Prayer.
Matt. vi. 9—13.

OUR Father, who | art in | heaven, || Hallowed | be — | Thy — | name.

Thy | kingdom | come. || Thy will be done on earth, | as it | is in | heaven.

Give us this day our | daily | bread. || And forgive us our debts, as | we for- | give our | debtors.

And lead us not | into temp- | tation, || But de- | liver | us from | evil:

For Thine is the kingdom, and the | power, and the | glory, || For- | ever. | A — | men.

HYMNS AND SONGS.

INVOCATION.

ITALIAN HYMN. 6, 4.   Felice Giardini. (1716—1796.) 1760.

1. Come, Thou al-might-y King, Help us Thy Name to sing, Help us to praise: Father all-glo-rious, O'er all vic-to-rious, Come, and reign over us, Ancient of days.

I   *The Trinity invoked.*

2 Jesus, our Lord, arise;
    Scatter our enemies,
      And make them fall:
    Let Thine almighty aid
    Our sure defence be made;
    Our souls on Thee be stayed;
      Lord, hear our call.

3 Come, Thou Incarnate Word,
    Gird on Thy mighty sword,
      Our prayer attend:
    Come, and Thy people bless,
    And give Thy Word success;
    Spirit of holiness,
      On us descend.

4 Come, Holy Comforter,
    Thy sacred witness bear
      In this glad hour:
    Thou who Almighty art,
    Now rule in every heart,
    And ne'er from us depart,
      Spirit of power.

5 To the great One and Three
    Eternal praises be
      Hence, evermore.
    His sovereign majesty
    May we in glory see,
    And to eternity
      Love and adore.
      Rev. Charles Wesley. (1708—1788.) 1757.

OPENING OF SERVICE.

MESSIAH. 7. D. Louis Joseph Ferdinand Herold. (1791—1833.) 1830.
Arr. by George Kingsley. (1811—) 1838.

1. Holy, holy, holy Lord God of Hosts! When heaven and earth, Out of darkness, at Thy word, Is-sued in-to glorious birth, All Thy works before Thee stood, And Thine eye beheld them good, While they sang with sweet accord, Ho-ly, ho-ly, ho-ly Lord!

2 *Thrice Holy.*
Is. vi. 3.

2 Holy, holy, holy! Thee,
One Jehovah evermore,
Father, Son, and Spirit, we,
Dust and ashes, would adore ;
Lightly by the world esteemed,
From that world by Thee redeemed,
Sing we here, with glad accord,
Holy, holy, holy Lord!

3 Holy, holy, holy! All
Heaven's triumphant choir shall sing,
When the ransomed nations fall
At the footstool of their King:
Then shall saints and seraphim,
Hearts and voices, swell one hymn,
Round the throne with full accord,
Holy, holy, holy Lord!
James Montgomery. (1771—1854.) 1836, 1853.

3 *The Song of the Ransomed.*
Rev. v. 13.

1 See the ransomed millions stand,
Palms of conquest in their hand ;
This before the throne their strain,
"Hell is vanquished, death is slain ;
Blessing, honor, glory, might,
Are the Conqueror's native right ;
Thrones and powers before Him fall.
Lamb of God, and Lord of all !"

2 Hasten, Lord, the promised hour ;
Come in glory and in power ;
Still Thy foes are unsubdued ;
Nature sighs to be renewed.
Time has nearly reached its sum ;
All things, with Thy bride, say "Come ;"
Jesus, whom all worlds adore,
Come, and reign for evermore.
Josiah Conder. (1789—1855.) 1836.

OPENING OF SERVICE. 3

HARWELL. 8, 7. D.   Lowell Mason. (1792—1872.) 1840.

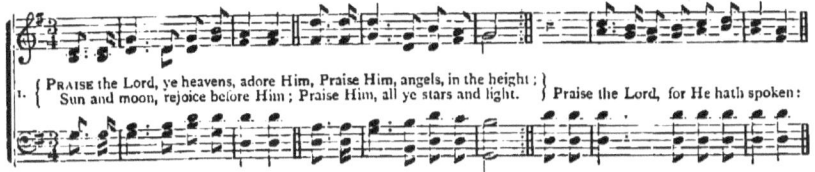

1. Praise the Lord, ye heavens, adore Him, Praise Him, angels, in the height;
Sun and moon, rejoice before Him; Praise Him, all ye stars and light.
Praise the Lord, for He hath spoken:

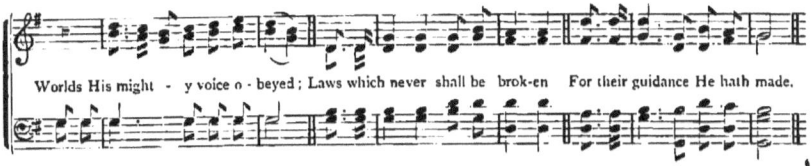

Worlds His might - y voice o - beyed; Laws which never shall be brok-en For their guidance He hath made.

4
Praise from the whole Creation.
Ps. cxlviii.

2 Praise the Lord, for He is glorious;
Never shall His promise fail;
God hath made His saints victorious;
Sin and death shall not prevail.
Praise the God of our salvation;
Hosts on high, His power proclaim;
Heaven and earth, and all creation,
Laud and magnify His name.

3 Worship, honor, glory, blessing,
Lord, we offer unto Thee;
Young and old, Thy praise confessing,
In glad homage bend the knee.
As the saints in heaven adore Thee,
We would bow before Thy throne;
As Thine angels serve before Thee,
So on earth Thy will be done.
Rev. John Kempthorne. (1775—1838.) 1809. vs. 1, 2.
Edward Osler. (1798—1863.) 1836. v. 3, alt.

5
Thrice Holy.
Is. vi. 1—3. John xii. 41.

1 ROUND the Lord in glory seated
Cherubim and seraphim

Filled His temple, and repeated
Each to each th' alternate hymn.
" Lord, Thy glory fills the heaven,
" Earth is with its fulness stored;
" Unto Thee be glory given,
" Holy, holy, holy Lord!"

2 Heaven is still with glory ringing;
Earth takes up the angels' cry,
" Holy, holy, holy," singing,
" Lord of Hosts, the Lord most High."
With His seraph train before Him,
With His holy Church below,
Thus conspire we to adore Him,
Bid we thus our anthem flow:

3 "Lord, Thy glory fills the heaven,
Earth is with its fulness stored:
Unto Thee be glory given,
Holy, holy, holy Lord!"
Thus Thy glorious name confessing,
We adopt the angels' cry,
Holy, holy, holy! blessing
Thee the Lord of Hosts most High.
Bp. Richard Mant. (1776—1848.) 1837. ab.

OPENING OF SERVICE.

DARWELL. H. M.   Rev. John Darwell. c. 1750.

1. I GIVE im-mor-tal praise To God the Fa-ther's love, For all my com-forts here, And bet-ter hopes a-bove; He sent His own E-ter-nal Son To die for sins That man had done.

6   *Praise to the Trinity.*

2 To God the Son belongs
    Immortal glory too ;
Who bought us with His blood
    From everlasting woe :
And now He lives, and now He reigns,
And sees the fruit of all His pains.

3 To God the Spirit's name
    Immortal worship give,
Whose new-creating power
    Makes the dead sinner live ;
His work completes the great design,
And fills the soul with joy divine.

4 Almighty God, to Thee
    Be endless honors done,
The undivided Three,
    And the mysterious One :
Where reason fails, with all her powers,
There faith prevails, and love adores.
        Rev. Isaac Watts. (1674—1748.) 1709.

7   *Praise to the Trinity.*

1 To Him that chose us first,
    Before the world began ;
To Him that bore the curse
    To save rebellious man ;
To Him that formed our hearts anew,
Is endless praise and glory due.

2 The Father's love shall run
    Through our immortal songs ;
We bring to God the Son
    Hosannas on our tongues :
Our lips address the Spirit's name
With equal praise and zeal the same.

3 Let every saint above,
    And angels round the throne,
Forever bless and love
    The Sacred Three in One :
Thus heaven shall raise His honors high,
When earth and time grow old and die.
        Rev. Isaac Watts. 1709.

OPENING OF SERVICE. 5

NICAEA. 11, 12, 12, 10. Rev. John Bacchus Dykes. 1861.

1. Ho-ly, ho-ly, ho-ly, Lord God Al-might-y! Ear-ly in the morn-ing our song shall rise to Thee; Ho-ly, ho-ly, ho-ly! Mer-ci-ful and Might-y! God in Three Per-sons, Bless-èd Trin-i-ty!

8

"*Which was, and is, and is to come.*"
Rev. iv. 8.

2 Holy, holy, holy! all the saints adore Thee,
    Casting down their golden crowns around the glassy sea;
    Cherubim and seraphim falling down before Thee,
    Which wert, and art, and evermore shalt be.

3 Holy, holy, holy! though the darkness hide Thee,
    Though the eye of sinful man Thy glory may not see,
    Only Thou art holy, there is none beside Thee,
    Perfect in power, in love, and purity.

4 Holy, holy, holy! Lord God Almighty!
    All Thy works shall praise Thy Name, in earth, and sky, and sea;
    Holy, holy, holy! Lord God Almighty!
    God in Three Persons, Blessèd Trinity!

Bp. Reginald Heber. (1783—1826.) 1827.

OPENING OF SERVICE.

ERNAN. L. M.   Lowell Mason. (1792—1872.) 1850.

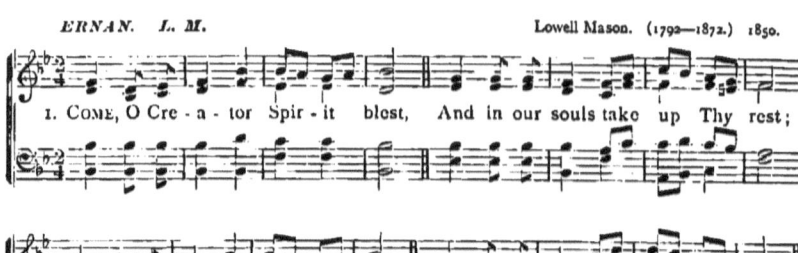

1. Come, O Cre-a-tor Spir-it blest, And in our souls take up Thy rest;

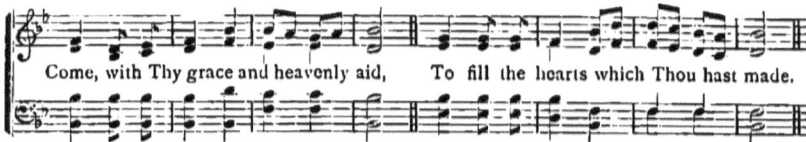

Come, with Thy grace and heavenly aid, To fill the hearts which Thou hast made.

9   *"Veni, Creator Spiritus."*

2 Great Comforter, to Thee we cry;
O highest gift of God most high,
O Fount of life, O Fire of love,
And sweet anointing from above!

3 Kindle our senses from above,
And make our hearts o'erflow with love;
With patience firm, and virtue high,
And weakness of our flesh supply.

4 Far from us drive the foe we dread,
And grant us Thy true peace instead;
So shall we not, with Thee for guide,
Turn from the path of life aside.
    Unknown Author of the 7th or 8th Century.
Tr. by Rev. Edward Caswall. (1814—) 1849. ab. and alt.

10   *The Operations of the Spirit.*

1 Eternal Spirit, we confess
And sing the wonders of Thy grace;
Thy power conveys our blessings down
From God the Father and the Son.

2 Enlightened by Thy heavenly ray,
Our shades and darkness turn to day;
Thine inward teachings make us know
Our danger and our refuge too.

3 Thy power and glory work within,
And break the chains of reigning sin;
Do our imperious lusts subdue,
And form our wretched hearts anew.

4 The troubled conscience knows Thy voice;
Thy cheering words awake our joys;
Thy words allay the stormy wind,
And calm the surges of the mind.
    Rev. Isaac Watts. (1674—1748.) 1709.

11   *"Where two or three."*
    Matt. xviii. 20.

1 "Where two or three, with sweet accord,
Obedient to their sovereign Lord,
Meet to recount His acts of grace,
And offer solemn prayer and praise;

2 "There," says the Saviour, "will I be,
Amid this little company;
To them unveil My smiling face,
And shed My glories round the place."

3 We meet at Thy command, dear Lord,
Relying on Thy faithful word:
Now send Thy Spirit from above,
Now fill our hearts with heavenly love.
    Rev. Samuel Stennett. (1727—1795.) 1778.

OPENING AND CLOSING OF SERVICE. 7

ROCKINGHAM. L. M.   Lowell Mason. 1832.

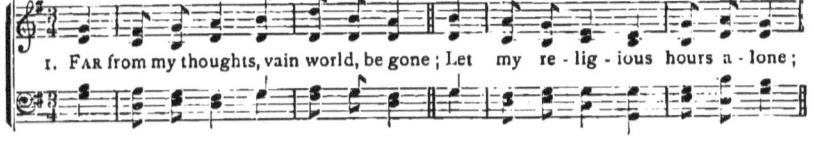

1. Far from my thoughts, vain world, be gone; Let my re-lig-ious hours a-lone;

Fain would mine eyes my Sav-iour see: I wait a vis-it, Lord, from Thee.

12   *Delight in Worship.*

2 My heart grows warm with holy fire,
And kindles with a pure desire;
Come, my dear Jesus, from above,
And feed my soul with heavenly love.

3 Blest Jesus, what delicious fare,
How sweet Thine entertainments are:
Never did angels taste above
Redeeming grace, and dying love.

4 Hail, great Immanuel, all-divine,
In Thee Thy Father's glories shine:
Thou brightest, sweetest, fairest One,
That eyes have seen, or angels known.
                 Rev. Isaac Watts. 1709. ab.

13   "*Jam lucis orto sidere.*"

1 While now the daylight fills the sky,
We lift our hearts to God on high,
That He, in all we do or say,
Would keep us free from harm to-day.

2 So when the daylight leaves the sky,
And night's dark hours once more are nigh,
May we, unsoiled by sinful stain,
Sing glory to our God again.
        Ambrose of Milan. (340—397.)
Tr. by Rev. John Mason Neale. (1818—1866.) ab. and alt.

14   *Christ always near His People.*

1 Jesus, where'er Thy people meet,
There they behold Thy mercy-seat;
Where'er they seek Thee, Thou art found,
And every place is hallowed ground.

2 For Thou, within no walls confined,
Inhabitest the humble mind;
Such ever bring Thee where they come,
And going, take Thee to their home.

3 Dear Shepherd of Thy chosen few,
Thy former mercies here renew;
Here to our waiting hearts proclaim
The sweetness of Thy saving name.

4 Here may we prove the power of prayer
To strengthen faith, and sweeten care,
To teach our faint desires to rise,
And bring all heaven before our eyes.

5 Lord, we are few, but Thou art near;
Nor short Thine arm, nor deaf Thine ear: [down,
O rend the heavens, come quickly
And make a thousand hearts Thine own.
           William Cowper. (1731—1800.) 1769. ab.

OPENING OF SERVICE.

OLMUTZ. S. M. Adapted by Lowell Mason. (1792—1872.) 1825.

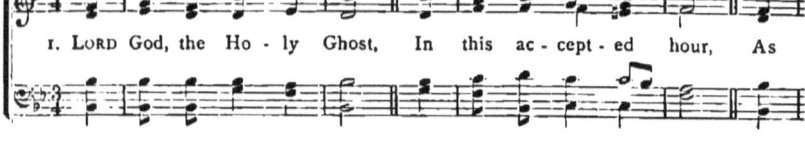

1. Lord God, the Ho-ly Ghost, In this ac-cept-ed hour,

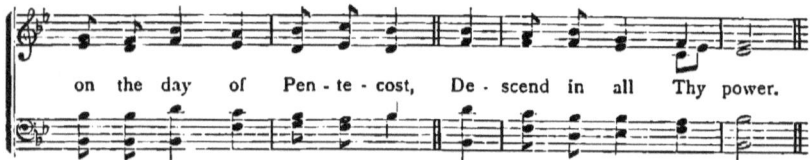

As on the day of Pen-te-cost, De-scend in all Thy power.

15 *The Descent of the Spirit.*

2 We meet with one accord
  In our appointed place,
And wait the promise of our Lord,
  The Spirit of all grace.

3 Like mighty rushing wind
  Upon the waves beneath,
Move with one impulse every mind,
  One soul, one feeling breathe.

4 The young, the old inspire
  With wisdom from above;
And give us hearts and tongues of fire
  To pray, and praise, and love.

5 Spirit of light, explore,
  And chase our gloom away,
With lustre shining more and more
  Unto the perfect day.

6 Spirit of truth, be Thou,
  In life and death, our guide;
O Spirit of adoption, now
  May we be sanctified.
        James Montgomery. (1771—1854.) 1819, 1825.

16 *To the Holy Spirit.*

1 Come, Holy Spirit, come,
  Let Thy bright beams arise,
Dispel the darkness from our minds,
  And open all our eyes.

2 Revive our drooping faith,
  Our doubts and fears remove,
And kindle in our breasts the flame
  Of never-dying love.

3 Convince us of our sin,
  Then lead to Jesus' blood,
And to our wondering view reveal
  The secret love of God.

4 Show us that loving Man
  That rules the courts of bliss,
The Lord of Hosts, the Mighty God,
  The Eternal Prince of Peace.

5 'Tis Thine to cleanse the heart,
  To sanctify the soul,
To pour fresh life in every part,
  And new-create the whole.
        Rev. Joseph Hart. (1712—1768.) 1759. ab.

OPENING AND CLOSING OF SERVICE.

MORNINGTON. S. M. — Lord Garret Wellesley Mornington. (1720—1781.) 1760. Arr. by Lowell Mason. 1822.

1. Be-hold the throne of grace! The prom-ise calls me near;
There Je-sus shows a smil-ing face, And waits to an-swer prayer.

17 *"Ask what thou wilt."* 1 Kings iii, 5.

2 That rich atoning blood,
Which sprinkled round I see,
Provides for those who come to God
An all-prevailing plea.

3 My soul, ask what thou wilt,
Thou canst not be too bold;
Since His own blood for thee He spilt,
What else can He withhold?

4 Thine image, Lord, bestow,
Thy presence and Thy love;
I ask to serve Thee here below,
And reign with Thee above.

5 Teach me to live by faith,
Conform my will to Thine,
Let me victorious be in death,
And then in glory shine.
Rev. John Newton. (1725—1807.) 1779. ab.

18 *"Thy work revive."*

1 O Lord, Thy work revive,
In Zion's gloomy hour,
And make her dying graces live
By Thy restoring power.

2 O let Thy chosen few
Awake to earnest prayer;
Their covenant again renew,
And walk in filial fear.

3 Thy Spirit then will speak
Through lips of humble clay,
Till hearts of adamant shall break,
Till rebels shall obey.

4 Now lend Thy gracious ear;
Now listen to our cry;
O come and bring salvation near;
Our souls on Thee rely.
Mrs. Phœbe Hinsdale Brown. (1783—1861.) 1819.

19 *Parting Hymn.*

1 O happy, happy place,
Where saints and angels meet:
There shall we see each others' face,
And all our brethren greet.

2 The Church of the first-born,
We shall with them be blest;
And, crowned with endless joy, return
To our eternal rest.
Rev. Charles Wesley. (1708—1788.) 1749. ab.

OPENING OF SERVICE.

AUTUMN. 8, 7. D. — Spanish Melody. From Marechio.

1. FA-THER, Thine E-lect who lov-est With an ev-er-last-ing love;
Sav-iour, who the bar re-mov-est From the ho-ly home a-bove;
D.S. List to Thy glad peo-ple sing-ing, "Ho-ly, ho-ly, ho-ly Lord!"
Spir-it, dai-ly meet-ness bring-ing For the glo-ry there up-stored;

20 "*Holy, holy, holy Lord.*"

2 Lord, with sin-bound souls Thou bearest,
Struggling towards this strain divine;
Glad on mortal lips Thou hearest
That thrice awful name of Thine.
But Thou listenest, O how sweetly!
When from holy lips outpoured,
Rings through heaven this strain full meetly,
"Holy, holy, holy Lord!" [

3 Shall we, Lord, meet voices never
Bring to that eternal hymn?
Hallow us to help the endeavor
Of Thy pure-lipped Seraphim:
Hark! their own high strain we bring Thee,
Listen to the full accord! [
Sweet the song we ever sing Thee,
"Holy, holy, holy Lord!"
Thomas Hornblower Gill. (1819—) 1860. ab.

21 *Praise on Earth and in Heaven.*
Rev. iv. 11.

1 PRAISE to Thee, Thou great Creator,
Praise be Thine from every tongue;
Join, my soul, with every creature,
Join the universal song.
Father, Source of all compassion,
Pure unbounded grace is Thine;
Hail the God of our salvation,
Praise Him for His love divine.

2 For ten thousand blessings given,
For the richest gifts bestowed,
Sound His praise through earth and heaven,
Sound Jehovah's praise aloud.
Joyfully on earth adore Him,
Till in heaven our song we raise;
There, enraptured fall before Him,
Lost in wonder, love, and praise.
Rev. John Fawcett. (1739—1817.) 1767. alt.

OPENING AND CLOSING OF SERVICE.

22 *"Lead us."*

1 GENTLY, Lord, O gently lead us,
Pilgrims in this vale of tears,
Through the trials yet decreed us,
Till our last great change appears.
When temptation's darts assail us,
When in devious paths we stray,
Let Thy goodness never fail us,
Lead us in Thy perfect way.

2 In the hour of pain and anguish,
In the hour when death draws near,
Suffer not our hearts to languish,
Suffer not our souls to fear;
And, when mortal life is ended,
Bid us in Thine arms to rest,
Till, by angel bands attended,
We awake among the blest.
Thomas Hastings. (1784—1872.) 1830, 1850, 1859.

ITALIAN HYMN. 6, 4.   Felice Giardini. (1716—1796.) 1760.

1. Shepherd of tender youth, Guiding in love... and truth Through devious ways; Christ, our triumphant King, We come Thy name to sing; Hither our children bring To shout Thy praise.

23 Στόμιον πώλων ἀδαῶν.

2 Thou art our Holy Lord,
The all-subduing Word,
Healer of strife :
Thou didst Thyself abase,
That from sin's deep disgrace
Thou mightest save our race,
And give us life.

3 Thou art the great High Priest,
Thou hast prepared the feast
Of heavenly love;
While in our mortal pain
None calls on Thee in vain ;
Help Thou dost not disdain,
Help from above.

4 Ever be Thou our Guide,
Our Shepherd and our Pride,
Our Staff and Song :
Jesus, Thou Christ of God,
By Thy perennial Word
Lead us where Thou hast trod,
Make our faith strong.

5 So now, and till we die,
Sound we Thy praises high,
And joyful sing :
Infants, and the glad throng
Who to Thy Church belong,
Unite to swell the song
To Christ our King.
From Clement of Alexandria. (—220.)
Tr. by Rev. Henry Martyn Dexter. (1821—) 1846, 1849

OPENING AND CLOSING OF SERVICE.

HURSLEY. L. M.
Francis Joseph Haydn. (1732—1809.) 1798.
Arr. by William Henry Monk. 1861.

1. Come, Holy Spirit, heavenly Dove, My sinful maladies remove; Be Thou my Light, be Thou my Guide, O'er every thought and step preside.

24 *Prayer for Light and Guidance.*

2 The light of truth to me display,
That I may know and choose my way;
Plant holy fear within my heart,
That I from God may ne'er depart.

3 Conduct me safe, conduct me far
From every sin and hurtful snare;
Lead me to God, my final Rest,
In His enjoyment to be blest.

4 Lead me to Christ, the Living Way,
Nor let me from His pastures stray;
Lead me to heaven, the seat of bliss,
Where pleasure in perfection is.

5 Lead me to holiness, the road
That I must take to dwell with God;
Lead to Thy Word, that rules must give,
And sure directions how to live.
Rev. Simon Browne. (1680—1732.) 1720. ab.

25 *Teachings of the Spirit.*

1 Come, blesséd Spirit, Source of light,
Whose power and grace are unconfined,
Dispel the gloomy shades of night,
The thicker darkness of the mind.

2 To mine illumined eyes display
The glorious truths Thy word reveals;
Cause me to run the heavenly way;
The book unfold, and loose the seals.

3 Thine inward teachings make me know
The mysteries of redeeming love,
The vanity of things below,
And excellence of things above.

4 While through this dubious maze I stray, [abroad,
Spread, like the sun, Thy beams
To show the dangers of the way,
And guide my feeble steps to God.
Rev. Benjamin Beddome. (1717—1795.) 1818.

26 *Thanks for the Gospel.*

1 Let everlasting glories crown
Thy head, my Saviour, and my Lord:
Thy hands have brought salvation down,
And writ the blessings in Thy word.

2 In vain the trembling conscience seeks
Some solid ground to rest upon;
With long despair the spirit breaks,
Till we apply to Christ alone.

OPENING AND CLOSING OF SERVICE. 13

3 How well Thy blessèd truths agree,
  How wise and holy Thy commands;
  Thy promises, how firm they be,
  How firm our hope and comfort stands!

4 Should all the forms that men devise
  Assault my faith with treacherous art,
  I'd call them vanity and lies,
  And bind the Gospel to my heart.

Isaac Watts. (1674—1748.) 1709. ab.

ERNAN. L. M.   Lowell Mason. (1792—1872.) 1850.

1. How blest the sa-cred tie that binds, In union sweet, ac-cord-ing minds;
   How swift the heavenly course they run, Whose hearts, whose faith, whose hopes are one!

27   *Christian Fellowship.*

2 To each the soul of each how dear,
  What jealous love, what holy fear!
  How doth the generous flame within
  Refine from earth, and cleanse from sin!

3 Their streaming eyes together flow
  For human guilt and mortal woe;
  Their ardent prayers together rise,
  Like mingling flames in sacrifice.

4 Together oft they seek the place
  Where God reveals His awful face;
  How high, how strong, their raptures swell,
  There's none but kindred souls can tell.

5 Nor shall the glowing flame expire,
  When nature droops her sickening fire;
  Then shall they meet in realms above,
  A heaven of joy, a heaven of love.

Mrs. Anna Lætitia Barbauld. (1743—1825.) 1795. sl. alt.

28   *The Christian Farewell.*
        2 Cor. xiii. 11.

1 THY presence, everlasting God,
  Wide o'er all nature spreads abroad;
  Thy watchful eyes, which cannot sleep,
  In every place Thy children keep.

2 While near each other we remain,
  Thou dost our lives and souls sustain;
  When absent, Thou dost make us share
  Thy smiles, Thy counsels, and Thy care.

3 To Thee we all our ways commit,
  And seek our comforts at Thy feet;
  Still on our souls vouchsafe to shine,
  And guard and guide us still as Thine.

4 Give us, O Lord, within Thy house
  Again to pay our thankful vows;
  Or if that joy no more be known.
  O let us meet around Thy throne.

Rev. Philip Doddridge. (1702—1751.) 1755. alt.

OPENING AND CLOSING OF SERVICE.

RETREAT. L. M. Thomas Hastings. (1784—1872.) 1840.

1. From ev-ery storm-y wind that blows, From ev-ery swell-ing tide of woes, There is a calm, a sure re-treat: 'Tis found be-neath the mer-cy-seat.

29 *The Mercy-Seat.*

2 There is a place where Jesus sheds
  The oil of gladness on our heads;
  A place than all besides more sweet:
  It is the blood-bought mercy-seat.

3 There is a spot where spirits blend,
  Where friend holds fellowship with friend; [meet
  Though sundered far, by faith they
  Around one common mercy-seat.

4 There, there, on eagle wings we soar,
  And time and sense seem all no more;
  And heaven comes down our souls to greet,
  And glory crowns the mercy-seat.

5 O may my hand forget her skill,
  My tongue be silent, cold, and still,
  This bounding heart forget to beat,
  If I forget the mercy-seat.
  Rev. Hugh Stowell. (1799—1865.) 1832. ab.

30 *"O quam juvat fratres, Deus."*

1 O Lord, how joyful 'tis to see
  The brethren join in love to Thee:
  On Thee alone their heart relies;
  Their only strength Thy grace supplies.

2 How sweet, within Thy holy place,
  With one accord to sing Thy grace,
  Besieging Thine attentive ear
  With all the force of fervent prayer.

3 The world without may rage, but we
  Will only cling more close to Thee,
  With hearts to Thee more wholly given,
  More weaned from earth, more fixed on heaven.

4 Lord, shower upon us from above
  The sacred gift of mutual love;
  Each other's wants may we supply,
  And reign together in the sky.
  Santolius Victorinus. (1630—1697.) 1736.
Tr. by Rev. John Chandler. (1806—) 1837.

31 *Retirement and Meditation.*
Titus ii. 12.

1 My God, permit me not to be
  A stranger to myself and Thee;
  Amidst a thousand thoughts I rove,
  Forgetful of my highest Love.

2 Why should my passions mix with earth,
  And thus debase my heavenly birth?
  Why should I cleave to things below,
  And let my God, my Saviour, go?

OPENING AND CLOSING OF SERVICE. 15

3 Call me away from flesh and sense,
One sovereign word can draw me thence.
I would obey the voice divine,
And all inferior joys resign.

4 Be earth, with all her scenes, withdrawn;
Let noise and vanity be gone;
In secret silence of the mind
My heaven, and there my God, I find.
Rev. Isaac Watts. (1674—1748.) 1709.

32 *Prayer for Rest in God.*
Tune—HURSLEY, p. 12.

1 COME, Holy Spirit, calm my mind,
And fit me to approach my God;
Remove each vain, each worldly thought,
And lead me to Thy blest abode.

2 Hast Thou imparted to my soul
A living spark of heavenly fire?
O kindle now the sacred flame;
Teach it to burn with pure desire.

3 A brighter faith and hope impart,
And let me now the Saviour see:
O soothe and cheer my burdened heart,
And bid my Spirit rest in Thee.
Rev. Henry Forster Burder's Coll. 1826.

ROSEFIELD. 7. 6 l.  Rev. Cæsar Henri Abraham Malan. (1787—1864.) 1830.

1. { BLESS-ED are the sons of God; They are bought with Christ's own blood;
   They are ransomed from the grave; Life e - ter - nal they shall have: }

With them numbered may we be, Here, and in e - ter - ni - ty.

33 *"Numbered with God's Sons."*

2 God did love them in His Son,
Long before the world begun;
All their sins are washed away;
They shall stand in God's great day:
With them numbered may we be,
Here, and in eternity.

3 They are lights upon the earth,
Children of a heavenly birth,
One with God, with Jesus one;
Glory is in them begun:
With them numbered may we be,
Here, and in eternity.
Rev. Joseph Humphreys. (1720—) 1743. ab.

OPENING OF SERVICE.

ALETTA. 7.   William Batchelder Bradbury. (1816—1868.) 1858.

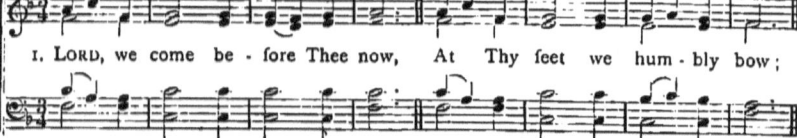

1. Lord, we come before Thee now, At Thy feet we humbly bow;

O do not our suit disdain; Shall we seek Thee, Lord, in vain?

34   *"Ye shall seek Me, and find Me."*
                  Jer. xxix. 13.

2 Lord, on Thee our souls depend,
In compassion, now descend ;
Fill our hearts with Thy rich grace,
Tune our lips to sing Thy praise.

3 In Thine own appointed way,
Now we seek Thee, here we stay :
Lord, we know not how to go,
Till a blessing Thou bestow.

4 Send some message from Thy word,
That may joy and peace afford ;
Let Thy Spirit now impart
Full salvation to each heart.

5 Comfort those who weep and mourn,
Let the time of joy return ;
Those that are cast down lift up,
Strong in faith, in love, and hope.
         Rev. William Hammond. (—1783.) 1745. ab.

35   *"Ask what I shall give thee."*
                1 Kings iii. 5.

1 Come, my soul, thy suit prepare,
Jesus loves to answer prayer ;
He Himself has bid thee pray,
Therefore will not say thee nay.

2 Thou art coming to a King,
Large petitions with thee bring ;
For His grace and power are such,
None can ever ask too much.

3 With my burden I begin,
Lord, remove this load of sin ;
Let Thy blood, for sinners spilt,
Set my conscience free from guilt.

4 Lord, I come to Thee for rest,
Take possession of my breast ;
There Thy blood-bought right maintain,
And without a rival reign.

5 While I am a pilgrim here,
Let Thy love my spirit cheer ;
As my Guide, my Guard, my Friend,
Lead me to my journey's end.

6 Show me what I have to do,
Every hour my strength renew ;
Let me live a life of faith,
Let me die Thy people's death.
         Rev. John Newton. (1725—1807.) 1779. ab.

OPENING AND CLOSING OF SERVICE. 17

PLEYEL'S HYMN. 7. Ignace Pleyel. (1757—1831.) 1800.

1. Soft-ly now the light of day Fades up-on my sight a-way;
Free from care, from la-bor free, Lord, I would com-mune with Thee.

36 *The fading Light.*

2 Thou, whose all-pervading eye
Naught escapes, without, within,
Pardon each infirmity,
Open fault, and secret sin.

3 Soon, for me, the light of day
Shall forever pass away;
Then, from sin and sorrow free,
Take me, Lord, to dwell with Thee.

4 Thou who, sinless, yet hast known
All of man's infirmity;
Then, from Thine eternal throne,
Jesus, look with pitying eye.
Bp. George Washington Doane. (1799—1859.) 1824.

37 *Sabbath Evening.*

1 For the mercies of the day
For this rest upon our way,
Thanks to Thee alone be given,
Lord of earth and King of Heaven.

2 Cold our services have been,
Mingled every prayer with sin;

But Thou canst and wilt forgive:
By Thy grace alone we live.

3 Whilst this thorny path we tread,
May Thy love our footsteps lead;
When our journey here is past,
May we rest with Thee at last.

4 Let these earthly Sabbaths prove
Foretastes of our joys above;
While their steps Thy pilgrims bend
To the rest which knows no end.
Unknown. Rev. Baptist Wriothesley Noel's Selection.
1832. ab.

38 *"Part in Peace."*

1 Part in peace, Christ's life was peace,
Let us live our life in Him:
Part in peace, Christ's death was peace;
Let us die our death in Him.

2 Part in peace, Christ promise gave
Of a life beyond the grave,
Where all mortal partings cease:
Brethren, sisters, part in peace.
Mrs. Sarah Flower Adams. (1805—1848.) 1841. alt.

OPENING OF SERVICE.

SWEET HOUR OF PRAYER. L. M. D. William Batchelder Bradbury. (1816—1868.) 1859.

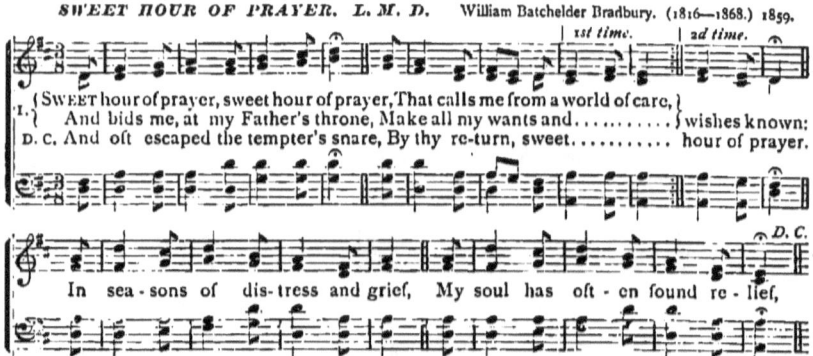

1. { Sweet hour of prayer, sweet hour of prayer, That calls me from a world of care, }
   { And bids me, at my Father's throne, Make all my wants and .... } wishes known:
   D. C. And oft escaped the tempter's snare, By thy re-turn, sweet .... hour of prayer.

In sea-sons of dis-tress and grief, My soul has oft-en found re-lief,

---

39 *"Sweet Hour of Prayer."*

2 Sweet hour of prayer, sweet hour of prayer,
Thy wings shall my petition bear
To Him, whose truth and faithfulness
Engage the waiting soul to bless:
And since He bids me seek His face,
Believe His word, and trust His grace,
I'll cast on Him my every care,
And wait for thee, sweet hour of prayer.

3 Sweet hour of prayer, sweet hour of prayer,
May I thy consolation share,
Till, from Mount Pisgah's lofty height,
I view my home, and take my flight:
This robe of flesh I'll drop, and rise,
To seize the everlasting prize;
And shout, while passing through the air,
Farewell, farewell, sweet hour of prayer.
Rev. W. W. Walford. 1846.

40 *Evening Prayer for Healing.*
Mark i. 32.

1 At even, ere the sun was set,
The sick, O Lord, around Thee lay;
O in what divers pains they met,
O with what joy they went away.

Once more 'tis eventide, and we,
Oppressed with various ills, draw near:
What if Thy form we cannot see?
We know and feel that Thou art here.

2 O Saviour Christ, our woes dispel,
For some are sick, and some are sad,
And some have never loved Thee well,
And some have lost the love they had;
And none, O Lord, have perfect rest,
For none are wholly free from sin;
And they who fain would serve Thee best,
Are conscious most of wrong within.

3 O Saviour Christ, Thou too art Man;
Thou hast been troubled, tempted, tried;
Thy kind but searching glance can scan
The very wounds that shame would hide;
Thy touch has still its ancient power,
No word from Thee can fruitless fall;
Hear in this solemn evening hour,
And in Thy mercy heal us all.
Rev. Henry Twells. (1823—) 1868. ab.

OPENING AND CLOSING OF SERVICE.

FOREST. L. M.   Aaron Chapin. 1813.

1. What va-rious hin-dran-ces we meet, In com-ing to a mer-cy-seat! Yet who that knows the worth of prayer, But wish-es to be oft-en there?

41   *Exhortation to Prayer.*
     Col. iv. 2.

2 Prayer makes the darkened cloud
withdraw,
Prayer climbs the ladder Jacob saw,
Gives exercise to faith and love,
Brings every blessing from above.

3 Restraining prayer, we cease to fight;
Prayer makes the Christian's armor
bright;
And Satan trembles when he sees
The weakest saint upon his knees.

4 Have you no words? Ah, think again,
Words flow apace when you complain,
And fill your fellow-creature's ear
With the sad tale of all your care.

5 Were half the breath thus vainly spent,
To heaven in supplication sent,
Our cheerful song would oftener be,
" Hear what the Lord has done for me."
     William Cowper. (1731—1800.) 1779. ab.

42   *The Love of God shed abroad in the Heart.*
     Eph. iii. 16.

1 Come, dearest Lord, descend and dwell,
By faith and love, in every breast;
Then shall we know, and taste, and
feel,
The joys that cannot be expressed.

2 Come, fill our hearts with inward
strength;
Make our enlarged souls possess,
And learn the height and breadth and
length
Of Thine unmeasurable grace.

3 Now to the God whose power can do
More than our thoughts or wishes know,
Be everlasting honors done,
By all the Church, through Christ, His
Son.
     Rev. Isaac Watts. (1674—1748.) 1709.

43   *Dismission.*

1 Dismiss us with Thy blessing, Lord;
Help us to feed upon Thy word;
All that has been amiss, forgive,
And let Thy truth within us live.

2 Though we are guilty, Thou art good;
Wash all our works in Jesus' blood;
Give every burdened soul release,
And bid us all depart in peace.

3 Praise God, from whom all blessings
flow,
Praise Him, all creatures here below;
Praise Him above, ye heavenly host;
Praise Father, Son, and Holy Ghost.
     Rev. Joseph Hart. (1712—1768.) 1762. vs. 1, 2.
     Bp. Thomas Ken. (1637—1711.) 1697. v. 3.

THE COMFORTER INVOKED.

NEW HAVEN. 6, 4.   Thomas Hastings. (1784—1872.) 1833.

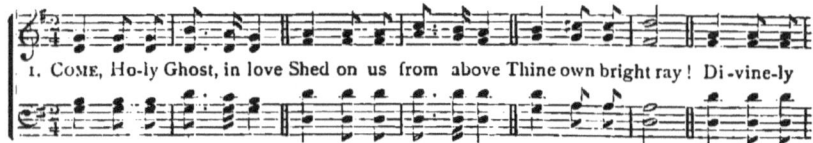

1. Come, Ho-ly Ghost, in love Shed on us from above Thine own bright ray! Di-vine-ly

good Thou art; Thy sa-cred gifts impart To gladden each sad heart: O come to-day!

44   *"Veni, Sancte Spiritus."*

2 Come, tenderest Friend, and best,
Our most delightful guest,
   With soothing power:
Rest, which the weary know,
Shade, 'mid the noontide glow,
Peace, when deep griefs o'erflow,
   Cheer us, this hour!

3 Come, Light serene, and still
Our inmost bosoms fill;
   Dwell in each breast;
We know no dawn but Thine;
Send forth Thy beams divine,
On our dark souls to shine,
   And make us blest!

4 Come, all the faithful bless;
Let all who Christ confess,
   His praise employ:
Give virtue's rich reward;
Victorious death accord,
And, with our glorious Lord,
   Eternal joy!

         Robert II, King of France. (972—1031.)
         Tr. by Rev. Ray Palmer. (1808—) 1858.

45   *Evening Prayer.*

1 Father of love and power,
Guard Thou our evening hour,
   Shield with Thy might:
For all Thy care this day
Our grateful thanks we pay,
And to our Father pray,
   Bless us to-night.

2 Jesus Immanuel,
Come in Thy love to dwell
   In hearts contrite:
For many sins we grieve,
But we Thy grace receive,
And in Thy word believe;
   Bless us to-night.

3 Spirit of truth and love,
Life-giving, holy Dove,
   Shed forth Thy light:
Heal every sinner's smart,
Still every throbbing heart,
And Thine own peace impart;
   Bless us to-night.

        George Rawson. (1807—) 1853.

THE COMFORTER INVOKED.

DALLAS. 7. From Maria Luigi Cherubini. (1760—1842.)

1. Gra-cious Spir-it, Dove Di-vine, Let Thy light with-in me shine;
All my guilt-y fears re-move, Fill me full of heaven and love.

46 *Prayer for Peace and Rest.*

2 Speak Thy pardoning grace to me,
Set the burdened sinner free,
Lead me to the Lamb of God,
Wash me in His precious blood.

3 Life and peace to me impart,
Seal salvation on my heart,
Breathe Thyself into my breast,
Earnest of immortal rest.

4 Let me never from Thee stray,
Keep me in the narrow way,
Fill my soul with joy divine,
Keep me, Lord, forever Thine.

John Stocker. 1776. ab.

47 *Light, Power, Joy.*

1 Holy Ghost, with light divine,
Shine upon this heart of mine;
Chase the shades of night away,
Turn the darkness into day.

2 Holy Ghost, with power divine,
Cleanse this guilty heart of mine;
Long has sin, without control,
Held dominion o'er my soul.

3 Holy Ghost, with joy divine,
Cheer this saddened heart of mine;

Bid my many woes depart,
Heal my wounded, bleeding heart.

4 Holy Spirit, all Divine,
Dwell within this heart of mine,
Cast down every idol-throne;
Reign supreme, and reign alone.

Rev. Andrew Reed. (1787—1862.) 1843. ab.

48 *"Granted is the Saviour's Prayer."*

1 Granted is the Saviour's prayer,
Sent the gracious Comforter,
Promise of our parting Lord,
Jesus, to His heaven restored.

2 God, the everlasting God,
Makes with mortals His abode;
Whom the heavens cannot contain,
He vouchsafes to dwell in man.

3 Come, divine and peaceful Guest,
Enter our devoted breast:
Holy Ghost, our hearts inspire,
Kindle there the gospel fire.

4 Crown the agonizing strife,
Principle and Lord of life:
Life divine in us renew,
Thou the Gift and Giver too!

Rev. Charles Wesley. (1708—1788.) 1739. ab.

OPENING HYMNS.

BYEFIELD. C. M. — Thomas Hastings. (1784—1872.) 1840.

1. Prayer is the soul's sincere desire,
Uttered or unexpressed,
The motion of a hidden fire
That trembles in the breast.

49 *Prayer.*

2 Prayer is the burden of a sigh,
The falling of a tear,
The upward glancing of an eye,
When none but God is near.

3 Prayer is the simplest form of speech
That infant lips can try;
Prayer the sublimest strains that reach
The Majesty on high.

4 Prayer is the contrite sinner's voice
Returning from his ways,
While angels in their songs rejoice,
And cry, " Behold he prays ! "

5 Prayer is the Christian's vital breath,
The Christian's native air,
His watchword at the gates of death;
He enters heaven with prayer.

6 O Thou, by whom we come to God,
The Life, the Truth, the Way,
The path of prayer Thyself hast trod;
Lord, teach us how to pray.
James Montgomery. (1771—1854.) 1819, 1853. ab.

50 *The witnessing and sealing Spirit.*

1 Why should the children of a King
Go mourning all their days?
Great Comforter, descend and bring
Some tokens of Thy grace.

2 Dost Thou not dwell in all the saints,
And seal the heirs of heaven?
When wilt Thou banish my complaints
And show my sins forgiven?

3 Assure my conscience of her part
In the Redeemer's blood;
And bear Thy witness with my heart,
That I am born of God.

4 Thou art the earnest of His love,
The pledge of joys to come;
And Thy soft wings, celestial Dove,
Will safe convey me home.
Rev. Isaac Watts. (1674—1748.) 1709.

51 *"Far from the world."*

1 Far from the world, O Lord, I flee,
From strife and tumult far;
From scenes where Satan wages still
His most successful war.

2 The calm retreat, the silent shade,
With prayer and praise agree,
And seem by Thy sweet bounty made
For those who follow Thee.

3 There, if Thy Spirit touch the soul,
   And grace her mean abode,
   O with what peace, and joy, and love,
   She communes with her God!
4 There, like the nightingale, she pours
   Her solitary lays;
   Nor asks a witness of her song,
   Nor thirsts for human praise.
5 Author, and Guardian of my life,
   Sweet Source of love Divine,
   And, all harmonious names in one,
   My Saviour, Thou art mine!
   William Cowper. (1731—1800.) 1793. ab.

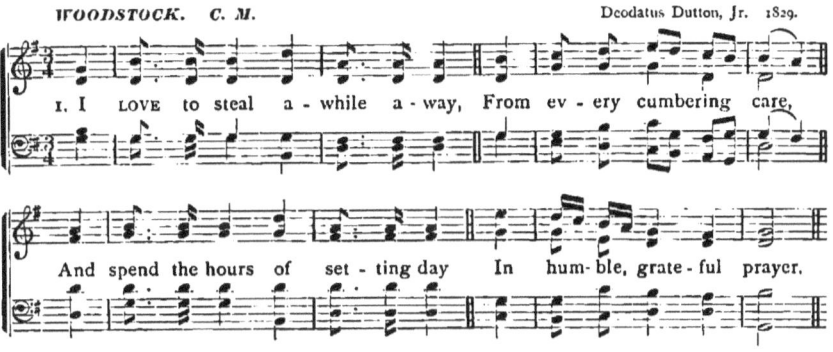

WOODSTOCK. C. M.   Deodatus Dutton, Jr. 1829.

1. I LOVE to steal a-while a-way, From ev-ery cumbering care, And spend the hours of set-ting day In hum-ble, grate-ful prayer.

52 *Evening Twilight.*

2 I love, in solitude, to shed
   The penitential tear;
   And all His promises to plead
   Where none but God can hear.

3 I love to think on mercies past,
   And future good implore;
   And all my cares and sorrows cast
   On Him whom I adore.

4 I love, by faith, to take a view
   Of brighter scenes in heaven;
   The prospect doth my strength renew,
   While here by tempests driven.

5 Thus, when life's toilsome day is o'er,
   May its departing ray
   Be calm as this impressive hour,
   And lead to endless day.
   Mrs. Phœbe Hinsdale Brown. (1783—1861.) 1824.

53 *The Spirit's Influences desired.*
Acts x. 44.

1 GREAT Father of each perfect gift,
   Behold Thy servants wait;
   With longing eyes and lifted hands,
   We flock around Thy gate.

2 O shed abroad that royal gift,
   Thy Spirit from above,
   To bless our eyes with sacred light,
   And fire our hearts with love.

3 Blest Earnest of eternal joy,
   Declare our sins forgiven;
   And bear, with energy divine,
   Our raptured thoughts to heaven.

4 Diffuse, O God, those copious showers,
   That earth its fruit may yield,
   And change the barren wilderness
   To Carmel's flowery field.
   Rev. Philip Doddridge. (1702—1751.) 1755. ab.

OPENING AND CLOSING HYMNS.

ADRIAN. S. M.   John Edgar Gould. (1822—) 1846.

1. Be-hold, the morn-ing sun Be-gins his glo-rious way;
His beams through all the na-tions run, And life and light con-vey.

54 *For a Lord's Day Morning.*
Ps. xix.

2 But where the Gospel comes,
It spreads diviner light;
It calls dead sinners from their tombs,
And gives the blind their sight.

3 How perfect is Thy word,
And all Thy judgments just;
For ever sure Thy promise, Lord,
And men securely trust.

4 My gracious God, how plain
Are Thy directions given:
O may I never read in vain,
But find the path to heaven.
    Rev. Isaac Watts. (1674—1748.) 1719. ab.

55 *"The Day-star from on high."*

1 We lift our hearts to Thee,
Thou Day-star from on high;
The sun itself is but Thy shade,
Yet cheers both earth and sky.

2 O let Thy rising beams
Dispel the shades of night;
And let the glories of Thy love
Come like the morning light.

3 How beauteous nature now,
How dark and sad before:

With joy we view the pleasing change,
And nature's God adore.

4 May we this life improve
To mourn for errors past;
And live, this short, revolving day,
As if it were our last.
    Rev. John Wesley? (1703—1791.) 1741. ab. and alt.

56 *The Sweetness of the Sabbath.*
Ps. xcii.

1 Sweet is the work, O Lord,
Thy glorious acts to sing,
To praise Thy name, and hear Thy
And grateful offerings bring. [word,

2 Sweet, at the dawning light,
Thy boundless love to tell;
And, when approach the shades of
Still on the theme to dwell. [night,

3 Sweet, on this day of rest,
To join in heart and voice
With those who love and serve Thee
And in Thy name rejoice. [best,

4 To songs of praise and joy,
Be every Sabbath given,
That such may be our blest employ
Eternally in heaven.
    Miss Harriet Auber. (1773—1862.) 1829. alt.

OPENING AND CLOSING HYMNS. 25

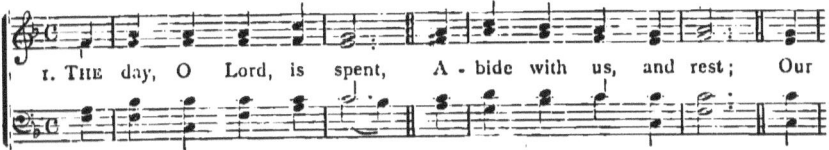

57 *"The Day is far spent."* Luke xxiv. 29.

2 We have not reached that land,
   That happy land, as yet,
Where holy angels round Thee stand,
   Whose sun can never set.

3 Our sun is sinking now,
   Our day is almost o'er;
O Sun of Righteousness, do Thou
   Shine on us evermore.
   Rev. John Mason Neale. (1818—1866.) 1854.

58 *The Worship that never ceases.*

1 OUR day of praise is done;
   The evening shadows fall;
Yet pass not from us with the sun,
   True Light that lightenest all.

2 Around the throne on high
   Where night can never be,
The white-robed harpers of the sky
   Bring ceaseless hymns to Thee.

3 Too faint our anthems here;
   Too soon of praise we tire;
But, O the strains, how full and clear,
   Of that eternal choir.

4 Yet, Lord, to Thy dear will
   If Thou attune the heart,
We in Thine angels' music still
   May bear our lower part.

5 'Tis Thine each soul to calm,
   Each wayward thought reclaim,
And make our daily life a psalm
   Of glory to Thy name.

6 A little while, and then
   Shall come the glorious end;
And songs of angels and of men
   In perfect praise shall blend.
   Rev. John Ellerton. (1826—) 1867.

59 *Praise to God from all Nations.* Ps. cxvii.

1 THY name, Almighty Lord,
   Shall sound through distant lands;
Great is Thy grace, and sure Thy word;
   Thy truth forever stands.

2 Far be Thine honor spread,
   And long Thy praise endure,
Till morning light and evening shade
   Shall be exchanged no more.
   Rev. Isaac Watts. 1719.

OPENING AND CLOSING HYMNS.

EVENING HYMN. L. M.   Thomas Tallis. (—1585.) c. 1567.

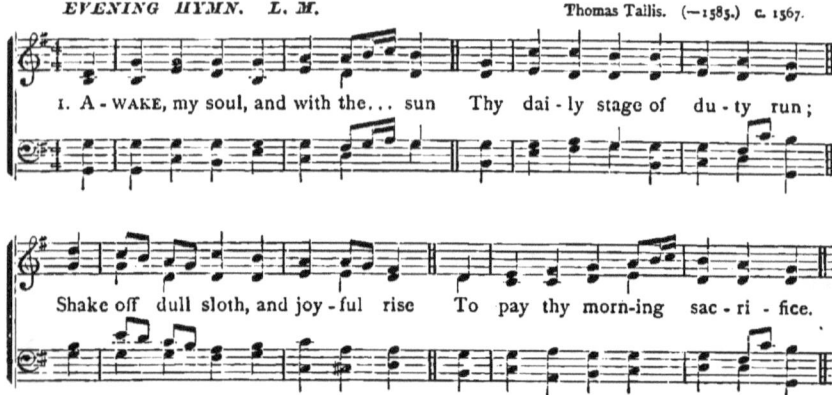

1. A-WAKE, my soul, and with the... sun Thy dai-ly stage of du-ty run; Shake off dull sloth, and joy-ful rise To pay thy morn-ing sac-ri-fice.

60   *A Morning Hymn.*

2 Wake, and lift up thyself, my heart,
And with the angels bear thy part,
Who, all night long, unwearied sing
High praise to the eternal King.

3 All praise to Thee who safe hast kept,
And hast refreshed me whilst I slept;
Grant, Lord, when I from death shall
I may of endless life partake. [wake,

4 Lord, I my vows to Thee renew;
Disperse my sins as morning dew;
Guide my first springs of thought and
And with Thyself my spirit fill. [will,

5 Direct, control, suggest this day,
All I design, or do, or say;
That all my powers, with all their might,
In Thy sole glory may unite.
    Bp. Thomas Ken. (1637—1711.) 1697, 1709. ab.

61   *An Evening Hymn.*

1 ALL praise to Thee, my God, this night,
For all the blessings of the light :
Keep me, O keep me, King of kings,
Beneath Thine own almighty wings.

2 Forgive me, Lord, for Thy dear Son,
The ill that I this day have done ;
That with the world, myself, and Thee,
I, ere I sleep, at peace may be.

3 Teach me to live, that I may dread
The grave as little as my bed ;
To die, that this vile body may
Rise glorious at the awful day.

4 O may my soul on Thee repose,
And may sweet sleep my eyelids close;
Sleep, that shall me more vigorous
   make,
To serve my God when I awake.

5 When in the night I sleepless lie,
My soul with heavenly thoughts supply,
Let no ill dreams disturb my rest,
No powers of darkness me molest.

6 Praise God, from whom all blessings
   flow ;
Praise Him, all creatures here below;
Praise Him above, ye heavenly host ;
Praise Father, Son, and Holy Ghost.
    Bp. Thomas Ken. 1697, 1709. ab.

CLOSING HYMNS. 27

NURSLEY. L. M.
Francis Joseph Haydn. (1732—1809.) 1798.
Arr. by William Henry Monk. 1861.

1. Sun of my soul, Thou Saviour dear,
   It is not night if Thou be near:
   O may no earth-born cloud arise
   To hide Thee from Thy servant's eyes.

62 *"Abide with us."* Luke xxiv. 29.

2 When the soft dews of kindly sleep
  My wearied eyelids gently steep,
  Be my last thought, how sweet to rest
  Forever on my Saviour's breast.

3 Abide with me from morn till eve,
  For without Thee I cannot live;
  Abide with me when night is nigh,
  For without Thee I dare not die.

4 If some poor wandering child of Thine
  Have spurned, to-day, the voice divine;
  Now, Lord, the gracious work begin;
  Let him no more lie down in sin.

5 Watch by the sick; enrich the poor
  With blessings from Thy boundless store;
  Be every mourner's sleep to-night,
  Like infant's slumbers, pure and light.

6 Come near and bless us when we wake,
  Ere through the world our way we take;
  Till, in the ocean of Thy love,
  We lose ourselves in heaven above.

  Rev. John Keble. (1792—1866.) 1827. ab.

63 *An Evening Hymn.* Ps. iv.

1 Thus far the Lord has led me on,
  Thus far His power prolongs my days;
  And every evening shall make known
  Some fresh memorial of His grace.

2 Much of my time has run to waste,
  And I perhaps am near my home;
  But He forgives my follies past,
  And gives me strength for days to come.

3 I lay my body down to sleep;
  Peace is the pillow for my head,
  While well-appointed angels keep
  Their watchful stations round my bed.

4 Faith in His name forbids my fear;
  O may Thy presence ne'er depart;
  And, in the morning, make me hear
  The love and kindness of Thy heart.

5 Thus, when the night of death shall come,
  My flesh shall rest beneath the ground;
  And wait Thy voice to rouse my tomb,
  With sweet salvation in the sound.

  Rev. Isaac Watts. (1674—1748.) 1709. ab.

CLOSING HYMNS.

STOCKWELL. 8. 7.   Rev. Darius Eliot Jones. (1815–) 1848.

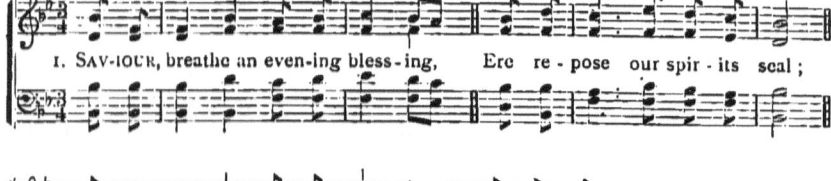

1. Saviour, breathe an evening blessing, Ere repose our spirits seal;

Sin and want we come confessing, Thou canst save, and Thou canst heal.

64   *Evening Blessing.*

2 Though destruction walk around us,
    Though the arrow past us fly,
Angel-guards from Thee surround us,
    We are safe, if Thou art nigh.

3 Though the night be dark and dreary,
    Darkness cannot hide from Thee;
Thou art He who, never weary,
    Watchest where Thy people be.

4 Should swift death this night o'ertake us,
    And our couch become our tomb,
May the morn in heaven awake us,
    Clad in light and deathless bloom.
             James Edmeston. (1791–1867.) 1820.

65   *Evening Shadows.*

1 Tarry with me, O my Saviour,
    For the day is passing by;
See, the shades of evening gather,
    And the night is drawing nigh.

2 Deeper, deeper grow the shadows,
    Paler now the glowing west;
Swift the night of death advances;
    Shall it be the night of rest?

3 Feeble, trembling, fainting, dying,
    Lord, I cast myself on Thee;
Tarry with me through the darkness;
    While I sleep, still watch by me.

4 Tarry with me, O my Saviour;
    Lay my head upon Thy breast
Till the morning, then awake me,—
    Morning of eternal rest.
          Mrs. Caroline Sprague Smith. 1855. ab.

66   *An Evening Prayer.*

1 Hear my prayer, O heavenly Father,
    Ere I lay me down to sleep:
Bid Thine angels, pure and holy,
    Round my bed their vigil keep.

2 Great my sins are, but Thy mercy
    Far outweighs them every one;
Down before Thy cross I cast them,
    Trusting in Thy help alone.

3 Pardon all my past transgressions;
    Give me strength for days to come;
Guide and guard me with Thy blessing,
    Till Thine angels bid me home.
          Miss Harriet Parr. 1856. ab. and sl. alt.

CLOSING HYMNS.

VESPERS. 8, 7. Arr. from Friedrich von Flotow. (1812—)

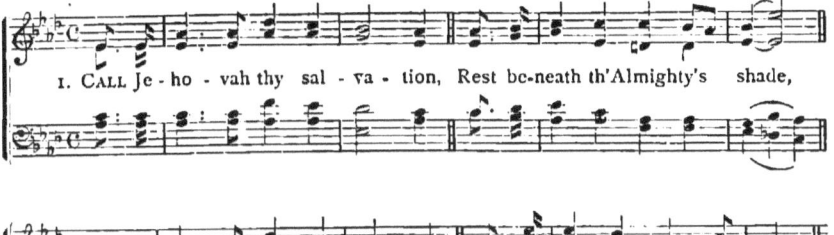

1. Call Je-ho-vah thy sal-va-tion, Rest be-neath th'Almighty's shade,

In His se-cret hab-i-ta-tion Dwell, and nev-er be dis-mayed.

67 *Safety in God.*
Ps. xci.

2 There no tumult can alarm thee,
  Thou shalt dread no hidden snare;
  Guile nor violence can harm thee,
  In eternal safeguard there.

3 From the sword, at noonday wasting,
  From the noisome pestilence,
  In the depth of midnight, blasting,
  God shall be thy sure defence.

4 God shall charge His angel legions
  Watch and ward o'er thee to keep;
  Though thou walk through hostile regions,
  Though in desert wilds thou sleep.

5 Since, with pure and firm affection,
  Thou on God hast set thy love,
  With the wings of His protection
  He will shield thee from above.

6 Thou shalt call on Him in trouble,
  He will hearken, He will save;
  Here for grief reward thee double,
  Crown with life beyond the grave.
  James Montgomery. (1771—1854.) 1822. ab.

68 *Our Need of God.*
Ps. cxxvii.

1 Vainly through night's weary hours,
  Keep we watch, lest foes alarm;
  Vain our bulwarks, and our towers,
  But for God's protecting arm.

2 Vain were all our toil and labor,
  Did not God that labor bless;
  Vain, without His grace and favor,
  Every talent we possess.

3 Vainer still the hope of heaven,
  That on human strength relies;
  But to him shall help be given,
  Who in humble faith applies.

4 Seek we, then, the Lord's Anointed;
  He will grant us peace and rest;
  Ne'er was suppliant disappointed,
  Who through Christ his prayer addressed.
  Miss Harriet Auber. (1773—1862.) 1829.

EVENING WORSHIP.

HALLE. 7. 6 l. From Francis Joseph Haydn. (1732—1809.) 1798.

1. FA-THER, by Thy love and power, Comes a-gain the eve-ning hour;
   Light has van-ished, la-bors cease, Wea-ry crea-tures rest in peace:
   We to Thee our-selves re-sign, Let our lat-est thoughts be Thine.

69 *Evening Hymn.*

2 Saviour, to Thy Father bear
This our feeble evening prayer;
Thou hast seen how oft to-day
We, like sheep, have gone astray;
Blessèd Saviour, we, through Thee,
Pray that we may pardoned be.

3 Holy Spirit, Breath of balm,
Fall on us in evening's calm;
Yet awhile, before we sleep,
We with Thee will vigil keep.
Melt our spirits, mould our will,
Soften, strengthen, comfort still.

4 Blessèd Trinity, be near
Through the hours of darkness drear;
Father, Son, and Holy Ghost,
Round us set th' angelic host,
Till the flood of morning rays
Wake us to a song of praise.

Prof. Joseph Anstice. (1808—1836.) 1836. ab. and alt.

70 *Evening Hymn.*

1 Now from labor and from care
Evening hours have set me free,
In the work of praise and prayer,
Lord, I would converse with Thee:
O behold me from above,
Fill me with a Saviour's love.

2 Sin and sorrow, guilt and woe
Wither all my earthly joys;
Naught can charm me here below,
But my Saviour's melting voice:
Lord, forgive, Thy grace restore,
Make me Thine forevermore.

3 For the blessings of this day,
For the mercies of this hour,
For the Gospel's cheering ray,
For the Spirit's quickening power,
Grateful notes to Thee I raise:
O accept the song of praise.

Thomas Hastings. (1784—1872.) 1832.

EVENING WORSHIP

EVENTIDE. 10. William Henry Monk. 1861.

1. A-BIDE with me: fast falls the eventide; The darkness deepens; Lord, with me abide;

When other helpers fail, and comforts flee, Help of the helpless, O a-bide with me.

71
"*Abide with me.*"

2 Swift to its close ebbs out life's little day;
Earth's joys grow dim, its glories pass away;
Change and decay in all around I see;
O Thou, who changest not, abide with me.

3 I need Thy presence every passing hour:
What but Thy grace can foil the tempter's power?
Who like Thyself my guide and stay can be?
Through cloud and sunshine, O abide with me.

4 I fear no foe, with Thee at hand to bless;
Ills have no weight, and tears no bitterness;
Where is death's sting? where, grave, thy victory?
I triumph still, if Thou abide with me.

5 Hold Thou Thy cross before my closing eyes;
Shine through the gloom and point me to the skies;
Heaven's morning breaks, and earth's vain shadows flee;
In life, in death, O Lord, abide with me.

Rev. Henry Francis Lyte. (1793—1847.) 1847. ab.

OPENING AND CLOSING HYMNS.

ALVAN. 8, 7, 4.   Lowell Mason. (1792—1872.) 1854.

1. { In Thy name, O Lord, as-sem-bling, We, Thy peo-ple, now draw near:
{ Teach us to re-joice with trembling; Speak, and let Thy ser-vants hear,

Hear with meekness, Hear with meekness, Hear Thy word with god-ly fear.

72   "*Speak, for Thy servant heareth.*"
               1 Sam. iii, 10.
2 While our days on earth are lengthened,
    May we give them, Lord, to Thee ;
    Cheered by hope, and daily strengthened,
    May we run, nor weary be,
       Till Thy glory
    Without clouds in heaven we see.
3 There in worship purer, sweeter,
    Thee Thy people shall adore ;
    Tasting of enjoyment greater
    Far than thought conceived before ;
       Full enjoyment,
    Full, unmixed, and evermore.
         Rev. Thomas Kelly. (1769—1855.) 1815.

73   *Dismission.*
1 Lord, dismiss us with Thy blessing,
    Fill our hearts with joy and peace ;
    Let us now, Thy love possessing,
    Triumph in redeeming grace :
       O refresh us,
    Travelling through this wilderness.
2 Thanks we give, and adoration,
    For Thy gospel's joyful sound :

    May the fruits of Thy salvation
    In our hearts and lives abound ;
       May Thy presence
    With us evermore be found.
3 So, whene'er the signal's given
    Us from earth to call away,
    Borne on angels' wings to heaven,
    Glad the summons to obey,
       May we ever
    Reign with Christ in endless day.
     Hon. and Rev. Walter Shirley. (1725—1786.) 1774.

74   "*Thine entirely.*"
1 Welcome, welcome, dear Redeemer,
    Welcome to this heart of mine :
    Lord, I make a full surrender,
    Every power and thought be Thine,
       Thine entirely,
    Through eternal ages Thine.
2 Known to all to be Thy mansion,
    Earth and hell will disappear ;
    Or in vain attempt possession,
    When they find the Lord is near ;
       Shout, O Zion,
    Shout, ye saints, the Lord is here.
         Rev. William Mason. (1725—1797.) 1794.

SABBATH PRAISE.

Safely, thro' an-oth-er week, God has brought us on our way; Let us now a blessing seek, Waiting in His courts to-day: Day of all the week the best, Emblem of e-ter-nal rest, Day of all the week the best, Emblem of e-ter-nal rest.

75   "*Safely, through another Week.*"

2 While we pray for pardoning grace,
    Through the dear Redeemer's name,
  Show Thy reconciled face,
  Take away our sin and shame;
From our worldly cares set free,
May we rest this day in Thee.

3 Here we come Thy name to praise;
    May we feel Thy presence near:
  May Thy glory meet our eyes,
  While we in Thy house appear:
Here afford us, Lord, a taste
Of our everlasting feast.

4 May Thy gospel's joyful sound
    Conquer sinners, comfort saints;
  Make the fruits of grace abound,
  Bring relief for all complaints:
Thus may all our Sabbaths prove,
Till we join the Church above.
    Rev. John Newton. (1725—1807.) 1779.

76   *Creator, Saviour, Comforter.*

1 GREAT Creator, who this day
    From Thy perfect work didst rest,
  By the souls that own Thy sway
    Hallowed be its hours and blest:
Cares of earth aside be thrown,
This day given to heaven alone.

2 Saviour, who this day didst break
    The dark prison of the tomb,
  Bid my slumbering soul awake,
    Shine through all its sin and gloom:
Let me, from my bonds set free,
Rise from sin, and live to Thee.

3 Blessèd Spirit, Comforter,
    Sent this day from Christ on high,
  Lord, on me Thy gifts confer,
    Cleanse, illumine, sanctify;
All Thine influence shed abroad,
Lead me to the truth of God.
    Mrs. Julia Anne Elliott. (—1841.) 1835.

SABBATH PRAISE.

EL PARAN. L. M.
Johann Abraham Peter Schulz. (1747—1800.)
Arr. by Lowell Mason. (1792—1872.) 1839.

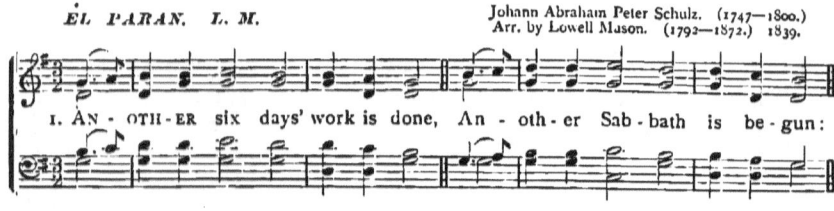

1. An-oth-er six days' work is done, An-oth-er Sab-bath is be-gun:

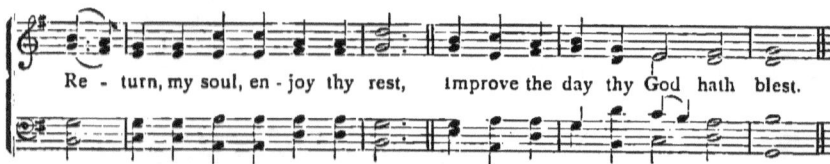

Re-turn, my soul, en-joy thy rest, Improve the day thy God hath blest.

77 *The Day of Holy Rest.*

2 Come, bless the Lord, whose love assigns
So sweet a rest to wearied minds ;
Provides an antepast of heaven,
And gives this day the food of seven.

3 O that our thoughts and thanks may rise,
As grateful incense, to the skies ;
And draw from heaven that sweet repose,
Which none but he that feels it knows.

4 This heavenly calm within the breast
Is the dear pledge of glorious rest,
Which for the Church of God remains,
The end of cares, the end of pains.

5 In holy duties let the day,
In holy pleasures, pass away ;
How sweet a Sabbath thus to spend,
In hope of one that ne'er shall end.

Rev. Joseph Stennett. (1663—1713.) 1732. ab. and much alt.

78 *"Sacred Rest."*
Ps. xcii.

1 SWEET is the work, my God, my King,
To praise Thy name, give thanks, and sing ;
To show Thy love by morning light,
And talk of all Thy truth at night.

2 Sweet is the day of sacred rest ;
No mortal cares shall seize my breast ;
O may my heart in tune be found,
Like David's harp of solemn sound.

3 My heart shall triumph in my Lord,
And bless His works, and bless His word ;
Thy works of grace, how bright they shine,
How deep Thy counsels, how divine !

4 Lord, I shall share a glorious part,
When grace hath well refined my heart,
And fresh supplies of joy are shed,
Like holy oil, to cheer my head.

5 Then shall I see, and hear, and know
All I desired or wished below ;
And every power find sweet employ,
In that eternal world of joy.

Rev. Isaac Watts. (1674—1748.) 1719. ab. and sl. alt.

SABBATH PRAISE. 35

AMES. L. M. Sigismund Neukomm. (1778—1858.) 1837.
Arr. by Lowell Mason. 1840.

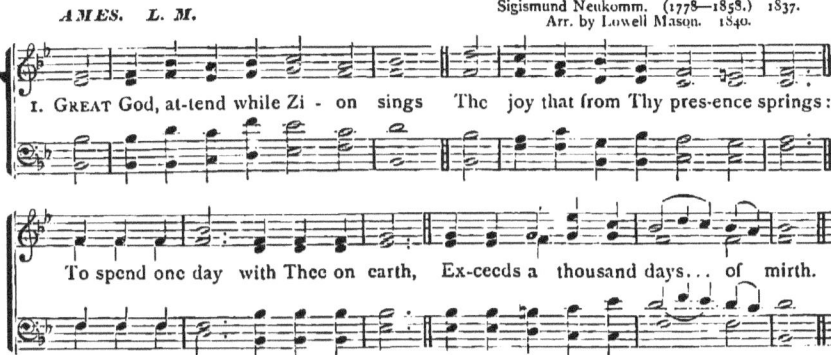

1. Great God, attend while Zion sings
The joy that from Thy presence springs:
To spend one day with Thee on earth,
Exceeds a thousand days of mirth.

79 *God and His Church.*
Ps. lxxxiv.

2 Might I enjoy the meanest place
Within Thy house, O God of grace,
Not tents of ease, nor thrones of power,
Should tempt my feet to leave Thy door.

3 God is our Sun, He makes our day;
God is our Shield, He guards our way
From all the assaults of hell and sin,
From foes without and foes within.

4 All needful grace will God bestow,
And crown that grace with glory too ;
He gives us all things, and withholds
No real good from upright souls.

5 O God, our King, whose sovereign sway
The glorious hosts of heaven obey,
And devils at Thy presence flee ;
Blest is the man that trusts in Thee.
Rev. Isaac Watts. 1719.

80 *An Exhortation to praise God.*
Ps. xcv. 1—6.

1 O come, loud anthems let us sing,
Loud thanks to our Almighty King ;
For we our voices high should raise,
When our salvation's Rock we praise.

2 Into His presence let us haste,
To thank Him for His favors past ;

To Him address, in joyful songs,
The praise that to His name belongs.

3 O let us to His courts repair,
And bow with adoration there ;
Down on our knees devoutly all
Before the Lord our Maker fall.
Tate and Brady. 1696. ab.

81 *The eternal Sabbath.*
Heb. iv. 9.

1 Thine earthly Sabbaths, Lord, we love;
But there's a nobler rest above :
To that our laboring souls aspire
With ardent hope and strong desire.

2 No more fatigue, no more distress.
Nor sin, nor hell, shall reach the place ;
No groans to mingle with the songs
Which warble from immortal tongues.

3 No rude alarms of raging foes ;
No cares to break the long repose ;
No midnight shade, no clouded sun,
But sacred, high, eternal noon.

4 O long-expected day, begin ;
Dawn on these realms of woe and sin :
Fain would we leave this weary road,
And sleep in death, to rest with God.
Rev. Philip Doddridge. (1702—1751.) 1755. ab. and alt.

SABBATH PRAISE.

LANESBORO. C. M. — William Dixon. 1790.

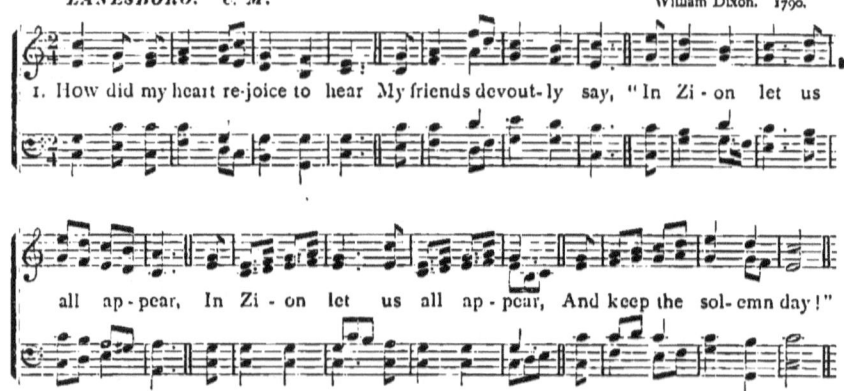

1. How did my heart rejoice to hear My friends devoutly say, "In Zion let us all appear, In Zion let us all appear, And keep the solemn day!"

82 *Going to Church.*
Ps. cxxii.

2 I love her gates, I love the road;
The Church, adorned with grace,
Stands like a palace built for God,
To show His milder face.

3 Up to her courts, with joys unknown,
The holy tribes repair;
The Son of David holds His throne,
And sits in judgment there.

4 He hears our praises, and complaints;
And while His awful voice
Divides the sinners from the saints,
We tremble and rejoice.

5 Peace be within this sacred place,
And joy a constant guest;
With holy gifts and heavenly grace,
Be her attendants blest.

6 My soul shall pray for Zion still,
While life or breath remains;
There my best friends, my kindred dwell,
There God, my Saviour, reigns.

Rev. Isaac Watts. (1674—1748.) 1719.

83 *Lord's Day Morning.*
Ps. lxiii.

1 EARLY, my God, without delay,
I haste to seek Thy face;
My thirsty spirit faints away,
Without Thy cheering grace.

2 So pilgrims on the scorching sand,
Beneath a burning sky,
Long for a cooling stream at hand,
And they must drink or die.

3 I've seen Thy glory and Thy power
Through all Thy temple shine:
My God repeat that heavenly hour,
That vision so divine.

4 Not life itself, with all its joys,
Can my best passions move;
Or raise so high my cheerful voice,
As Thy forgiving love.

5 Thus, till my last expiring day,
I'll bless my God and King;
Thus will I lift my hands to pray,
And tune my lips to sing.

Rev. Isaac Watts. 1719. ab. and sl. alt.

SABBATH PRAISE.

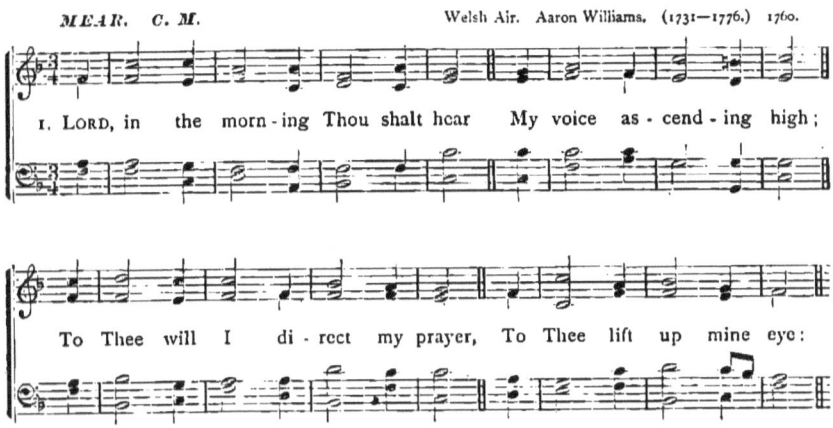

MEAR. C. M.   Welsh Air. Aaron Williams. (1731—1776.) 1760.

1. Lord, in the morning Thou shalt hear My voice ascending high;
To Thee will I direct my prayer, To Thee lift up mine eye:

84 *For the Lord's Day Morning.*
Ps. v.

2 Up to the hills, where Christ is gone
To plead for all His saints,
Presenting, at His Father's throne,
Our songs and our complaints.

3 Thou art a God, before whose sight
The wicked shall not stand;
Sinners shall ne'er be Thy delight,
Nor dwell at Thy right hand.

4 But to Thy house will I resort,
To taste Thy mercies there;
I will frequent Thy holy court,
And worship in Thy fear.

5 O may Thy Spirit guide my feet
In ways of righteousness;
Make every path of duty straight,
And plain before my face.
Rev. Isaac Watts. 1719.

85 *"The Day the Lord hath made."*
Ps. cxviii.

1 This is the day the Lord hath made,
He calls the hours His own;

Let heaven rejoice, let earth be glad,
And praise surround the throne.

2 To-day He rose and left the dead,
And Satan's empire fell;
To-day the saints His triumphs spread,
And all His wonders tell.

3 Hosanna to th' anointed King,
To David's holy Son;
Help us, O Lord, descend and bring
Salvation from the throne.

4 Blest be the Lord, who comes to men
With messages of grace;
Who comes in God His Father's name,
To save our sinful race.

5 Hosanna, in the highest strains
The Church on earth can raise;
The highest heavens, in which He reigns,
Shall give Him nobler praise.
Rev. Isaac Watts. 1719.

SABBATH PRAISE.

LISBON. S. M.   Daniel Read. (1757—1836.) 1785.

1. Welcome, sweet day of rest, That saw the Lord arise; Welcome to this reviving breast, And these rejoicing eyes.

86   *The Lord's Day welcomed.*

2 The King Himself comes near,
   And feasts His saints to-day;
Here we may sit, and see Him here,
   And love, and praise, and pray.

3 One day amidst the place
   Where my dear God hath been,
Is sweeter than ten thousand days
   Of pleasurable sin.

4 My willing soul would stay
   In such a frame as this,
And sit, and sing herself away
   To everlasting bliss.
         Rev. Isaac Watts. (1674—1748.) 1709.

87   *"Bless the Lord."*
       Neh. ix. 5.

1 Stand up, and bless the Lord,
   Ye people of His choice;
Stand up, and bless the Lord your God,
   With heart, and soul, and voice.

2 O for the living flame,
   From His own altar brought,
To touch our lips, our minds inspire,
   And wing to heaven our thought.

3 God is our strength and song,
   And His salvation ours;
Then be His love in Christ proclaimed
   With all our ransomed powers.

4 Stand up, and bless the Lord,
   The Lord your God adore;
Stand up, and bless His glorious name
   Henceforth for evermore.
      James Montgomery. (1771—1854.) 1825. ab.

88   *The Pleasures of Worship.*

1 How charming is the place,
   Where my Redeemer God
Unveils the beauties of His face,
   And sheds His love abroad.

2 Here, on the mercy-seat,
   With radiant glory crowned,
Our joyful eyes behold Him sit,
   And smile on all around.

3 To Him their prayers and cries
   Each humble soul presents:
He listens to their broken sighs,
   And grants them all their wants.

SABBATH PRAISE.   39

4 To them His sovereign will
    He graciously imparts;
  And in return accepts, with smiles,
    The tribute of their hearts.

5 Give me, O Lord, a place
    Within Thy blest abode,
  Among the children of Thy grace,
    The servants of my God.
              Rev. Samuel Stennett. (1727—1795.) 1778. ab.

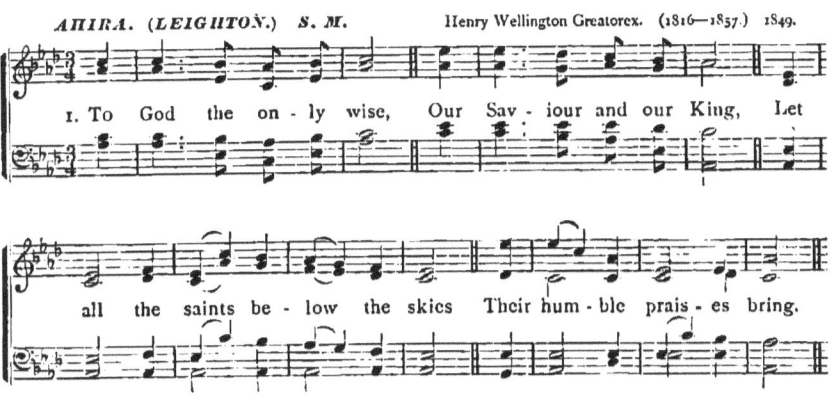

AHIRA. (LEIGHTON.) S. M.   Henry Wellington Greatorex. (1816—1857.) 1849.

1. To God the on-ly wise, Our Sav-iour and our King, Let all the saints be-low the skies Their hum-ble prais-es bring.

89 "*The only Wise.*"
      Jude 24, 25.

2 'Tis His almighty love,
    His counsel and His care,
  Preserves us safe from sin and death,
    And every hurtful snare.

3 He will present our souls,
    Unblemished and complete,
  Before the glory of His face,
    With joys divinely great.

4 Then all the chosen seed
    Shall meet around the throne,
  Shall bless the conduct of His grace,
    And make His wonders known.

5 To our Redeemer God
    Wisdom and power belongs,
  Immortal crowns of majesty,
    And everlasting songs.
              Rev. Isaac Watts. 1709.

90 *A holy God worshipped with Reverence.*
        Ps. xcix.

1 EXALT the Lord our God,
    And worship at His feet;
  His nature is all holiness,
    And mercy is His seat.

2 When Israel was His church,
    When Aaron was His priest,
  When Moses cried, when Samuel prayed,
    He gave His people rest.

3 Oft He forgave their sins,
    Nor would destroy their race;
  And oft He made His vengeance known
    When they abused His grace.

4 Exalt the Lord our God,
    Whose grace is still the same;
  Still He's a God of holiness,
    And jealous for His name.
              Rev. Isaac Watts. 1719.

SABBATH PRAISE.

BEMERTON. C. M. Henry Wellington Greatorex. (1816—1857.) 1849.

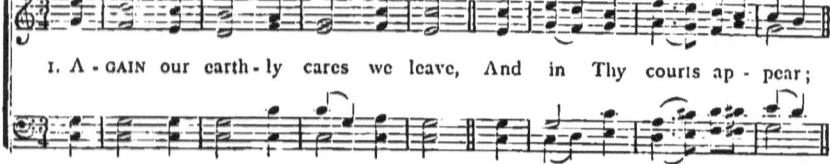

1. A-GAIN our earth-ly cares we leave, And in Thy courts ap-pear;
A-gain, with joy-ful feet, we come To meet our Sav-iour here.

91 *God's Presence in the Sanctuary.*

2 Within these walls let holy peace,
  And love, and concord dwell;
Here give the troubled conscience ease,
  The wounded spirit heal.

3 The feeling heart, the melting eye,
  The humble mind bestow;
And shine upon us from on high,
  To make our graces grow.

4 May we in faith receive Thy word,
  In faith present our prayers;
And, in the presence of our Lord,
  Unbosom all our cares.

5 Show us some token of Thy love,
  Our fainting hope to raise;
And pour Thy blessing from above,
  That we may render praise.
        Rev. John Newton. (1725—1807.) 1779. alt.

92 *Sincerity in Worship.*

1 LORD, when we bend before Thy throne,
  And our confessions pour,
Teach us to feel the sins we own,
  And hate what we deplore.

2 Our broken spirits, pitying, see,
  And penitence impart;
Then let a kindling glance from Thee
  Beam hope upon the heart.

3 When we disclose our wants in prayer,
  May we our wills resign;
And not a thought our bosom share
  Which is not wholly Thine.

4 Let faith each meek petition fill,
  And waft it to the skies;
And teach our hearts, 'tis goodness still
  That grants it, or denies.
        Rev. Joseph Dacre Carlyle. (1759—1804.) 1805. ab.

SABBATH PRAISE. 41

93 *Christ's Triumph.*
1 AGAIN the Lord of life and light
   Awakes the kindling ray,
   Unseals the eyelids of the morn,
   And pours increasing day.
2 O what a night was that which wrapt
   A heathen world in gloom;
   O what a sun which broke this day
   Triumphant from the tomb.
3 The powers of darkness leagued in vain
   To bind our Lord in death;
   He shook their kingdom, when He fell,
   With His expiring breath.
4 And now His conq'ring chariot wheels
   Ascend the lofty skies;
   While, broke beneath His powerful
   Death's iron sceptre lies.   [cross,
5 This day be grateful homage paid,
   And loud hosannas sung;
   Let gladness dwell in every heart,
   And praise on every tongue.
6 Ten thousand differing lips shall join
   To hail this welcome morn,
   Which scatters blessings from its wings
   On nations yet unborn.

Mrs. Anna Lætitia Barbauld. (1743—1825.) 1773, 1825. ab. and alt.

BROWNELL. L. M. 6 l.   Arr. from Francis Joseph Haydn. (1732—1809.)

1. FORTH from the dark and stormy sky, Lord, to Thine al-tar's shade we fly;
Forth from the world, its hope and fear, Sav-iour, we seek Thy shelter here:
Wear-y and weak, Thy grace we pray; Turn not, O Lord, Thy guests a-way.

94 *Flying to the Shadow of the Altar.*
2 Long have we roamed in want and pain,
  Long have we sought Thy rest in vain;
  Wildered in doubt, in darkness lost,
  Long have our souls been tempest-tost:
  Low at Thy feet our sins we lay;
  Turn not, O Lord, Thy guests away.

Bp. Reginald Heber. (1783—1826.) 1827.

SABBATH PRAISE.

HENDON. 7.   Rev. Cæsar Henri Abraham Malan. (1787—1864.) 1830.

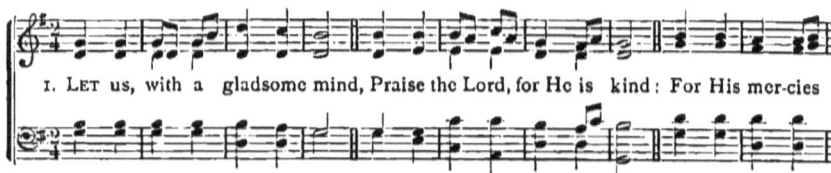

1. Let us, with a gladsome mind, Praise the Lord, for He is kind: For His mer-cies

shall en-dure, Ev-er faith-ful, ev-er sure, Ev-er faith-ful, ev-er sure.

95 *Wonders of Creation, Providence, and Grace.*
Ps. cxxxvi.

2 He, with all-commanding might,
Filled the new-made world with light:
For His mercies shall endure,
Ever faithful, ever sure.

3 He His chosen race did bless
In the wasteful wilderness:
For His mercies shall endure,
Ever faithful, ever sure.

4 He hath, with a piteous eye,
Looked upon our misery:
For His mercies shall endure,
Ever faithful, ever sure.

5 All things living He doth feed,
His full hand supplies their need:
For His mercies shall endure,
Ever faithful, ever sure.

6 Let us therefore warble forth
His high majesty and worth:
For His mercies shall endure,
Ever faithful, ever sure.

John Milton. (1608—1674.) 1624. ab. and alt.

96 *A Day in the Lord's Courts.*

1 To Thy temple I repair;
Lord, I love to worship there;
When within the veil I meet
Christ before the mercy-seat.

2 While Thy glorious praise is sung,
Touch my lips, unloose my tongue,
That my joyful soul may bless
Thee, the Lord my Righteousness.

3 While the prayers of saints ascend,
God of love, to mine attend;
Hear me, for Thy Spirit pleads,
Hear, for Jesus intercedes.

4 While Thy ministers proclaim
Peace and pardon in Thy Name,
Through their voice, by faith, may I
Hear Thee speaking from the sky.

5 From Thy house when I return,
May my heart within me burn;
And at evening let me say,
"I have walked with God to-day."

James Montgomery. (1771—1854.) 1825. ab.

SABBATH PRAISE. 43

MENDEBRAS. 7, 6. D. German Melody. Arr. by Lowell Mason. (1792—1872.) 1839.

1. { O DAY of rest and glad-ness, O day of joy and light, }
   { O balm of care and sad-ness, Most beau-ti - ful, most bright: } On thee, the high and low - ly,
   Through a - ges joined in tune, Sing ho - ly, ho - ly, ho - ly, To the Great God Tri - une.

97 *"The Day which the Lord hath made."*
Ps. cxviii. 24.

2 On thee, at the creation,
   The light first had its birth;
On thee, for our salvation,
   Christ rose from depths of earth;
On thee our Lord, victorious,
   The Spirit sent from heaven,
And thus on thee, most glorious,
   A triple light was given.

3 To-day on weary nations
   The heavenly manna falls;
To holy convocations
   The silver trumpet calls,
Where gospel light is glowing
   With pure and radiant beams,
And living water flowing
   With soul-refreshing streams.

4 New graces ever gaining
   From this our day of rest,
We reach the rest remaining
   To spirits of the blest;
To Holy Ghost be praises,
   To Father, and to Son;
The Church her voice upraises
   To Thee, blest Three in One.

Bp. Christopher Wordsworth. (1807—) 1862. ab. and alt.

98 Ἀναστάσεως ἡμέρα.

1 THE day of resurrection,
   Earth, tell it out abroad:
The Passover of gladness,
   The Passover of God.
From death to life eternal,
   From earth unto the sky,
Our Christ hath brought us over,
   With hymns of victory.

2 Our hearts be pure from evil,
   That we may see aright
The Lord in rays eternal
   Of resurrection-light;
And, listening to His accents,
   May hear, so calm and plain,
His own " All hail!" and, hearing,
   May raise the victor-strain.

3 Now let the heavens be joyful;
   Let earth her song begin;
Let the round world keep triumph,
   And all that is therein;
Invisible and visible,
   Their notes let all things blend,
For Christ the Lord hath risen,
   Our Joy that hath no end.
        John of Damascus. (—c. 780.)
Tr. by Rev. John Mason Neale. (1818—1866.) 1862.

SABBATH PRAISE.

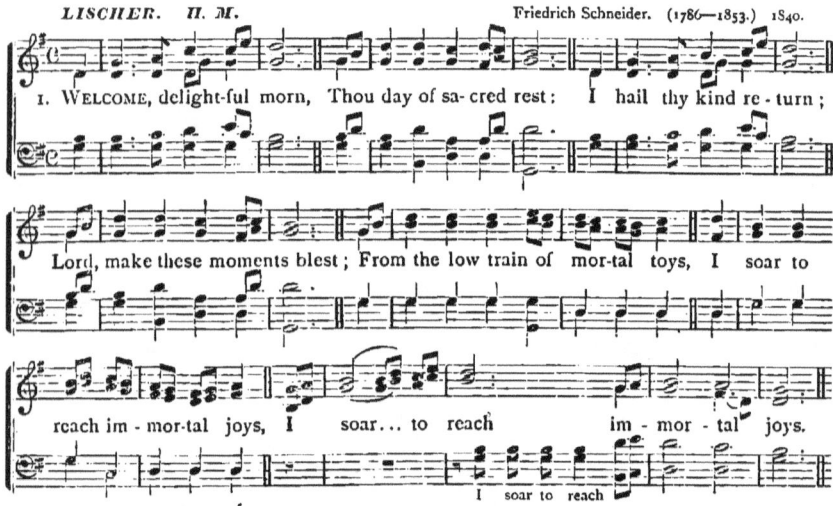

LISCHER. H. M.   Friedrich Schneider. (1786—1853.) 1840.

1. Welcome, delight-ful morn, Thou day of sa-cred rest: I hail thy kind re-turn; Lord, make these moments blest; From the low train of mor-tal toys, I soar to reach im-mor-tal joys, I soar... to reach im - mor - tal joys.

99   *Sabbath Morning.*

2 Now may the King descend,
   And fill His throne with grace;
Thy sceptre, Lord, extend,
   While saints address Thy face;
Let sinners feel Thy quickening word,
And learn to know and fear the Lord.

3 Descend, celestial Dove,
   With all Thy quickening powers,
Disclose a Saviour's love,
   And bless these sacred hours;
Then shall my soul new life obtain,
Nor Sabbaths e'er be spent in vain.
       Hayward. In John Dobell's Collection. 1806.

100   *Longing for the House of God.*
       Ps. lxxxiv.

1 Lord of the worlds above,
   How pleasant and how fair,
The dwellings of Thy love,
   Thine earthly temples are!
To Thine abode my heart aspires,
With warm desires, to see my God.

2 O happy souls that pray
   Where God appoints to hear;
O happy men that pay
   Their constant service there!
They praise Thee still; and happy they
That love the way to Zion's hill.

3 They go from strength to strength,
   Through this dark vale of tears,
Till each arrives at length,
   Till each in heaven appears:
O glorious seat, when God our King
Shall thither bring our willing feet!

4 The Lord His people loves;
   His hand no good withholds,
From those His heart approves,
   From pure and upright souls:
Thrice happy he, O God of hosts,
Whose spirit trusts alone in Thee.
       Rev. Isaac Watts. (1674—1748.) 1719. ab.

SABBATH PRAISE. 45

HADDAM. H. M.   Arr. by Lowell Mason. (1792—1872.) 1822.

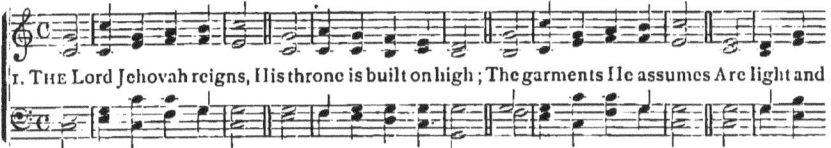

1. The Lord Jehovah reigns, His throne is built on high; The garments He assumes Are light and

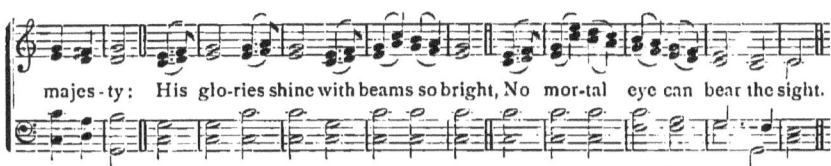

majes-ty: His glo-ries shine with beams so bright, No mor-tal eye can bear the sight.

101   *"The Lord reigneth."*   Ps. xciii; xcvii.

2 The thunders of His hand
   Keep the wide world in awe;
   His wrath and justice stand
   To guide His holy law;
And where His love resolves to bless,
His truth confirms and seals the grace.

3 Through all His ancient works,
   Surprising wisdom shines;
   Confounds the powers of hell,
   And breaks their cursed designs:
Strong is His arm, and shall fulfil
His great decrees, His sovereign will.

4 And can this mighty King
   Of glory condescend?
   And will He write His name,
   My Father and my Friend?
I love His name, I love His word;
Join, all my powers, and praise the Lord.
                      Rev. Isaac Watts. 1709.

102   *God our Preserver.*   Ps. cxxi.

1 Upward I lift mine eyes,
   From God is all my aid;
   The God that built the skies,
   And earth and nature made:
God is the tower to which I fly;
His grace is nigh in every hour.

2 My feet shall never slide,
   And fall in fatal snares,
   Since God, my guard and guide,
   Defends me from my fears:
Those wakeful eyes, that never sleep,
Shall Israel keep when dangers rise.

3 No burning heats by day,
   Nor blasts of evening air,
   Shall take my health away,
   If God be with me there:
Thou art my sun, and Thou my shade,
To guard my head by night or noon.

4 Hast Thou not given Thy word
   To save my soul from death?
   And I can trust my Lord
   To keep my mortal breath:
I'll go and come, nor fear to die,
Till from on high Thou call me home.
                      Rev. Isaac Watts. 1719.

SABBATH PRAISE.

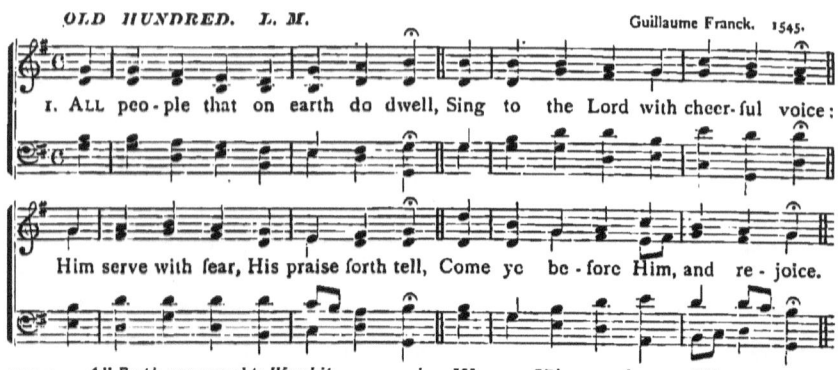

103 *All People summoned to Worship.*
Ps. c.

2 The Lord, ye know, is God indeed,
    Without our aid He did us make :
    We are His flock, He doth us feed,
    And for His sheep He doth us take.

3 O enter then His gates with praise,
    Approach with joy His courts unto :
    Praise, laud, and bless His name always,
    For it is seemly so to do.

4 For why? the Lord our God is good,
    His mercy is forever sure :
    His truth at all times firmly stood,
    And shall from age to age endure.
                Rev. William Kethe. 1561.

104 *Grateful Adoration.*
Ps. c.

1 BEFORE Jehovah's awful throne,
    Ye nations, bow with sacred joy;
    Know that the Lord is God alone ;
    He can create, and He destroy.

2 His sovereign power, without our aid,
    Made us of clay, and formed us men ;
    And when, like wand'ring sheep, we strayed,
    He brought us to His fold again.

3 We are His people, we His care,
    Our souls and all our mortal frame :
    What lasting honors shall we rear,
    Almighty Maker, to Thy name ?

4 We'll crowd Thy gates with thankful songs,
    High as the heavens our voices raise ;
    And earth, with her ten thousand tongues,   [praise.
    Shall fill Thy courts with sounding

5 Wide as the world is Thy command,
    Vast as eternity Thy love ;
    Firm as a rock Thy truth must stand,
    When rolling years shall cease to move.
    Rev. Isaac Watts. (1674—1748.) 1719. ab. and alt.
        Rev. John Wesley. (1703—1791.) 1741.

105 *Praise from all Nations.*
Ps. cxvii.

1 FROM all that dwell below the skies,
    Let the Creator's praise arise :
    Let the Redeemer's name be sung
    Through every land, by every tongue.

2 Eternal are Thy mercies, Lord ;
    Eternal truth attends Thy word ;
    Thy praise shall sound from shore to shore
    Till suns shall rise and set no more.
                Rev. Isaac Watts. 1719.

SABBATH PRAISE.

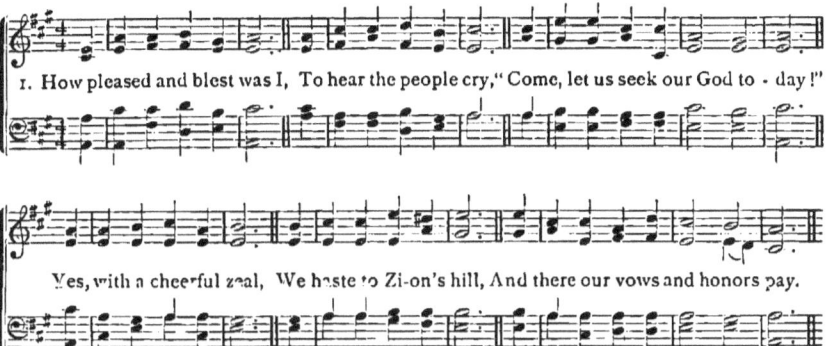

DALSTON. S. P. M.   Aaron Williams. (1731—1776.) 1760.

1. How pleased and blest was I, To hear the people cry," Come, let us seek our God to - day!"
Yes, with a cheerful zeal, We haste to Zi-on's hill, And there our vows and honors pay.

106   *Going to Church.*
Ps. cxxii.

2 Zion, thrice happy place,
Adorned with wondrous grace,
And walls of strength embrace thee round :
In thee our tribes appear,
To pray, and praise, and hear
The sacred gospel's joyful sound.

3 There David's greater Son
Has fixed His royal throne ;
He sits for grace and judgment there ;
He bids the saints be glad ;
He makes the sinner sad ;
And humble souls rejoice with fear.

4 May peace attend thy gate,
And joy within thee wait,
To bless the soul of every guest :
The man that seeks thy peace,
And wishes thine increase,
A thousand blessings on him rest !

5 My tongue repeats her vows,
" Peace to this sacred house ! "
For there my friends and kindred dwell ;

And since my glorious God
Makes thee His blest abode,
My soul shall ever love thee well.
       Rev. Isaac Watts. 1719.

107   *" Heaven begun below."*

1 'Tis Heaven begun below
To hear Christ's praises flow
In Zion, where His name is known :
What will it be above
To sing redeeming love,
And cast our crowns before His throne !

2 O what sweet company
We then shall hear and see ;
What harmony will there abound,
When souls unnumbered sing
The praise of Zion's King,
Nor one dissenting voice is found !

3 Till that blest period come,
Zion shall be my home ;
And may I never thence remove,
Till from the Church below
To that on high I go,
And there commune in perfect love.
Rev. Joseph Swain. (1761—1796.) 1792. ab. and alt.

LYONS. 5, 5, 6, 5. Francis Joseph Haydn. (1732—1809.) 1770.

1. O WORSHIP the King, All glorious above; O grateful-ly sing His power and His love;

Our Shield and Defender, The Ancient of days, Pavilioned in splendor, And girded with praise.

108 *The Majesty and Mercy of God.*
Ps. civ.

2 Frail children of dust,
 And feeble as frail,
In Thee do we trust,
 Nor find Thee to fail:
Thy mercies how tender,
 How firm to the end,
Our Maker, Defender,
 Redeemer, and Friend.

3 O measureless Might,
 Ineffable Love,
While angels delight
 To hymn Thee above,
The humbler creation,
 Though feeble their lays,
With true adoration
 Shall lisp to Thy praise.
Sir Robert Grant. (1785—1838.) 1839. ab.

109 *Jesus worshipped.*

1 YE servants of God,
 Your Master proclaim,
And publish abroad
 His wonderful name;
The name all-victorious
 Of Jesus extol;
His kingdom is glorious,
 And rules over all.

2 God ruleth on high,
 Almighty to save:
And still He is nigh;
 His presence we have.
The great congregation,
 His triumph shall sing,
Ascribing salvation
 To Jesus our King.

3 "Salvation to God
 Who sits on the throne,"
Let all cry aloud,
 And honor the Son:
The praises of Jesus
 The angels proclaim,
Fall down on their faces,
 And worship the Lamb.

4 Then let us adore,
 And give Him His right,
All glory, and power,
 And wisdom and might;
All honor and blessing,
 With angels above,
And thanks never ceasing
 And infinite love.
Rev. Charles Wesley. (1708—1788.) 1744.

SABBATH PRAISE.

ST. GERVAIS. 7. Arr. by Rev. William Henry Havergal. (1793—1870.)

1. Songs of praise the an-gels sang, Heaven with hal-le-lu-jahs rang,

When Je-ho-vah's work be-gun, When He spake, and it was done.

110   *"Glory to God in the highest."* Luke ii. 13.

2 Songs of praise awoke the morn,
When the Prince of Peace was born;
Songs of praise arose, when He
Captive led captivity.

3 Heaven and earth must pass away,
Songs of praise shall crown that day;
God will make new heavens, new earth,
Songs of praise shall hail their birth.

4 And can man alone be dumb
Till that glorious kingdom come?
No; the Church delights to raise
Psalms, and hymns, and songs of praise.

5 Saints below, with heart and voice,
Still in songs of praise rejoice;
Learning here, by faith and love,
Songs of praise to sing above.

6 Borne upon their latest breath,
Songs of praise shall conquer death;
Then, amidst eternal joy,
Songs of praise their powers employ.

James Montgomery. (1771—1854.) 1819, 1853.

111   *The unfailing Mercies of God.*

1 HOLY, holy, holy Lord,
Be Thy glorious name adored:
Lord, Thy mercies never fail;
Hail, celestial Goodness, hail!

2 Though unworthy, Lord, Thine ear,
Deign our humble songs to hear;
Purer praise we hope to bring,
When around Thy throne we sing.

3 While on earth ordained to stay,
Guide our footsteps in Thy way,
Till we come to dwell with Thee,
Till we all Thy glory see.

4 Then with angel-harps again
We will wake a nobler strain;
There, in joyful songs of praise,
Our triumphant voices raise.

5 Lord, Thy mercies never fail:
Hail, celestial Goodness, hail!
Holy, holy, holy Lord,
Be Thy glorious name adored.

Rev. Benjamin Williams. 1778. ab.

SABBATH PRAISE.

MISSIONARY CHANT. L. M.   Charles Zeuner. (1795—1857.) 1832.

1. Praises to Him whose love has given, In Christ, His Son, the Life of Heaven;
Who for our darkness gives us light, And turns to day our deepest night.

112   *Praise for Salvation.*

2 Praises to Him, in grace who came,
To bear our woe, and sin, and shame ;
Who lived to die, who died to rise,
The God-accepted sacrifice.

3 Praises to Him the chain who broke,
Opened the prison, burst the yoke,
Sent forth its captives glad and free,
Heirs of an endless liberty.

4 Praises to Him who sheds abroad
Within our hearts the love of God ;
The Spirit of all truth and peace,
Fountain of joy and holiness !

5 To Father, Son, and Spirit now
The hands we lift, the knees we bow ;
To Thee, Jehovah, thus we raise
The sinner's endless song of praise.
   Rev. Horatius Bonar. (1808—) 1861. ab. and alt.

113   *"Vexilla Regis prodeunt."*

1 The royal banners forward go,
The cross shines forth in mystic glow ;
Where He in flesh, our flesh who made,
Our sentence bore, our ransom paid ;

2 Where deep for us the spear was dy'd,
Life's torrent rushing from His side,
To cleanse us in the precious flood
Of water mingled with His blood.

3 O tree of glory, tree most fair,
Ordained those holy limbs to bear,
How bright in purple robe it stood,
The purple of a Saviour's blood !

4 Upon its arms, so widely flung,
The weight of this world's ransom hung :
The price which none but He could pay,
And spoiled the spoiler of his prey.

5 To Thee Eternal Three in One,
Let homage meet by all be done :
As by the cross Thou dost restore,
So rule and guide us evermore.
   Venantius Fortunatus. (530—609.) c. 575.
   Tr. by Rev. John Mason Neale. (1818—1866.) 1851. ab. & alt.

SABBATH PRAISE.   51

114 *The Trinity humbly worshipped.*

1 FATHER of Heaven, whose love profound
A ransom for our souls hath found,
Before Thy throne we sinners bend :
To us Thy pardoning love extend.

2 Almighty Son, incarnate Word,
Our Prophet, Priest, Redeemer, Lord,
Before Thy throne we sinners bend :
To us Thy saving grace extend.

3 Eternal Spirit, by whose breath
The soul is raised from sin and death,
Before Thy throne we sinners bend :
To us Thy quickening power extend.

4 Jehovah,—Father, Spirit, Son,—
Mysterious Godhead, Three in one,
Before Thy throne we sinners bend :
Grace, pardon, life, to us extend.
John Cooper. 1810.

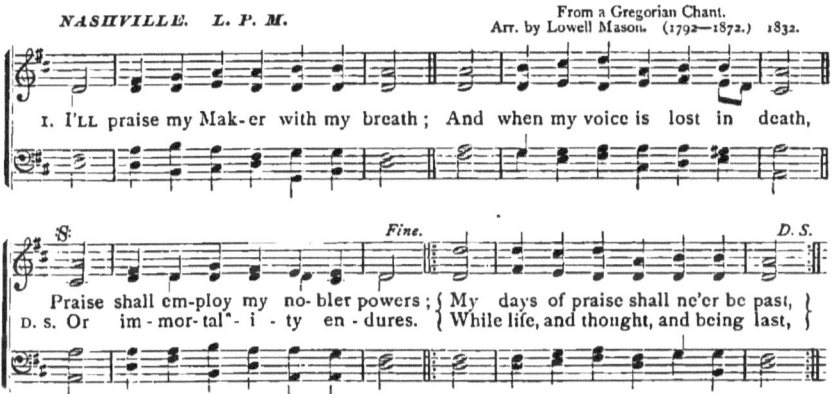

NASHVILLE. L. P. M.   From a Gregorian Chant. Arr. by Lowell Mason. (1792—1872.) 1832.

1. I'll praise my Maker with my breath ; And when my voice is lost in death,
Praise shall employ my nobler powers ; My days of praise shall ne'er be past,
D. S. Or immortal'-i-ty endures. While life, and thought, and being last,

115 *God praised for His Goodness and Truth.*
Ps. cxlvi.

2 Happy the man whose hopes rely
On Israel's God: He made the sky,
And earth, and seas, with all their train ;
His truth forever stands secure ;
He saves the opprest, He feeds the poor,
And none shall find His promise vain.

3 The Lord hath eyes to give the blind ;
The Lord supports the sinking mind ;
He sends the laboring conscience peace ;

He helps the stranger in distress,
The widow and the fatherless,
And grants the prisoner sweet release.

4 I'll praise Him while He lends me breath ;
And when my voice is lost in death,
Praise shall employ my nobler powers :
My days of praise shall ne'er be past,
While life and thought and being last,
Or immortality endures.
Rev. Isaac Watts. (1674—1748.) 1719. ab.

SABBATH PRAISE.

HUMMEL. C. M.   Charles Zeuner. (1795—1857.) 1832.

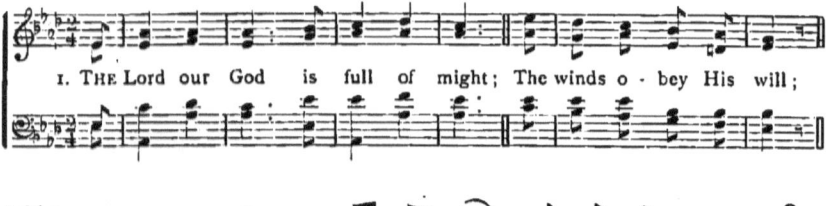

1. The Lord our God is full of might; The winds o-bey His will;
He speaks, and in His heaven-ly height The roll-ing sun stands still.

116   *The Majesty of God.*

2 Rebel, ye waves, and o'er the land
    With threatening aspect roar:
The Lord uplifts His awful hand,
    And chains you to the shore.

3 Howl, winds of night, your force com-
    Without His high behest,   [bine;
Ye shall not in the mountain pine
    Disturb the sparrow's nest.

4 His voice sublime is heard afar,
    In distant peals it dies;
He yokes the whirlwind to His car,
    And sweeps the howling skies.

5 Ye nations, bend, in reverence bend;
    Ye monarchs wait His nod;
And bid the choral song ascend,
    To celebrate our God.
        Henry Kirke White. (1785—1806.) 1806.

117   *The Divine Decrees.*

1 KEEP silence, all created things,
    And wait your Master's nod;
My soul stands trembling while she
    The honors of her God.   [sings

2 Life, death, and hell, and worlds un-
    known,
    Hang on His firm decree;
He sits on no precarious throne,
    Nor borrows leave to be.

3 Chained to His throne a volume lie,
    With all the fates of men;
With every angel's form and size,
    Drawn by the eternal pen.

4 His providence unfolds the book,
    And makes His counsels shine;
Each opening leaf, and every stroke,
    Fulfils some deep design.

5 My God, I would not long to see
    My fate with curious eyes,
What gloomy lines are writ for me,
    Or what bright scenes shall rise.

6 In Thy fair book of life and grace
    O may I find my name,
Recorded in some humble place,
    Beneath my Lord, the Lamb.
      Rev. Isaac Watts. (1674—1748.) 1706. ab. and alt.

SABBATH PRAISE. 53

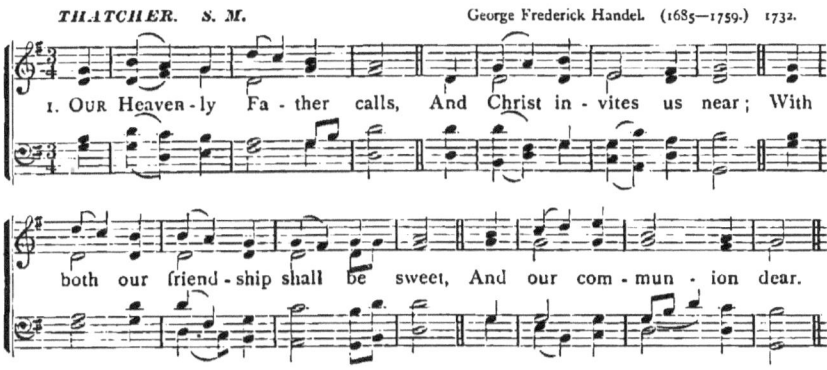

THATCHER. S. M. George Frederick Handel. (1685—1759.) 1732.

1. Our Heaven-ly Fa-ther calls, And Christ in-vites us near; With both our friend-ship shall be sweet, And our com-mun-ion dear.

118 *Communion with God and Christ.*
1 John i. 3.

2 God pities all my griefs ;
He pardons every day ;
Almighty to protect my soul,
And wise to guide my way.

3 Jesus, my living Head,
We bless Thy faithful care ;
Mine Advocate before the throne,
And my Forerunner there.

4 Here fix, my roving heart,
Here wait, my warmest love,
Till the communion be complete,
In nobler scenes above.
Rev. Philip Doddridge. (1702—1751.) 1755. ab.

119 *Abounding Compassion of God.*
Ps. ciii. 8—12.

1 My soul, repeat His praise
Whose mercies are so great ;
Whose anger is so slow to rise,
So ready to abate.

2 God will not always chide ;
And when His strokes are felt,
His strokes are fewer than our crimes,
And lighter than our guilt.

3 High as the heavens are raised
Above the ground we tread,

So far the riches of His grace
Our highest thoughts exceed.

4 His power subdues our sins,
And His forgiving love,
Far as the east is from the west,
Doth all our guilt remove.
Rev. Isaac Watts. 1719.

120 *"He knoweth our Frame."*
Ps. ciii. 13—18.

1 The pity of the Lord
To those that fear His name,
Is such as tender parents feel :
He knows our feeble frame.

2 He knows we are but dust,
Scattered with every breath ;
His anger, like a rising wind,
Can send us swift to death.

3 Our days are as the grass,
Or like the morning flower ;
If one sharp blast sweep o'er the field,
It withers in an hour.

4 But Thy compassions, Lord,
To endless years endure ;
And children's children ever find
Thy words of promise sure.
Rev. Isaac Watts. 1719.

SABBATH PRAISE.

TRURO. L. M. Charles Burney. (1726—1814.) 1760.

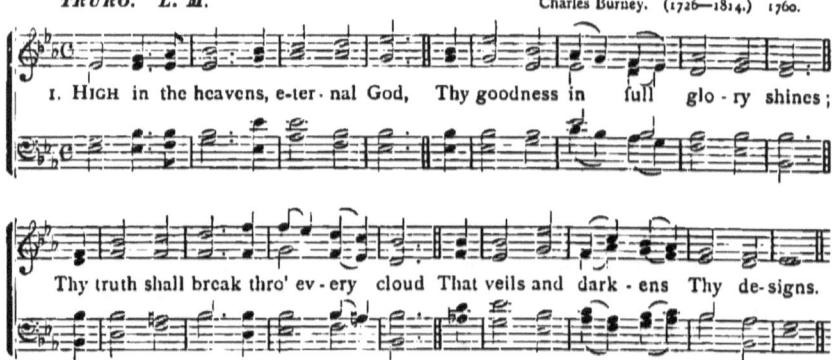

1. High in the heavens, e-ter-nal God, Thy goodness in full glo-ry shines;
Thy truth shall break thro' ev-ery cloud That veils and dark-ens Thy de-signs.

121 *General Providence and special Grace.*
Ps. xxxvi. 5—9.

2 Forever firm Thy justice stands,
As mountains their foundations keep;
Wise are the wonders of Thy hands;
Thy judgments are a mighty deep.

3 My God, how excellent Thy grace,
Whence all our hope and comfort
The sons of Adam in distress [springs;
Fly to the shadow of Thy wings.

4 From the provisions of Thy house
We shall be fed with sweet repast:
There mercy like a river flows,
And brings salvation to our taste.

5 Life, like a fountain rich and free,
Springs from the presence of my Lord;
And in Thy light our souls shall see
The glories promised in Thy word.
Rev. Isaac Watts. (1674—1748.) 1719. ab.

122 *"Bless the Lord."*
Ps. ciii.

1 Bless, O my soul, the living God,
Call home thy thoughts that rove abroad;
Let all the powers within me join
In work and worship so divine.

2 Bless, O my soul, the God of grace;
His favors claim thy highest praise:
Why should the wonders He hath
Be lost in silence and forgot? [wrought

3 'Tis He, my soul, that sent his Son
To die for crimes which thou hast done;
He owns the ransom, and forgives
The hourly follies of our lives.

4 Let the whole earth His power confess;
Let the whole earth adore His grace:
The Gentile with the Jew shall join
In work and worship so divine.
Rev. Isaac Watts. 1719. ab.

123 *God's unspeakable Glory.*

1 Come, O my soul, in sacred lays
Attempt thy great Creator's praise:
But O, what tongue can speak His fame?
What mortal verse can reach the theme?

2 Enthroned amid the radiant spheres,
He glory like a garment wears;
To form a robe of light divine,
Ten thousand suns around Him shine.

SABBATH PRAISE. 55

3 In all our Maker's grand designs,
  Almighty power with wisdom shines;
  His works, through all this wondrous frame,
  Declare the glory of His name.

4 Raised on devotion's lofty wing,
  Do thou, my soul, His glories sing;
  And let His praise employ thy tongue,
  Till listening worlds shall join the song.
  Rev. Thomas Blacklock. (1721—1791.) 1754.

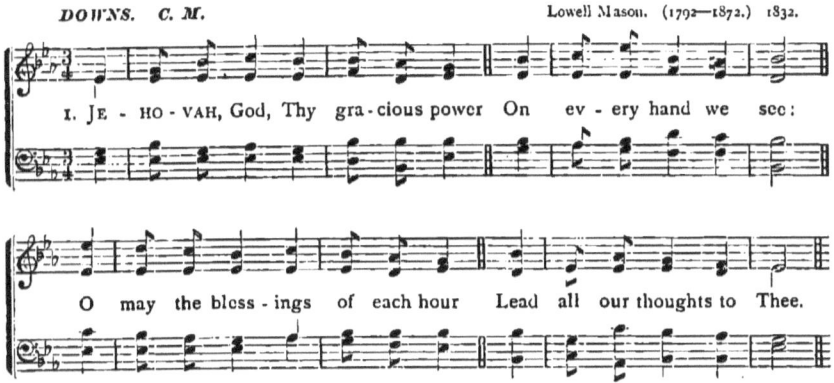

DOWNS. C. M.   Lowell Mason. (1792—1872.) 1832.

1. JE-HO-VAH, God, Thy gra-cious power On ev-ery hand we see:
O may the bless-ings of each hour Lead all our thoughts to Thee.

124 *Omnipresence and Omniscience of God.*
        Ps. cxxxix.

2 Thy power is in the ocean deeps,
  And reaches to the skies;
  Thine eye of mercy never sleeps,
  Thy goodness never dies.

3 From morn till noon, till latest eve,
  Thy hand, O God, we see;
  And all the blessings we receive,
  Proceed alone from Thee.

4 In all the varying scenes of time,
  On Thee our hopes depend;
  Through every age, in every clime,
  Our Father, and our Friend.
  Rev. John Thomson. (1782—1818.) 1810.

125 *Resignation to God's Will.*

1 SINCE all the varying scenes of time
  God's watchful eye surveys,

O who so wise to choose our lot,
Or to appoint our ways?

2 Good, when He gives, supremely good;
  Nor less when He denies;
  E'en crosses, from His sovereign hand,
  Are blessings in disguise.

3 Why should we doubt a Father's love,
  So constant and so kind?
  To His unerring gracious will
  Be every wish resigned.

4 In Thy fair book of life divine,
  My God, inscribe my name;
  There let it fill some humble place
  Beneath my Lord, the Lamb.
  Rev. James Hervey. (1714—1758.) 1746. alt.

BALERMA. C. M. — Scotch Melody. Hugh Wilson. 1768. Arr. by Lowell Mason. (1792–1872.) 1836.

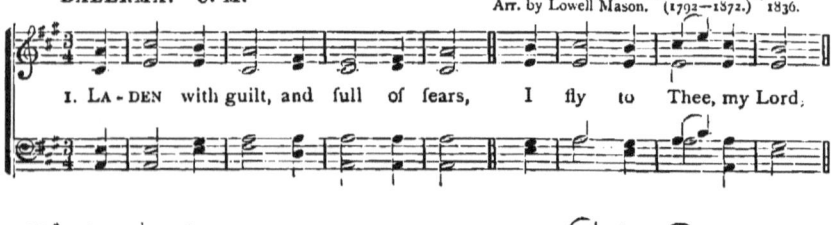
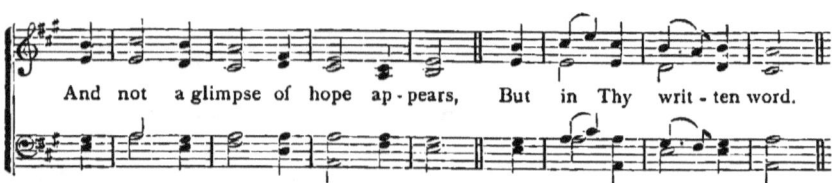

1. LA-DEN with guilt, and full of fears, I fly to Thee, my Lord; And not a glimpse of hope appears, But in Thy writ-ten word.

126 *The Scriptures our only Help and Guide.*

2 The volume of my Father's grace,
Does all my grief assuage ;
Here I behold my Saviour's face
Almost in every page.

3 This is the judge that ends the strife,
Where wit and reason fail ;
My guide to everlasting life,
Through all this gloomy vale.

4 O may Thy counsels, mighty God,
My roving feet command ;
Nor I forsake the happy road,
That leads to Thy right hand.
Rev. Isaac Watts. (1674–1748.) 1709. ab.

127 *The Light and Glory of the Word.*
Ps. cxix. 130. 2 Cor. iv. 4.

1 A GLORY gilds the sacred page,
Majestic, like the sun ;
It gives a light to every age,
It gives, but borrows none.

2 The hand, that gave it, still supplies
The gracious light and heat ;
Its truths upon the nations rise,
They rise, but never set.

3 Let everlasting thanks be Thine,
For such a bright display,
As makes a world of darkness shine,
With beams of heavenly day.

4 My soul rejoices to pursue
The steps of Him I love,
Till glory breaks upon my view,
In brighter worlds above.
William Cowper. (1731–1800.) 1779. ab.

128 *A Lamp, and a Light.*
Ps. cxix. 105. 2 Tim. iii. 16.

1 How precious is the book divine,
By inspiration given :
Bright as a lamp its doctrines shine,
To guide our souls to heaven.

2 Its light, descending from above,
Our gloomy world to cheer,
Displays a Saviour's boundless love,
And brings His glories near.

3 It shows to man his wandering ways,
And where his feet have trod ;
And brings to view the matchless grace
Of a forgiving God.

GOD'S WORD.   57

4 It sweetly cheers our drooping hearts,
    In this dark vale of tears;
    Life, light, and joy it still imparts,
    And quells our rising fears.

5 This lamp, thro' all the tedious night
    Of life, shall guide our way,
    Till we behold the clearer light
    Of an eternal day.
        Rev. John Fawcett. (1739—1817.) 1782. ab.

DUKE STREET. L. M. John Hatton. c. 1790.

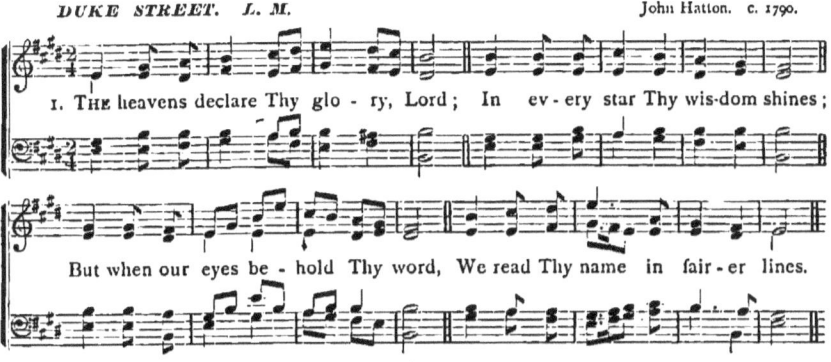

1. The heavens declare Thy glo - ry, Lord; In ev - ery star Thy wis-dom shines;
But when our eyes be - hold Thy word, We read Thy name in fair - er lines.

129   *The two Revelations.*
         Ps. xix.

2 The rolling sun, the changing light,
    And nights and days, Thy power confess,
    But the blest volume Thou hast writ,
    Reveals Thy justice and Thy grace.

3 Sun, moon, and stars, convey Thy praise   [stand:
    Round the whole earth, and never
    So when Thy truth began its race,
    It touched and glanced on every land.

4 Nor shall Thy spreading gospel rest,
    Till thro' the world Thy truth has run;
    Till Christ has all the nations blessed
    That see the light, and feel the sun.

5 Great Sun of Righteousness, arise,
    Bless the dark world with heavenly light;
    Thy gospel makes the simple wise,
    Thy laws are pure, Thy judgments right.
        Rev. Isaac Watts. 1719. ab.

130   *God's Word our Guide."*

1 God, in the gospel of His Son,
    Makes His eternal counsels known:
    Where love in all its glory shines,
    And truth is drawn in fairest lines.

2 Here sinners, of an humble frame,
    May taste His grace, and learn His name;
    May read, in characters of blood,
    The wisdom, power, and grace of God.

3 Here faith reveals to mortal eyes
    A brighter world beyond the skies;
    Here shines the light which guides our way
    From earth to realms of endless day.

4 O grant us grace, Almighty Lord,
    To read and mark Thy holy word;
    Its truth with meekness to receive,
    And by its holy precepts live.
        Rev. Benjamin Beddome. (1717—1795.) 1787. ab. and alt.
        Rev. Thomas Cotterill. (1779—1823.) 1819. ab.

GOD'S WORD.

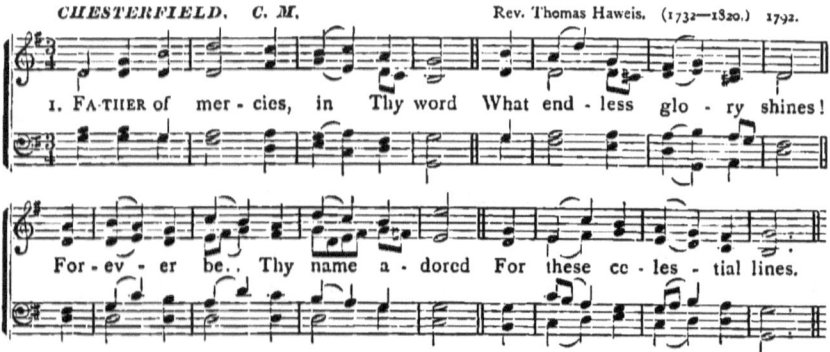

CHESTERFIELD. C. M.   Rev. Thomas Haweis. (1732—1820.) 1792.

1. Father of mercies, in Thy word
What endless glory shines!
For ever be Thy name adored
For these celestial lines.

131   *The Riches of God's Word.*
Ps. cxix.

2 Here may the wretched sons of want
Exhaustless riches find;
Riches above what earth can grant,
And lasting as the mind.

3 Here the Redeemer's welcome voice
Spreads heavenly peace around;
And life and everlasting joys
Attend the blissful sound.

4 O may these heavenly pages be
My ever dear delight;
And still new beauties may I see,
And still increasing light.

5 Divine Instructor, gracious Lord,
Be Thou forever near;
Teach me to love Thy sacred word,
And view my Saviour there.
Miss Anne Steele. (1717—1778.) 1760. ab.

132   *"Lamp of our Feet."*

1 Lamp of our feet, whereby we trace
Our path when wont to stray;
Stream from the Fount of heavenly grace,
Brook by the traveller's way;

2 Bread of our souls, whereon we feed,
True manna from on high;

Our guide and chart, wherein we read
Of realms beyond the sky;

3 Word of the Everlasting God,
Will of His glorious Son;
Without thee how could earth be trod,
Or heaven itself be won?

4 Lord, grant us all aright to learn
The wisdom it imparts;
And to its heavenly teaching turn,
With simple, child-like hearts.
Bernard Barton. (1784—1849.) 1827. ab.

133   *"Hail, sacred Truth."*

1 Hail, sacred truth, whose piercing rays
Dispel the shades of night;
Diffusing, o'er the mental world,
The healing beams of light.

2 Jesus, Thy word, with friendly aid,
Restores our wandering feet;
Converts the sorrows of the mind
To joys divinely sweet.

3 O send Thy light and truth abroad,
In all their radiant blaze;
And bid the admiring world adore
The glories of Thy grace.
John Buttress. 1820.

GOD'S WORD AND SALVATION.

SALVATION. 7, 6. D. — Johann C. W. A. Mozart, (1756—1791.)

1. O Word of God In-carn-ate, O Wisdom from on high, O Truth unchanged, un-changing, O Light of our dark sky; We praise Thee for the ra-diance That from the hallowed page, A lan-tern to our footsteps, Shines on from age to age.

134 *"O Word of God incarnate."*

2 The Church from Thee, her Master,
Received the gift divine;
And still that light she lifteth
O'er all the earth to shine.
It is the golden casket
Where gems of truth are stored;
It is the heaven-drawn picture
Of Thee, the living Word.

3 It floateth like a banner
Before God's host unfurled;
It shineth like a beacon
Above the darkling world;
It is the chart and compass,
That o'er life's surging sea,
Mid mists, and rocks, and quick-sands,
Still guide, O Christ, to Thee.

3 O make Thy Church, dear Saviour,
A lamp of burnished gold,
To bear before the nations
Thy true light, as of old.

O teach Thy wandering pilgrims
By this their path to trace,
Till, clouds and darkness ended,
They see Thee face to face.
Rev. William Walsham How. (1823—) 1867.

135 *"Mighty to save."* Is. lxiii. 1.

1 He comes in blood-stained garments;
Upon His brow a crown;
The gates of brass fly open,
The iron bands drop down;
From off the fettered captive
The chains of Satan fall,
While angels shout triumphant,
That Christ is Lord of all.

2 O Christ, His love is mighty,
Long-suffering is His grace;
And glorious is the splendor
That beameth from His face.
Our hearts up-leap in gladness
When we behold that love,
As we go singing onward
To dwell with Him above.
Mrs. Charitie Lees Bancroft. (1841—) 1860. ab.

THE GREAT SALVATION.

HENRY. C. M.   Sylvanus Billings Pond. (1815—1871.) 1835.

1. Sal-va-tion, O...... the joy-ful sound! 'Tis pleasure to...... our ears;
A sov-ereign balm for ev-ery wound, A cor-dial for our fears.

136   *Salvation.*
2 Buried in sorrow and in sin,
   At hell's dark door we lay;
   But we arise, by grace divine,
   To see a heavenly day.

3 Salvation! Let the echo fly
   The spacious earth around,
   While all the armies of the sky
   Conspire to raise the sound.
              Rev. Isaac Watts. (1674—1748.) 1709.

137   *Praise to the Redeemer.*
1 Plunged in a gulf of dark despair,
   We wretched sinners lay,
   Without one cheerful beam of hope,
   Or spark of glimmering day.

2 With pitying eyes the Prince of grace
   Beheld our helpless grief;
   He saw, and (O amazing love!)
   He ran to our relief.

3 Down from the shining seats above,
   With joyful haste He fled,
   Entered the grave in mortal flesh,
   And dwelt among the dead.

4 O for this love, let rocks and hills
   Their lasting silence break;

And all harmonious human tongues
   The Saviour's praises speak.

5 Angels, assist our mighty joys,
   Strike all your harps of gold;
   But when you raise your highest notes,
   His love can ne'er be told.
              Rev. Isaac Watts. 1709. ab.

138   *"The Way, the Truth, the Life."*
               John xiv. 6.
1 Thou art the Way: To Thee alone
   From sin and death we flee;
   And he who would the Father seek,
   Must seek Him, Lord, by Thee.

2 Thou art the Truth: Thy word alone
   True wisdom can impart;
   Thou only canst inform the mind,
   And purify the heart.

3 Thou art the Life: the rending tomb
   Proclaims Thy conquering arm,
   And those who put their trust in Thee
   Nor death, nor hell shall harm.

4 Thou art the Way, the Truth, the Life:
   Grant us that Way to know,
   That Truth to keep, that Life to win,
   Whose joys eternal flow.
      Bp. George Washington Doane. (1799—1859.) 1824.

THE GREAT SALVATION. 61

139 *Trust in Christ.*

1 O Jesus, when I think of Thee,
Thy manger, cross, and throne,
My spirit trusts exultingly
In Thee, and Thee alone.

2 For me Thou didst become a man,
For me didst weep and die ;
For me achieve Thy wondrous plan,
For me ascend on high.

3 O let me share Thy holy birth,
Thy faith, Thy death to sin !
And, strong amidst the toils of earth,
My heavenly life begin.

4 Then shall I know what means the
Triumphant of Saint Paul : [strain
" To live is Christ, to die is gain ; "
"Christ is my All in all."
Rev. George Washington Bethune. (1805—1862.) 1847. ab.

VALENTIA. C. M.
Traugott Maximilian Eberwein. (1775—1831.)
Arr. by George Kingsley. (1811—) 1853.

1. The Sav-iour calls, let ev-ery ear At-tend the heavenly sound;
Ye doubting souls, dis-miss your fear, Hope smiles re-viv-ing round.

140 *"The Saviour calls."* John vii. 37.

2 For every thirsty, longing heart,
Here streams of bounty flow,
And life, and health, and bliss impart,
To banish mortal woe.

3 Ye sinners, come, 'tis mercy's voice,
The gracious call obey ;
Mercy invites to heavenly joys,
And can you yet delay ?

4 Dear Saviour, draw reluctant hearts,
To Thee let sinners fly,
And take the bliss Thy love imparts,
And drink and never die.
Miss Anne Steele. (1717—1778.) 1760 ab.

141 *"The Incarnate Mystery."* 1 Cor. i. 22—29.

1 Dearest of all the names above,
My Jesus and my God,
Who can resist Thy heavenly Love,
Or trifle with Thy blood ?

2 Till God in human flesh I see,
My thoughts no comfort find :
The holy, just, and sacred Three
Are terrors to my mind.

3 But if Immanuel's face appear,
My hope, my joy, begins :
His name forbids my slavish fear ;
His grace removes my sins.

4 While Jews on their own law rely,
And Greeks of wisdom boast,
I love the incarnate Mystery,
And there I fix my trust.
Rev. Isaac Watts. 1709. ab.

GRACE AND MERCY.

SILVER STREET. S. M. Isaac Smith. 1770.

1. Grace, 'tis a charming sound, Harmonious to mine ear; Heaven with the echo shall resound, And all.... the earth shall hear.

142 *Saving Grace.*
Eph. ii. 5.

2 Grace first contrived a way
  To save rebellious man,
And all the steps that grace display,
  Which drew the wondrous plan.

3 Grace taught my wandering feet
  To tread the heavenly road ;
And new supplies each hour I meet,
  While pressing on to God.

4 Grace all the work shall crown,
  Through everlasting days ;
It lays in heaven the topmost stone,
  And well deserves the praise.
  Rev. Philip Doddridge. (1702—1751.) 1755.

143 "*The Song of Moses and the Lamb.*"
Rev. xv. 3.

1 Awake, and sing the song
  Of Moses and the Lamb ;
Wake every heart and every tongue,
  To praise the Saviour's name.

2 Sing of His dying love ;
  Sing of His rising power ;
Sing how He intercedes above
  For those whose sins he bore.

3 Sing till we feel our hearts
  Ascending with our tongues ;

Sing till the love of sin departs,
  And grace inspires our songs.

4 Sing on your heavenly way,
  Ye ransomed sinners, sing ;
Sing on, rejoicing every day
  In Christ the eternal King.

5 Soon shall ye hear Him say,
  "Ye blessed children, come ; "
Soon will He call you hence away,
  And take His wanderers home.

6 There shall our raptured tongue
  His endless praise proclaim,
And sweeter voices swell the song
  Of Moses and the Lamb.
  Rev. William Hammond. (—1783.) 1745. ab. and alt.
  Rev. Martin Madan. (1726—1790.) 1760. First 5 vs.

144 "*Sweet is Thy Mercy.*"
Ps. cix. 20.

1 Sweet is Thy mercy, Lord ;
  Before Thy mercy-seat
My soul, adoring, pleads Thy word,
  And owns Thy mercy sweet.

2 Where'er Thy name is blest,
  Where'er Thy people meet,
There I delight in Thee to rest,
  And find Thy mercy sweet.

GRACE AND MERCY. 63

3 Light Thou my weary way,
Place Thou my weary feet,
That while I stray on earth I may
Still find Thy mercy sweet.

4 Thus shall the heavenly host
Hear all my songs repeat
To Father, Son, and Holy Ghost,
My joy, Thy mercy sweet.
Rev. John Samuel Bewley Monsell. (1811—) 1862. ab.

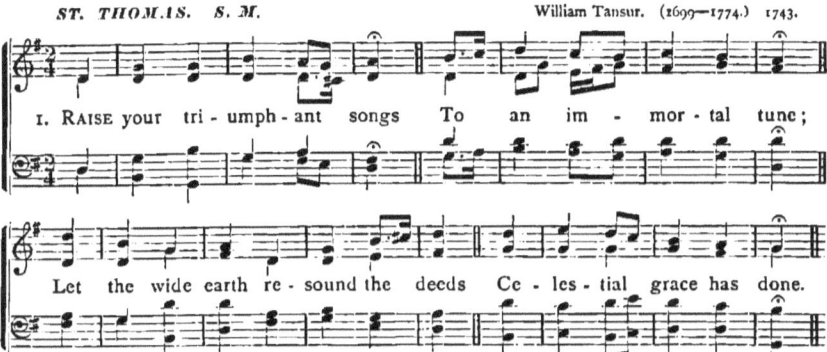

ST. THOMAS. S. M. — William Tansur. (1699—1774.) 1743.

1. Raise your triumphant songs To an immortal tune;
Let the wide earth resound the deeds Celestial grace has done.

145 *Christ sent to save us.*

2 Sing how Eternal Love
Its chief belovèd chose,
And bade Him raise our wretched race
From their abyss of woes.

3 'Twas mercy filled the throne,
And wrath stood silent by,
When Christ was sent with pardons
To rebels doomed to die. [down

4 Now, sinners, dry your tears,
Let hopeless sorrow cease ;
Bow to the sceptre of His love,
And take the offered peace.

5 Lord, we obey Thy call ;
We lay a humble claim
To the salvation Thou hast brought,
And love and praise Thy name.
Rev. Isaac Watts. (1674—1748.) 1709. ab.

146 *Christ our Righteousness.*

1 How heavy is the night
That hangs upon our eyes,
Till Christ, with His reviving light,
Over our souls arise !

2 Our guilty spirits dread
To meet the wrath of heaven ;
But, in His righteousness arrayed,
We see our sins forgiven.

3 Unholy and impure
Are all our thoughts and ways ;
His hands infected nature cure,
With sanctifying grace.

4 The powers of hell agree
To hold our souls in vain ;
He sets the sons of bondage free,
And breaks the cursèd chain.

5 Lord, we adore Thy ways
To bring us near to God ;
Thy sovereign power, Thy healing grace,
And Thine atoning blood.
Rev. Isaac Watts. 1709.

THE SAVIOUR BORN.

ZERAH. C. M. — Lowell Mason. (1792—1872.) 1837.

1. The race that long in darkness pined Have seen a glorious Light; The people dwell in Day, who dwelt In Death's surrounding night, The people dwell in Day, who dwelt In Death's surrounding night.

147 *The Messiah's Coming and Kingdom.*
Is. ix. 1—7.

2 To hail Thy rise, Thou better Sun,
  The gathering nations come,
  Joyous as when the reapers bear
  The harvest-treasures home.

3 To us a Child of Hope is born,
  To us a Son is given;
  Him shall the tribes of earth obey,
  Him all the hosts of heaven.

4 His name shall be the Prince of Peace
  Forevermore adored,
  The Wonderful, the Counsellor,
  The great and mighty Lord.

5 His power increasing still shall spread;
  His reign no end shall know:
  Justice shall guard His throne above,
  And Peace abound below.
  Rev. John Morrison. (1749—1798.) 1770. ab.

148 *Song of the Angels.*
Luke ii. 7—15.

1 While shepherds watched their flocks
    by night,
  All seated on the ground,
  The angel of the Lord came down,
  And glory shone around.

2 "Fear not," said he, for mighty dread
  Had seized their troubled mind;

"Glad tidings of great joy I bring
To you, and all mankind.

3 "To you, in David's town, this day,
  Is born of David's line,
  The Saviour, who is Christ, the Lord;
  And this shall be the sign:

4 "The heavenly babe you there shall find
  To human view displayed,
  All meanly wrapped in swathing bands,
  And in a manger laid."

5 Thus spake the seraph, and forthwith
  Appeared a shining throng
  Of angels, praising God, and thus
  Addressed their joyful song:

6 "All glory be to God on high,
  And to the earth be peace;
  Good-will henceforth from heaven to
  Begin, and never cease."   [men
  Tate and Brady's Supplemen.. 1703.

149 *The Saviour's Errand.*
Is. lxi.

1 Hark, the glad sound, the Saviour
    comes,
  The Saviour promised long;
  Let every heart prepare a throne,
  And every voice a song.

JOY TO THE WORLD. 65

2 He comes, the prisoners to release
  In Satan's bondage held ;
  The gates of brass before Him burst,
  The iron fetters yield.

3 He comes, from thickest films of vice
  To clear the mental ray,
  And on the eyeballs of the blind
  To pour celestial day.

4 He comes, the broken heart to bind,
  The bleeding soul to cure,
  And with the treasures of His grace
  To enrich the humble poor.

5 Our glad hosannas, Prince of Peace,
  Thy welcome shall proclaim,
  And heaven's eternal arches ring
  With Thy beloved name.

  Rev. Philip Doddridge. (1702—1751.) 1735.

ANTIOCH. C. M.   From George Frederick Handel. Arr. by Lowell Mason. 1836.

150 "*Joy to the World.*"
         Ps. xcviii.

2 Joy to the earth, the Saviour reigns :
  Let men their songs employ ;
  While fields and floods, rocks, hills,
      and plains,
  Repeat the sounding joy.

3 No more let sins and sorrows grow,
  Nor thorns infest the ground :
  He comes to make His blessings flow
  Far as the curse is found.

4 He rules the world with truth and
  And makes the nations prove [grace,
  The glories of His righteousness,
  And wonders of His love.

       Rev. Isaac Watts. (1674—1748.) 1709.

151   *Christ's Coming.*
           Ps. xcvi.

1 SING to the Lord, ye distant lands,
  Ye tribes of every tongue :
  His new discovered grace demands
  A new and nobler song.

2 Say to the nations, Jesus reigns,
  God's own almighty Son ;
  His power the sinking world sustains,
  And grace surrounds His throne.

3 Behold He comes, He comes to bless
  The nations as their God ;
  To show the world His righteousness,
  And send His truth abroad.

       Rev. Isaac Watts. 1719. ab.

THE DAWN OF HOPE.

MORNING STAR. 7. D.   Lowell Mason. (1792—1872.) 1830.

1. Watchman, tell us of the night, What its signs of promise are: Traveller, o'er yon mountain's height See that glo-ry-beaming star! Watchman, does its beauteous ray Aught of joy or hope foretell? Traveller, yes; it brings the day, Promised day of Is-ra-el.

152   "*What of the Night?*"
         Is. xxi. 11.

2 Watchman, tell us of the night;
    Higher yet that star ascends:
Traveller, blessedness and light,
    Peace and truth, its course portends.
Watchman, will its beams alone
    Gild the spot that gave them birth?
Traveller, ages are its own,
    See, it bursts o'er all the earth.

3 Watchman, tell us of, the night,
    For the morning seems to dawn:
Traveller, darkness takes its flight,
    Doubt and terror are withdrawn.
Watchman, let thy wanderings cease;
    Hie thee to thy quiet home:
Traveller, lo, the Prince of Peace,
    Lo, the Son of God is come!
         Sir John Bowring. (1792—1872.) 1825. sl. alt.

153   "*The Herald Angels.*"

1 Hark! the herald angels sing,
    "Glory to the new-born King:
Peace on earth, and mercy mild,
    God and sinners reconciled!"
Joyful, all ye nations, rise,
    Join the triumph of the skies;
Universal nature say,
    Christ, the Lord, is born to-day!

2 Hail, the heavenly Prince of Peace!
    Hail, the Sun of Righteousness!
Light and life to all He brings,
    Risen with healing in His wings.
Mild He lays His glory by,
    Born that man no more may die,
Born to raise the sons of earth,
    Born to give them second birth
      Rev. Charles Wesley. (1708—1788.) 1739. ab. and alt.

154   *The Names and Offices of Christ.*

1 Bright and joyful is the morn,
    For to us a Child is born:
From the highest realms of heaven
    Unto us a Son is given.
On His shoulder He shall bear
    Power and majesty, and wear
On His vesture and His thigh
    Names most awful, names most high.

2 Wonderful in counsel, He,
The incarnate Deity:
Sire of ages ne'er to cease,
King of kings, and Prince of Peace.

Come and worship at His feet,
Yield to Christ the homage meet;
From His manger to His throne,
Homage due to God alone.

James Montgomery. (1771—1854.) 1853.

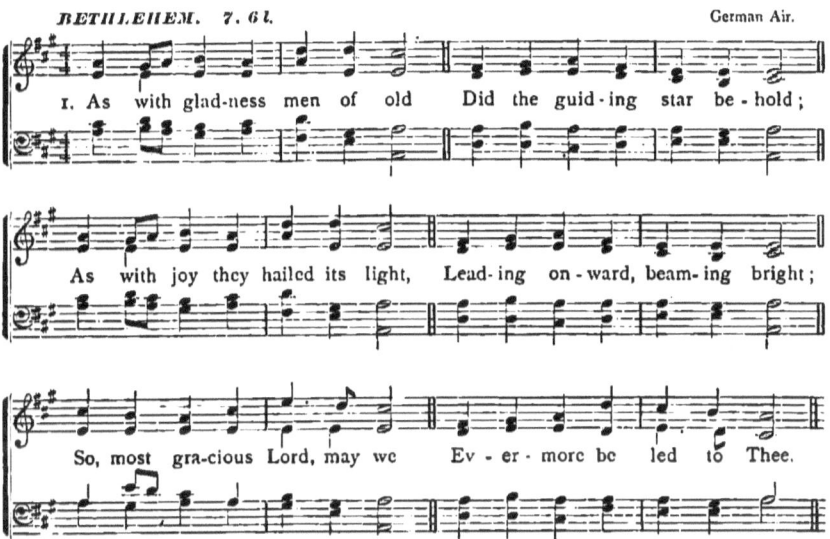

BETHLEHEM. 7. 6 l. German Air.

1. As with gladness men of old Did the guiding star behold;
As with joy they hailed its light, Leading onward, beaming bright;
So, most gracious Lord, may we Evermore be led to Thee.

155 *The guiding Star.*
Matt. ii. 10.

2 As with joyful steps they sped
To that lowly manger-bed,
There to bend the knee before
Him whom heaven and earth adore;
So may we with willing feet
Ever seek the mercy-seat.

3 As they offered gifts more rare
At that manger rude and bare;
So may we with holy joy,
Pure, and free from sin's alloy,
All our costliest treasures bring,
Christ, to Thee, our heavenly King.

4 Holy Jesus, every day
Keep us in the narrow way;
And, when earthly things are past,
Bring our ransomed souls at last
Where they need no star to guide,
Where no clouds Thy glory hide.

5 In the heavenly country bright
Need they no created light;
Thou its Light, its Joy, its Crown,
Thou its Sun, which goes not down:
There forever may we sing
Alleluias to our King.

William Chatterton Dix. (1837—) 1860.

STAR OF BETHLEHEM.

CAPELLO. L. M.   Rudolf Kreutzer. (1766—1831.)

1. When marshalled on the night-ly plain, The glittering host be-stud the sky, One star a-lone of all the train Can fix the sin-ner's wandering eye.

156   *The Star of Bethlehem.*

2 Hark, hark! to God the chorus breaks
From every host, from every gem;
But one alone the Saviour speaks,
It is the Star of Bethlehem.

3 Once on the raging seas I rode,
The storm was loud, the night was dark,
The ocean yawned, and rudely blowed
The wind that tossed my foundering bark.

4 Deep horror then my vitals froze;
Death-struck, I ceased the tide to stem :
When suddenly a star arose,
It was the Star of Bethlehem.

5 It was my guide, my light, my all,
It bade my dark forebodings cease ;
And, through the storm and danger's thrall,
It led me to the port of peace.

6 Now safely moored, my perils o'er,
I'll sing, first in night's diadem,
Forever and for evermore,
The Star, the Star of Bethlehem.
        Henry Kirke White. (1785—1806.) 1806.

157   *"Quæ stella sole pulchrior."*

1 What star is this, with beams so bright,
Which shame the sun's less radiant light?
It shines to announce a new-born King,
Glad tidings of our God to bring.

2 'Tis now fulfilled what God decreed,
"From Jacob shall a star proceed:"
And lo, the Eastern sages stand,
To read in heaven the Lord's command.

3 O Jesus, while the star of grace,
Invites us now to seek Thy face,
May we no more that grace repel,
Or quench that light which shines so well.
    Prof. Charles Coffin. (1676—1749.) 1736. alt.
    Tr. by Rev. John Chandler. (1806—) 1837. ab.

158   *The Birth at Bethlehem.*

1 When Jordan hushed his waters still,
And silence slept on Zion's hill;
When Bethlehem's shepherds thro' the night
Watched o'er their flocks by starry light;

2 Hark! from the midnight hills around,
A voice of more than mortal sound
In distant hallelujahs stole,
Wild murmuring o'er the raptured soul.

3 On wheels of light, on wings of flame,
The glorious hosts of Zion came ;
High heaven with songs of triumph rung,
While thus they struck their harps, and sung:

STAR OF THE EAST. 69

4 "O Zion, lift thy raptured eye,
The long-expected hour is nigh;
Renewed, creation smiles again,
The Prince of Salem comes to reign.

5 "He comes to cheer the trembling heart,
Bid Satan and his host depart;
Again the Daystar gilds the gloom,
Again the bowers of Eden bloom."
Thomas Campbell. (1777—1844.) 1820. ab.

FOLSOM. 11, 10. Johann C. W. A. Mozart. (1756—1791.)

1. Brightest and best of the sons of the morn-ing, Dawn on our dark-ness, and lend us thine aid;
Star of the East, the ho-ri-zon a-dorn-ing, Guide where our in-fant Re-deem-er is laid.

159 *"Star of the East."*

2 Cold on His cradle the dew-drops are shining,
  Low lies His head with the beasts of the stall;
Angels adore Him in slumber reclining,
  Maker, and Monarch, and Saviour of all.

3 Say, shall we yield Him, in costly devotion,
  Odors of Edom, and offerings divine,
Gems of the mountain, and pearls of the ocean,
  Myrrh from the forest, or gold from the mine?

4 Vainly we offer each ample oblation;
  Vainly with gifts would His favor secure:
Richer by far is the heart's adoration;
  Dearer to God are the prayers of the poor.

5 Brightest and best of the sons of the morning,
  Dawn on our darkness, and lend us Thine aid;
Star of the East, the horizon adorning,
  Guide where our infant Redeemer is laid.
            Bp. Reginald Heber. (1783—1826.) 1811.

SONG OF THE ANGELS.

WILMOT. 8, 7.   Carl Maria von Weber. (1786—1826.)

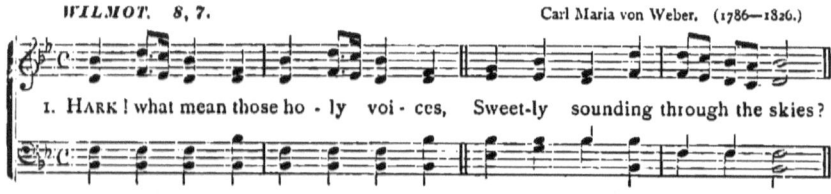

1. Hark! what mean those ho-ly voi-ces, Sweet-ly sounding through the skies?

Lo, the an-gel-ic host re-joic-es; Heavenly hal-le-lu-jahs rise.

160   *The holy Voices.*

2 Listen to the wondrous story,
   Which they chant in hymns of joy:
"Glory in the highest, glory,
   Glory be to God most high.

3 "Peace on earth, good-will from heaven,
   Reaching far as man is found;
Souls redeemed, and sins forgiven,
   Loud our golden harps shall sound.

4 "Christ is born, the great Anointed;
   Heaven and earth His glory sing:
Glad receive whom God appointed
   For your Prophet, Priest, and King.

5 "Hasten, mortals, to adore Him;
   Learn His name and taste His joy:
Till in heaven you sing before Him,
   'Glory be to God most high.'"
        Rev. John Cawood. (1775—1852.) 1819. ab.

161   *Desired of all Nations.*

1 Come, Thou long-expected Jesus,
   Born to set Thy people free:
From our fears and sins release us,
   Let us find our rest in Thee.

2 Israel's Strength and Consolation,
   Hope of all the earth Thou art;
Dear Desire of every nation,
   Joy of every longing heart.

3 Born Thy people to deliver,
   Born a Child, and yet a King,
Born to reign in us for ever,
   Now Thy gracious kingdom bring.

4 By Thine own eternal Spirit,
   Rule in all our hearts alone;
By Thine all-sufficient merit,
   Raise us to Thy glorious throne.
        Rev. Charles Wesley. (1708—1788.) 1744.

162   *Christ praised.*

1 Brightness of the Father's glory,
   Shall Thy praise unuttered lie?
Fly, my tongue, such guilty silence,
   Sing the Lord who came to die.

2 Did archangels sing Thy coming?
   Did the shepherds learn their lays?
Shame would cover me ungrateful,
   Should my tongue refuse to praise.

SONG OF THE ANGELS. 71

3 From the highest throne of glory,
To the cross of deepest woe—
All to ransom guilty captives :
Flow, my praise, forever flow.

4 Go, return, immortal Saviour,
Leave Thy footstool, take Thy throne
Thence return and reign forever;
Be the Kingdom all Thine own.
Rev. Robert Robinson. (1735—1790.) 1774. sl. alt.

FINNEY. 8, 7, 4.   Carl Maria von Weber.

1. { ANGELS, from the realms of glory, Wing your flight o'er all the earth, }
   { Ye who sang crea-tion's sto-ry, Now proclaim Messiah's birth : } Come and worship,

Come and worship, Worship Christ, the new-born King, Worship Christ, the new-born King.

163   *"Good Tidings of great Joy."* Luke ii. 10.

2 Shepherds, in the field abiding,
Watching o'er your flocks by night,
God with man is now residing;
Yonder shines the infant-light :
Come and worship,
Worship Christ, the new-born King.

3 Saints, before the altar bending,
Watching long in hope and fear,
Suddenly the Lord, descending,
In His temple shall appear:
Come and worship,
Worship Christ, the new-born King.

4 Sinners, wrung with true repentance,
Doomed for guilt to endless pains,
Justice now revokes the sentence ;
Mercy calls you, break your chains :
Come and worship,
Worship Christ, the new-born King.
James Montgomery. (1771—1854.) 1819, 1825. ab.

164   *Christ's Coming.*

1 JESUS came, the heavens adoring,
Came with peace from realms on high;
Jesus came for man's redemption,
Lowly came on earth to die ;
Hallelujah ! Hallelujah !
Came in deep humility.

2 Jesus comes to hearts rejoicing,
Bringing news of sins forgiven ;
Jesus comes in sounds of gladness,
Leading souls redeemed to heaven;
Hallelujah ! Hallelujah !
Now the gate of death is riven.

3 Jesus comes on clouds triumphant,
When the heavens shall pass away ;
Jesus comes again in glory ;
Let us then our homage pay,
Hallelujah ! ever singing,
Till the dawn of endless day.
Rev. Godfrey Thring. (1823—) 1866. ab.

SONG OF THE ANGELS.

CAROL. C. M. D. — Richard Storrs Willis. (1819—.)

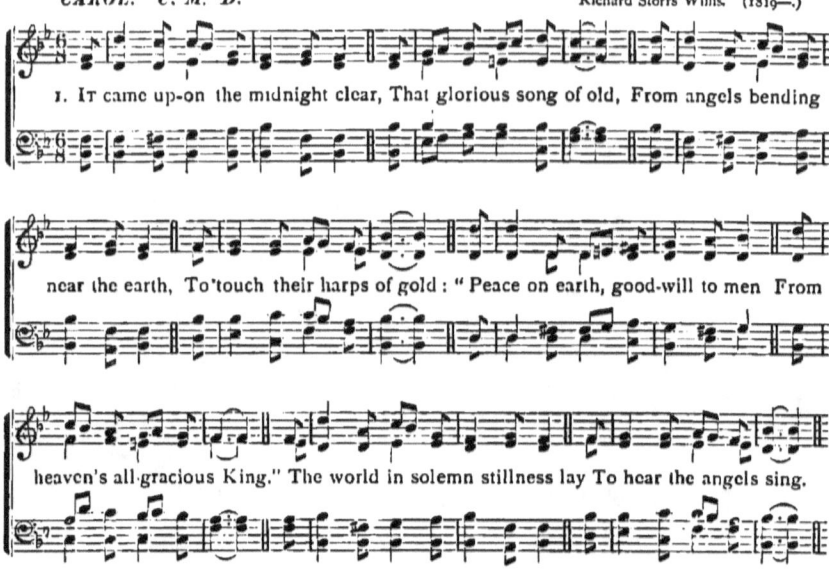

1. It came up-on the midnight clear, That glorious song of old, From angels bending near the earth, To 'touch their harps of gold: "Peace on earth, good-will to men From heaven's all-gracious King." The world in solemn stillness lay To hear the angels sing.

165 *Christmas Carol.*

2 Still thro' the cloven skies they come,
   With peaceful wings unfurled;
And still their heavenly music floats
   O'er all the weary world:
Above its sad and lowly plains
   They bend on hovering wing,
And ever o'er its Babel sounds
   The blessèd angels sing.

3 But with the woes of sin and strife
   The world has suffered long;
Beneath the angel-strain have rolled
   Two thousand years of wrong;
And man, at war with man, hears not
   The love-song which they bring:
O hush the noise, ye men of strife,
   And hear the angels sing.

4 And ye, beneath life's crushing load
   Whose forms are bending low,
Who toil along the climbing way,
   With painful steps and slow,—
Look now; for glad and golden hours
   Come swiftly on the wing:
O rest beside the weary road,
   And hear the angels sing.

5 For lo, the days are hastening on
   By prophet bards foretold,
When with the ever circling years
   Comes round the age of gold:
When Peace shall over all the earth
   Its ancient splendors fling,
And the whole world give back the song
   Which now the angels sing.

Rev. Edmund Hamilton Sears. (1810—). 1850.

CHRIST'S ADVENT AND ERRAND.

166 *Christmas Song.*

1 CALM on the listening ear of night
   Come heaven's melodious strains,
   Where wild Judea stretches far
   Her silver-mantled plains;
   Celestial choirs from courts above
   Shed sacred glories there;
   And angels, with their sparkling lyres,
   Make music on the air.

2 The answering hills of Palestine
   Send back the glad reply,
   And greet from all their holy heights
   The day-spring from on high:

O'er the blue depths of Galilee
There comes a holier calm;
And Sharon waves in solemn praise
Her silent groves of palm.

3 Glory to God! the lofty strain
   The realm of ether fills;
   How sweeps the song of solemn joy
   O'er Judah's sacred hills!
   "Glory to God!" the sounding skies
   Loud with their anthems ring:
   "Peace on the earth; good-will to men,
   From heaven's eternal King."

   Rev. Edmund Hamilton Sears. 1835. ab.

167 *"Who went about doing Good."* Acts x. 38.

2 To spread the rays of heavenly light,
   To give the mourner joy,
   To preach glad tidings to the poor,
   Was His divine employ.

3 Lowly in heart, to all His friends
   A Friend and Servant found, [tears,
   He washed their feet, He wiped their
   And healed each bleeding wound.

4 'Midst keen reproach, and cruel scorn,
   Patient and meek He stood;
   His foes, ungrateful, sought His life:
   He labored for their good.

5 To God He left His righteous cause,
   And still His task pursued;
   With humble prayer, and holy faith,
   His fainting strength renewed.

6 In the last hour of deep distress,
   Before His Father's throne,
   With soul resigned, He bowed, and said,
   "Thy will, not mine, be done."

7 Be Christ our pattern and our guide,
   His image may we bear;
   O may we tread His holy steps,
   His joy and glory share.

   Prof. William Enfield. (1741—1797.) 1771. alt.

CHRIST'S LIFE.

HAMBURG. (GREGORIAN.) *L. M.*   Arr. by Lowell Mason. (1792—1872.) 1825.

1. My dear Redeem-er, and my Lord, I read my du-ty in Thy word.

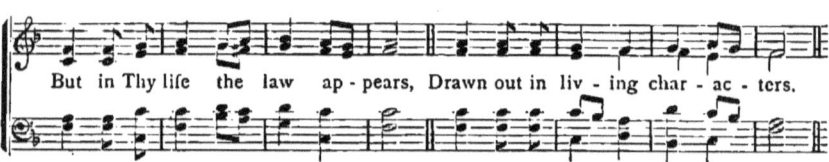

But in Thy life the law ap-pears, Drawn out in liv-ing char-ac-ters.

168   *Christ's Example.*
              1 Pet. ii. 21.

2 Such was Thy truth, and such Thy zeal,
Such deference to Thy Father's will,
Such love, and meekness so divine,
I would transcribe and make them mine.

3 Cold mountains and the midnight air
Witnessed the fervor of Thy prayer;
The desert Thy temptations knew,
Thy conflict and Thy victory too.

4 Be Thou my pattern; make me bear
More of Thy gracious image here;
Then God, the Judge, shall own my name
Amongst the followers of the Lamb.
      Rev. Isaac Watts. (1674—1748.) 1709.

169   *Christ in the Desert.*

1 AWHILE in spirit, Lord, to Thee
Into the desert would we flee;
Awhile upon the barren steep
Thy Fast with Thee in spirit keep;

2 Awhile from Thy temptation learn
The daily snares of sin to spurn,
And in our hearts to feel and own
Man liveth not by bread alone.

3 And while at Thy command we pray,
Give us our bread from day to day,
May we with Thee, O Christ, be fed,
Thou Word of God, Thou Living Bread.

4 Incarnate Lord, we come to Thee,
Thou knowest our infirmity;
Be Thou our Helper in the strife,
Be Thou our True, our inward Life.
      Rev. Joseph Francis Thrupp. 1860?

170   *Christ's Works of Mercy.*

1 WHEN, like a stranger on our sphere,
The lowly Jesus sojourned here,
Where'er He went, affliction fled,
And sickness reared her drooping head.

2 The eye that rolled in irksome night
Beheld His face, for He was light;
The opening ear, the loosened tongue,
His precepts heard, His praises sung.

3 Demoniac madness, dark and wild,
With melancholy transport smiled;
The storm of horror ceased to roll,
And reason lightened through the soul.

CHRIST'S LIFE AND MIRACLES.

4 His touch the outcast leper healed,
His lips the sinner's pardon sealed;
Warm tears o'er Lazarus He shed,
Then spake the word that raised the dead.
James Montgomery. (1771—1854.) 1797. ab.

171 *The Meekness of Christ.* L. M.

1 How beauteous were the marks divine,
That in Thy meekness used to shine,
That lit Thy lonely pathway, trod
In wondrous love, O Son of God.

2 O who like Thee, so calm, so bright,
So pure, so made to live in light?
O who like Thee did ever go
So patient, through a world of woe?

3 O who like Thee, so humbly bore
The scorn, the scoffs of men, before?
So meek, forgiving, godlike, high,
So glorious in humility?

4 And death, that sets the prisoner free,
Was pang, and scoff, and scorn to Thee,
Yet love thro' all Thy torture glowed,
And mercy with Thy life-blood flowed.

5 O in Thy light be mine to go,
Illuming all my way of woe;
And give me ever, on the road,
To trace Thy footsteps, O my God.
Bp. Arthur Cleveland Coxe. (1818—) 1840. ab.

VARINA. C. M. D.
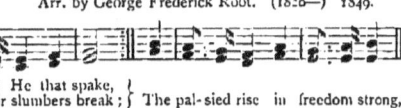
Johann C. H. Rink. (1770—1846.)
Arr. by George Frederick Root. (1820—) 1849.

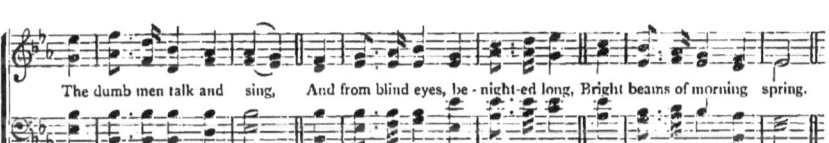

1. { O, WHERE is He that trod the sea, O, where is He that spake, }
   { And demons from their victims flee, The dead their slumbers break; } The pal-sied rise in freedom strong,

The dumb men talk and sing, And from blind eyes, be-night-ed long, Bright beams of morning spring.

172 *"O, where is He that trod the Sea?"*

2 O, where is He that trod the sea,
'Tis only He can save;
To thousands hungering wearily,
A wondrous meal He gave:
Full soon, celestially fed,
Their mystic fare they take; [bread,
'Twas springtide when He blest the
And harvest when He brake.

3 O, where is He that trod the sea,
My soul, the Lord is here:
Let all Thy fears be hushed in thee;
To leap, to look, to hear,
Be thine: thy needs He'll satisfy:
Art thou diseased, or dumb?
Or dost thou in thy hunger cry?
"I come," said Christ, "I come."
Rev. Thomas Toke Lynch. (1818—1871.) 1855. ab.

GETHSEMANE AND CALVARY.

OLIVE'S BROW. L. M.   William Batchelder Bradbury. (1816—1868.) 1853.

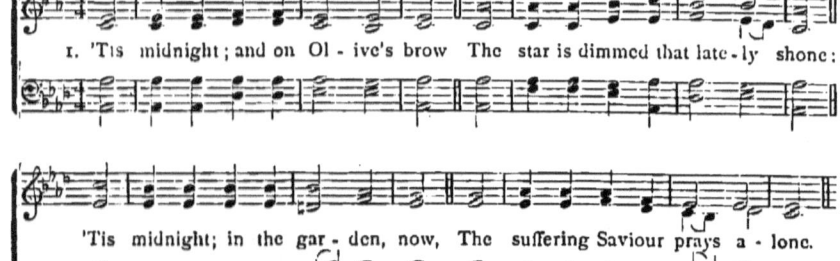

1. 'Tis midnight; and on Olive's brow The star is dimmed that lately shone:
'Tis midnight; in the garden, now, The suffering Saviour prays alone.

173   *Christ in Gethsemane.*

2 'Tis midnight; and from all removed,
The Saviour wrestles lone with fears;
E'en that disciple whom He loved
Heeds not his Master's grief and tears.

3 'Tis midnight; and for others' guilt
The Man of Sorrows weeps in blood;
Yet He that hath in anguish knelt
Is not forsaken by His God.

4 'Tis midnight; and from ether-plains
Is borne the song that angels know;
Unheard by mortals are the strains
That sweetly soothe the Saviour's woe.
Rev. William Bingham Tappan. (1794—1849.) 1819.

174   *"Behold the Man!"*

1 YE that pass by, behold the Man,
The Man of Griefs condemned for you:
The Lamb of God for sinners slain,
Weeping to Calvary pursue.

2 His sacred limbs they stretch, they tear;
With nails they fasten to the wood;
His sacred limbs, exposed and bare,
Or only covered with His blood.

3 See there, His temples crowned with thorn,
His bleeding hands extended wide,
His streaming feet transfixed and torn,
The fountain gushing from His side.

4 O Thou dear suffering Son of God,
How doth Thy heart to sinners move:
Sprinkle on us Thy precious blood,
And melt us with Thy dying love.

5 The rocks could feel Thy powerful death,
And tremble and asunder part:
O rend with Thine expiring breath
The harder marble of my heart.
Rev. Charles Wesley. (1708—1788.) 1742. ab.

175   *Gazing upon the Cross.*

1 LORD Jesus, when we stand afar
And gaze upon Thy holy cross,
In love of Thee and scorn of self,
O may we count the world as loss.

2 When we behold Thy bleeding wounds,
And the rough way that Thou hast trod,
Make us to hate the load of sin
That lay so heavy on our God.

GETHSEMANE AND CALVARY.

3 O Holy Lord, uplifted high
    With outstretched arms, in mortal woe,
    Embracing in Thy wondrous love
    The sinful world that lies below;

4 Give us an ever-living faith
    To gaze beyond the things we see;
    And, in the mystery of Thy death,
    Draw us and all men unto Thee.
    Rev. William Walsham How. (1823—) 1854.

REDHEAD. 7. 6 l.   Richard Redhead. 1853.

1. Go to dark Gethsemane, Ye that feel the tempter's power; Your Redeemer's conflict see, Watch with Him one bitter hour: Turn not from His griefs away, Learn of Jesus Christ to pray.

176 *Christ our Example in Suffering.*

2 Follow to the judgment-hall,
    View the Lord of life arraigned;
    O the wormwood and the gall!
    O the pangs His soul sustained!
    Shun not suffering, shame, or loss;
    Learn of Him to bear the cross.

3 Calvary's mournful mountain climb;
    There, adoring at His feet,
    Mark that Miracle of time,
    God's own sacrifice complete:
    "It is finished," hear the cry;
    Learn of Jesus Christ to die.

4 Early hasten to the tomb,
    Where they laid His breathless clay:
    All is solitude and gloom;
    Who hath taken Him away?
    Christ is risen; He meets our eyes;
    Saviour, teach us so to rise.
    James Montgomery. (1771—1854.) 1822, 1853.

177 *"By Thy Night of Agony."*

1 LORD, in this Thy mercy's day,
    Ere from us it pass away,
    On our knees we fall and pray.
    Holy Jesus, grant us tears,
    Fill us with heart-searching fears,
    Ere that day of doom appears.

2 By Thy night of agony,
    By Thy supplicating cry,
    By Thy willingness to die,
    By Thy tears of bitter woe
    For Jerusalem below,
    Let us not Thy love forego.

3 Lord, on us Thy Spirit pour,
    Kneeling lowly at the door,
    Ere it close for evermore.
    Judge and Saviour of our race,
    Grant us, when we see Thy face,
    With Thy ransomed ones a place.
    Rev. Isaac Williams. (1802—1865.) 1844. ab. and alt.

THE DYING SAVIOUR.

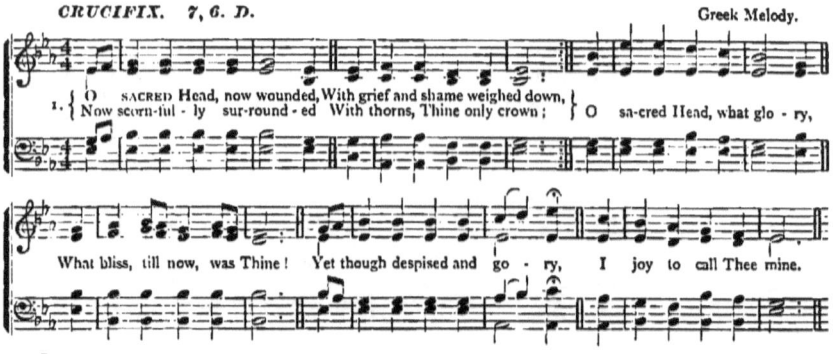

CRUCIFIX. 7, 6. D. Greek Melody.

O sacred Head, now wounded, With grief and shame weighed down,
Now scornfully surrounded With thorns, Thine only crown;
O sacred Head, what glory, What bliss, till now, was Thine!
Yet though despised and gory, I joy to call Thee mine.

178 *"Salve, caput cruentatum."*

2 What Thou, my Lord, hast suffered
  Was all for sinners' gain:
Mine, mine was the transgression,
  But Thine the deadly pain:
Lo, here I fall, my Saviour!
  'Tis I deserve Thy place;
Look on me with Thy favor,
  Vouchsafe to me Thy grace.

3 What language shall I borrow
  To thank Thee, dearest Friend,
For this Thy dying sorrow,
  Thy pity without end?
O make me Thine forever;
  And should I fainting be,
Lord, let me never, never,
  Outlive my love to Thee.

4 Be near me when I'm dying,
  O show Thy cross to me;
And for my succor flying,
  Come, Lord, and set me free:
These eyes, new faith receiving,
  From Jesus shall not move;
For he who dies believing,
  Dies safely, through Thy love.

Bernard of Clairvaux. (1091—1153.)
Rev. Paul Gerhardt. (1606—1676.) 1659.
Rev. James Waddell Alexander. (1804—1859.) 1849. ab.

179 *Standing at the Door.*

1 O JESUS, Thou art standing
  Outside the fast-closed door,
In lowly patience waiting
  To pass the threshold o'er:
Shame on us, Christian brethren,
  His Name and sign who bear,
O shame, thrice shame upon us,
  To keep Him standing there!

2 O Jesus, Thou art knocking:
  And lo, that hand is scarred,
And thorns Thy brow encircle,
  And tears Thy face have marred.
O love that passeth knowledge,
  So patiently to wait!
O sin that hath no equal,
  So fast to bar the gate!

3 O Jesus, Thou art pleading
  In accents meek and low,
"I died for you, My children,
  And will ye treat Me so?"
O Lord, with shame and sorrow
  We open now the door:
Dear Saviour, enter, enter,
  And leave us never more.

Rev. William Walsham How. (1823—) 1854.

CROSS AND PASSION. 79

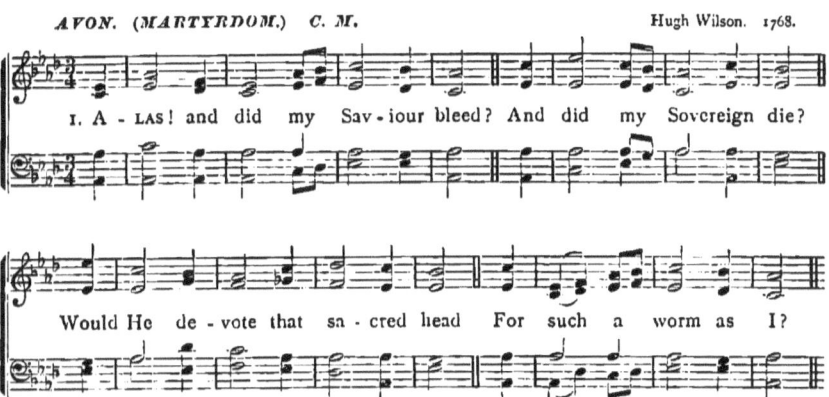

AVON. (MARTYRDOM.) C. M. Hugh Wilson. 1768.

1. A-LAS! and did my Sav-iour bleed? And did my Sovereign die?
Would He de-vote that sa-cred head For such a worm as I?

180 *Godly Sorrow in View of Christ's Sufferings.*

2 Was it for crimes that I had done
 He groaned upon the tree?
 Amazing pity! grace unknown!
 And love beyond degree!

3 Well might the sun in darkness hide,
 And shut his glories in,
 When God, the mighty Maker, died
 For man the creature's sin.

4 Thus might I hide my blushing face,
 While His dear cross appears:
 Dissolve, my heart, in thankfulness,
 And melt, mine eyes, to tears.

5 But drops of grief can ne'er repay
 The debt of love I owe:
 Here, Lord, I give myself away;
 'Tis all that I can do.
  Rev. Isaac Watts. (1674—1748.) 1709. ab.

181 *Kneeling at the Cross.*

1 O JESUS, sweet the tears I shed,
 While at Thy cross I kneel,
 Gaze on Thy wounded, fainting head,
 And all Thy sorrows feel.

2 My heart dissolves to see Thee bleed,
 This heart so hard before;
 I hear Thee for the guilty plead,
 And grief o'erflows the more.

3 'Twas for the sinful Thou didst die,
 And I a sinner stand:
 What love speaks from Thy dying eye,
 And from each piercéd hand.

4 I know this cleansing blood of Thine
 Was shed, dear Lord, for me:
 For me, for all, O grace divine!
 Who look by faith on Thee.

5 O Christ of God, O spotless Lamb,
 By love my soul is drawn;
 Henceforth, for ever, Thine I am;
 Here life and peace are born.

6 In patient hope, the cross I'll bear,
 Thine arm shall be my stay;
 And Thou, enthroned, my soul shalt spare,
 On Thy great judgment-day.
  Rev. Ray Palmer. (1808—) 1867.

CROSS AND PASSION.

FEDERAL STREET. L. M.   Henry Kemble Oliver. (1800—) 1832.

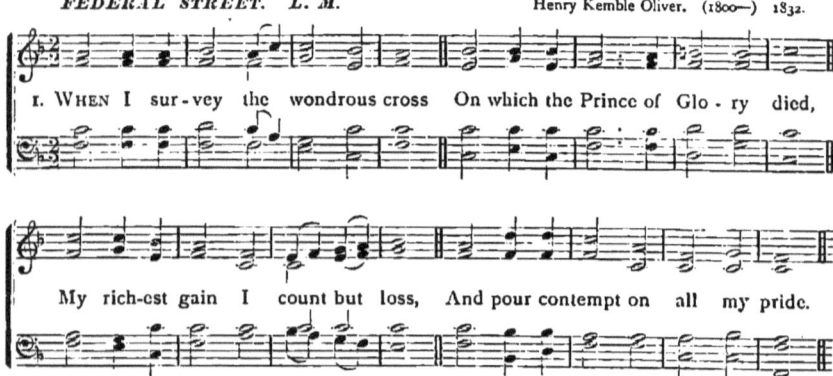

1. When I survey the wondrous cross
On which the Prince of Glory died,
My richest gain I count but loss,
And pour contempt on all my pride.

182   *Crucifixion to the World.*

2 Forbid it, Lord, that I should boast,
Save in the death of Christ, my God:
All the vain things that charm me most,
I sacrifice them to His blood.

3 See, from His head, His hands, His feet,
Sorrow and love flow mingled down:
Did e'er such love and sorrow meet,
Or thorns compose so rich a crown?

4 His dying crimson, like a robe,
Spreads o'er His body on the tree;
Then I am dead to all the globe,
And all the globe is dead to me.

5 Were the whole realm of nature mine,
That were a present far too small;
Love so amazing, so divine,
Demands my soul, my life, my all.
Rev. Isaac Watts. (1672—1748.) 1709.

183   *"'Tis finished!"*
John xix. 30.

1 "'Tis finished!" so the Saviour cried,
And meekly bowed His head, and died:
"'Tis finished!" yes, the race is run,
The battle fought, the victory won.

2 'Tis finished! all that heaven decreed,
And all the ancient Prophets said,
Is now fulfilled, as was designed,
In Me, the Saviour of mankind.

3 'Tis finished! this My dying groan
Shall sins of every kind atone;
Millions shall be redeemed from death,
By this My last expiring breath.

4 'Tis finished! let the joyful sound
Be heard through all the nations round;
'Tis finished! let the echo fly
Thro' heaven and hell, thro' earth and sky.
Rev. Samuel Stennett. (1727—1795.) 1778. ab.

184   *"Our Lord is crucified."*

1 O come, and mourn with me awhile;
O come ye to the Saviour's side;
O come, together let us mourn;
Jesus, our Lord, is crucified.

2 Have we no tears to shed for Him,
While soldiers scoff and Jews deride?
Ah, look how patiently He hangs;
Jesus, our Lord, is crucified.

3 How fast His hands and feet are
  nailed; [dried;
  His throat with parching thirst is
  His failing eyes are dimmed with blood:
  Jesus, our Lord, is crucified.
4 Seven times He spake, seven words of
  love;
  And all three hours His silence cried
  For mercy on the souls of men:
  Jesus, our Lord, is crucified.
Rev. Frederick William Faber. (1814—1863.) 1849. ab. and alt.

185 *The Song of Songs.*

1 COME, let us sing the song of songs,
  The saints in heaven began the strain,
  The homage which to Christ belongs:
  "Worthy the Lamb, for He was slain!"
2 Slain to redeem us by His blood,
  To cleanse from every sinful stain,
  And make us kings and priests to God:
  "Worthy the Lamb, for He was slain!"
3 To Him who suffered on the tree,
  Our souls at His soul's price to gain,
  Blessing, and praise, and glory be:
  "Worthy the Lamb, for He was slain!"
4 To Him, enthroned by filial right,
  All power in heaven and earth proclaim,
  Honor, and majesty, and might:
  "Worthy the Lamb, for He was slain!"
5 Long as we live, and when we die,
  And while in heaven with Him we reign,
  This song our song of songs shall be:
  "Worthy the Lamb, for He was slain!"
James Montgomery. (1771—1854.) 1853. ab. and alt.

186 *Our Priest and King.*

1 Now to the Lord, who makes us know
  The wonders of His dying love,
  Be humble honors paid below,
  And strains of noble praise above.
2 'Twas He who cleansed our foulest sins,
  And washed us in His precious blood;

'Tis He who makes us priests and kings,
  And brings us rebels near to God.
3 To Jesus, our atoning Priest,
  To Jesus, our eternal King,
  Be everlasting power confessed,
  And every tongue His glory sing.
4 Behold, on flying clouds He comes,
  And every eye shall see Him move;
  Though with our sins we pierced Him once,
  He now displays His pard'ning love.
Rev. Isaac Watts. 1707. ab. and sl. alt.

187 *The enthroned High Priest.*

1 WHERE high the heavenly temple
  stands, [hands,
  The house of God not made with
  A great High Priest our nature wears,
  The Patron of mankind appears.
2 He who for men in mercy stood,
  And poured on earth His precious blood,
  Pursues in heaven His plan of grace,
  The Guardian God of human race.
3 Though now ascended up on high,
  He bends on earth a brother's eye;
  Partaker of the human name,
  He knows the frailty of our frame.
4 Our fellow-sufferer yet retains
  A fellow-feeling of our pains;
  And still remembers in the skies
  His tears, and agonies, and cries.
5 In every pang that rends the heart,
  The Man of sorrows had a part;
  He sympathizes in our grief,
  And to the sufferer sends relief.
6 With boldness, therefore, at the throne,
  Let us make all our sorrows known,
  And ask the aids of heavenly power,
  To help us in the evil hour.
Michael Bruce. (1746—1767.) 1781.

ALL IS FINISHED.

BREST. 8, 7, 4.   Lowell Mason. (1792—1872.) 1836.

1. Hark, the voice of love and mercy Sounds aloud from Calvary;
See, it rends the rocks asunder, Shakes the earth, and veils the sky:
"It is finished!" "It is finished!" Hear the dying Saviour cry.

---

188   *"It is finished!"*

2 "It is finished!" O what pleasure
Do these charming words afford!
Heavenly blessings without measure
Flow to us from Christ, the Lord:
  "It is finished!"
Saints, the dying words record.

3 Finished all the types and shadows
Of the ceremonial law!
Finished all that God had promised;
Death and hell no more shall awe:
  "It is finished!"
Saints, from hence your comfort draw.

4 Tune your harps anew, ye seraphs,
Join to sing the pleasing theme;
All on earth and all in heaven,
Join to praise Immanuel's name:
  Hallelujah!
Glory to the bleeding Lamb.

Rev. Jonathan Evans. (1749—1809.) 1787. ab.

---

189   *"Thou art worthy, O Lord."*
            Rev. iv. 11.

1 Glory, glory everlasting
Be to Him who bore the cross!
Who redeemed our souls, by tasting
Death, the death deserved by us:
  Spread His glory,
Who redeemed His people thus.

2 His is love, 'tis love unbounded,
Without measure, without end;
Human thought is here confounded,
'Tis too vast to comprehend:
  Praise the Saviour!
Magnify the sinner's Friend.

3 While we hear the wondrous story
Of the Saviour's cross and shame,
Sing we "Everlasting glory
Be to God, and to the Lamb:"
  Saints and angels,
Give ye glory to His name.

Rev. Thomas Kelly. (1769—1855.) 1809.

190 *"He hath borne our Griefs."*
Is. liii. 4, 5, 12.

2 Weary sinner, keep thine eyes
On the atoning sacrifice:
There the incarnate Deity
Numbered with transgressors see;
There His Father's absence mourns,
Nailed, and bruised, and crowned with thorns.

3 See thy God His head bow down,
Hear the Man of Sorrows groan;
For thy ransom, there condemned,
Stripped, derided, and blasphemed;
Bleeds the guiltless for the unclean,
Made an offering for thy sin.

4 Cast thy guilty soul on Him,
Find Him mighty to redeem;
At His feet thy burden lay,
Look thy doubts and cares away;
Now by faith the Son embrace,
Plead His promise, trust His grace.

Rev. Augustus Montague Toplady. (1740—1778.) 1759, 1770. ab.

191 *The Heart breaking before the Cross.*

1 HEART of stone, relent, relent;
Break, by Jesus' cross subdued!
See His body mangled, rent,
Covered with a gore of blood;
Sinful soul, what hast thou done?
Crucified the Incarnate Son.

2 Yes, thy sins have done the deed,
Driven the nails that fixed Him there,
Crowned with thorns His sacred head,
Pierced Him with the cruel spear,
Made His soul a sacrifice,
While for sinful man He dies.

3 Wilt thou let Him bleed in vain?
Still to death thy Lord pursue?
Open all His wounds again,
And the shameful cross renew?
No; with all my sins I'll part;
Break, O break, my bleeding heart!

Rev. Charles Wesley. (1708—1788.) 1745. alt.

The Lord of glory dies for men;
But lo, what sudden joys I see,
Jesus, the dead, revives again.

3 The rising God forsakes the tomb,
Up to His Father's court He flies;
Cherubic legions guard Him home,
And shout Him welcome to the skies.

4 Break off your tears, ye saints, and tell
How high our great Deliverer reigns;
Sing how He spoiled the hosts of hell,
And led the monster death in chains.

5 Say, "Live forever, wondrous King,
Born to redeem, and strong to save!"
Then ask the monster, "Where's thy sting?"
"And where's thy victory, boasting grave?"

Rev. Isaac Watts. (1674—1748.) 1706. ab.
Alt. by Rev. John Wesley. (1703—1791.)

What joy the blest assurance gives;
And now, before His Father, God,
Pleads the full merits of His blood.

2 Repeated crimes awake our fears,
And justice armed with frowns appears;
But in the Saviour's loving face
Sweet mercy smiles, and all is peace.

3 Hence then, ye black, despairing thoughts;
Above our fears, above our faults,
His powerful intercessions rise,
And guilt recedes, and terror dies.

4 In every dark, distressful hour;
When sin and Satan join their power,
Let this dear hope repel the dart,
That Jesus bears us on His heart.

5 Great Advocate, Almighty Friend,
On Him our humble hopes depend;
Our cause can never, never fail,
For Jesus pleads, and must prevail.

Miss Anne Steele. (1717—1778.) 1760.

CHRIST RISING AND REIGNING.

MIGDOL. L. M.   Lowell Mason. (1792—1872.) 1841.

1. Our Lord is ris-en from the dead, Our Jesus is gone up on high; The powers of hell are captive led, Dragged to the portals of the sky.

194   *"Our Lord is risen."* Ps. xxiv.

2 There His triumphal chariot waits,
And angels chant the solemn lay: —
" Lift up your heads, ye heavenly gates,
Ye everlasting doors, give way."

3 " Loose all your bars of massy light,
And wide unfold the ethereal scene ;
He claims these mansions as His right;
Receive the King of glory in."

4 "Who is this King of glory, who?"
"The Lord that all His foes o'ercame;
The world, sin, death, and hell o'erthrew ;
And Jesus is the conqueror's name."

5 Lo, His triumphal chariot waits,
And angels chant the solemn lay :—
" Lift up your heads, ye heavenly gates,
Ye everlasting doors, give way."

6 " Who is this King of glory, who?"
"The Lord of glorious power possessed,
The King of saints and angels, too :
God over all, forever blest."

Rev. Charles Wesley. (1708—1788.) 1743. ab.

195   *"He lives."*

1 " I know that my Redeemer lives: "
What comfort this sweet sentence
gives,
He lives, He lives, who once was dead,
He lives, my ever-living head.

2 He lives to bless me with His love,
He lives to plead for me above,
He lives my hungry soul to feed,
He lives to help in time of need.

3 He lives to silence all my fears,
He lives to stoop and wipe my tears,
He lives to calm my troubled heart,
He lives all blessings to impart.

4 He lives, my kind, my faithful Friend,
He lives and loves me to the end,
He lives, and while He lives I'll sing,
He lives, my Prophet, Priest, and
King.

5 He lives, all glory to His Name ;
He lives, my Jesus, still the same:
O the sweet joy this sentence gives,
" I know that my Redeemer lives."

Rev. Samuel Medley. (1738—1799.) 1789. ab. and sl. al.

CHRIST RISING AND REIGNING.

STOW. II. M. English Melody. Arr. by Lowell Mason. (1792—1872.) 1833.

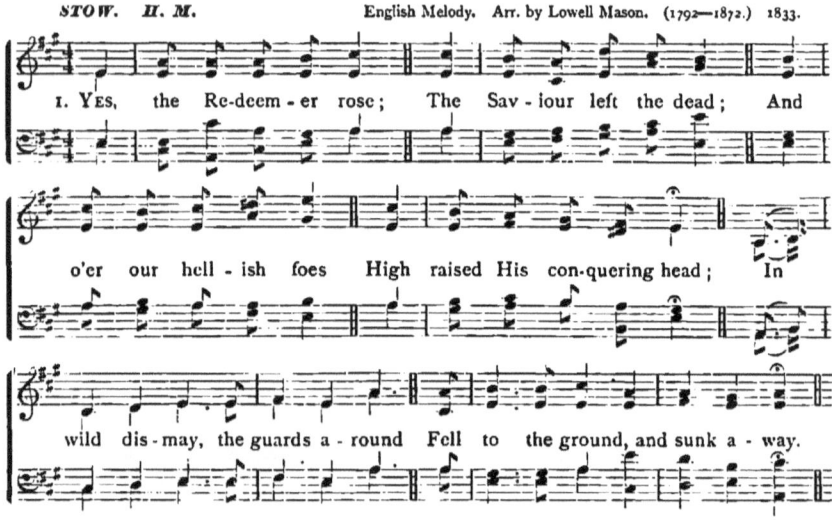

1. Yes, the Redeemer rose; The Saviour left the dead; And o'er our hellish foes High raised His conquering head; In wild dismay, the guards around Fell to the ground, and sunk away.

196 *The Resurrection of Christ.*
Luke xxiv. 34.

2 Lo, the angelic bands
   In full assembly meet,
To wait His high commands,
   And worship at His feet :
Joyful they come, and wing their way,
From realms of day, to such a tomb.

3 Then back to heaven they fly,
   And the glad tidings bear ;
Hark! as they soar on high,
   What music fills the air :
Their anthems say, 'Jesus, who bled,
Hath left the dead ; He rose to-day.'

4 Ye mortals, catch the sound,
   Redeemed by Him from hell ;
And send the echo round
   The globe on which you dwell :
Transported cry, 'Jesus, who bled,
Hath left the dead, no more to die.'

5 All hail, triumphant Lord,
   Who savest us with Thy blood !
Wide be Thy name adored,
   Thou rising, reigning God.
With Thee we rise, with Thee we reign,
And empires gain beyond the skies.
     Rev. Philip Doddridge. (1702—1751.) 1755.

197 *Captivity led captive.*
Ps. lxviii. 18. Eph. iv. 8.

1 The happy morn is come ;
   The Saviour leaves the grave ;
His glorious work is done,
   Almighty now to save :
Captivity is captive led,
Since Jesus liveth that was dead.

2 Hail the triumphant Lord!
   The resurrection Thou !
We bless Thy sacred word,
   Before Thy throne we bow :
Captivity is captive led,
Since Jesus liveth that was dead.
     Rev. Thomas Haweis. (1732—1820.) 1792. ab.

CHRIST RISING AND REIGNING. 87

198 *The Work that saves.*

1 DONE is the work that saves,
  Once and forever done;
  Finished the righteousness
  That clothes the unrighteous one:
  The love that blesses us below
  Is flowing freely to us now.

2 The sacrifice is o'er,
  The veil is rent in twain,
  The mercy-seat is red
  With blood of victim slain:
  Why stand we then without, in fear?
  The blood divine invites us near.

3 The gate is open wide,
  The new and living way
  Is clear, and free, and bright,
  With love, and peace, and day:
  Into the holiest now we come,
  Our present and our endless home.

4 Upon the mercy-seat
  The High Priest sits within;
  The blood is in His hand
  Which makes and keeps us clean:
  With boldness let us now draw near;
  That blood has banished every fear.

  Rev. Horatius Bonar. (1808—) 1866. ab.

HASTINGS. C. L. M.   Thomas Hastings. (1784—1872.) 1832.

1. How calm and beau-ti-ful the morn, That gilds the sa-cred tomb, Where Christ the cru-ci-fied was borne,
And veiled in midnight gloom! O weep no more the Saviour slain, The Lord is risen, He lives a-gain.

199 *The Sepulchre on Sabbath Morning.*

2 Ye mourning saints, dry every tear
  For your departed Lord;
  "Behold the place, He is not here,"
  The tomb is all unbarred:
  The gates of death were closed in vain,
  The Lord is risen, He lives again.

3 Now cheerful to the house of prayer
  Your early footsteps bend;
  The Saviour will Himself be there,
  Your Advocate and Friend:
  Once by the law your hopes were slain,
  But now in Christ ye live again.

4 How tranquil now the rising day!
  'Tis Jesus still appears,
  A risen Lord, to chase away
  Your unbelieving fears:
  O weep no more your comforts slain,
  The Lord is risen, He lives again.

5 And when the shades of evening fall,
  When life's last hour draws nigh,
  If Jesus shines upon the soul,
  How blissful then to die!
  Since He has risen that once was slain,
  Ye die in Christ to live again.

  Thomas Hastings. 1832.

CHRIST RISING AND REIGNING.

MOZART. 7. Johann C. W. A. Mozart. (1756—1791.)

1. "Christ, the Lord, is risen to-day," Sons of men and an-gels say. Raise your joys and

triumphs high; Sing, ye heavens; and earth, reply; Sing, ye heavens; and earth, reply.

200   "*He is risen.*"
Mark xvi. 6.

2 Love's redeeming work is done,
Fought the fight, the battle won.
Lo, our Sun's eclipse is o'er;
Lo, He sets in blood no more.

3 Vain the stone, the watch, the seal;
Christ has burst the gates of hell;
Death in vain forbids His rise:
Christ has opened paradise.

4 Lives again our glorious King:
Where, O death, is now thy sting?
Once He died our souls to save:
Where thy victory, O grave?

5 Soar we now where Christ has led,
Following our exalted Head:
Made like Him, like Him we rise;
Ours the cross, the grave, the skies.

6 Hail, the Lord of earth and heaven!
Praise to Thee by both be given:
Thee we greet triumphant now;
Hail, the Resurrection Thou!

Rev. Charles Wesley. (1708—1788.) 1739. ab.

201   "*Christus ist erstanden.*"

1 Christ, the Lord, is risen again,
Christ hath broken every chain:
Hark, the angels shout for joy,
Singing evermore on high.

2 He who bore all pain and loss
Comfortless upon the cross,
Lives in glory now on high,
Pleads for us, and hears our cry.

3 He who slumbered in the grave,
Is exalted now to save;
Now through Christendom it rings,
That the Lamb is King of kings.

4 Now He bids us tell abroad,
How the lost may be restored,
How the penitent forgiven,
How we, too, may enter heaven.

5 Thou our Paschal Lamb indeed,
Christ, to-day Thy people feed;
Take our sins and guilt away;
Let us sing by night and day.

Rev. Michael Weisse. (—1540.) 1531.
Tr. by Miss Catherine Winkworth. (1829—) 1858. ab.

CHRIST ASCENDING.

HERALD ANGELS. 7. D.   Felix Mendelssohn-Bartholdy. (1809—1847.) 1846.

1. Hail the day that sees Him rise, Ravished from our wish-ful eyes; Christ, a-while to mor-tals given,
Re-as-cends His na-tive heaven. { There the glo-rious tri-umph waits; Lift your heads, e-ter-nal gates; } Wide un-fold the ra-diant scene, Take the King of Glo-ry in, Wide un-fold the ra-diant scene, Take the King of Glo-ry in.

202 *Christ ascending.*

2 Him though highest heaven receives,
Still He loves the earth He leaves:
Though returning to His throne,
Still He calls mankind His own.
See, He lifts His hands above;
See, He shows the prints of love;
Hark, His gracious lips bestow
Blessings on His Church below.

3 Still for us His death He pleads;
Prevalent, He intercedes;
Near Himself prepares our place,
Harbinger of human race.
Lord, though parted from our sight,
High above yon azure height,
Grant our hearts may thither rise,
Following Thee beyond the skies.

Rev. Charles Wesley. 1739. ab.

203 *The Shout of Triumph.*

1 Sons of Zion, raise your songs,
Praise to Zion's King belongs;
His the victor's crown and fame,
Glory to the Saviour's name.
Sore the strife, but rich the prize,
Precious in the Victor's eyes;
Glorious is the work achieved,
Satan vanquished, man relieved.

2 Sing we then the Victor's praise,
Go ye forth and strew the ways;
Bid Him welcome to His throne,
He is worthy, He alone.
Place the crown upon His brow;
Every knee to Him shall bow;
Him the brightest seraph sings,
Heaven proclaims Him "King of kings."

Rev. Thomas Kelly. (1769—1855.) 1839.

WORTHY THE LAMB.

DORT. 6, 4. Lowell Mason. (1792—1872.) 1832.

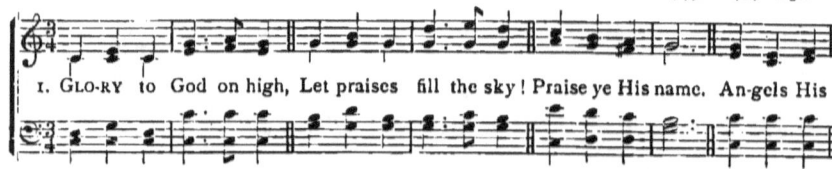

1. Glo-ry to God on high, Let praises fill the sky! Praise ye His name. An-gels His

name a-dore, Who all our sorrows bore, And saints cry ev-ermore," Worthy the Lamb!"

204   *"Worthy the Lamb."*

2 All they around the throne
  Cheerfully join in one,
    Praising His name.
  We who have felt His blood
  Sealing our peace with God,
  Spread His dear fame abroad:
    "Worthy the Lamb!"

3 To Him our hearts we raise;
  None else shall have our praise;
    Praise ye His name!
  Him, our exalted Lord,
  By us below adored,
  We praise with one accord,
    "Worthy the Lamb!"

4 Though we must change our place,
  Our souls shall never cease
    Praising His name;
  To Him we'll tribute bring,
  Laud Him our gracious King,
  And without ceasing sing,
    "Worthy the Lamb!"
      Rev. James Allen. (1734—1804.) 1761. ab.

205   *Praise to Jesus.*

1 Come, all ye saints of God,
  Wide through the earth abroad
    Spread Jesus' fame;
  Tell what His love has done;
  Trust in His name alone;
  Shout to His lofty throne,
    "Worthy the Lamb!"

2 Hence, gloomy doubts and fears;
  Dry up your mournful tears;
    Join our glad theme;
  Beauty for ashes bring;
  Strike each melodious string;
  Join heart and voice to sing,
    "Worthy the Lamb!"

3 Hark how the choirs above,
  Filled with the Saviour's love
    Dwell on His name;
  There too may we be found,
  With light and glory crowned,
  While all the heavens resound,
    "Worthy the Lamb!"
      Rev. James Boden. (1757—1841.) 1801. sl. alt.

CHRIST IN GLORY. 91

206. *Christ ascending.*

1 RISE, glorious Conqueror, rise
    Into Thy native skies ;
    Assume Thy right ;
    And where, in many a fold,
    The clouds are backward rolled,
    Pass through those gates of gold,
    And reign in light.

2 Victor o'er death and hell,
    Cherubic legions swell
    The radiant train :
    Praises all heaven inspire ;
    Each angel sweeps his lyre,
    And claps his wings of fire,
    Thou Lamb once slain.

3 Enter, Incarnate God !
    No feet but Thine have trod
    The serpent down :
    Blow the full trumpets, blow,
    Wider yon portals throw,
    Saviour, triumphant, go,
    And take Thy crown.

4 Lion of Judah, Hail !
    And let Thy name prevail
    From age to age :
    Lord of the rolling years,
    Claim for Thine own the spheres,
    For Thou hast bought with tears
    Thy heritage.

        Matthew Bridges. (1800—) 1848. ab.

ALEXANDER. S. M.   Charles Zeuner. (1795—1857.) 1832.

1. The Lord on high as-cends, Once more to take His seat: Ce-
les-tial powers re-joic-ing fly, His glad re-turn to greet.

207 *"Ascendens in altum Dominus."*

2 The mighty battle gained,
    The world's great Prince undone,
    Before His Father He presents
    The mortal palm He won.

3 Upborne above the clouds,
    Sweet hope He sheds on all ;
    He flings the gates of Eden back,
    Shut fast by Adam's fall.

4 To our Redeemer's name
    All thanks and praise be given,
    That He hath borne our mortal shape,
    To tread the courts of heaven.

5 May we, while waiting Christ,
    To heavenly works arise,
    And ever live such saintly lives,
    That we may reach the skies.

        Ambrose of Milan. (340—397.)
        Tr. by Robert Corbet Singleton. 1870. ab.

CROWNED AND ADORED.

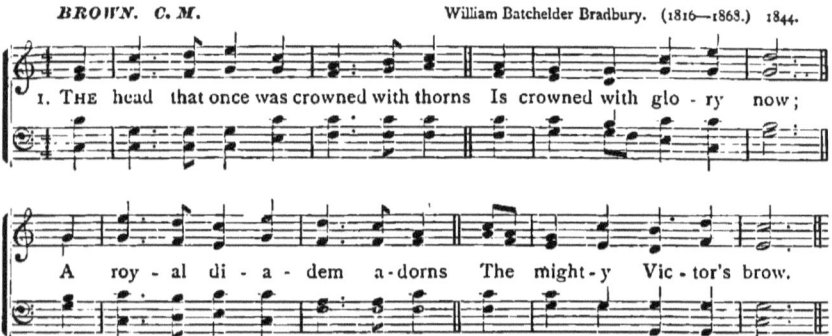

1. The head that once was crowned with thorns Is crowned with glory now;
A royal diadem adorns The mighty Victor's brow.

208 *"Perfect through Sufferings."*
Heb. ii. 10.

2 The highest place that heaven affords
Is His, is His by right,
"The King of kings, and Lord of lords,"
And heaven's eternal light.

3 The joy of all who dwell above,
The joy of all below
To whom He manifests His love,
And grants His name to know:

4 To them the cross, with all its shame,
With all its grace, is given;
Their name, an everlasting name,
Their joy, the joy of heaven.

5 They suffer with their Lord below,
They reign with Him above;
Their profit and their joy to know
The mystery of His love.

6 The cross He bore is life and health,
Though shame and death to Him;
His people's hope, His people's wealth,
Their everlasting theme.

Rev. Thomas Kelly. (1769—1855.) 1820.

209 *The Gates opened.*

1 Come, let us lift our joyful eyes
Up to the courts above,
And smile to see our Father there,
Upon a throne of love.

2 Now we may bow before His feet,
And venture near the Lord:
No fiery cherub guards His seat,
Nor double flaming sword.

3 The peaceful gates of heavenly bliss
Are opened by the Son;
High let us raise our notes of praise,
And reach the almighty throne.

4 To Thee ten thousand thanks we bring
Great Advocate on high;
And glory to the eternal King,
That lays His fury by.

Rev. Isaac Watts. (1674—1748.) 1709. ab.

210 *"The Desire of all Nations."*
Hag. ii. 7.

1 Infinite excellence is Thine,
Thou glorious Prince of Grace!
Thy uncreated beauties shine
With never-fading rays.

2 Sinners, from earth's remotest end,
Come bending at Thy feet;
To Thee their prayers and songs ascend,
In Thee their wishes meet.

MIGHTY AND MERCIFUL. 93

3 Millions of happy spirits live
On Thy exhaustless store;
From Thee they all their bliss receive,
And still Thou givest more.

4 Thou art their triumph, and their joy;
They find their all in Thee;
Thy glories will their tongues employ
Through all eternity.
Rev. John Fawcett. (1739—1817.) 1782. ab.

BRADFORD. C. M.   George Frederick Handel. (1685—1759.) 1741.

1. I know that my Re-deem-er lives, And ev - er prays for me;
A to-ken of His love He gives, A pledge of lib - er - ty.

211 *Rejoicing in Hope.*
Rom. xii. 12.

2 I find Him lifting up my head,
He brings salvation near;
His presence makes me free indeed,
And He will soon appear.

3 He wills that I should holy be:
What can withstand His will?
The counsel of His grace in me
He surely shall fulfil.

4 Jesus, I hang upon Thy word;
I steadfastly believe
Thou wilt return, and claim me, Lord,
And to Thyself receive.

5 When God is mine, and I am His,
Of paradise possessed,
I taste unutterable bliss,
And everlasting rest.
Rev. Charles Wesley. (1708—1788.) 1742. ab.

212 *Christ's Compassion to the Weak and Tempted.*
Heb. iv. 16; v. 7. Matt. xii. 20.

1 With joy we meditate the grace
Of our High Priest above;
His heart is made of tenderness,
His bosom glows with love.

2 Touched with a sympathy within,
He knows our feeble frame;
He knows what sore temptations mean,
For He hath felt the same.

3 He, in the days of feeble flesh,
Poured out His cries and tears;
And, in His measure, feels afresh
What every member bears.

4 He'll never quench the smoking flax,
But raise it to a flame;
The bruisèd reed He never breaks,
Nor scorns the meanest name.

5 Then let our humble faith address
His mercy and His power;
We shall obtain delivering grace
In the distressing hour.
Rev. Isaac Watts. 1709. alt.

OUR KINSMAN.

SILOAM. C. M.   Isaac Beverly Woodbury. (1819—1858.) 1842.

1. O MEAN may seem this house of clay, Yet 'twas the Lord's a-bode;

Our feet may mourn this thorn-y way, Yet here Em-man-uel trod.

213   *Our double Kindred to Emmanuel.*
       1 Cor. xv. 47, 49.

2 This fleshly robe the Lord did wear;
     This watch the Lord did keep;
     These burdens sore the Lord did bear;
     These tears the Lord did weep.

3 O vale of tears no longer sad,
     Wherein the Lord did dwell!
     O happy robe of flesh that clad
     Our own Emmanuel!

4 But not this fleshly robe alone
     Shall link us, Lord, to Thee;
     Not only in the tear and groan
     Shall the dear kindred be.

5 We shall be reckoned for Thine own,
     Because Thy heaven we share,
     Because we sing around Thy throne,
     And Thy bright raiment wear.

6 O mighty grace, our life to live,
     To make our earth divine!
     O mighty grace, Thy heaven to give,
     And lift our life to Thine!

        Thomas Hornblower Gill. (1819—) 1860. ab.

214   *"Clothed with our Nature still."*

1 COME, let us join in songs of praise
     To our ascended Priest;
     He entered heaven, with all our names
     Engraven on His breast.

2 Below He washed our guilt away,
     By His atoning blood;
     Now He appears before the throne,
     And pleads our cause with God.

3 Clothed with our nature still, He knows
     The weakness of our frame,
     And how to shield us from the foes
     Which He Himself o'ercame.

4 Nor time, nor distance, e'er shall quench
     The fervors of His love;
     For us He died in kindness here,
     Nor is less kind above.

5 O may we ne'er forget His grace,
     Nor blush to wear His name;
     Still may our hearts hold fast His faith,
     Our mouths His praise proclaim.

        Rev. Alexander Pirie. (—1804.) 1786.

GLORY TO THE LAMB. 95

215 *"Enthroned in Glory."*

2 Paschal Lamb, by God appointed,
  All our sins on Thee were laid;
  By Almighty Love anointed,
  Thou hast full atonement made:
  All Thy people are forgiven
  Through the virtue of Thy blood;
  Opened is the gate of heaven;
  Peace is made 'twixt man and God.

3 Jesus, hail, enthroned in glory,
  There forever to abide;
  All the heavenly hosts adore Thee,
  Seated at Thy Father's side.
  There for sinners Thou art pleading;
  There Thou dost our place prepare;
  Ever for us interceding
  Till in glory we appear.

Rev. John Bakewell. (1721—1819.) 1760. alt.
Rev. Augustus Montague Toplady. (1740—1778.) 1776.

216 *"Thou art worthy."*
(Second Part of preceding Hymn.)

1 WORSHIP, honor, power, and blessing,
  Thou art worthy to receive:
  Loudest praises, without ceasing,
  Meet it is for us to give.
  Help, ye bright angelic spirits,
  Bring your sweetest, noblest lays;
  Help to sing our Saviour's merits,
  Help to chant Immanuel's praise.

2 Soon we shall, with those in glory,
  His transcendent grace relate;
  Gladly sing the amazing story
  Of His dying love so great:
  In that blessed contemplation
  We for evermore shall dwell,
  Crowned with bliss and consolation,
  Such as none below can tell.

Rev. John Bakewell. 1760. alt.
Rev. Augustus Montague Toplady. 1776.

CROWN HIM.

CORONATION. C. M.   Oliver Holden. (1756—1831.) 1793.

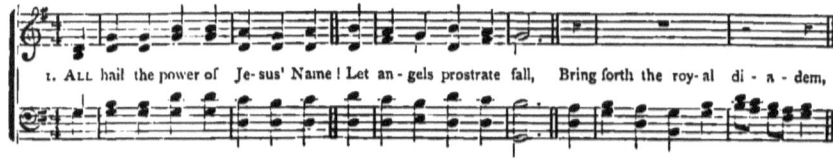

1. All hail the power of Jesus' Name! Let angels prostrate fall, Bring forth the royal diadem, And crown Him Lord of all, Bring forth the royal diadem, And crown Him Lord of all.

217   "*Lord of all.*"
Acts x. 36.

2 Crown Him, ye morning stars of light,
   Who fixed this floating ball;
Now hail the strength of Israel's might,
   And crown Him Lord of all.

3 Crown Him, ye martyrs of your God,
   Who from His altar call;
Extol the stem of Jesse's rod,
   And crown Him Lord of all.

4 Ye seed of Israel's chosen race,
   Ye ransomed of the fall,
Hail Him, who saves you by His grace,
   And crown Him Lord of all.

5 Sinners, whose love can ne'er forget
   The wormwood and the gall,
Go, spread your trophies at His feet,
   And crown Him Lord of all.

6 Let every kindred, every tribe,
   On this terrestrial ball,
To Him all majesty ascribe,
   And crown Him Lord of all.

Rev. Edward Perronet. (—1792.) 1780. ab. and alt.

218   *The Lamb worshipped by all Creatures.*
Rev. v. 11—13.

1 Come, let us join our cheerful songs
   With angels round the throne;
Ten thousand thousand are their tongues,
   But all their joys are one.

2 "Worthy the Lamb that died," they cry,
   "To be exalted thus;"
"Worthy the Lamb," our lips reply,
   "For He was slain for us."

3 Jesus is worthy to receive
   Honor and power divine;
And blessings, more than we can give,
   Be, Lord, forever Thine.

4 Let all that dwell above the sky,
   And air, and earth, and seas,
Conspire to lift Thy glories high,
   And speak Thine endless praise.

5 The whole creation join in one,
   To bless the sacred name
Of Him that sits upon the throne,
   And to adore the Lamb.

Rev. Isaac Watts. (1674—1748.) 1709.

GLORY OF THE LAMB.

MILES LANE. C. M. Rev. William Shrubsole. (1729—1797.) 1793.
Har. by Rev. John Bacchus Dykes. 1861.

1. Behold the glories of the Lamb, A-midst His Father's throne: Prepare new honors for His name, And songs be-fore un-known, And songs be-fore un-known.

219 *To the Lamb that was slain.*
Rev. v. 6—12.

2 Let elders worship at His feet,
  The church adore around,
With vials full of odors sweet,
  And harps of sweeter sound.

3 Those are the prayers of all the saints,
  And these the hymns they raise:
Jesus is kind to our complaints,
  He loves to hear our praise.

4 Now to the Lamb that once was slain,
  Be endless blessings paid ;
Salvation, glory, joy remain
  Forever on Thy head.

5 Thou hast redeemed our souls with blood,
  Hast set the prisoners free,
Hast made us kings and priests to God,
  And we shall reign with Thee.
      Rev. Isaac Watts. 1709. ab.

220 *"Our great High Priest above."*
1 Now let our cheerful eyes survey
  Our great High Priest above,
And celebrate His constant care,
  And sympathetic love.

2 Though raised to a superior throne,
  Where angels bow around,
And high o'er all the shining train
  With matchless honors crowned;

3 The names of all His saints He bears,
  Deep graven on His heart:
Nor shall the meanest Christian say
  That he hath lost his part.

4 Those characters shall fair abide,
  Our everlasting trust,
When gems, and monuments, and crowns,
Are mouldered down to dust.

5 So, gracious Saviour, on my breast
  May Thy dear name be worn,
A sacred ornament and guard,
  To endless ages borne.
      Rev. Philip Doddridge. (1702—1751.) 1755.

GLORY OF THE LAMB.

LENOX. H. M.   Jonathan Edson. 1782.

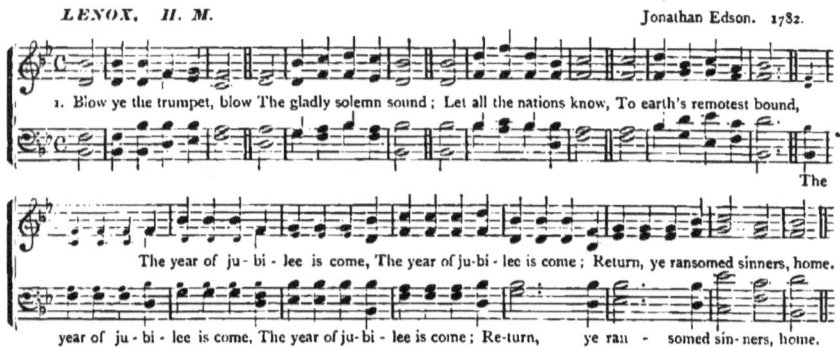

221   *"The Year of Jubilee is come."*

2 Jesus, our great High-Priest.
    Hath full atonement made;
    Ye weary spirits, rest,
    Ye mournful souls, be glad:
The year of jubilee is come;
Return, ye ransomed sinners, home.

3 Extol the Lamb of God,
    The all-atoning Lamb;
    Redemption in His blood
    Throughout the world proclaim:
The year of jubilee is come;
Return, ye ransomed sinners, home.

4 Ye, who have sold for naught
    Your heritage above,
    Shall have it back unbought,
    The gift of Jesus' love:
The year of jubilee is come;
Return, ye ransomed sinners, home.

5 The gospel trumpet hear,
    The news of heavenly grace;
    And, saved from earth, appear
    Before your Saviour's face:
The year of jubilee is come;
Return, ye ransomed sinners, home.
       Rev. Charles Wesley. (1708—1788.) 1750. ab.

WARSAW. H. M.   Thomas Clark. 1804.

GLORY OF THE LAMB.

222   *"The Lord is King."*

2 Jesus the Saviour reigns,
    The God of truth and love ;
  When He had purged our stains,
    He took His seat above :
  Lift up your heart, lift up your voice,
  Rejoice, again I say, rejoice.

3 His kingdom cannot fail,
    He rules o'er earth and heaven ;
  The keys of death and hell
    Are to our Jesus given :
  Lift up your heart, lift up your voice,
  Rejoice, again I say, rejoice.

4 He all His foes shall quell,
    Shall all our sins destroy,
  And every bosom swell
    With pure seraphic joy :
  Lift up your heart, lift up your voice.
  Rejoice, again I say, rejoice.

5 Rejoice in glorious hope ;
    Jesus, the Judge, shall come,
  And take His servants up
    To their eternal home :
  We soon shall hear the archangel's voice,
  The trump of God shall sound, Rejoice.
        Rev. Charles Wesley. 1748. ab.

HARWELL. 8, 7. 6 l.   Lowell Mason. (1792—1872.) 1840.

Come, ye faithful, raise the anthem, Cleave the skies with shouts of praise :
Sing to Him Who found the ransom, Ancient of e-ter-nal days : God Eter - nal, Word In-car-nate,
Whom the Heaven of heavens o-beys : God E-ter-nal, Word In-car-nate, Whom the Heaven of heavens obeys.

223   *A Hymn of Praise to the Redeemer.*

2 Ere He raised the lofty mountains,
    Formed the sea, or built the sky,
  Love eternal, free, and boundless,
    Forced the Lord of Life to die ;
  Lifted up the Prince of princes
    On the throne of Calvary.

3 Now on those eternal mountains
    Stands the sapphire throne, all bright,
  Where unceasing hallelujahs
    They upraise, the sons of light :
  Zion's people tell His praises,
    Victor after hard-won fight.

4 Bring your harps and bring your incense,
  Sweep the string and pour the lay ;
  Let the earth proclaim His wonders,
    King of that celestial day :
  He, the Lamb once slain, is worthy,
    Who was dead and lives for aye.
        Rev. Job Hupton. (1762—1849.) 1805. ab.
  Alt. by Rev. John Mason Neale. (1818—1866.) 1851.

FREE SALVATION.

MARLOW. C. M. English Melody. Arr. by Lowell Mason. (1792—1872.) 1832.

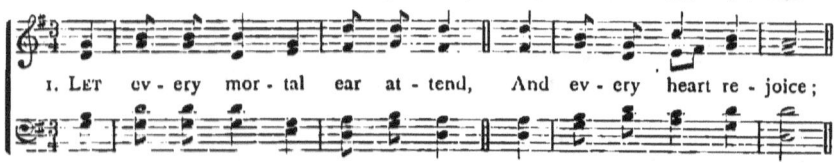

1. Let ev-ery mor-tal ear at-tend, And ev-ery heart re-joice;

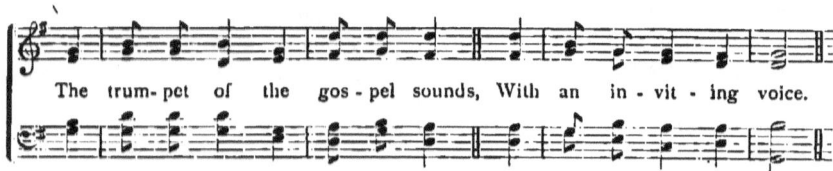

The trum-pet of the gos-pel sounds, With an in-vit-ing voice.

224 *Without Money and without Price.*
Is. lv. 1, 2.

2 Ho, all ye hungry, starving souls,
  That feed upon the wind,
  And vainly strive, with earthly toys,
  To fill an empty mind;

3 Eternal wisdom has prepared
  A soul-reviving feast,
  And bids your longing appetites
  The rich provision taste.

4 Ho, ye that pant for living streams,
  And pine away and die,
  Here you may quench your raging thirst
  With springs that never dry.

5 Rivers of love and mercy here
  In a rich ocean join;
  Salvation in abundance flows,
  Like floods of milk and wine.

6 The happy gates of gospel grace
  Stand open night and day;
  Lord, we are come to seek supplies,
  And drive our wants away.

Rev. Isaac Watts. (1674—1748.) 1709.

225 *Christ's Commission.*
John iii. 16, 17.

1 Come, happy souls, approach your God
  With new, melodious songs;
  Come, render to almighty grace
  The tribute of your tongues.

2 So strange, so boundless, was the love
  That pitied dying men,
  The Father sent His equal Son
  To give them life again.

3 Thy hands, dear Jesus, were not armed
  With a revenging rod,
  No hard commission to perform
  The vengeance of a God.

4 But all was mercy, all was mild,
  And wrath forsook the throne,
  When Christ on the kind errand came,
  And brought salvation down.

5 Here, sinners, you may heal your wounds,
  And wipe your sorrows dry;
  Trust in the mighty Saviour's name,
  And you shall never die.

Rev. Isaac Watts. 1709. ab.

FREE SALVATION.

SCOTLAND. 12, 11.   John Clarke. (1770—1818.) 1800.

1. The voice of free grace cries, Es-cape to the mountain; For A-dam's lost race, Christ has opened a fount-ain; { For sin, and un-cleanness, and ev-ery trans-gres-sion, His blood flows most free-ly, in streams of sal-va-tion, His blood flows most free-ly, in streams of sal-va-tion. { Hal-le-lu-jah to the Lamb, who hath purchased our par-don, We'll praise Him a-gain, when we pass o-ver Jor-dan, We'll praise Him a-gain, when we pass o-ver Jor-dan.

226   "*The Voice of Free Grace.*"

2 Ye souls that are wounded, O flee to the Saviour;
He calls you in mercy, 'tis infinite favor;
Your sins are increaséd as high as a mountain,
His blood can remove them, it flows from the fountain. Hallelujah, etc.

3 Now Jesus, our King, reigns triumphantly glorious;
O'er sin, death, and hell, He is more than victorious;
With shouting proclaim it, O trust in His passion,
He saves us most freely, O glorious salvation! Hallelujah, etc.
              Rev. Richard Burdsall. (1735—1824.) 1796. ab. and alt.

227   "*The merciful Saviour.*"

1 O come to the merciful Saviour that calls you,
O come to the Lord who forgives and forgets;
Though dark be the fortune on earth that befalls you,
There's a bright home above, where the sun never sets.

2 O come then to Jesus, whose arms are extended
To fold His dear children in closest embrace.
O come, for your exile will shortly be ended,
And Jesus will show you His beautiful face.

3 Then come to the Saviour, whose mercy grows brighter
The longer you look at the depths of His love;
And fear not, 'tis Jesus, and life's cares grow lighter
As you think of the home and the glory above.
              Rev. Frederick William Faber. (1814—1863.) 1849. ab.

INVITATION AND WARNING.

HENLEY. 11, 10. Lowell Mason. (1792—1872.) 1854.

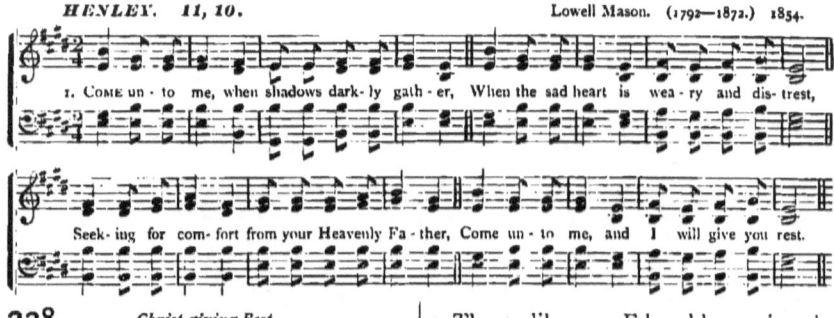

1. Come un-to me, when shadows dark-ly gath-er, When the sad heart is wea-ry and dis-trest,
Seek-ing for com-fort from your Heavenly Fa-ther, Come un-to me, and I will give you rest.

228 *Christ giving Rest.*

2 Large are the mansions in thy Father's
    dwelling,   [dim,
  Glad are the homes that sorrows never
  Sweet are the harps in holy music
    swelling,   .   [enly hymn.
  Soft are the tones which raise the heav-

3 There, like an Eden blossoming in
    gladness,   [rudely pressed;
  Bloom the fair flowers the earth too
  Come unto me all ye who droop in sad-
    ness,   [rest.
  Come unto me, and I will give you
            Unknown Author. 1854. ab.

EXPOSTULATION. 11. Rev. Josiah Hopkins. (1786—1862.) 1830.

1. De-lay not, de-lay not; O sin-ner, draw near, The wa-ters of life are now flow-ing for thee;
No price is de-mand-ed, the Sav-iour is here, Re-demption is purchased, sal-va-tion is free.

229 *"Delay not!"*

2 Delay not, delay not; why longer abuse
    The love and compassion of Jesus, thy
        God?   [refuse
  A fountain is opened:—how canst thou
    To wash and be cleansed in His pard-
        'ning blood?
3 Delay not, delay not, O sinner, to come,
    For mercy still lingers and calls thee
        to-day;

  Her voice is not heard in the vale of
        the tomb,   [away.
  Her message, unheeded, will soon pass
4 Delay not, delay not; the Spirit of
        grace,   [its sad flight;
  Long grieved and resisted, may take
  And leave thee in darkness to finish
        thy race,
  To sink in the vale of eternity's night.
            Thomas Hastings. (1784—1872.) 1831.

INVITATION ACCEPTED. 103

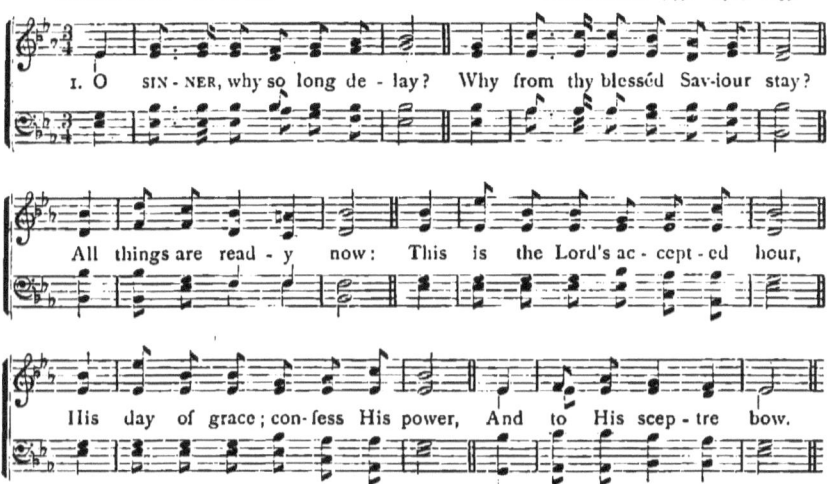

MERIBAH. C. P. M.   Lowell Mason. (1792—1872.) 1839.

1. O sinner, why so long delay?
Why from thy blessèd Saviour stay?
All things are ready now:
This is the Lord's accepted hour,
His day of grace; confess His power,
And to His sceptre bow.

230   *The gracious Call.*

2 Why wilt thou thus His Spirit grieve;
Why wilt thou not at once believe?
Say wherefore dost thou doubt?
Come, weary one, to Him for rest,
O come to Jesus and be blest;
He will not cast thee out.

3 Come gladly now to Him who died,
Come to the Saviour crucified;
He waits with outstretched hands.
The nail-prints in those hands I see:
They plead with God, they plead with thee,
To join His chosen band.

4 Obey thy Master's gracious call,
Low at His feet for mercy fall;
He waits to welcome thee:
O sinner, ere it be too late,
Flee thou to mercy's open gate;
Christ waits to welcome thee.

Rev. Eli Corwin. (1824—) 1874.

231   *The Response.*
Acts ix. 6.

1 Lord, Thou hast won, at length I yield;
My heart, by mighty grace compelled,
Surrenders all to Thee;
Against Thy terrors long I strove,
But who can stand against Thy love?
Love conquers even me.

2 If Thou hadst bid Thy thunders roll,
And lightnings flash to blast my soul,
I still had stubborn been;
But mercy has my heart subdued,
A bleeding Saviour I have viewed,
And now I hate my sin.

3 Now, Lord, I would be Thine alone,
Come, take possession of Thine own,
For Thou hast set me free;
Released from Satan's hard command,
See all my powers in waiting stand,
To be employed by Thee.

Rev. John Newton. (1725—1807.) 1779. ab.

ENTREATY.

BAVARIA. 8, 7. 6 l. German Melody.

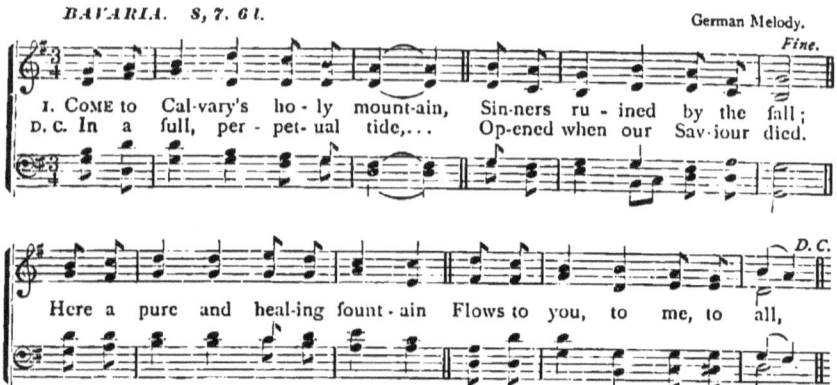

1. Come to Calvary's holy mountain,
Sinners ruined by the fall;
Here a pure and healing fountain
Flows to you, to me, to all,
D. C. In a full, perpetual tide,...
Opened when our Saviour died.

232 *A Fountain opened.*

2 Come in poverty and meanness,
  Come defiled, without, within ;
From infection and uncleanness,
From the leprosy of sin,
Wash your robes and make them white:
Ye shall walk with God in light.

3 Come, in sorrow and contrition,
  Wounded, impotent, and blind ;
Here the guilty, free remission,
Here the troubled, peace may find ;
Health this fountain will restore,
He that drinks shall thirst no more:

4 He that drinks shall live forever ;
  'Tis a soul-renewing flood :
God is faithful ; God will never
Break His covenant in blood,
Signed when our Redeemer died,
Sealed when He was glorified.

* James Montgomery. (1771—1854.) 1819.

BELMONT. 8, 7, 4. Jeremiah Ingalls. (1764—1838.) 1805.

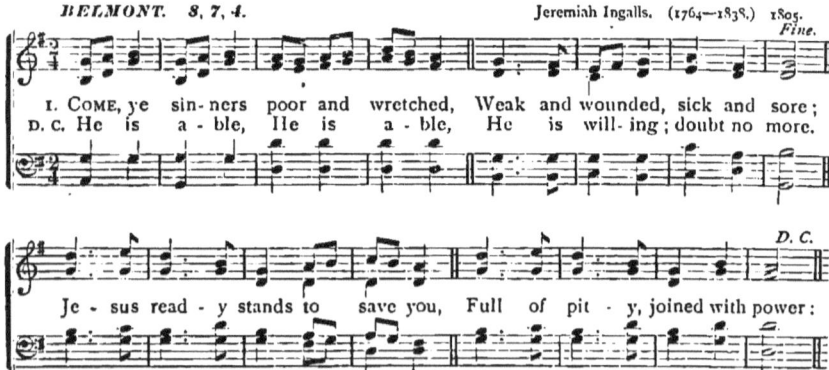

1. Come, ye sinners poor and wretched, Weak and wounded, sick and sore;
Jesus ready stands to save you, Full of pity, joined with power:
D. C. He is able, He is able, He is willing; doubt no more.

ENTREATY. 105

GREENVILLE. 8, 7, 4.   Jean Jacques Rousseau. (1712—1778.) 1750.

1. Come, ye sinners, poor and wretched, Weak and wounded, sick and sore: Jesus ready stands to save you, Full of pity, joined with power: He is able, He is able, He is willing; doubt no more.

233 *"Come, and welcome."*

2 Let not conscience make you linger,
  Nor of fitness fondly dream;
  All the fitness He requireth
    Is to feel your need of Him:
      This He gives you;
  'Tis the Spirit's rising beam.

3 Come, ye weary, heavy-laden,
    Bruised and mangled by the fall;
  If you tarry till you're better,
    You will never come at all:
      Not the righteous,
  Sinners, Jesus came to call.

4 Lo, the Incarnate God, ascended,
    Pleads the merit of His blood:
  Venture on Him, venture wholly,
    Let no other trust intrude;
      None but Jesus
  Can do helpless sinners good.

Rev. Joseph Hart. (1712—1768.) 1759. ab.

234 *"Hear, and live."*

1 Sinners, will you scorn the message
    Sent in mercy from above?
  Every sentence, O how tender!
  ' Every line is full of love:
      Listen to it;
  Every line is full of love.

2 Hear the heralds of the gospel
    News from Zion's King proclaim:
  "Pardon to each rebel sinner,
    Free forgiveness in His name:"
      How important!
  "Free forgiveness in His name."

3 O ye angels, hovering round us,
    Waiting spirits, speed your way;
  Haste ye to the court of heaven,
    Tidings bear without delay,
      Rebel sinners
  Glad the message will obey.

Rev. Jonathan Allen. 1801. ab.

ENTREATY.

SESSIONS. L. M.   Luther Orlando Emerson. (1820—) 1847.

1. Come, sinners, to the gos-pel feast, Let ev-ery soul be Je-sus' guest;

You need not one be left be-hind, For God has bid-den all man-kind.

235   *"The Gospel Feast."*
Luke xiv. 16—24.

1 Sent by my Lord, on you I call,
The invitation is to all:
Come, all the world; come sinner, thou;
All things in Christ are ready now.

3 Come, then, ye souls by sin opprest,
Ye restless wanderers after rest;
Ye poor, and maimed, and halt, and blind,
In Christ a hearty welcome find.
Rev. Charles Wesley. (1708—1788.) 1747. ab.

236   *"All Things are now ready."*
Luke xiv. 17.

1 Sinners, obey the gospel word;
Haste to the supper of my Lord;
Be wise to know your gracious day;
All things are ready, come away.

2 Ready the Father is to own
And kiss His late-returning son;
Ready your loving Saviour stands,
And spreads for you His bleeding hands.

3 Ready for you the angels wait,
To triumph in your blest estate;
Tuning their harps, they long to praise
The wonders of redeeming grace.

4 The Father, Son, and Holy Ghost,
Are ready, with their shining host:
All heaven is ready to resound,
"The dead's alive, the lost is found!"
Rev. Charles Wesley. 1749. ab.

237   *No Hope after Death.*

1 While life prolongs its precious light,
Mercy is found and peace is given;
But soon, ah, soon approaching night
Shall blot out every hope of heaven.

2 Soon, borne on time's most rapid wing,
Shall death command you to the grave,
Before His bar your spirits bring,
And none be found to hear or save.

3 Now God invites, how blest the day!
How sweet the gospel's charming sound!
Come, sinners, haste, O haste away,
While yet a pardoning God is found.
Rev. Timothy Dwight. (1752—1817.) 1800. ab.

ENTREATY. 107

COME, YE DISCONSOLATE. 11, 10. Samuel Webbe. (1740—1816.) 1800.

1. COME, ye disconsolate, where'er ye languish, Come to the mercy-seat, fervently kneel; Here bring your wounded hearts, here tell your anguish, Earth has no sorrows that heaven cannot heal.

238 *"Come, ye disconsolate."*

2 Joy of the desolate, Light of the straying,
Hope of the penitent, fadeless and pure,
Here speaks the Comforter, tenderly saying,
Earth has no sorrows that heaven cannot cure.

3 Here see the Bread of Life, see waters flowing
Forth from the throne of God, pure from above;
Come to the feast prepared, come, ever knowing
Earth has no sorrows but heaven can remove.

Thomas Moore. (1779—1852.) 1816. vs. 1, 2. alt.
Thomas Hastings. (1784—1872.) v. 3.

TO-DAY. 6, 4. Lowell Mason. (1792—1872.) 1831.

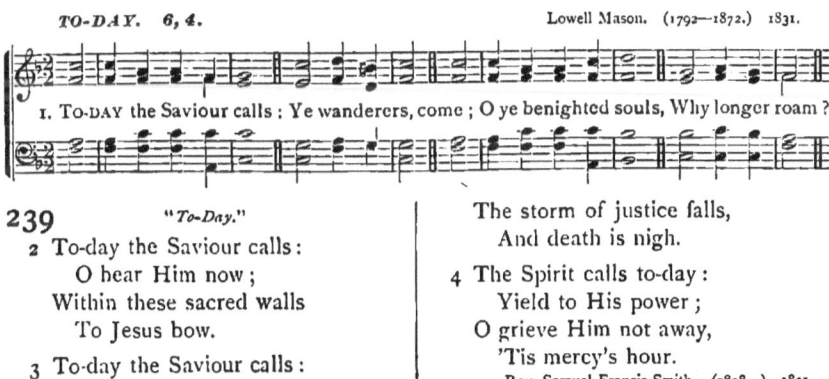

1. TO-DAY the Saviour calls: Ye wanderers, come; O ye benighted souls, Why longer roam?

239 *"To-Day."*

2 To-day the Saviour calls:
  O hear Him now;
  Within these sacred walls
  To Jesus bow.

3 To-day the Saviour calls:
  For refuge fly;

The storm of justice falls,
And death is nigh.

4 The Spirit calls to-day:
  Yield to His power;
  O grieve Him not away,
  'Tis mercy's hour.

Rev. Samuel Francis Smith. (1808—) 1831.
Alt. by Thomas Hastings. 1831.

ENTREATY.

HORTON. 7.   Xavier Schnyder von Wartensee. (1786—)

1. Come, said Jesus' sacred voice, Come, and make My paths your choice;

I will guide you to your home, Weary pilgrim, hither come.

240   *The gracious Call.*
Matt. xi. 28—30.

2 Thou who, houseless, sole, forlorn,
Long hast borne the proud world's scorn,
Long hast roamed the barren waste,
Weary pilgrim, hither haste.

3 Ye who, tossed on beds of pain,
Seek for ease, but seek in vain;
Ye, by fiercer anguish torn,
In remorse for guilt who mourn;

4 Hither come, for here is found
Balm that flows for every wound,
Peace that ever shall endure,
Rest eternal, sacred, sure.
Mrs. Anna Lætitia Barbauld. (1743—1825.) 1825. ab. and alt.

241   *"Why will ye die?"*
Tune, MARTYN. 7. D.

1 SINNERS, turn, why will ye die?
God, your Maker, asks you why;
God, who did your being give,
Made you with Himself to live;
He the fatal cause demands,
Asks the work of His own hands,
Why, ye thankful creatures, why
Will ye cross His love, and die?

2 Sinners, turn, why will ye die?
God, your Saviour, asks you why;
God who did your souls retrieve,
Died Himself that ye might live:
Will you let Him die in vain?
Crucify your Lord again?
Why, ye ransomed sinners, why
Will you slight His grace, and die?

3 Sinners, turn, why will ye die?
God, the Spirit, asks you why;
He, who all your lives hath strove,
Wooed you to embrace His love:
Will you not His grace receive?
Will you still refuse to live?
Why, ye long-sought sinners, why
Will ye grieve your God, and die?
Rev. Charles Wesley. (1708—1788.) 1745. ab.

ENTREATY.   109

ROSEFIELD. 7. 6 l. Rev. Cæsar Henri Abraham Malan. (1787—1864.) 1830.

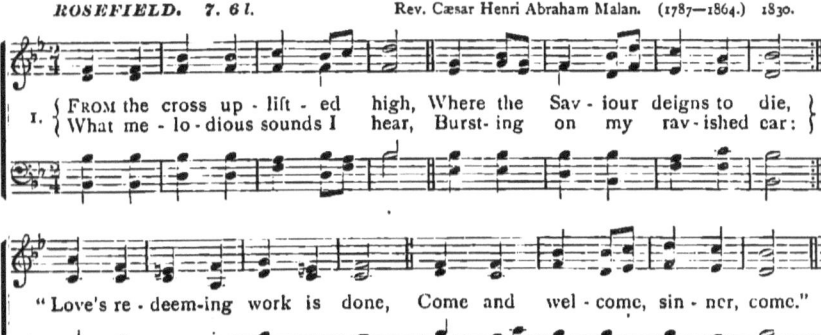

1. From the cross up-lift-ed high, Where the Sav-iour deigns to die,
   What me-lo-dious sounds I hear, Burst-ing on my rav-ished ear:
   "Love's re-deem-ing work is done, Come and wel-come, sin-ner, come."

242 *"Let him come unto Me."*
John vii. 37.

2 "Sprinkled now with blood the throne;
Why beneath thy burdens groan?
On My pierced body laid,
Justice owns the ransom paid:
Bow the knee, and kiss the Son,
Come and welcome, sinner, come.

3 "Spread for thee, the festal board
See with richest dainties stored;
To thy Father's bosom prest,
Yet again a child confest,
Never from His house to roam;
Come and welcome, sinner, come.

4 "Soon the days of life shall end;
Lo I come, your Saviour, Friend,
Safe your spirits to convey
To the realms of endless day,

Up to My eternal home:
Come and welcome, sinner, come."
Rev. Thomas Haweis. (1732—1820.) 1792.

243 *"Take the Peace the Gospel brings."*
Ps. cxxxv. 2.

1 Ye that in His courts are found,
Listening to the joyful sound,
Lost and helpless as ye are,
Sons of sorrow, sin, and care;
Glorify the King of kings,
Take the peace the gospel brings.

2 Turn to Christ your longing eyes,
View His bloody sacrifice;
See, in Him, your sins forgiven,
Pardon, holiness, and heaven;
Glorify the King of kings,
Take the peace the gospel brings.
Rev. Rowland Hill. (1744—1833.) 1774.

MARTYN. 7. D. Simeon Butler Marsh. (1798—) 1834.

ENTREATY.

OLNEY. S. M.   Lowell Mason. (1792—1872.) 1832.

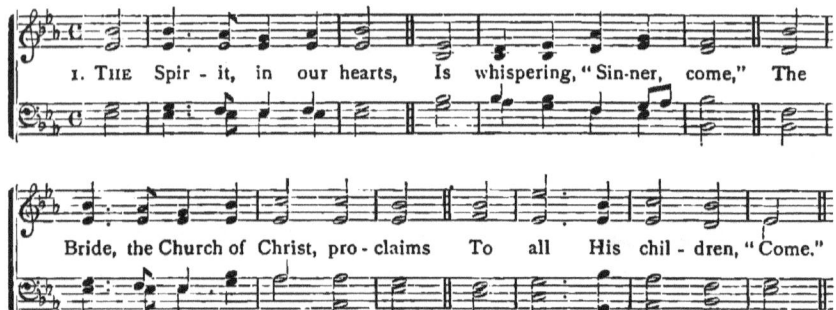

1. The Spir-it, in our hearts, Is whispering, "Sin-ner, come," The Bride, the Church of Christ, pro-claims To all His chil-dren, "Come."

244   *"And the Spirit and the Bride say, Come."* Rev. xxii. 17—20.

2 Let him that heareth, say
    To all about him, "Come;"
Let him that thirsts for righteousness,
    To Christ, the Fountain, come.

3 Yes, whosoever will,
    O let him freely come,
And freely drink the stream of life:
    'Tis Jesus bids him come.

4 Lo, Jesus, who invites,
    Declares, "I quickly come;"
Lord, even so; I wait Thine hour;
    Jesus, my Saviour, come.

Bp. Henry Ustick Onderdonk. (1789—1858.) 1826.

245   *"The Land of Peace."*

1 Come to the land of peace;
    From shadows come away;
Where all the sounds of weeping cease,
    And storms no more have sway.

2 Fear hath no dwelling here;
    But pure repose and love
Breathe through the bright, celestial air
    The spirit of the dove.

3 Come to the bright and blest,
    Gathered from every land;
For here thy soul shall find its rest
    Amid the shining band.

4 In this divine abode
    Change leaves no saddening trace;
Come, trusting spirit, to thy God,
    Thy holy resting-place.

5 "Come to our peaceful home,"
    The saints and angels say,
"Forsake the world, no longer roam;
    O wanderer, come away!"

Briggs' Collection.

246   *The Uncertainty of Life.* James iv. 13—15.

1 To-morrow, Lord, is Thine,
    Lodged in Thy sovereign hand;
And if its sun arise and shine,
    It shines by Thy command.

2 Since on this wingèd hour,
    Eternity is hung,
Waken, by Thine almighty power,
    The aged and the young.

3 To Jesus may we fly,
    Swift as the morning light,
Lest life's young golden beams should
    die
In sudden, endless night.

Rev. Philip Doddridge. (1702—1751.) 1755. ab.

THE ACCEPTED TIME.

GORTON. S. M.   Ludwig von Beethoven. (1770—1827)

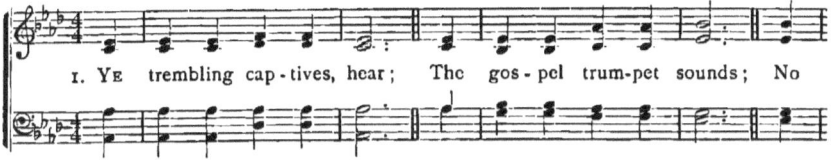

1. Ye trembling cap-tives, hear; The gos-pel trum-pet sounds; No

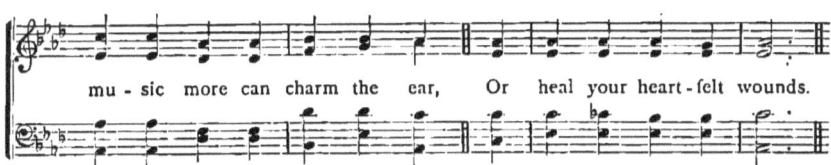

mu-sic more can charm the ear, Or heal your heart-felt wounds.

247   *The Gospel Trumpet.*

2 'Tis not the trump of war,
   Nor Sinai's awful roar;
Salvation's news is spread afar,
   And vengeance is no more.

3 Forgiveness, love, and peace,
   Glad heaven aloud proclaims;
And earth the jubilee's release
   With eager rapture claims.

4 Far, far to distant lands
   The saving news shall spread;
And Jesus all His willing bands
   In glorious triumph lead.
                 Samuel Boyce. 1801. sl. alt.

248   *"Now is the accepted Time."*
                 2 Cor. vi. 2.
1 Now is the accepted time,
   Now is the day of grace;
Now, sinners, come without delay,
   And seek the Saviour's face.

2 Now is the accepted time,
   The Saviour calls to-day;
Pardon and peace He freely gives;
   Then why should you delay?

3 Now is the accepted time,
   The gospel bids you come;
And every promise in His word
   Declares there yet is room.

4 Lord, draw reluctant souls,
   And feast them with Thy love:
Then will the angels clap their wings,
   And bear the news above.
             John Dobell. (1757—1840.) 1806. ab.

249   *"Behold the Ark of God."*
1 O cease, my wandering soul,
   On restless wing to roam;
All the wide world, to either pole,
   Has not for thee a home.

2 Behold the Ark of God,
   Behold the open door;
Hasten to gain that dear abode,
   And rove, my soul, no more.

3 There, safe thou shalt abide,
   There, sweet shall be thy rest,
And every longing satisfied,
   With full salvation blest.
       Rev. William Augustus Muhlenberg. (1796—). 1826. ab.

CHRIST AT THE DOOR.

ZEPHYR. L. M.   William Batchelder Bradbury. (1816—1868.) 1844.

1. Be-hold, a stran-ger's at the door: He gen-tly knocks, has knocked before;

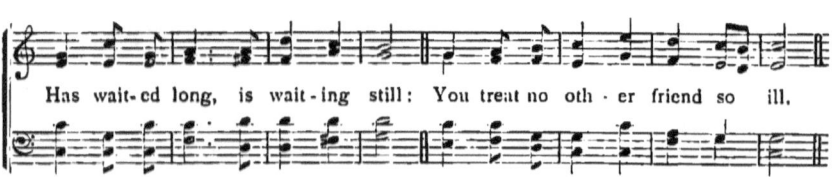

Has wait-ed long, is wait-ing still: You treat no oth-er friend so ill.

250   *Christ knocking at the Door.*
Cant. v. 2. Rev. iii. 20.

2 But will He prove a friend indeed?
He will, the very friend you need;
The Man of Nazareth, 'tis He,
With garments dyed at Calvary.

3 O lovely attitude! He stands
With melting heart, and laden hands:
O matchless kindness! and He shows
This matchless kindness to His foes.

4 Rise, touched with gratitude divine;
Turn out His enemy and thine,
That soul-destroying monster, Sin;
And let the Heavenly Stranger in.

5 Admit Him, ere His anger burn;
His feet, departed, ne'er return!
Admit Him; or the hour's at hand
When at His door denied you'll stand.
Rev. Joseph Grigg. (—1768.) 1765. ab. and alt.

251   *"Return!"*
Jer. xxxi. 18—20.

1 Return, O wanderer, return,
And seek thine injured Father's face;
Those new desires that in thee burn,
Were kindled by reclaiming grace.

2 Return, O wanderer, return,
And seek a Father's melting heart;
Whose pitying eyes thy grief discern,
Whose hand can heal thine inward smart.

3 Return, O wanderer, return,
He heard thy deep repentant sigh,
He saw thy softened spirit mourn,
When no intruding ear was nigh.

4 Return, O wanderer, return,
Thy Saviour bids thy spirit live;
Go to His bleeding feet, and learn
How freely Jesus can forgive.

5 Return, O wanderer, return,
And wipe away the falling tear;
'Tis God who says, "No longer mourn,"
'Tis mercy's voice invites thee near.
Rev. William Bengo Collyer. (1782—1854.) 1812. ab.

THE SAD AND WEARY INVITED. 113

AVA. 6, 4, 6, 4, 4.   Thomas Hastings. (1784—1872.) 1832.

1. Child of sin and sorrow, Filled with dismay,
Wait not for tomorrow, Yield thee today;
Heaven bids thee come, While yet there's room.
Child of sin and sorrow, Hear and obey.

252   *"Child of Sin and Sorrow."*

2 Child of sin and sorrow,
  Why wilt thou die?
Come while thou canst borrow
  Help from on high:
Grieve not that love
  Which from above,
Child of sin and sorrow,
  Would bring thee nigh.

3 Child of sin and sorrow,
  Thy moments glide,
Like the flitting arrow,
  Or the rushing tide;
Ere time is o'er,
  Heaven's grace implore;
Child of sin and sorrow,
  In Christ confide.
          Thomas Hastings. 1832.

STEPHANOS. 8, 5, 8, 3.   William Henry Monk. 1861.

1. Art thou weary, art thou languid, Art thou sore distrest?
"Come to me," saith One, "and coming Be at rest!"

253   Κόπον τε καὶ κάματον.

2 Hath He marks to lead me to Him,
  If He be my Guide?   [prints,
"In His feet and hands are wounded
  And His side."

3 Is there diadem, as Monarch,
  That His brow adorns?
"Yea, a crown in very surety,
  But of thorns!"

4 If I still hold closely to Him,
  What hath He at last?
"Sorrow vanquished, labor ended,
  Jordan past!"

5 If I ask Him to receive me,
  Will He say me nay?
"Not till earth, and not till heaven
  Pass away!"
      Stephen of St. Sabas. (725—794.)
Tr. by Rev. John Mason Neale. (1818—1866.) 1862. ab.

MEDITATION AND PRAYER.

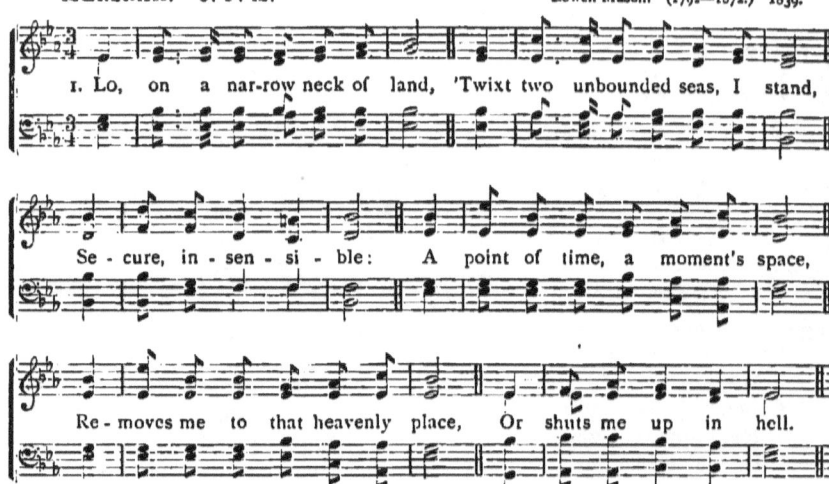

MERIBAH. C. P. M.   Lowell Mason. (1792—1872.) 1839.

1. Lo, on a narrow neck of land, 'Twixt two unbounded seas, I stand, Secure, insensible: A point of time, a moment's space, Removes me to that heavenly place, Or shuts me up in hell.

254 *Death and Judgment anticipated.*

2 O God, mine inmost soul convert,
And deeply on my thoughtful heart
   Eternal things impress ;
Give me to feel their solemn weight,
And tremble on the brink of fate,
   And wake to righteousness.

3 Before me place, in dread array,
The pomp of that tremendous day,
   When Thou with clouds shalt come
To judge the nations at Thy bar ;
And tell me, Lord, shall I be there
   To meet a joyful doom?

4 Be this my one great business here,
With holy trembling, holy fear,
   To make my calling sure,
Thine utmost counsel to fulfil,
And suffer all Thy righteous will,
   And to the end endure.

Rev. Charles Wesley. (1708—1788.) 1749. ab. and alt. v. 4.

255 *The Prayer of Faith.*

1 O THOU that hear'st the prayer of faith,
Wilt Thou not save a soul from death,
   That casts itself on Thee?
I have no refuge of my own,
But fly to what my Lord hath done,
   And suffered once for me.

2 Slain in the guilty sinner's stead,
His spotless righteousness I plead,
   And His availing blood :
Thy merit, Lord, my robe shall be,
Thy merit shall atone for me,
   And bring me near to God.

3 Then snatch me from eternal death,
The Spirit of adoption breathe,
   His consolations send :
By Him some word of life impart,
And sweetly whisper to my heart,
   "Thy Maker is Thy Friend."

Rev. Augustus Montague Toplady. (1740—1778.) 1759. ab.

MUST BE BORN AGAIN. 115

GANGES. C. P. M. S. Chandler. 1790.

1. When Thou, my righteous Judge, shalt come To fetch Thy ran-somed peo-ple home, Shall I a-mong them stand? Shall such a worth-less worm as I, Who some-times am a-fraid to die, Be found at Thy right hand?

256 *The Judgment anticipated.*

2 I love to meet among them now,
  Before Thy gracious feet to bow,
    Though vilest of them all;
  But can I bear the piercing thought,
  What if my name should be left out,
    When Thou for them shalt call?

3 Prevent, prevent it by Thy grace;
  Be Thou, dear Lord, my hiding-place,
    In this th' accepted day;
  Thy pardoning voice, O let me hear,
  To still my unbelieving fear,
    Nor let me fall, I pray.

Selina, Countess of Huntingdon. (1707—1791.) 1772. ab. and alt.

257 *Sinai, and the Saviour.*

1 Awaked by Sinai's awful sound,
  My soul in bonds of guilt I found,
    And knew not where to go;
  Eternal truth did loud proclaim,
  "The sinner must be born again,
    Or sink to endless woe."

2 When to the law I trembling fled,
  It poured its curses on my head,
    I no relief could find;
  This fearful truth increased my pain,
  "The sinner must be born again,"
    And whelmed my tortured mind.

3 The saints I heard with rapture tell
  How Jesus conquered death and hell,
    And broke the fowler's snare;
  Yet, when I found this truth remain,
  "The sinner must be born again,"
    I sunk in deep despair.

4 But while I thus in anguish lay,
  The gracious Saviour passed this way,
    And felt His pity move;
  The sinner, by His justice slain,
  Now by His grace is born again,
    And sings redeeming love.

Rev. Sampson Occum. (1723—1792.) 1760. alt.
Rev. Asahel Nettleton. (1783—1844.) 1824. ab.

THE SINNER AWAKENED.

BRADEN. S. M.   William Batchelder Bradbury. (1816—1868.) 1844.

1. O WHERE shall rest be found, Rest for the wea-ry soul? 'Twere

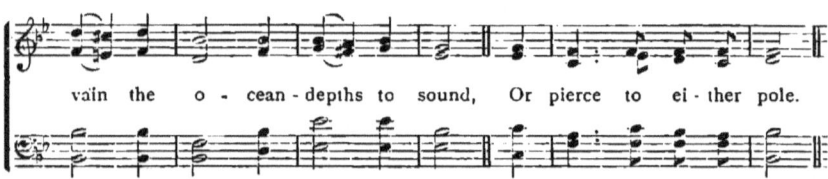

vain the o-cean-depths to sound, Or pierce to ei-ther pole.

258   *The Issues of Life and Death.*

2 The world can never give
   The bliss for which we sigh;
'Tis not the *whole* of life to live,
   Nor *all* of death to die.

3 Beyond this vale of tears
   There is a life above,
Unmeasured by the flight of years;
   And all that life is love.

4 There is a death, whose pang
   Outlasts the fleeting breath:
O what eternal horrors hang
   Around the second death!

5 Lord God of truth and grace,
   Teach us that death to shun,
Lest we be banished from Thy face,
   And evermore undone.
      James Montgomery. (1771—1854.) 1819, 1853. ab.

259   *The Shining Light.*

1 My former hopes are fled,
   My terror now begins;
I feel, alas, that I am dead
   In trespasses and sins.

2 Ah, whither shall I fly?
   I hear the thunder roar;
The law proclaims destruction nigh,
   And vengeance at the door.

3 When I review my ways,
   I dread impending doom;
But sure a friendly whisper says,
   "Flee from the wrath to come."

4 I see, or think I see,
   A glimmering from afar;
A beam of day, that shines for me,
   To save me from despair.

5 Forerunner of the sun,
   It marks the pilgrim's way;
I'll gaze upon it while I run,
   And watch the rising day.
      William Cowper. (1731—1800.) 1779.

PENITENCE.

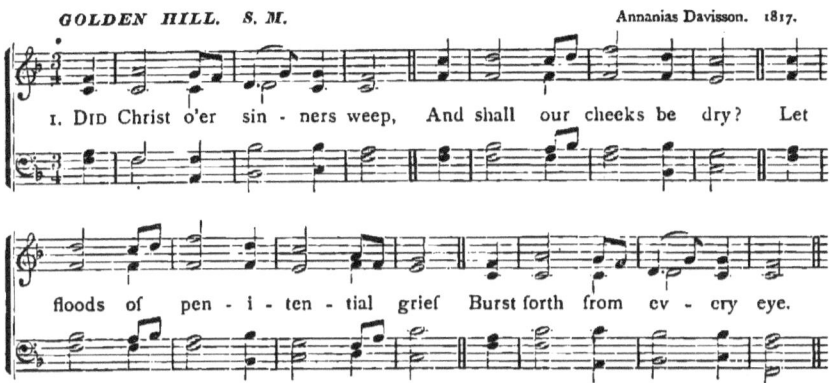

GOLDEN HILL. S. M.   Annanias Davisson. 1817.

1. Did Christ o'er sin-ners weep, And shall our cheeks be dry? Let floods of pen-i-ten-tial grief Burst forth from ev-ery eye.

260   *Tears of Penitence.*

2 The Son of God in tears
   Angels with wonder see :
   Be thou astonished, O my soul,
   He shed those tears for thee.

3 He wept that we might weep ;
   Each sin demands a tear ;
   In heaven alone no sin is found,
   And there's no weeping there.
   Rev. Benjamin Beddome. (1717—1795.) 1787.

261 *God's Goodness leading to Repentance.*
      Rom. ii. 4.
1 Is this the kind return,
   And these the thanks we owe,
   Thus to abuse eternal love,
   Whence all our blessings flow?

2 To what a stubborn frame
   Hath sin reduced our mind!
   What strange, rebellious wretches we,
   And God as strangely kind?

3 Turn, turn us, mighty God,
   And mould our souls afresh ;
   Break, sovereign grace, these hearts of stone,
   And give us hearts of flesh.

4 Let old ingratitude
   Provoke our weeping eyes ;
   And hourly, as new mercies fall,
   Let hourly thanks arise.
   Rev. Isaac Watts. (1674—1748.) 1709. ab.

262   *Mercy implored.*

1 Thou Lord of all above,
   And all below the sky,
   Prostrate before Thy feet I fall,
   And for Thy mercy cry.

2 Forgive my follies past,
   The crimes which I have done ;
   Bid a repenting sinner live,
   Through Thine incarnate Son.

3 Guilt, like a heavy load,
   Upon my conscience lies ;
   To Thee I make my sorrows known,
   And lift my weeping eyes.

4 One gracious look of Thine
   Will ease my troubled breast ;
   O let me know my sins forgiven,
   And I shall then be blest.
   Rev. Benjamin Beddome. 1818. ab.

PROBATION AND CONTRITION.

WINDHAM. L. M.   Daniel Read. (1757—1836.) 1785.

1. Broad is the road that leads to death, And thousands walk to-geth-er there; But wisdom shows a nar-row path, With here and there a trav-el-ler.

263   *The broad Road.*

2 "Deny thyself, and take thy cross,"
Is the Redeemer's great command ;
Nature must count her gold but dross,
If she would gain this heavenly land.

3 The fearful soul, that tires and faints,
And walks the ways of God no more,
Is but esteemed almost a saint,
And makes his own destruction sure.

4 Lord, let not all my hopes be vain ;
Create my heart entirely new—
Which hypocrites could ne'er attain,
Which false apostates never knew.
Rev. Isaac Watts. (1674—1748.) 1719. ab.

264   *Sin confessed.*
Ps. li.

1 Lord, I am vile, conceived in sin,
And born unholy and unclean ;
Sprung from the man whose guilty fall
Corrupts the race, and taints us all.

2 Behold, I fall before Thy face ;
My only refuge is Thy grace ;
No outward forms can make me clean;
The leprosy lies deep within.

3 No bleeding bird, nor bleeding beast,
Nor hyssop branch, nor sprinkling priest,
Nor running brook, nor flood, nor sea,
Can wash the dismal stain away.

4 Jesus, my God, Thy blood alone,
Hath power sufficient to atone ;
Thy blood can make me white as snow ;
No Jewish types could cleanse me so.
Rev. Isaac Watts. 1719. ab.

265   *Pleading for Pardon.*
Ps. li.

1 Show pity, Lord, O Lord, forgive ;
Let a repenting rebel live :
Are not Thy mercies large and free ?
May not a sinner trust in Thee ?

2 My crimes are great, but don't surpass
The power and glory of Thy grace ;
Great God, Thy nature hath no bound,
So let Thy pardoning love be found.

3 O wash my soul from every sin,
And make my guilty conscience clean ;
Here on my heart the burden lies,
And past offences pain mine eyes.

4 My lips with shame my sins confess,
Against Thy law, against Thy grace ;
Lord, should Thy judgments grow severe,
I am condemned, but Thou art clear.

5 Yet save a trembling sinner, Lord,
Whose hope, still hovering round Thy word,   [there,
Would light on some sweet promise
Some sure support against despair.
Rev. Isaac Watts. 1719. ab.

PROBATION AND CONTRITION.

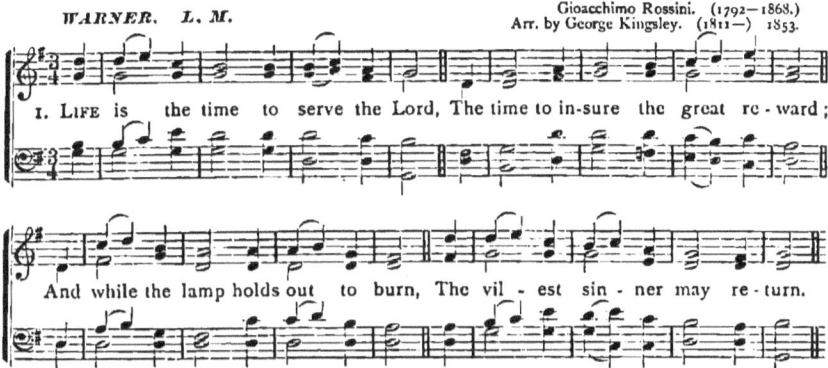

WARNER. L. M.
Gioacchimo Rossini. (1792—1868.)
Arr. by George Kingsley. (1811—) 1853.

1. Life is the time to serve the Lord, The time to insure the great reward; And while the lamp holds out to burn, The vilest sinner may return.

266 *This our only Probation.*
Eccl. ix. 10.

2 Life is the hour that God has given
T' escape from hell and fly to heaven;
The day of grace, and mortals may
Secure the blessings of the day.

3 Then what my thoughts design to do,
My hands, with all your might pursue,
Since no device, nor work is found,
Nor faith, nor hope, beneath the ground.

4 There are no acts of pardon passed
In the cold grave to which we haste;
But darkness, death, and long despair
Reign in eternal silence there.
Rev. Isaac Watts. 1709. ab.

267 *Seeking Rest in Christ.*
Matt. xi. 28.

1 O that my load of sin were gone!
O that I could at last submit
At Jesus' feet to lay it down,
To lay my soul at Jesus' feet!

2 Rest for my soul I long to find;
Saviour of all, if mine Thou art,
Give me Thy meek and lowly mind,
And stamp Thine image on my heart.

3 Break off the yoke of inbred sin,
And fully set my spirit free;
I cannot rest till pure within,
Till I am wholly lost in Thee.

4 Fain would I learn of Thee, my God;
Thy light and easy burden prove,
The cross all stained with hallowed blood,
The labor of Thy dying love.
Rev. Charles Wesley. (1708—1788.) 1742. ab.

268 *A contrite Heart.*
Ps. li.

1 A BROKEN heart, my God, my King,
Is all the sacrifice I bring;
The God of grace will ne'er despise
A broken heart for sacrifice.

2 My soul lies humbled in the dust,
And owns Thy dreadful sentence just;
Look down, O Lord, with pitying eye,
And save the soul condemned to die.

3 O may Thy love inspire my tongue!
Salvation shall be all my song;
And all my powers shall join to bless
The Lord, my strength and righteousness.
Rev. Isaac Watts. 1719. ab. and alt.

CONTRITION.

WOODWORTH. L. M. William Batchelder Bradbury. (1816—1868.) 1849.

1. God call-ing yet! shall I not hear? Earth's pleasures shall I still hold dear? Shall life's swift passing years all fly, And still my soul in slum-bers lie?...

269 *"Gott rufet noch."*

2 God calling yet! shall I not rise?
Can I His loving voice despise,
And basely His kind care repay?
He calls me still; can I delay?

3 God calling yet! and shall He knock,
And I my heart the closer lock?
He still is waiting to receive,
And shall I dare His Spirit grieve?

4 God calling yet! and shall I give
No heed, but still in bondage live?
I wait, but He does not forsake;
He calls me still; my heart, awake!

5 God calling yet! I cannot stay;
My heart I yield without delay:
Vain world, farewell, from Thee I part; [heart.
The voice of God hath reached my

Gerhard Tersteegen. (1697—1769.) 1730.
Tr. by Miss Jane Borthwick. 1854. ab. and alt.

270 *"Come to Me!"*

1 With tearful eyes I look around;
Life seems a dark and stormy sea;
Yet 'midst the gloom I hear a sound,
A heavenly whisper, "Come to Me!"

2 It tells me of a place of rest,
It tells me where my soul may flee:

O, to the weary, faint, opprest,
How sweet the bidding, "Come to Me!"

3 "Come, for all else must fail and die;
Earth is no resting-place for thee;
Heavenward direct thy weeping eye;
I am thy portion; Come to Me!"

4 O voice of mercy, voice of love,
In conflict, grief, and agony,
Support me, cheer me from above,
And gently whisper, Come to Me!"

Miss Charlotte Elliott. (1789—1871.) 1841. ab.

271 *Help only in Christ.*
            Gal. iii. 22.

1 Jesus, the sinner's Friend, to Thee,
Lost and undone, for aid I flee,
Weary of earth, myself, and sin:
Open Thine arms and take me in.

2 Pity and heal my sin-sick soul,
'Tis Thou alone canst make me whole;
Dark, till in me Thine image shine,
And lost I am, till Thou art mine.

3 At last I own it cannot be
That I should fit myself for Thee:
Here, then, to Thee I all resign;
Thine is the work, and only Thine.

Rev. Charles Wesley. (1708—1788.) 1739. ab.

CONTRITION. 121

LOUVAN. L. M.   Virgil Corydon Taylor. (1817—) 1847.

1. With brok-en heart and con-trite sigh, A trembling sin-ner, Lord, I cry: Thy pardoning grace is rich and free; O God, be mer-ci-ful to me.

272   *The Prayer of the Publican.*
         Luke xviii. 13.

2 I smite upon my troubled breast,
With deep and conscious guilt opprest,
Christ and His cross my only plea;
O God, be merciful to me.

3 Far off I stand with tearful eyes,
Nor dare uplift them to the skies;
But Thou dost all my anguish see;
O God, be merciful to me.

4 Nor alms, nor deeds that I have done,
Can for a single sin atone;
To Calvary alone I flee;
O God, be merciful to me.

5 And when, redeemed from sin and hell,
With all the ransomed throng I dwell,
My raptured song shall ever be,
God has been merciful to me.
        Rev. Cornelius Elven. (1797—) 1852.

273   *The Spirit entreated to stay.*

1 Stay, Thou insulted Spirit, stay,
Tho' I have done Thee such despite,
Nor cast the sinner quite away,
Nor take Thine everlasting flight.

2 Though I have steeled my stubborn heart,
And shaken off my guilty fears;
And vexed, and urged Thee to depart,
For many long rebellious years;

3 Though I have most unfaithful been
Of all who e'er Thy grace received;
Ten thousand times Thy goodness seen,
Ten thousand times Thy goodness grieved;

4 Yet, O the chief of sinners spare,
In honor of my great High Priest;
Now in Thy righteous anger swear
To exclude me from Thy people's rest.

5 Now, Lord, my weary soul release,
Upraise me with Thy gracious hand,
And guide into Thy perfect peace,
And bring me to the promised land.
        Rev. Charles Wesley. 1749. ab.

REPENTANCE AT THE CROSS.

HERMON. C. M. — Lowell Mason. (1792–1872.) 1839.

1. In evil long I took delight,
Unawed by shame or fear,
Till a new object struck my sight,
And stopped my wild career.

274 *At the Cross.*

2 I saw One hanging on a tree,
In agonies and blood;
Who fixed His languid eyes on me,
As near His cross I stood.

3 Sure, never till my latest breath,
Can I forget that look;
It seemed to charge me with His death,
Though not a word He spoke.

4 My conscience felt and owned the guilt,
And plunged me in despair;
I saw my sins His blood had spilt,
And helped to nail Him there.

5 Alas, I knew not what I did,
But all my tears were vain;
Where could my trembling soul be hid,
For I the Lord had slain. [hid,

6 A second look He gave, that said,
"I freely all forgive;
This blood is for thy ransom paid,
I die that thou mayest live."

Rev. John Newton. (1725–1807.) 1779. ab.

275 *In Pilate's Hall.*

1 I SEE the crowd in Pilate's hall,
I mark their wrathful mien;
Their shouts of "crucify" appall,
With blasphemy between.

2 And of that shouting multitude
I feel that I am one;
And in that din of voices rude,
I recognize my own.

3 I see the scourges tear His back,
I see the piercing crown,
And of that crowd who smite and mock
I feel that I am one.

4 Around yon cross the throng I see,
Mocking the Sufferer's groan;
Yet still my voice it seems to be,
As if I mocked alone.

5 'Twas I that shed the sacred blood,
I nailed Him to the tree,
I crucified the Christ of God,
I joined the mockery.

6 Yet not the less that blood avails
To cleanse away my sin;
And not the less that cross prevails
To give me peace within.

Rev. Horatius Bonar. (1808–) 1857.

PLEADING FOR MERCY. 123

PASS ME NOT. 8, 5. William Howard Doane. (1832—) 1869.

1. Pass me not, O gentle Saviour, Hear my humble cry;
While on others Thou art smiling,
Do not pass me by.

CHORUS.
Saviour, Saviour, Hear my humble cry.

276 *"Pass me not."*

2 Let me at a throne of mercy
  Find a sweet relief,
Kneeling there in deep contrition,
  Help my unbelief!

3 Trusting only in Thy merits,
  Would I seek Thy face,
Heal my wounded, broken spirit,
  Save me by Thy grace!

4 Thou the Spring of all my comfort,
  More than life to me,
Whom on earth have I besides Thee,
  Whom in heaven but Thee!

Mrs. Fanny Jane Crosby Van Alstyne. (1823—) 1869.

EVEN ME. 8, 7. Arr. by William Batchelder Bradbury. (1816—1868.) 1862.

1. Lord, I hear of showers of blessing
   Thou art scattering full and free;
   Showers, the thirsty land refreshing;
   Let some droppings fall on me,
   Even me, Even me,
   Let some droppings fall on me.

277 *"Bless me, even me also."*
Gen. xxvii. 34.

2 Pass me not, O gracious Father,
  Sinful though my heart may be;
Thou might'st curse me, but the rather
  Let Thy mercy light on me,
    Even me.

3 Pass me not, O tender Saviour,
  Let me love and cling to Thee;
I am longing for Thy favor;
  When Thou comest, call for me,
    Even me.

4 Pass me not, O mighty Spirit,
  Thou canst make the blind to see;
Witnesser of Jesus' merit,
  Speak the word of power to me,
    Even me.

5 Love of God, so pure and changeless,
  Blood of God, so rich and free,
Grace of God, so strong and boundless
  Magnify them all in me,
    Even me.

Mrs. Elizabeth Codner. 1860. ab.

PLEADING FOR MERCY.

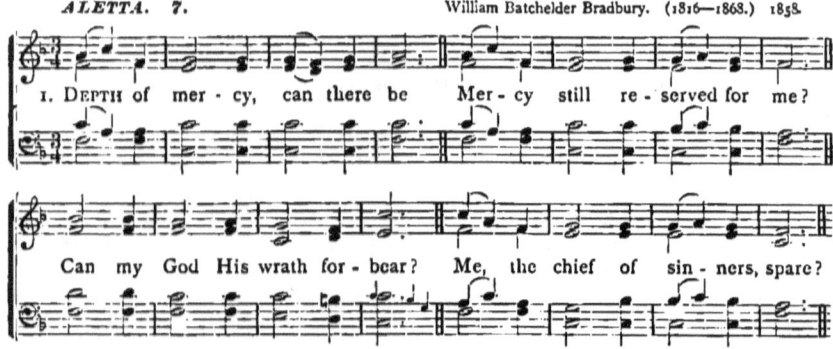

ALETTA. 7. William Batchelder Bradbury. (1816—1868.) 1858.

1. Depth of mer-cy, can there be Mer-cy still re-served for me?
Can my God His wrath for-bear? Me, the chief of sin-ners, spare?

278 *After a Relapse into Sin.*
Heb. x. 29.

2 I have long withstood His grace,
Long provoked Him to His face ;
Would not hearken to His calls ;
Grieved Him by a thousand falls.

3 Kindled His relentings are ;
Me He now delights to spare ;
Cries, " How shall I give thee up ? "
Lets the lifted thunder drop.

4 There for me the Saviour stands,
Shows His wounds, and spreads His hands ;
God is love : I know, I feel ;
Jesus weeps, but loves me still.
Rev. Charles Wesley. (1708—1788.) 1740. ab.

279 *The Penitent pardoned.*

1 Sovereign Ruler, Lord of all,
Prostrate at Thy feet I fall ;
Hear, O hear my ardent cry,
Frown not, lest I faint and die.

2 Vilest of the sons of men,
Worst of rebels I have been ;
Oft abused Thee to Thy face,
Trampled on Thy richest grace.

3 Justly might Thy vengeful dart
Pierce this bleeding, broken heart ;
Justly might Thy kindled ire
Blast me in eternal fire.

4 But with Thee there's mercy found,
Balm to heal my every wound :
Thou canst soothe the troubled breast,
Give the weary wanderer rest.
Rev. Thomas Raffles. (1788—1863.) 1812. ab.

280 *Rest in Christ.*

1 Jesus, full of truth and love,
We Thy kindest word obey :
Faithful let Thy mercies prove,
Take our load of guilt away.

2 Weary of this war within,
Weary of this endless strife,
Weary of ourselves and sin,
Weary of a wretched life ;

3 Burdened with a world of grief,
Burdened with our sinful load,
Burdened with this unbelief,
Burdened with the wrath of God ;

4 Lo, we come to Thee for ease,
True and gracious as Thou art ;
Now our groaning soul release,
Write forgiveness on our heart.
Rev. Charles Wesley. 1747. ab. and alt.
Rev. John Wesley. (1703—1791.) 1779.

COMING TO JESUS. 125

TENNESSEE. C. M.   Robert Boyd. 1817.

1. Come, humble sinner, in whose breast, A thousand thoughts revolve; Come, with your guilt and fear oppressed, And make this last resolve: 2. "I'll go to Jesus, though my sin Hath like a mountain rose; I know His courts, I'll enter in, What-ever may oppose.

281   *"I'll go to Jesus."*

3 "Prostrate I'll lie before His throne,
And there my guilt confess;
I'll tell Him I'm a wretch undone,
Without His sovereign grace.

4 "I'll to the gracious King approach,
Whose sceptre pardon gives;
Perhaps He may command my touch,
And then the suppliant lives.

5 "Perhaps He will admit my plea,
Perhaps will hear my prayer;
But, if I perish, I will pray,
And perish only there.

6 "I can but perish if I go,
I am resolved to try;
For if I stay away, I know
I must forever die."
Rev. Edmund Jones. (1732—1765.) c. 1760.

WOODLAND. C. M.   Nathaniel D. Gould. (1781—1864.) 1832.

1. Jesus, Thou art the sinner's Friend; As such I look to Thee; Now, in the fulness of Thy love, Now, in the fulness of Thy love, O Lord, remember me.

282   *"Remember me."*

2 Remember Thy pure word of grace,
Remember Calvary;
Remember all Thy dying groans,
And then remember me.

3 Thou wondrous Advocate with God,
I yield myself to Thee;
While Thou art sitting on Thy throne,
Dear Lord, remember me.

4 Lord, I am guilty, I am vile,
But Thy salvation's free;
Then in Thine all-abounding grace,
Dear Lord, remember me.

5 And when I close my eyes in death,
When creature-helps all flee,
Then, O my dear Redeemer God,
I pray, remember me.
Rev. Richard Burnham. (1749—1810.) 1783. ab.

PLEADING AND BELIEVING.

DORRNANCE. (TALMAR.) 8, 7.   Isaac Beverly Woodbury. (1819—1858.) 1850.

1. Je-sus, full of all com-pas-sion, Hear Thy hum-ble suppliant's cry;

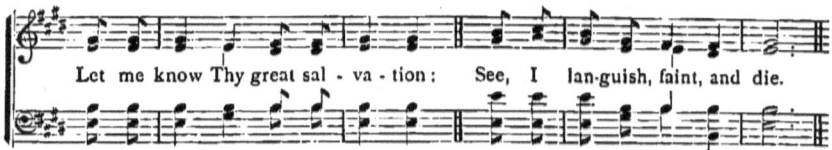

Let me know Thy great sal-va-tion: See, I lan-guish, faint, and die.

283 *"Have Mercy."* Mark x. 47.

2 Guilty, but with heart relenting,
 Overwhelmed with helpless grief,
 Prostrate at Thy feet repenting,
 Send, O send me quick relief.

3 Whither should a wretch be flying,
 But to Him who comfort gives?
 Whither, from the dread of dying,
 But to Him who ever lives?

4 On the word Thy blood hath sealed
 Hangs my everlasting all;
 Let Thy arm be now revealed;
 Stay, O stay me, lest I fall.

5 In the world of endless ruin,
 Let it never, Lord, be said,
 "Here's a soul that perished sueing
 For the boasted Saviour's aid.

6 *Saved!*—the deed shall spread new glory
 Through the shining realms above ;
 Angels sing the pleasing story,
 All enraptured with Thy love.
 Rev. Daniel Turner. (1710—1798.) 1787. ab.

284 *"Take me."*

1 Take me, O my Father, take me,
 Take me, save me, thro' Thy Son;
 That, which Thou wouldst have me,
   make me,
 Let Thy will in me be done.

2 Long from Thee my footsteps stray-
   ing,
 Thorny proved the way I trod ;
 Weary come I now, and praying,
 Take me to Thy love, my God.

3 Fruitless years with grief recalling,
 Humbly I confess my sin ;
 At Thy feet, O Father, falling,
 To Thy household take me in.

4 Freely now to Thee I proffer
 This relenting heart of mine :
 Freely, life and soul I offer,
 Gift unworthy love like Thine.

5 Once the world's Redeemer dying,
 Bore our sins upon the tree;
 On that sacrifice relying,
 Now I look in hope to Thee;

6 Father, take me; all forgiving,
 Fold me to Thy loving breast ;
 In Thy love for ever living,
 I must be for ever blest.
   Rev. Ray Palmer. (1808—) 1865.

JUST AS I AM. 127

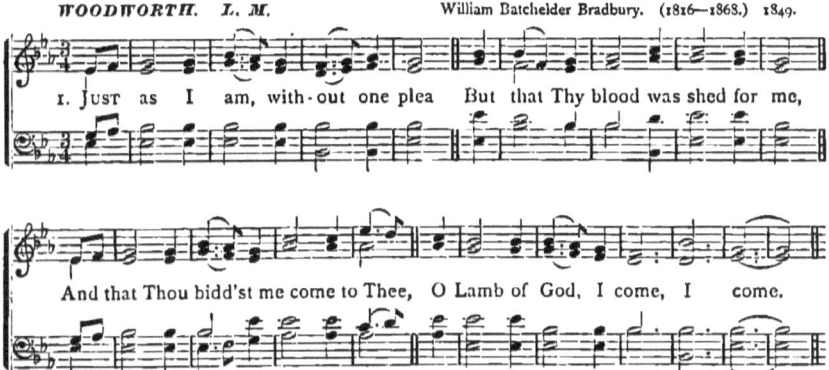

285   "*Just as I am.*" John vi. 37.

2 Just as I am, and waiting not
To rid my soul of one dark blot,
To Thee, whose blood can cleanse each spot,
O Lamb of God, I come.

3 Just as I am, though tossed about
With many a conflict, many a doubt,
With fears within, and foes without,
O Lamb of God, I come.

4 Just as I am, poor, wretched, blind ;
Sight, riches, healing of the mind,
Yea, all I need, in Thee to find,
O Lamb of God, I come.

5 Just as I am, Thou wilt receive,
Wilt welcome, pardon, cleanse, relieve:
Because Thy promise I believe,
O Lamb of God, I come.

6 Just as I am, Thy love unknown
Has broken every barrier down :
Now, to be Thine, yea, *Thine alone,*
O Lamb of God, I come.

    Miss Charlotte Elliot. (1789—1871.) 1836.

286   "*Entirely Thine.*"

1 LORD, I am Thine, entirely Thine,
Purchased and saved by blood divine ;
With full consent Thine I would be,
And own Thy sovereign right in me.

2 Grant one poor sinner more a place,
Among the children of Thy grace ;
A wretched sinner, lost to God,
But ransomed by Immanuel's blood.

3 Thine would I live, Thine would I die,
Be Thine through all eternity ;
The vow is past beyond repeal ;
Now will I set the solemn seal.

4 Here, at that cross where flows the blood
That bought my guilty soul for God,
Thee my new Master now I call,
And consecrate to Thee my all.

5 Do Thou assist a feeble worm
The great engagement to perform ;
Thy grace can full assistance lend,
And on that grace I dare depend.

    Rev. Samuel Davies. (1724—1761.) 1769.

FAITH AND LOVE.

ROCK OF AGES. 7. 6 l. — Rev. John Bacchus Dykes. 1861.

1. Rock of ages, cleft for me, Let me hide myself in Thee; Let the water and the blood, From Thy riven side which flowed, Be of sin the double cure, Cleanse me from its guilt and power.

287   *"Rock of Ages."*

2 Not the labors of my hands
Can fulfil Thy law's demands;
Could my zeal no respite know,
Could my tears for ever flow,
All for sin could not atone;
Thou must save, and Thou alone.

3 Nothing in my hand I bring;
Simply to Thy cross I cling;
Naked, come to Thee for dress;
Helpless, look to Thee for grace;
Foul, I to the fountain fly;
Wash me, Saviour, or I die.

4 While I draw this fleeting breath,
When my eye-lids close in death,
When I soar to worlds unknown,
See Thee on Thy judgment throne,
Rock of ages, cleft for me,
Let me hide myself in Thee.

Rev. Augustus Montague Toplady. (1740—1778.) 1776. sl. alt.

288   *"Only Thee."*

1 ONCE again beside the cross,
All my gain I count but loss;
Earthly pleasures fade away,
Clouds they are that hide my day:
Hence, vain shadows! let me see
Jesus crucified for me.

2 From beneath that thorny crown
Trickle drops of cleansing down;
Pardon from Thy piercèd hand
Now I take, while here I stand:
Only then I live to Thee,
When Thy wounded side I see.

3 Blessèd Saviour, Thine am I,
Thine to live, and Thine to die;
Height or depth, or earthly power
Ne'er shall hide my Saviour more:
Ever shall my glory be,
Only, only, only Thee!

Rev. George Duffield. (1818—) 1859. ab.

TOPLADY. 7. 6 l. — Thomas Hastings. (1784—1872.) 1830. D. C.

FAITH AND LOVE.

OLIVET. 6, 4.   Lowell Mason. (1792—1872.) 1830.

1. My faith looks up to Thee, Thou Lamb of Calvary, Saviour Divine: Now hear me

while I pray, Take all my guilt away, O let me from this day Be wholly Thine.

289   *"My Faith looks up to Thee."*

2 May Thy rich grace impart
    Strength to my fainting heart,
      My zeal inspire;
   As Thou hast died for me,
   O may my love to Thee,
   Pure, warm, and changeless be,
      A living fire.

3 While life's dark maze I tread,
   And griefs around me spread,
      Be Thou my Guide;
   Bid darkness turn to day,
   Wipe sorrow's tears away,
   Nor let me ever stray
      From Thee aside.

4 When ends life's transient dream,
   When death's cold, sullen stream
      Shall o'er me roll;
   Blest Saviour, then, in love,
   Fear and distrust remove;
   O, bear me safe above,
      A ransomed soul.
            Rev. Ray Palmer. (1808—) 1830.

290   *"Jesus, my Lord!"*

1 JESUS, Thy name I love,
   All other names above,
      Jesus, my Lord!
   O Thou art all to me;
   Nothing to please I see,
   Nothing apart from Thee,
      Jesus, my Lord!

2 When unto Thee I flee,
   Thou wilt my refuge be,
      Jesus, my Lord!
   What need I now to fear?
   What earthly grief or care,
   Since Thou art ever near,
      Jesus, my Lord!

3 Soon Thou wilt come again:
   I shall be happy then,
      Jesus, my Lord!
   Then Thine own face I'll see,
   Then I shall like Thee be,
   Then evermore with Thee,
      Jesus, my Lord!
            James George Deck. 1837. ab.

THE BLIND SEE.

291 *Prayer for Sight.*
Mark x. 47, 48.

2 Many for his crying chid him,
But he called the louder still ;
Till the gracious Saviour bid him
"Come, and ask Me what you will."

3 Money was not what he wanted,
Though by begging used to live ;
But he asked, and Jesus granted,
Alms which none but He could give.

4 " Lord, remove this grievous blindness,
Let mine eyes behold the day ! "
Straight he saw and, won by kindness,
Followed Jesus in the way.

5 O methinks I hear him praising,
Publishing to all around,
" Friends, is not my case amazing?
What a Saviour I have found ! "

6 " O that all the blind but knew Him,
And would be advised by me,
Surely they would hasten to Him,
He would cause them all to see."
Rev. John Newton. (1725—1807.) 1779.

292 *"He received his sight."*
Mark x. 51, 52.

1 Lord, I know Thy grace is nigh me,
Though Thyself I cannot see ;
Jesus, Master, pass not by me ;
Son of David, pity me.

2 While I sit in weary blindness,
Longing for the blessèd light,
Many taste Thy loving-kindness ;
" Lord, I would receive my sight."

3 I would see Thee and adore Thee,
And Thy word the power can give ;
Hear the sightless soul implore Thee :
Let me see Thy face and live.

4 Ah, what touch is this that thrills me?
What this burst of strange delight?
Lo, the rapturous vision fills me !
This is Jesus ! this is sight !

5 Room, ye saints that throng behind Him !
Let me follow in the way ;
I will teach the blind to find Him
Who can turn their night to day.
Rev. Hervey Doddridge Ganse. (1822—) 1869.

THE JOY OF FAITH.

293 *"How happy are they."*
2 That sweet comfort was mine,
 When the favor divine
I first found in the blood of the Lamb;
 When my heart it believed,
 What a joy it received,
What a heaven in Jesus's name!

3 'T was a heaven below
 My Redeemer to know,
And the angels could do nothing more

Than to fall at His feet,
 And the story repeat,
And the Lover of sinners adore.

4 O the rapturous height
 Of that holy delight,
Which I felt in the life-giving blood!
 Of my Saviour possessed,
 I was perfectly blest,
As if filled with the fulness of God.
Rev. Charles Wesley. (1708—1788.) 1749. ab. and sl. alt.

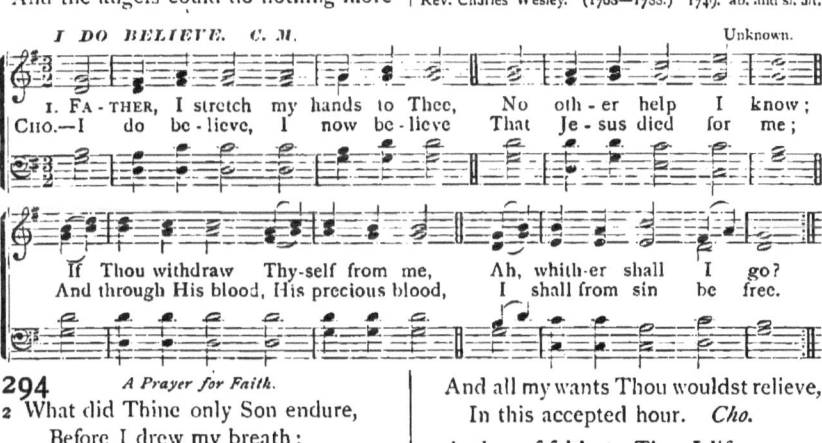

294 *A Prayer for Faith.*
2 What did Thine only Son endure,
 Before I drew my breath;
 What pain, what labor, to secure
 My soul from endless death! *Cho.*

3 O Jesus, could I this believe,
 I now should feel Thy power;

And all my wants Thou wouldst relieve,
 In this accepted hour. *Cho.*

4 Author of faith, to Thee I lift
 My weary, longing eyes:
 O let me now receive that gift;
 My soul without it dies. *Cho.*
Rev. Charles Wesley. 1741. ab., alt. and Cho. added.

NONE BUT CHRIST.

PENITENCE. 7, 6. D. — William Henry Oakley. (1808—) 1835.

1. Vain, de-lu-sive world, adieu, With all of creature good; Only Je-sus I pur-sue,
D. S. On-ly Je-sus will I know,

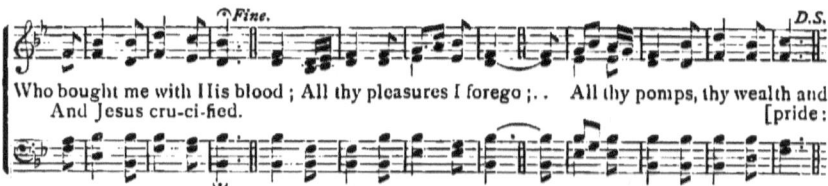

Who bought me with His blood; All thy pleasures I forego;.. All thy pomps, thy wealth and
And Jesus cru-ci-fied. [pride:

295 *Only Jesus, and Him crucified.*
1 Cor. ii. 2.

2 Other knowledge I disdain,
  'Tis all but vanity;
Christ, the Lamb of God, was slain,
  He tasted death for me;
Me to save from endless woe,
  Christ, th' atoning Victim died:
Only Jesus will I know,
  And Jesus crucified.

3 Him to know is life and peace
  And pleasure without end;
This is all my happiness,
  On Jesus to depend;
Daily in His grace to grow,
  Ever in His faith abide:
Only Jesus will I know,
  And Jesus crucified.

4 Him in all my works I seek,
  Who hung upon the tree;
Only of His love I speak,
  Who freely died for me;

While I sojourn here below,
  Nothing will I seek beside;
Only Jesus will I know,
  And Jesus crucified.

Rev. Charles Wesley. (1708—1788.) 1742. ab. and al't.

296 *"Look upon me, Lord."*

1 Saviour, see me from above,
  Nor suffer me to die;
Life, and happiness, and love,
  Drop from Thy gracious eye;
Speak the reconciling word,
  And let Thy mercy melt me down:
Turn, and look upon me, Lord,
  And break my heart of stone.

2 Look, as when Thine eye pursued
  The first apostate man,
Saw him welt'ring in his blood,
  And bade him rise again;
Speak my paradise restored;
  Redeem me by Thy grace alone;
Turn, and look upon me, Lord,
  And break my heart of stone.

Rev. Charles Wesley. 1749. ab.

BELIEVING AND YIELDING. 133

SHAWMUT. S. M.   Arr. by Lowell Mason. (1792—1872.) 1833.

1. Not all the blood of beasts On Jew-ish al-tars slain,

Could give the guilt-y con-science peace, Or wash a-way the stain.

297   *Faith in Christ our Sacrifice.*
2 But Christ, the heavenly Lamb,
   Takes all our sins away;
   A sacrifice of nobler name,
   And richer blood, than they.

3 My faith would lay her hand
   On that dear head of Thine,
   While like a penitent I stand,
   And there confess my sin.

4 My soul looks back to see
   The burdens Thou didst bear,
   When hanging on the curs'd tree,
   And hopes her guilt was there.

5 Believing, we rejoice
   To see the curse remove;
   We bless the Lamb with cheerful voice,
   And sing His bleeding love.
          Rev. Isaac Watts. (1674—1748.) 1709.

298   *"And can I yet delay?"*
1 AND can I yet delay
   My little all to give?
   To tear my soul from earth away,
   For Jesus to receive?

2 Nay, but I yield, I yield,
   I can hold out no more;
   I sink, by dying love compelled,
   And own Thee Conqueror.

3 Though late, I all forsake,
   My friends, my all resign:
   Gracious Redeemer, take, O take,
   And seal me ever Thine.

4 Come, and possess me whole,
   Nor hence again remove;
   Settle and fix my wavering soul
   With all Thy weight of love.

5 My one desire be this,
   Thine only love to know;
   To seek and taste no other bliss,
   No other good below.

6 My Life, my Portion Thou,
   Thou all-sufficient art;
   My Hope, my heavenly Treasure, now
   Enter, and keep my heart.
          Rev. Charles Wesley. 1740. ab.

JOY IN CHRIST.

COWPER. C. M.   Lowell Mason. (1792—1872.) 1830.

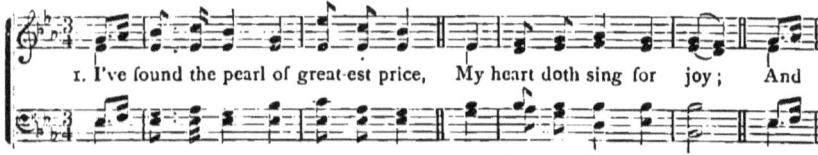

1. I've found the pearl of greatest price, My heart doth sing for joy; And sing I must, for Christ is mine, Christ shall my song employ, Christ shall my song employ.

299   *Singing for Joy.*

2 Christ is my Prophet, Priest, and King;
   A Prophet full of light,
My great High-Priest before the throne,
   My King of heavenly might.

3 For He indeed is Lord of lords,
   And He the King of kings;
He is the Sun of righteousness,
   With healing in His wings.

4 Christ is my Peace; He died for me,
   For me He gave His blood;
And as my wondrous Sacrifice,
   Offered Himself to God.

5 Christ Jesus is my All in all,
   My Comfort and my Love,
My Life below, and He shall be
   My Joy and Crown above.
      Rev. John Mason. (—1694.) 1683. ab. and alt.

300   *Fear disarmed.*

1 THE Saviour! O what endless charms
   Dwell in the blissful sound!
Its influence every fear disarms,
   And spreads sweet comfort round.

2 Wrapt in the gloom of dark despair,
   We helpless, hopeless lay;
But sovereign mercy reached us there,
   And smiled despair away.

3 The almighty Former of the skies
   Stooped to our vile abode;
While angels viewed with wondering eyes,
   And hailed the incarnate God.

4 O the rich depths of love divine,
   Of bliss a boundless store!
Dear Saviour, let me call Thee mine;
   I cannot wish for more.

5 On Thee alone my hope relies,
   Beneath Thy cross I fall,
My Lord, my Life, my Sacrifice,
   My Saviour, and my All.
      Miss Anne Steele. (1717—1778.) 1760. ab.

301   *"Old Things are passed away."*
       2 Cor. v. 17.

1 LET worldly minds the world pursue,
   It has no charms for me;
Once I admired its trifles too,
   But grace has set me free.

2 As by the light of opening day
   The stars are all concealed,
So earthly pleasures fade away,
   When Jesus is revealed.

3 Creatures no more divide my choice,
  I bid them all depart;
  His name, and love, and gracious voice,
  Have fixed my roving heart.

4 Now, Lord, I would be Thine alone,
  And wholly live to Thee:
  For if Thou hadst not loved me first,
  I had refused Thee still.

  Rev. John Newton. (1725—1807.) 1779. ab.

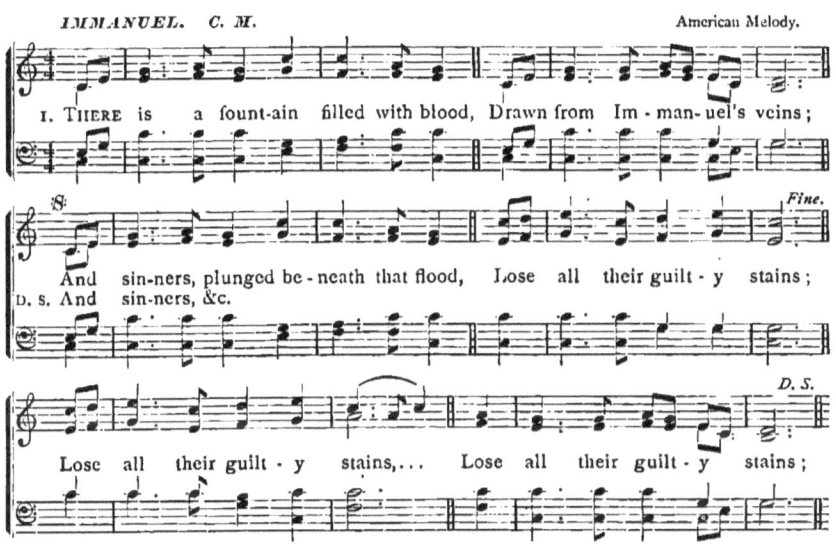

IMMANUEL. C. M.   American Melody.

1. There is a fount-ain filled with blood, Drawn from Im-man-uel's veins;
And sin-ners, plunged be-neath that flood, Lose all their guilt-y stains;
D. S. And sin-ners, &c.
Lose all their guilt-y stains,... Lose all their guilt-y stains;

302   "*A Fountain opened.*" Zech. xiii. 1.

2 The dying thief rejoiced to see
  That fountain in his day:
  And there have I, as vile as he,
  Washed all my sins away.

3 Dear dying Lamb, Thy precious Blood
  Shall never lose its power,
  Till all the ransomed Church of God
  Be saved, to sin no more.

4 E'er since, by faith, I saw the stream
  Thy flowing wounds supply,
  Redeeming love has been my theme,
  And shall be till I die.

5 Then in a nobler, sweeter song,
  I'll sing Thy power to save,
  When this poor lisping, stammering tongue,
  Lies silent in the grave.

6 Lord, I believe Thou hast prepared,
  Unworthy though I be,
  For me a blood-bought free reward,
  A golden harp for me.

7 'Tis strung, and tuned for endless years,
  And formed by power divine,
  To sound in God the Father's ears
  No other name but Thine.

  William Cowper. (1731—1800.) 1779.

SOUGHT AND FOUND.

LEBANON. S. M. D. John Zundel. (1815—) 1855.

1. I was a wandering sheep,
   I did not love the fold;
   I did not love my Shepherd's voice,
   D. S. I did not love my Father's voice,
   I would not be controlled;
   I was a wayward child,
   I did not love my home,
   I loved afar to roam.

303 *Lost but found.*

2 The Shepherd sought His sheep,
   The Father sought His child,
   They followed me o'er vale and hill,
   O'er deserts waste and wild :
   They found me nigh to death,
   Famished, and faint, and lone ;
   They bound me with the bands of love ;
   They saved the wandering one.

3 Jesus my Shepherd is,
   'Twas He that loved my soul,
   'Twas He that washed me in His blood,
   'Twas He that made me whole ;
   'Twas He that sought the lost,
   That found the wandering sheep,
   'Twas He that brought me to the fold,
   'Tis He that still doth keep.
   Rev. Horatius Bonar. (1808—) 1844. ab.

TRUSTING. 7. William Gustavus Fischer. (1835—) 1869.

1. I am coming to the cross;
   I am poor, and weak, and blind;

Cho. I am trusting, Lord, in Thee,
   Dear.. Lamb of Calvary;
   I am counting all but dross;
   I shall Thy salvation find,
   Humbly at Thy cross I bow;
   Save me, Jesus, save me now.

304

2 Here I give my all to Thee,
   Friends, and time, and earthly store ;
   Soul and body Thine to be,
   Wholly Thine for evermore. *Cho.*

3 In the promises I trust :
   Now I feel the blood applied ;
   I am prostrate in the dust ;
   I with Christ am crucified. *Cho.*
   Rev. William McDonald. (1820—) 1869. ab.

AMAZING GRACE.

ATHENS. C. M. D.   Felice Giardini. (1716—1796.) 1760.

1. I heard the voice of Jesus say, "Come unto Me and rest;
Lay down, thou weary one, lay down Thy head upon my breast."
I came to Jesus as I was, Weary, and worn, and sad;
I found in Him a resting-place, And He has made me glad.

305   *The Voice from Galilee.*
           John i. 16.

2 I heard the voice of Jesus say,
"Behold, I freely give
The living water; thirsty one,
Stoop down, and drink, and live."
I came to Jesus, and I drank
Of that life-giving stream;
My thirst was quenched, my soul revived,
And now I live in Him.

3 I heard the voice of Jesus say,
"I am this dark world's Light;
Look unto Me, thy morn shall rise,
And all thy day be bright."
I looked to Jesus, and I found
In Him my Star, my Sun;
And in that Light of Life I'll walk
Till all my journey's done.

         Rev. Horatius Bonar. 1857. sl. alt.

306   *"Amazing Grace."*

1 Amazing grace, how sweet the sound
That saved a wretch like me!
I once was lost, but now am found,
Was blind, but now I see.
'Twas grace that taught my heart to fear,
And grace my fears relieved;
How precious did that grace appear
The hour I first believed!

2 Thro' many dangers, toils, and snares,
I have already come;
'Tis grace has brought me safe thus far,
And grace will lead me home.
The Lord has promised good to me,
His word my hope secures;
He will my Shield and Portion be,
As long as life endures.

         Rev. John Newton. (1725—1807.) 1779. ab.

GRATEFUL PRAISE.

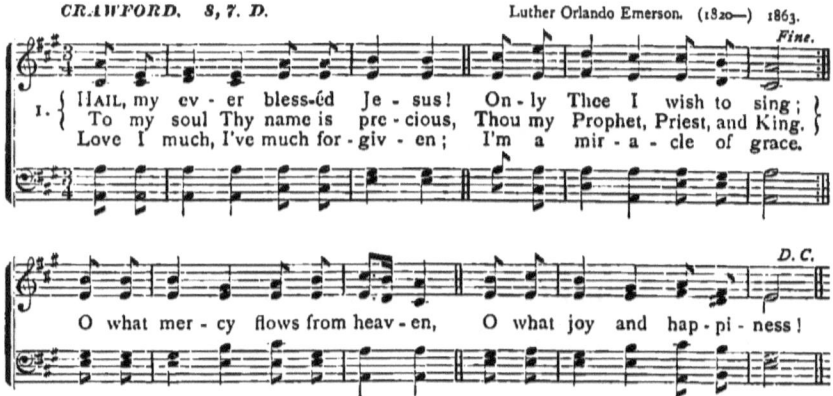

CRAWFORD. 8, 7. D.   Luther Orlando Emerson. (1820—) 1863.

1. Hail, my ever blessèd Jesus!
   Only Thee I wish to sing;
   To my soul Thy name is precious,
   Thou my Prophet, Priest, and King.
   Love I much, I've much forgiven;
   I'm a miracle of grace.
   O what mercy flows from heaven,
   O what joy and happiness!

307   "*A Miracle of Grace.*"

2 Once with Adam's race in ruin,
    Unconcerned in sin I lay,
Swift destruction still pursuing,
    Till my Saviour passed that way.
Witness, all ye host of heaven,
    My Redeemer's tenderness.
Love I much, I've much forgiven;
    I'm a miracle of grace.

3 Shout, ye bright, angelic choir,
    Praise the Lamb enthroned above,
While, astonished, I admire
    God's free grace and boundless love.
That blest moment I received Him
    Filled my soul with joy and peace.
Love I much, I've much forgiven;
    I'm a miracle of grace.
                    John Wingrove. 1806.

308   *Praise for pardoning Grace.*

1 Lord, with glowing heart I'd praise
    Thee
For the bliss Thy love bestows,
For the pardoning grace that saves me,
And the peace that from it flows.

Help, O God, my weak endeavor,
    This dull soul to rapture raise;
Thou must light the flame, or never
    Can my love be warmed to praise.

2 Praise, my soul, the God that sought
    thee,
Wretched wanderer, far astray;
Found thee lost, and kindly brought
    thee
From the paths of death away.
Praise, with love's devoutest feeling,
    Him who saw thy guilt-born fear,
And, the light of hope revealing,
    Bade the blood-stained cross appear.

3 Lord, this bosom's ardent feeling
    Vainly would my lips express;
Low before Thy footstool kneeling,
    Deign Thy suppliant's prayer to bless:
Let Thy grace, my soul's chief treasure,
    Love's pure flame within me raise;
And since words can never measure,
    Let my life show forth Thy praise.
                Francis Scott Key. (1799—1843.) 1857.

GRATEFUL PRAISE. 139

JESU BONE PASTOR. (AMOR.) 8, 7, 6l.   John Henry Willcox. (1827—)

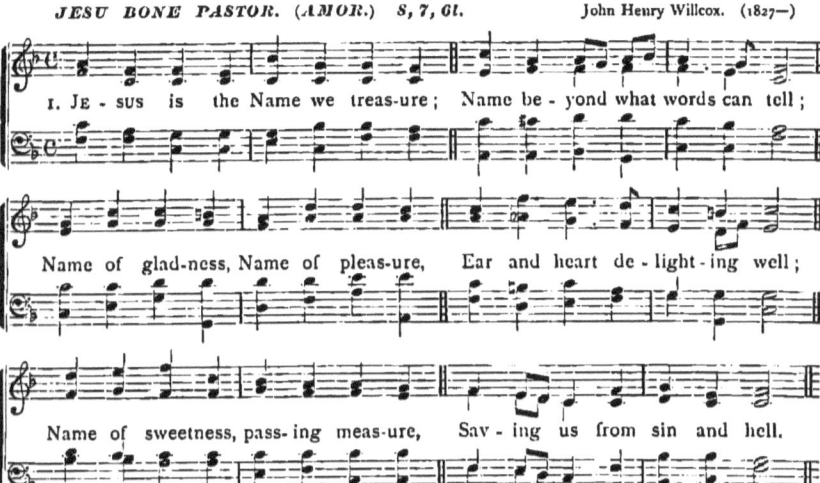

1. Jesus is the Name we treasure; Name beyond what words can tell;
Name of gladness, Name of pleasure, Ear and heart delighting well;
Name of sweetness, passing measure, Saving us from sin and hell.

309   *Christ's Name precious.*

2 'Tis the name for adoration,
   Name for songs of victory,
Name for holy meditation
   In this vale of misery,
Name for joyful veneration
   By the citizens on high.

3 Jesus is the Name exalted
   Over every other name;
In this Name, whene'er assaulted,
   We can put our foes to shame;
Strength to them who else had halted,
   Eyes to blind, and feet to lame.

4 Therefore we in love adoring,
   This most blessèd Name revere;
Holy Jesus, Thee imploring
   So to write it in us here,
That hereafter heavenward soaring,
   We may sing with angels there.

Unknown Author of the 14th and 15th Century.
Tr. by Rev. John Mason Neale. (1818—1866.) 1851. ab. and alt.

310   *"Ich will Dich lieben."* 1 Pet. i. 8.

1 I WILL love Thee, all my treasure;
   I will love Thee, all my strength;
I will love Thee without measure,
   And will love Thee right at length:
I will love Thee, Light Divine,
   Till I die and find Thee mine.

2 I will praise Thee, Sun of Glory,
   For Thy beams have gladness bro't;
I will praise Thee, will adore Thee,
   For the light I vainly sought;
Praise Thee that Thy words so blest
   Spake my sin-sick soul to rest.

3 I will love in joy or sorrow,
   Crowning joy! will love Thee well;
I will love to-day, to-morrow,
   While I in this body dwell:
I will love Thee, Light Divine,
   Till I die, and find Thee mine.

Johann Angelus Silesius. (1624—1677.) 1657.
Tr. by Miss Jane Borthwick. 1854. ab.

140 GRATEFUL PRAISE.

NETTLETON. 8, 7. D.   Rev. Asahel Nettleton. (1783—1844.) 1824.

1. Come, Thou Fount of every blessing, Tune my heart to sing Thy grace;
Streams of mercy never ceasing, Call for songs of loudest praise:
Teach me some melodious sonnet, Sung by flaming tongues above;
Praise the mount, I'm fixed upon it, Mount of God's unchanging love.

311   *Grateful Recollection.*

2 Here I raise my Ebenezer,
  Hither by Thy help I'm come;
And I hope, by Thy good pleasure,
  Safely to arrive at home:
Jesus sought me, when a stranger,
  Wandering from the fold of God;
He, to rescue me from danger,
  Interposed His precious blood.

3 O to grace how great a debtor,
  Daily I'm constrained to be:
Let that grace now, like a fetter,
  Bind my wandering heart to Thee:
Prone to wander, Lord, I feel it,
  Prone to leave the God I love;
Here's my heart, O take and seal it,
  Seal it from Thy courts above.
    Rev. Robert Robinson. (1735—1790.) 1758.

312   *"Bless the Lord, O my Soul."*
     Ps. ciii.

1 Praise, my soul, the King of Heaven;
  To His feet thy tribute bring,
Ransomed, healed, restored, forgiven,
  Evermore His praises sing:
Alleluia! Alleluia!
  Praise the everlasting King.

2 Praise Him for His grace and favor
  To our fathers in distress;
Praise Him still the same as ever,
  Slow to chide, and swift to bless:
Alleluia! Alleluia!
  Glorious in His faithfulness.

3 Father-like, He tends and spares us,
  Well our feeble frame He knows;
In His hands He gently bears us,
  Rescues us from all our foes:
Alleluia! Alleluia!
  Praise with us the God of grace.
    Rev. Henry Francis Lyte. (1793—1847.) 1834. ab. and alt.
    Rev. Sir Henry Williams Baker. (1821—) 1861.

BEFORE THE CROSS.

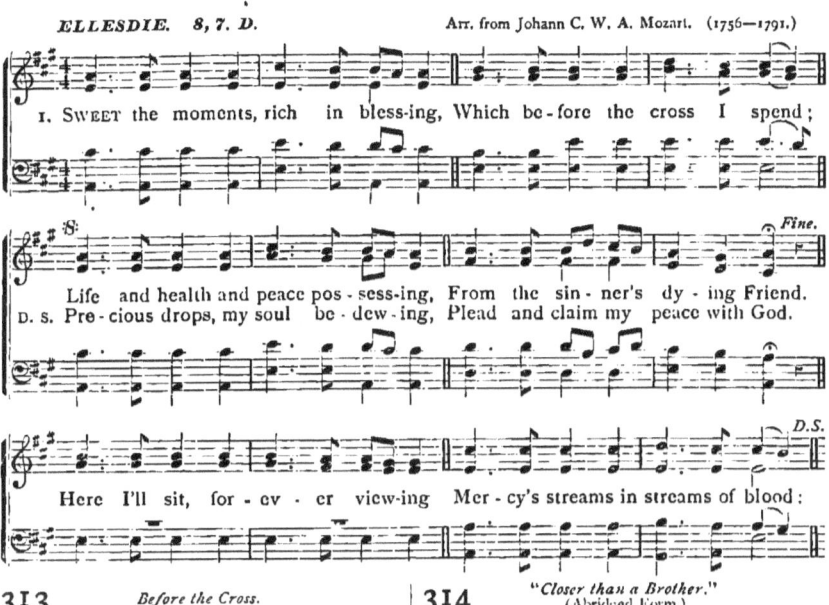

ELLESDIE. 8, 7. D. Arr. from Johann C. W. A. Mozart. (1756—1791.)

1. Sweet the moments, rich in blessing,
Which before the cross I spend;
Life and health and peace possessing,
From the sinner's dying Friend.
Here I'll sit, forever viewing
Mercy's streams in streams of blood:
Precious drops, my soul bedewing,
Plead and claim my peace with God.

313 *Before the Cross.*

2 Truly blessèd is this station,
Low before His cross to lie,
While I see divine compassion
Floating in His languid eye.
Here it is I find my heaven,
While upon the Lamb I gaze;
Love I much? I've much forgiven;
I'm a miracle of grace.

3 Love and grief my heart dividing,
With my tears His feet I'll bathe,
Constant still, in faith abiding,
Life deriving from His death.
May I still enjoy this feeling,
In all need to Jesus go;
Prove His blood each day more healing,
And Himself most deeply know.

Rev. James Allen. (1734—1804.) 1757. alt.
Hon. and Rev. Walter Shirley. (1725—1786.) 1771.

314 "*Closer than a Brother.*"
(Abridged Form.)

1 One there is, above all others,
Well deserves the name of Friend;
His is love beyond a brother's,
Costly, free, and knows no end.
Which of all our friends, to save us,
Could or would have shed his blood?
But our Jesus died to have us
Reconciled in Him to God.

2 When He lived on earth abasèd,
Friend of sinners was His name;
Now above all glory raisèd,
He rejoices in the same.
O for grace our hearts to soften;
Teach us, Lord, at length to love;
We, alas, forget too often
What a Friend we have above.

Rev. John Newton. (1725—1807.) 1779. ab.

142. THE LORD HATH DONE GREAT THINGS.

HEBRON. L. M.   Lowell Mason. (1792—1872.) 1830.

1. Je-sus, my All, to Heaven is gone, He that I placed my hopes up-on;

His track I see, and I'll pur-sue The nar-row way till Him I view.

315   *"The Way to God."*

2 The way the holy Prophets went,
    The way that leads from banishment,
    The King's highway of holiness,
    I'll go; for all the paths are peace.

3 This is the way I long have sought,
    And mourned because I found it not;
    My grief, my burden, long have been
    Because I could not cease from sin.

4 The more I strove against its power
    I sinned and stumbled but the more;
    Till late I heard my Saviour say,
    "Come hither, soul, for I'm the Way."

5 Lo, glad I come; and Thou, dear Lamb,
    Shalt take me to Thee, as I am:
    Nothing but sin I Thee can give;
    Yet help me, and Thy praise I'll live.

6 I'll tell to all poor sinners round
    What a dear Saviour I have found;
    I'll point to Thy redeeming blood,
    And say, "Behold the way to God!"

     Rev. John Cennick. (1717—1755.) 1743. ab.

316   *Christ, our Light and Life.*

1 LORD, I was blind! I could not see
    In Thy marred visage any grace;
    But now the beauty of Thy face
    In radiant vision dawns on me.

2 Lord, I was deaf! I could not hear
    The thrilling music of Thy voice;
    But now I hear Thee and rejoice,
    And all Thy uttered words are dear.

3 Lord, I was dumb! I could not speak
    The grace and glory of Thy name;
    But now, as touched with living flame,
    My lips Thine eager praises wake.

4 Lord, I was dead! I could not stir
    My lifeless soul to come to Thee;
    But now, since Thou hast quickened me,
    I rise from sin's dark sepulchre.

5 For Thou hast made the blind to see,
    The deaf to hear, the dumb to speak,
    The dead to live, and lo, I break
    The chains of my captivity.

     Rev. William Tidd Matson. 1866.

317
The new Joy.

1 THE Saviour smiles; upon my soul
New tides of hope tumultuous roll;
His voice proclaims my pardon found,
Seraphic transport wings the sound.

2 Earth has a joy unknown to heaven,
The new-born peace of sins forgiven;
Tears of such pure and deep delight,
Ye angels, never dimmed your sight.

3 Loud is the song, the heavenly plain
Is shaken with the choral strain;
And dying echoes, floating far,
Draw music from each chiming star.

4 But I amid your choirs shall shine,
And all your knowledge shall be mine;
Ye on your harps must lean to hear
A secret chord that mine will bear.

Abraham Lucas Hillhouse. (1792—1859.) 1822. ab.

318
Parting with earthly Joys.

1 I SEND the joys of earth away;
Away, ye tempters of the mind,
False as the smooth, deceitful sea,
And empty as the whistling wind.

2 Your streams were floating me along
Down to the gulf of dark despair;
And while I listened to your song,
Your streams had e'en conveyed me there.

3 Lord, I adore Thy matchless grace,
That warned me of that dark abyss,
That drew me from those treacherous seas,
And bade me seek superior bliss.

4 Now to the shining realms above
I stretch my hands and glance my eyes;
O for the pinions of a dove,
To bear me to the upper skies!

Rev. Isaac Watts. (1674—1748.) 1709. ab.

319
Longing for Communion with Christ.

1 O THAT I could for ever dwell
With Mary at my Saviour's feet,
And view the form I love so well,
And all His tender words repeat.

2 The world shut out from all my soul,
And heaven brought in with all its bliss,
O, is there aught, from pole to pole,
One moment to compare with this?

3 This is the hidden life I prize,
A life of penitential love,
When most my follies I despise,
And raise the highest thoughts above.

4 Thus would I live till nature fail,
And all my former sins forsake;
Then rise to God within the vail,
And of eternal joys partake.

Rev. Andrew Reed. (1787—1862.) 1842. ab.

320
Jesus the Best Beloved.

1 JESUS, this heart within me burns,
To tell Thee all its conscious love;
And from earth's low delights it turns,
To taste a joy like that above.

2 Though oft these lips my love have told,
They still the story would repeat;
To me the rapture ne'er grows old
That thrills me bending at Thy feet.

3 I breathe my words into Thine ear;
I seem to fix mine eyes on Thine;
And sure that Thou dost wait to hear,
I dare in faith to call Thee mine.

4 Reign Thou sole Sovereign of my heart,
My all I yield to Thy control;
O let me never from Thee part,
Thou Best Belovéd of my soul.

Rev. Ray Palmer. (1808—) 1869. ab.

144

ADORING LOVE.

PENUEL. 8, 6 l. American Melody.

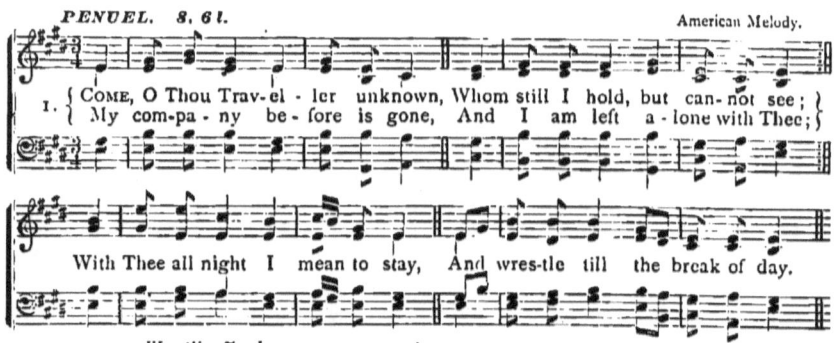

1. { Come, O Thou Trav-el-ler unknown, Whom still I hold, but can-not see;
   { My com-pa-ny be-fore is gone, And I am left a-lone with Thee;
   With Thee all night I mean to stay, And wres-tle till the break of day.

321   *Wrestling Jacob.*
Gen. xxxii. 24.

2 I need not tell Thee who I am?
My sin and misery declare;
Thyself hast called me by my name;
Look on Thy hands, and read it there:
But who, I ask Thee, who art Thou?
Tell me Thy name, and tell me now.

3 I know Thee, Saviour, who Thou art,
Jesus, the feeble sinner's Friend;
Nor wilt Thou with the night depart,
But stay and love me to the end:
Thy mercies never shall remove;
Thy nature and Thy name is Love.
Rev. Charles Wesley. (1703—1788.) 1742. ab.

BRADEN. S. M. William Batchelder Bradbury. (1816—1868.) 1844.

1. I bless the Christ of God; I rest on love di-vine; And
   with un-falt-ering lip and heart, I call this Sav-iour mine.

322   *"I bless the Christ of God."*

2 His cross dispels each doubt;
   I bury in His tomb
Each thought of unbelief and fear,
   Each lingering shade of gloom.

3 I praise the God of grace;
   I trust His truth and might;
He calls me His, I call Him mine,
   My God, my joy, my light.

4 'Tis He who saveth me,
   And freely pardon gives;
I love because He loveth me,
   I live because He lives.

5 My life with Him is hid,
   My death has passed away,
My clouds have melted into light,
   My midnight into day.
Rev. Horatius Bonar. (1808—) 1863. ab.

ADORING LOVE. 145

COLLINS. L. M. D. Jeremiah Ingalls. (1764—1838.) 1805.

1. { Je - sus, my Lord, my God, my All, Hear me, blest Sav-iour, when I call;
    Hear me, and from Thy dwell-ing place Pour down the rich - es of Thy grace; }
Je - sus, my Lord, I Thee a - dore, O make me love Thee more and more;
Je - sus, my Lord, I Thee a - dore, O make me love Thee more and more.

323 "*O make me love Thee more and more.*"

2 Jesus, too late I Thee have sought,
How can I love Thee as I ought;
And how extol Thy matchless fame,
The glorious beauty of Thy name?
Jesus, my Lord, I Thee adore,
O make me love Thee more and more.

3 Jesus, what didst Thou find in me,
That Thou hast dealt so lovingly?
How great the joy that Thou hast brought,
So far exceeding hope or thought!
Jesus, my Lord, I Thee adore,
O make me love Thee more and more.

4 Jesus, of Thee shall be my song,
To Thee my heart and soul belong;
All that I have or am is Thine,
And Thou, blest Saviour, Thou art mine;
Jesus, my Lord, I Thee adore, [
O make me love Thee more and more.
        Rev. Henry Collins. 1852.

324 "*Ich habe nun den Grund gefunden.*"

1 Now I have found the ground wherein
Sure my soul's anchor may remain:
The wounds of Jesus, for my sin
Before the world's foundation slain;
Whose mercy shall unshaken stay
When heaven and earth are fled away.

2 O Love, Thou bottomless abyss!
My sins are swallowed up in Thee;
Covered is my unrighteousness,
Nor spot of guilt remains in me:
While Jesus' blood thro' earth and skies,
Mercy, free, boundless mercy, cries!

3 With faith I plunge me in this sea;
Here is my hope, my joy, my rest;
Hither, when hell assails, I flee,
I look into my Saviour's breast.
Away, sad doubt and anxious fear!
Mercy is all that's written there.
  Rev. John Andrew Rothe. (1688—1758.) 1728.
Tr. by Rev. John Wesley. (1703—1791.) 1740. ab.

ADORING LOVE.

ORTONVILLE. C. M. Thomas Hastings. (1784—1872.) 1837.

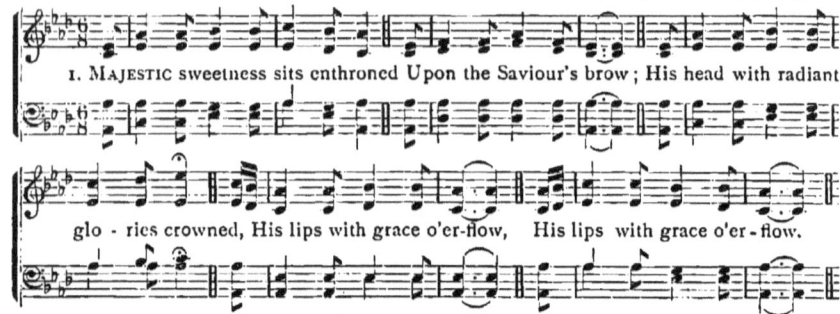

1. Majestic sweetness sits enthroned Upon the Saviour's brow; His head with radiant glo-ries crowned, His lips with grace o'er-flow, His lips with grace o'er-flow.

325 *"Majestic Sweetness."*

2 No mortal can with Him compare
Among the sons of men;
Fairer is He than all the fair
That fill the heavenly train.

3 He saw me plunged in deep distress,
He flew to my relief;
For me He bore the shameful cross,
And carried all my grief.

4 To Him I owe my life and breath,
And all the joys I have;
He makes me triumph over death,
He saves me from the grave.

5 To heaven, the place of His abode,
He brings my weary feet,
Shows me the glories of my God,
And makes my joy complete.

6 Since from His bounty I receive
Such proofs of love divine,
Had I a thousand hearts to give,
Lord, they should all be Thine.
Rev. Samuel Stennett. (1727—1795.) 1787.

326 *Christ precious.*
1 Pet. ii. 7

1 Jesus, I love Thy charming name,
'Tis music to mine ear:
Fain would I sound it out so loud
That earth and heaven should hear.

2 Yes, Thou art precious to my soul,
My Transport and my Trust;
Jewels to Thee are gaudy toys,
And gold is sordid dust.

3 All my capacious powers can wish,
In Thee doth richly meet;
Not to mine eyes is light so dear,
Nor friendship half so sweet.

4 Thy grace still dwells upon my heart,
And sheds its fragrance there;
The noblest balm of all its wounds,
The cordial of its care.

5 I'll speak the honors of Thy name
With my last,laboring breath;
Then, speechless, clasp Thee in mine arms,
The antidote of death.
Rev. Philip Doddridge. (1702—1751.) 1755.

327 *" Jesu, Rex admirabilis."*

1 O Jesus, King most wonderful,
Thou Conqueror renowned,
Thou sweetness most ineffable,
In whom all joys are found;

2 When once Thou visitest the heart,
Then truth begins to shine,
Then earthly vanities depart,
Then kindles love divine.

ADORING LOVE.

3 O Jesus, Light of all below,
Thou Fount of life and fire,
Surpassing all the joys we know,
All that we can desire;

4 May every heart confess Thy name,
And ever Thee adore;

And seeking Thee, itself inflame
To seek Thee more and more.

5 Thee may our tongues forever bless;
Thee may we love alone;
And ever in our lives express
The image of Thine own.
Bernard of Clairvaux. (1091—1153.) 1140.
Tr. by Rev. Edward Caswall. (1814—) 1849.

DEDHAM. C. M.   William Gardiner. (1770—1853.) 1830.

1. O for a thousand tongues to sing My dear Redeemer's praise;
The glories of my God and King, The triumphs of his grace.

---

328 *Converting Grace commemorated.*

2 My gracious Master and my God,
Assist me to proclaim,
To spread thro' all the earth abroad,
The honors of Thy name.

3 Jesus, the name that charms our fears,
That bids our sorrows cease;
'Tis music in the sinner's ears,
'Tis life, and health, and peace.

4 He breaks the power of cancelled sin,
He sets the prisoners free;
His blood can make the foulest clean,
His blood availed for *me*.
Rev. Charles Wesley. (1708—1788.) 1740. ab.

329   "*Jesu, dulcis memoria.*"

1 JESUS, the very thought of Thee
With sweetness fills my breast;

But sweeter far Thy face to see,
And in Thy presence rest.

2 Nor voice can sing, nor heart can frame,
Nor can the memory find
A sweeter sound than Thy blest name,
O Saviour of mankind!

3 O Hope of every contrite heart,
O Joy of all the meek,
To those who fall, how kind Thou art!
How good to those who seek!

4 Jesus, our only Joy be Thou,
As Thou our Prize wilt be;
Jesus, be Thou our Glory now,
And through eternity.
Bernard of Clairvaux. 1140.
Tr. by Rev. Edward Caswall. 1849.

LOVE TO CHRIST.

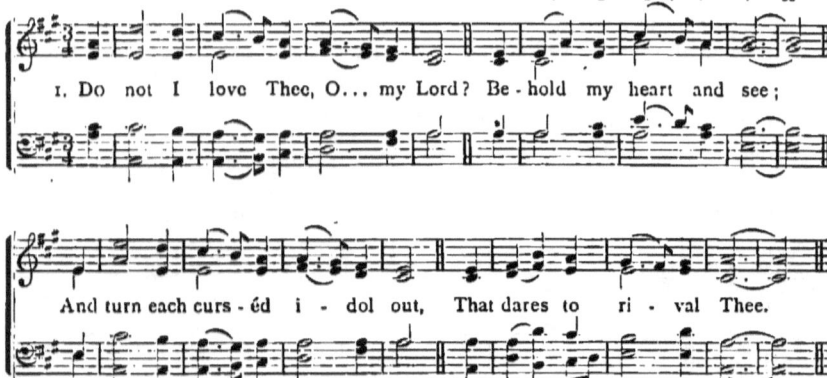

BOARDMAN. C. M. Devereux. Arr. by George Kingsley. (1811—) 1853.

1. Do not I love Thee, O... my Lord? Be-hold my heart and see;
And turn each curs-èd i-dol out, That dares to ri-val Thee.

330 *"Thou knowest that I love Thee."*
John xxi. 15.

2 Do not I love Thee from my soul?
Then let me nothing love;
Dead be my heart to every joy,
When Jesus cannot move.

3 Is not Thy Name melodious still
To mine attentive ear?
Doth not each pulse with pleasure bound
My Saviour's voice to hear?

4 Hast Thou a lamb in all Thy flock
I would disdain to feed?
Hast Thou a foe before whose face
I fear Thy cause to plead?

5 Would not my heart pour forth its blood
In honor of Thy Name,
And challenge the cold hand of death
To damp the immortal flame?

6 Thou know'st I love Thee, dearest Lord,
But O, I long to soar
Far from the sphere of mortal joys,
And learn to love Thee more.

Rev. Philip Doddridge. (1702—1751.) 1755. ab.

331 *Unseen, but loved.*
1 Pet. i. 8.

1 JESUS, these eyes have never seen
That radiant form of Thine;
The veil of sense hangs dark between
Thy blessèd face and mine.

2 I see Thee not, I hear Thee not,
Yet art Thou oft with me;
And earth hath ne'er so dear a spot,
As where I meet with Thee.

3 Like some bright dream that comes unsought
When slumbers o'er me roll,
Thine image ever fills my thought,
And charms my ravished soul.

4 Yet though I have not seen, and still
Must rest in faith alone,
I love Thee, dearest Lord,—and will,
Unseen, but not Unknown.

5 When death these mortal eyes shall seal,
And still this throbbing heart,
The rending veil shall Thee reveal,
All-glorious as Thou art.

Rev. Ray Palmer. (1808—) 1858.

LOVE TO CHRIST.

1. How sweet the Name of Jesus sounds In a believer's ear;
It soothes his sorrows, heals his wounds, And drives away his fear.

332 *The sweet Name.*

2 It makes the wounded spirit whole,
And calms the troubled breast ;
'Tis manna to the hungry soul,
And to the weary rest.

3 Dear Name! the rock on which I build,
My shield and hiding-place,
My never-failing treasury, filled
With boundless stores of grace.

4 By Thee my prayers acceptance gain,
Although with sin defiled ;
Satan accuses me in vain,
And I am owned a child.

5 Weak is the effort of my heart,
And cold my warmest thought ;
But when I see Thee as Thou art,
I'll praise Thee as I ought.

6 Till then I would Thy love proclaim
With every fleeting breath ;
And may the music of Thy Name
Refresh my soul in death.
Rev. John Newton. (1725—1807.) 1779. ab.

333 *"O Deus, ego amo Te."*

1 My God, I love Thee : not because
I hope for heaven thereby,

Nor yet because who love Thee not
Must die eternally.

2 Thou, O my Jesus, Thou didst me
Upon the cross embrace;
For me didst bear the nails, and spear,
And manifold disgrace ;

3 And griefs, and torments numberless,
And sweat of agony ;
Yea, death itself; and all for me
Who was Thine enemy.

4 Then why, O blessèd Jesus Christ,
Should I not love Thee well ?
Not for the hope of winning heaven,
Nor of escaping hell.

5 Not with the hope of gaining aught,
Not seeking a reward ;
But as Thyself hast lovéd me,
O ever-loving Lord.

6 So would I love Thee, dearest Lord,
And in Thy praise will sing ;
Solely because Thou art my God,
And my Eternal King.
Francis Xavier. (1506—1552.) 1552.
Tr. by Rev. Edward Caswall. (1814—) 1849. sl. alt.

LOVE AND PRAISE.

ARIEL. C. P. M.   Arr. from Mozart by Lowell Mason. (1792–1872.) 1836.

1. O could I speak the match-less worth, O could I sound the glories forth, Which in my Saviour shine, I'd soar, and touch the heavenly strings, And vie with Gabriel while he sings In notes al-most di-vine, In notes al-most di-vine.

334   "*Make His Praise glorious.*"
Ps. lxvi. 2.

2 I'd sing the precious blood He spilt,
My ransom from the dreadful guilt
   Of sin, and wrath divine ;
I'd sing His glorious righteousness,
In which all-perfect, heavenly dress
   My soul shall ever shine.

3 I'd sing the characters He bears,
And all the forms of love He wears,
   Exalted on His throne ;
In loftiest songs of sweetest praise,
I would to everlasting days
   Make all His glories known.

4 Well, the delightful day will come
When my dear Lord will bring me home,
   And I shall see His face ;
Then with my Saviour, Brother, Friend,
A blest eternity I'll spend,
   Triumphant in His grace.

      Rev. Samuel Medley. (1738–1799.) 1789. ab.

335   *Desiring to love.*

1 O Love divine, how sweet Thou art!
When shall I find my willing heart
   All taken up by Thee ?
I thirst, and faint, and die to prove
The greatness of redeeming love,
   The love of Christ to me.

2 God only knows the love of God ;
O that it now were shed abroad
   In this poor, stony heart !
For love I sigh, for love I pine :
This only portion, Lord, be mine,
   Be mine this better part.

3 O that I could forever sit
With Mary at the Master's feet !
   Be this my happy choice,
My only care, delight, and bliss,
My joy, my heaven on earth, be this,
   To hear the Bridegroom's voice.

      Rev. Charles Wesley. (1708–1788.) 1749. ab.

FAITH, LOVE, JOY. 151

ZEBULON. H. M.   Lowell Mason. 1830.

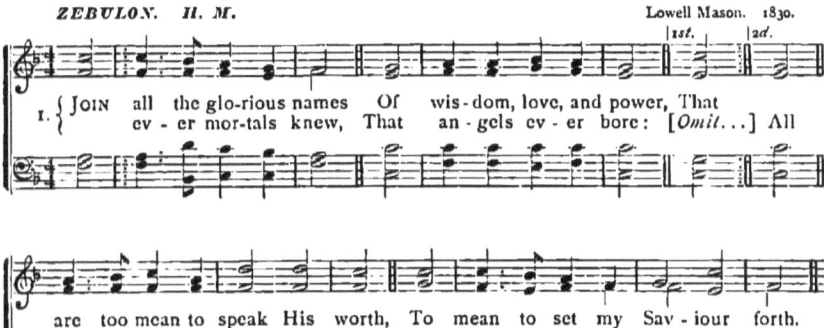

1. Join all the glo-rious names Of wis-dom, love, and power, That ev-er mor-tals knew, That an-gels ev-er bore: [*Omit*...] All are too mean to speak His worth, To mean to set my Sav-iour forth.

336   *Prophet, Priest, and King.*
2 Great Prophet of my God,
   My tongue would bless Thy name;
   By Thee the joyful news
   Of our salvation came:
   The joyful news of sins forgiven,
   Of hell subdued, and peace with heaven.

3 Jesus, my great High Priest,
   Offered His blood and died;
   My guilty conscience seeks
   No sacrifice beside:
   His powerful blood did once atone,
   And now it pleads before the throne.

4 My dear Almighty Lord,
   My Conqueror and my King,
   Thy sceptre and Thy sword,
   Thy reigning grace I sing:
   Thine is the power; behold, I sit,
   In willing bonds, beneath Thy feet.
          Rev. Isaac Watts. (1674—1748.) 1709. ab.

337   *"Behold the Man."*
      Tune, WARSAW, p. 98.
1 Arise, my soul, arise,
   Shake off thy guilty fears;

   The bleeding Sacrifice
   In my behalf appears;
   Before the throne my Surety stands,
   My name is written on His hands.

2 He ever lives above,
   For me to intercede,
   His all-redeeming love,
   His precious blood, to plead;
   His blood atoned for all our race,
   And sprinkles now the throne of grace.

3 The Father hears Him pray,
   His dear anointed One:
   He cannot turn away
   The presence of His Son:
   His Spirit answers to the blood,
   And tells me I am born of God.

4 My God is reconciled,
   His pardoning voice I hear,
   He owns me for His child;
   I can no longer fear,
   With confidence I now draw nigh,
   And Father, Abba, Father, cry.
          Rev. Charles Wesley. 1742. ab.

JOYFUL LAYS.

LOVING-KINDNESS. L. M. Christian Lyre. 1830.

1 Awake, my soul, to joyful lays, And sing thy great Redeemer's praise; He justly claims a song from me, His loving-kind-ness is so free; Loving-kindness, Loving-kindness, His loving-kind-ness is so free.

338 '*The Loving-Kindness of the Lord.*"
Is. lxiii. 7.

2 He saw me ruined in the fall,
Yet loved me notwithstanding all,
And saved me from my lost estate,
His loving-kindness is so great.

3 Through mighty hosts of cruel foes,
Where earth and hell my way oppose,
He safely leads my soul along,
His loving-kindness is so strong.

Rev. Samuel Medley. (1738—1799.) 1787. ab.

THE SWEETEST NAME. 8, 7. William Batchelder Bradbury. (1816—1868.) 1860.

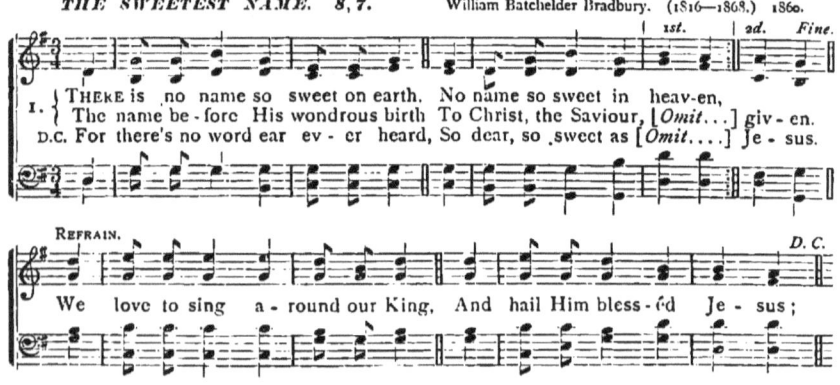

1. { There is no name so sweet on earth, No name so sweet in heav-en,
     The name be-fore His wondrous birth To Christ, the Saviour, [*Omit*...] giv-en.
D.C. For there's no word ear ev-er heard, So dear, so sweet as [*Omit*...] Je-sus.

REFRAIN.
We love to sing a-round our King, And hail Him bless-èd Je-sus;

339 "*No Name so sweet.*"

2 And when He hung upon the tree,
    They wrote His name above Him,
    That all might see the reason we
        For evermore must love Him. *Cho.*

3 So now upon His Father's throne,
    Almighty to release us
    From sin and pains, He gladly reigns,
        The Prince and Saviour, Jesus. *Cho.*

Rev. George Washington Bethune. (1805—1862.) 1858. ab.

SINGING OF JESUS.

SONG. 8, 5. German Melody. Adams' Church Pastorals. 1864.

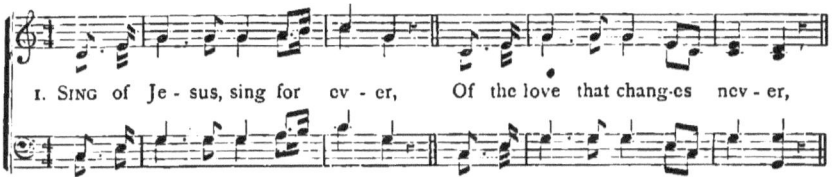

1. Sing of Jesus, sing for ev - er, Of the love that chang-es nev - er,

Who or what from Him can sev - er Those He makes His own?

340
"Sing unto the Lord."
Ps. xxvi. 2.

2 With His blood the Lord has bought them;
When they knew Him not, He sought them,
And from all their wanderings brought them;
His the praise alone.

3 Through the desert Jesus leads them,
With the bread of heaven He feeds them,
And through all the way He speeds them
To their home above.

4 There they see the Lord who bought them,
Him who came from heaven, and sought them,
Him who by His Spirit taught them,
Him they serve and love.

Rev. Thomas Kelly. (1767—1855.) 1815. ab.

341
Our Song on Earth and in Heaven.

1 Saints in glory, we together
Know the song that ceases never;
Song of songs, Thou art, O Saviour,
All that endless day.

2 Theme of Adam, when forgiven,
Theme of Abraham, David, Stephen;
Souls, ye chant it entering heaven,
Now, henceforth, alway.

3 Come, ye angels, round us gather,
While to Jesus we draw nearer;
In His throne He'll seat forever
Those for whom He died.

4 Underneath His throne a river,
Clear as crystal, flows forever,
Like His fulness, failing never:
Hail enthronéd Lamb!

5 O the unsearchable Redeemer!
Shoreless Ocean, sounded never!
Yesterday, to-day, forever,
Jesus Christ, the same.

S. P. Mahmied. ab.

PERENNIAL JOY.

CONTRAST. 8. D. — Jonathan Edson. 1782.

1. How tedious and tasteless the hours
   When Jesus no longer I see!
   Sweet prospects, sweet birds, and sweet flowers
   Have all lost their sweetness to me.
   But when I am happy in Him,
   December's as pleasant as May.
   The midsummer sun shines but dim,
   The fields strive in vain to look gay;

342 *None but Jesus.*
Ps. lxxiii. 25.

2 His name yields the richest perfume,
And sweeter than music His voice;
His presence disperses my gloom,
And makes all within me rejoice.
I should, were He always thus nigh,
Have nothing to wish or to fear;
No mortal so happy as I,
My summer would last all the year.

3 Content with beholding His face,
My all to His pleasure resigned,
No changes of season or place
Would make any change in my mind.
While blest with a sense of His love,
A palace a toy would appear;
And prisons would palaces prove,
If Jesus would dwell with me there.

Rev. John Newton. (1725—1807.) 1779. ab.

REVIVE US AGAIN. 11, 12. — English Melody.

1. We praise Thee, O God, for the Son of Thy love,
   For Jesus who died, and is now gone above.
   Hallelujah! Thine the glory, Hallelujah! Amen.
   Hallelujah! Thine the glory, Revive us again.

343
2 We praise Thee, O God, for Thy Spirit of Light,
Who has shown us our Saviour, and scattered our night.

3 All glory and praise to the Lamb that was slain,
Who has borne all our sins, and has cleansed every stain.

4 All glory and praise to the God of all grace,
Who has bought us, and sought us, and guided our ways.

5 Revive us again; fill each heart with Thy love;
May each soul be rekindled with fire from above.

Rev. W. P. Mackay. 1863.

ALL IN CHRIST.

ALL TO CHRIST I OWE. 6.   John Thomas Grape. (1833—) 1865.

1. I... hear the Sav-iour say, Thy strength in-deed is small;
Child of weakness, watch and pray, [Omit................] Find in Me thine All in all. Je-sus paid it all; All to Him I owe; Sin had left a crim-son stain: He washed it white as snow.

344   "*Jesus paid it all.*"

2 Lord, now indeed I find
   Thy faith, and Thine alone,
   Can change the leper's spots,
   And melt the heart of stone. *Cho.*

3 For nothing good have I
   Whereby Thy grace to claim ;
   I'll wash my garment white
   In the blood of Calv'ry's Lamb. *Cho.*

4 When from my dying bed,
   My ransomed soul shall rise,
   Then " Jesus paid it all,"
   Shall rend the vaulted skies. *Cho.*

5 And when before the throne
   I stand, in Him complete,
   I'll lay my trophies down,
   All down at Jesus' feet. *Cho.*
                Mrs. E. M. Hall.

345   *Wounded for us.*

1 Thy tears, not mine, O Christ,
   Have wept my guilt away ;
   And turned this night of mine
   Into a blessèd day.—*Cho.*

2 Thy wounds, not mine, O Christ,
   Can heal my bruisèd soul ;
   Thy stripes, not mine, contain
   The balm that makes me whole. *Cho.*

3 Thy cross, not mine, O Christ,
   Has borne the awful load
   Of sins that none could bear
   But the incarnate God.—*Cho.*

4 Thy death, not mine, O Christ,
   Has paid the ransom due ;
   Ten thousand deaths like mine
   Would have been all too few.—*Cho.*
      Rev. Horatius Bonar. (1808—) 1857. ab.

PILGRIM SONGS.

NUREMBURG. 7.   Johann Rudolph Ahle. (1625—1673.) 1664.

1. Chil-dren of the Heaven-ly King, As ye jour-ney, sweet-ly sing;

Sing your Sav-iour's wor-thy praise, Glo-rious in His works and ways.

346   *Rejoicing on our Way.*

2 We are travelling home to God,
In the way the fathers trod:
They are happy now, and we
Soon their happiness shall see.

3 Shout, ye little flock, and blest,
You on Jesus' throne shall rest;
There your seat is now prepared,
There your kingdom and reward.

4 Fear not, brethren, joyful stand
On the borders of your land;
Jesus Christ, your Father's Son,
Bids you undismayed go on.

5 Lord, obediently we go,
Gladly leaving all below;
Only Thou our Leader be,
And we still will follow Thee.
      Rev. John Cennick. (1717—1755.) 1742. ab.

347   *Redeeming Love.*

1 Now begin the heavenly theme,
Sing aloud in Jesus' name;
Ye who Jesus' kindness prove,
Triumph in redeeming love.

2 Ye who see the Father's grace
Beaming in the Saviour's face,
As to Canaan on ye move,
Praise and bless redeeming love.

3 Mourning souls, dry up your tears;
Banish all your guilty fears;
See your guilt and curse remove,
Cancelled by redeeming love.

4 Welcome, all by sin opprest,
Welcome to His sacred rest;
Nothing brought Him from above,
Nothing but redeeming love.

5 Hither, then, your music bring,
Strike aloud each joyful string;
Mortals, join the host above,
Join to praise redeeming love.
      Rev. Martin Madan? (1726—1790.) 1763. ab.

PILGRIM SONGS. 157

SILVER STREET. S. M.   Isaac Smith. 1770.

1. From Egypt lately come, Where death and darkness reign, We seek our new, our better home, Where we our rest shall gain. Hal-le-lu-jah! hal-le-lu-jah! We are on our way to God.

348   *Seeking a Country.*
            Heb. xi. 14.

2 To Canaan's sacred bound
We haste with songs of joy;
Where peace and liberty are found,
And sweets that never cloy.
   Hallelujah!
   We are on our way to God.

3 There, in celestial strains,
Enraptured myriads sing;
There love in every bosom reigns,
For God Himself is King.
   Hallelujah!
   We are on our way to God.

4 We soon shall join the throng;
Their pleasures we shall share,
And sing the everlasting song
With all the ransomed there.
   Hallelujah!
   We are on our way to God.
     Rev. Thomas Kelly. (1769—1855.) 1812, 1853. ab.

349   *Pressing on.*

1 This is the day of toil
Beneath earth's sultry noon;
This is the day of service true,
But the rest cometh soon.
   Hallelujah!
   There remains a rest for us.

2 Spend and be spent would we,
While lasteth time's brief day;
No turning back in coward fear,
No lingering by the way.
   Hallelujah!
   There remains a rest for us.

3 Onward we press in haste,
Upward our journey still;
Ours is the path the Master trod,
Through good report and ill.
   Hallelujah!
   There remains a rest for us.

4 The way may rougher grow,
The weariness increase;
We gird our loins, and hasten on:
The end, the end in peace.
   Hallelujah!
   There remains a rest for us.
     Rev. Horatius Bonar. (1808—) 1866. ab.

PILGRIM SONGS.

HE LEADETH ME. L. M.   William Batchelder Bradbury. (1816—1868.) 1864.

350   *"He leadeth me."*

2 Sometimes 'mid scenes of deepest gloom,
Sometimes where Eden's bowers bloom,
By waters still, o'er troubled sea,
Still 'tis His hand that leadeth me. *Cho.*

3 Lord, I would clasp Thy hand in mine,
Nor ever murmur nor repine ;
Content, whatever lot I see,
Since 'tis my God that leadeth me. *Cho.*

4 And when my task on earth is done,
When, by Thy grace, the victory's won,
E'en death's cold wave I will not flee,
Since God thro' Jordan leadeth me. *Cho.*
             Rev. Joseph H. Gilmore. 1859.

351   *Home in View.*

1 As when the weary traveller gains
The height of some o'erlooking hill,
His heart revives, if 'cross the plains
He eyes his home, though distant still.

2 So when the Christian pilgrim views,
By faith, his mansion in the skies,
The sight his fainting strength renews,
And wings his speed to reach the prize.

3 The thought of home his spirit cheers ;
No more he grieves for troubles past,
Nor any future trial fears,
So he may safe arrive at last.

4 'Tis there, he says, I am to dwell
With Jesus, in the realms of day ;
Then I shall bid my cares farewell,
And He will wipe my tears away.
    Rev. John Newton. (1725—1807). 1779. ab. and alt.

PILGRIM SONGS.

THE LORD WILL PROVIDE. 11, 6, 5. Calvin Sears Harrington. c. 1864.

1. In some way or other the Lord will provide: It may not be *my* way,
It may not be *thy* way, And yet, in His *own* way, "The Lord will provide."

352 "*The Lord will provide.*"

2 At some time or other the Lord will
provide:
It may not be *my* time,
It may not be *thy* time,
And yet, in His *own* time,
"The Lord will provide."

3 Despond then no longer; the Lord
will provide:
And this be the token,

No word He hath spoken
Was ever yet broken;
"The Lord will provide."

4 March on, then, right boldly, the sea
shall divide:
The pathway made glorious,
With shoutings victorious,
We'll join in the chorus,
"The Lord will provide."

Mrs. Martha Walker Cook. (1807—1874) c. 1864.

I'M A PILGRIM. 9, 11, 10, 10. German Melody.

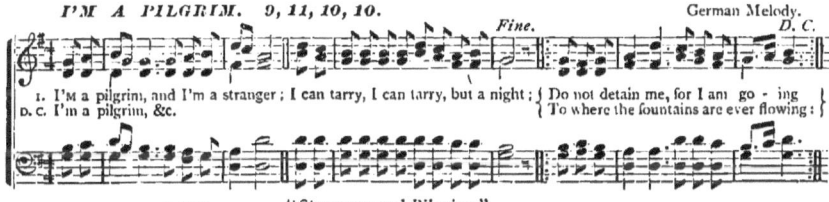

1. I'm a pilgrim, and I'm a stranger; I can tarry, I can tarry, but a night; Do not detain me, for I am go-ing
D.C. I'm a pilgrim, &c. To where the fountains are ever flowing:

353 "*Strangers and Pilgrims.*" Heb. xi. 13.

2 There the glory is ever shining:
O, my longing heart, my longing heart is there;
Here in this country so dark and dreary,
I long have wandered forlorn and weary.

3 There's the city to which I journey;
My Redeemer, my Redeemer is its light:
There is no sorrow, nor any sighing,
Nor any tears there, nor any dying.

Mrs. Mary S. B. Dana. (1810—) 1840.

PILGRIM SONGS.

OLIPHANT. 8, 7, 4.   Pierre-Marie-François de Sales Baillot. (1771—1842.) 1830.
Arr. by Lowell Mason. (1792—1872.) 1832.

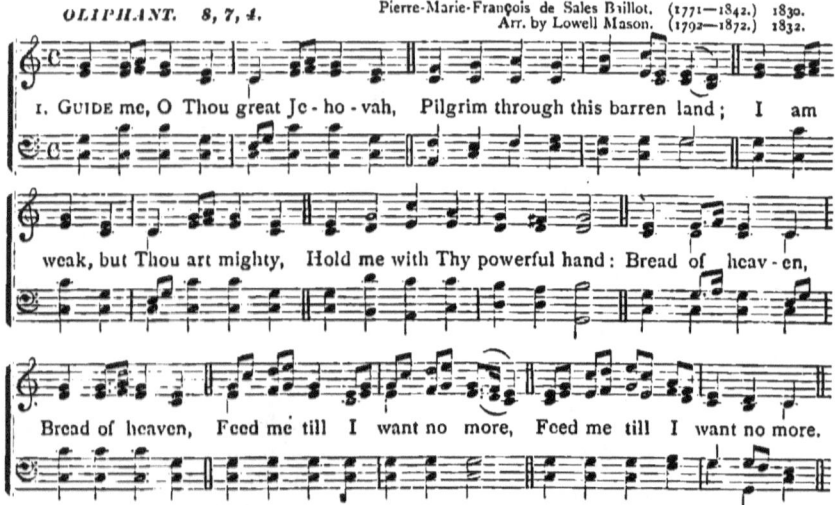

1. Guide me, O Thou great Jehovah, Pilgrim through this barren land; I am weak, but Thou art mighty, Hold me with Thy powerful hand: Bread of heaven, Bread of heaven, Feed me till I want no more, Feed me till I want no more.

354 *Prayer for Guidance.*

2 Open now the crystal fountain,
   Whence the healing stream doth flow;
   Let the fire and cloudy pillar
   Lead me all my journey through:
     Strong Deliverer,
   Be Thou still my strength and shield.

3 When I tread the verge of Jordan,
   Bid my anxious fears subside;
   Death of deaths, and hell's destruction,
   Land me safe on Canaan's side:
     Songs of praises,
   I will ever give to Thee.

    Rev. Peter Williams. (1719—1796.) 1771. v. 1.
    Rev. William Williams. (1717—1791.) 1773. ab.

355 *"And He led them on safely."*
Ps. lxxviii. 53.

1 Saviour, through the desert lead us,
   Without Thee we cannot go;
   Thou from cruel chains hast freed us,
   Thou hast laid the tyrant low:
     Let Thy presence
   Cheer us all our journey through.

2 When we halt, no track discovering,
   Fearful lest we go astray,
   O'er our path the pillar hovering,
   Fire by night, and cloud by day,
     Shall direct us;
   Thus we shall not miss our way.

3 When we hunger, Thou wilt feed us,
   Manna shall our camp surround;
   Faint and thirsty, Thou wilt feed us;
   Streams shall from the rock abound:
     Happy Israel,
   What a Saviour thou hast found!

4 When our foes in arms assemble,
   Ready to obstruct our way,
   Suddenly their hearts shall tremble,
   Thou wilt strike them with dismay;
     And Thy people,
   Led by Thee, shall win the day.

    Rev. Thomas Kelly. (1769—1855.) 1812. ab.

PILGRIM SONGS.

SHEPHERD. 8, 7, 4. William Batchelder Bradbury. (1816—1868.) 1862.

1. Sav-iour, like a shepherd lead us,
   Much we need Thy ten-der care;
   In Thy pleasant pastures feed us,
   For our use Thy folds pre-pare.
   Bless-èd Jesus, Bless-èd Jesus,
   Thou hast bought us, Thine we are;
   Bless-èd Jesus, Bless-èd Jesus,
   Thou hast bought us, Thine we are.

356 *Prayer for Guidance.*

2 We are Thine, do Thou befriend us,
   Be the guardian of our way;
Keep Thy flock, from sin defend us,
   Seek us when we go astray;
       Blessèd Jesus,
   Hear the children when they pray.

3 Thou hast promised to receive us,
   Poor and sinful though we be;
Thou hast mercy to relieve us,
   Grace to cleanse, and power to free;
       Blessèd Jesus,
   Let us early turn to Thee.

4 Early let us seek Thy favor,
   Early let us do Thy will;
Holy Lord, our only Saviour,
   With Thy grace our bosoms fill;
       Blessèd Jesus,
   Thou hast loved us, love us still.
   Miss Dorothy Ann Thrupp. (1779—1847.) 1838.

357 *Prayer for Guidance.*
Numbers x. 33.

1 Lead us, Heavenly Father, lead us
   O'er the world's tempestuous sea;
Guard us, guide us, keep us, feed us,
   For we have no help but Thee;
       Yet possessing every blessing,
   If our God our Father be.

2 Saviour, breathe forgiveness o'er us;
   All our weakness Thou dost know;
Thou didst tread this earth before us;
   Thou didst feel its keenest woe;
       Lone and dreary, faint and weary,
   Through the desert Thou didst go.

3 Spirit of our God, descending,
   Fill our hearts with heavenly joy,
Love with every passion blending,
   Pleasure that can never cloy;
       Thus provided, pardoned, guided,
   Nothing can our peace destroy.
   James Edmeston. (1791—1867.) 1820.

PILGRIM SONGS.

AMSTERDAM. 7, 6. D. James Nares. (1715—1783.) 1760.

Rise, my soul, and stretch thy wings, Thy better portion trace;
Rise from transitory things Towards heaven, thy native place:
Sun and moon and stars decay;

Time shall soon this earth remove; Rise, my soul, and haste away
To seats prepared above.

358 *The Pilgrim's Song.*
Heb. xi. 13.

2 Rivers to the ocean run,
  Nor stay in all their course;
Fire, ascending, seeks the sun;
  Both speed them to their source:
So, a soul, that's born of God,
  Pants to view His glorious face,
Upward tends to His abode,
  To rest in His embrace.

3 Fly me, riches, fly me, cares,
  Whilst I that coast explore;
Flattering world, with all thy snares
  Solicit me no more!
Pilgrims fix not here their home;
  Strangers tarry but a night;
When the last dear morn is come,
  They'll rise to joyful light.

4 Cease, ye pilgrims, cease to mourn,
  Press onward to the prize;
Soon our Saviour will return
  Triumphant in the skies:
Yet a season, and you know
  Happy entrance will be given,
All our sorrows left below,
  And earth exchanged for heaven.
Rev. Robert Seagrave. (1693—) 1742 ab.

359 *"Time is winging us away."*

1 Time is winging us away
  To our eternal home;
Life is but a winter's day,
  A journey to the tomb;
Youth and vigor soon will flee,
  Blooming beauty lose its charms;
All that's mortal soon shall be
  Enclosed in death's cold arms.

2 Time is winging us away
  To our eternal home;
Life is but a winter's day,
  A journey to the tomb;
But the Christian shall enjoy
  Health and beauty soon, above,
Far beyond the world's annoy,
  Secure in Jesus' love.
John Burton. (1773—1822.) 1815.

PILGRIM SONGS. 163

GUIDE. 5, 8. American Melody.

1. Jesus, still lead on, Till our rest be won; And although the way be cheerless, We will follow, calm and fearless: Guide us by Thy hand To our Father - land, To our Father - land.

360 *"Jesu, geh voran."*

2 If the way be drear,
If the foe be near,
Let not faithless fears o'ertake us,
Let not faith and hope forsake us;
For, through many a foe,
To our home we go.

3 When we seek relief
From a long-felt grief,
When temptations come alluring,

Make us patient and enduring;
Show us that bright shore
Where we weep no more.

4 Jesus, still lead on,
Till our rest be won;
Heavenly Leader, still direct us,
Still support, console, protect us,
Till we safely stand
In our Fatherland.

Nicolaus Ludwig Zinzendorf. (1700—1760.) 1721.
Tr. by Miss Jane Borthwick. 1853. sl. alt.

JESUS, GUIDE. 10, 8. William Howard Doane. (1832—) 1870.

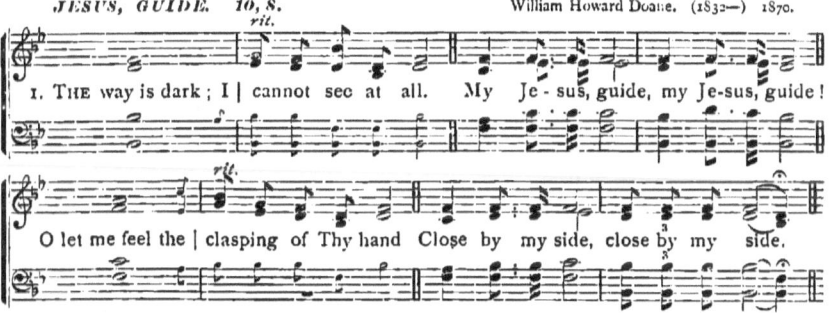

1. The way is dark; I cannot see at all. My Jesus, guide, my Jesus, guide! O let me feel the clasping of Thy hand Close by my side, close by my side.

361 *"My Jesus, guide."*

2 The way is rough; my | feet are very sore,
My Jesus, aid ! my Jesus, aid !
O let me lean while | yet Thou leadest on,
Nor me upbraid ! nor me upbraid !

3 The way is long; I | fear I yet may fall.
My Jesus, keep ! my Jesus, keep !

O let my faith out- | last the weary road,
No more to weep ! no more to weep !

4 The way, it ends ; the | radiant gate appears!
All trials past ! all trials past !
My spirit hastes and | bounds with joy, to be
At home at last ! at home at last !

James Upham. 1869.

PILGRIM SONGS.

STRACATHRO. C. M.  Scotch Melody.

1. O God of Beth-el, by whose hand Thy peo-ple still are fed;
Who through this wea-ry pil-grim-age Hast all our fa-thers led;

362 *Jacob's Vow.*
Gen. xxviii. 20—22.

2 Our vows, our prayers, we now present
Before Thy throne of grace :
God of our fathers, be the God
Of their succeeding race.

3 Through each perplexing path of life
Our wandering footsteps guide ;
Give us each day our daily bread,
And raiment fit provide.

4 O spread Thy covering wings around,
Till all our wanderings cease,
And, at our Father's loved abode,
Our souls arrive in peace.

5 Such blessings from Thy gracious hand
Our humble prayers implore ;
And Thou shalt be our chosen God,
And portion evermore.
Rev. Philip Doddridge. (1702—1751.) 1737.
Michael Bruce. (1746—1767.) 1781. alt.

363 *The hard Way.*

1 Our journey is a thorny maze,
But we march upward still,
Forget these troubles of the ways,
And reach at Zion's hill.

2 See the kind angels, at the gates,
Inviting us to come !
There Jesus, the Forerunner, waits
To welcome travellers home.

3 There, on a green and flowery mount,
Our weary souls shall sit,
And, with transporting joys, recount
The labors of our feet.

4 Eternal glories to the King,
Who brought us safely through,
Our tongues shall never cease to sing,
And endless praise renew.
Rev. Isaac Watts. (1674—1748.) 1709. ab.

364 *"A Priest for ever."*
Ps. cx. 4. Heb. v. 6.

1 Thou dear Redeemer, dying Lamb,
I love to hear of Thee ;
No music's like Thy charming name,
Nor half so sweet can be.

2 O let me ever hear Thy voice
In mercy to me speak ;
In Thee, my Priest, will I rejoice,
And Thy salvation seek.

PILGRIM SONGS. 165

3 My Jesus shall be still my theme,
While on this earth I stay;
I'll sing my Jesus' lovely name,
When all things else decay.

4 When I appear in yonder cloud,
With all His favored throng,
Then will I sing more sweet, more
And Christ shall be my song. [loud,
Rev. John Cennick. (1717—1755.) 1745. alt.

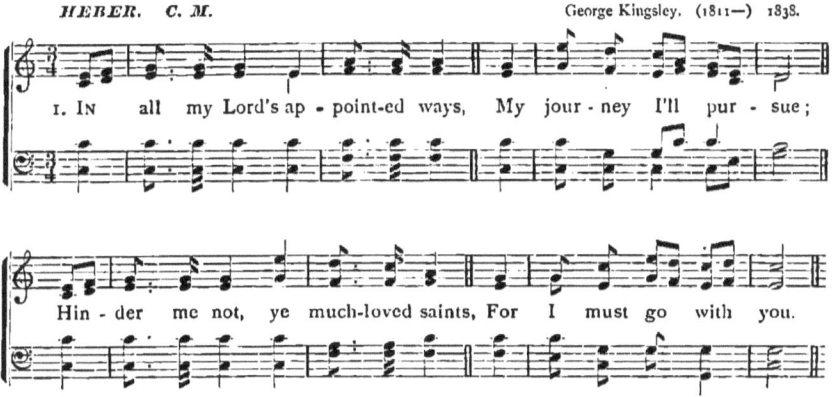

HEBER. C. M. George Kingsley. (1811—) 1838.

1. In all my Lord's ap-point-ed ways, My jour-ney I'll pur-sue;
Hin-der me not, ye much-loved saints, For I must go with you.

365 *"Hinder me not."* Gen. xxiv. 56.

2 Thro' floods and flames, if Jesus lead,
I'll follow where He goes;
Hinder me not! shall be my cry,
Though earth and hell oppose.

3 Through duty, and through trials too,
I'll go at His command;
Hinder me not, for I am bound
To my Immanuel's land.

4 And when my Saviour calls me home,
Still this my cry shall be,
Hinder me not! come, welcome death!
I'll gladly go with thee.
Rev. John Ryland. (1753—1825.) 1773. ab.

366 *The High-way to Zion.* Is. xxxv. 8—10.

1 Sing, ye redeemed of the Lord,
Your great Deliverer sing:
Pilgrims for Zion's city bound,
Be joyful in your King.

2 A band divine shall lead you on
Through all the blissful road,
Till to the sacred mount you rise,
And see your smiling God.

3 There garlands of immortal joy
Shall bloom on every head;
While sorrow, crying, and distress,
Like shadows all are fled.

4 March on in your Redeemer's strength;
Pursue His footsteps still;
And let the prospect cheer your eye,
While laboring up the hill.
Rev. Philip Doddridge. 1755.

PILGRIM SONGS.

NEARER MY HOME. 6, 6, 6, 4.   John M. Evans. 1863.

1. A CROWN of glo-ry bright, By faith's clear eyes I see, In yon-der realms of light Prepared for me. I'm near-er my home, nearer my home, nearer my home to-day; Yes, nearer my home in heaven to-day, Than ev-er I've been be-fore.

367   *"A Crown of Glory."*
2 Jesus, be Thou my Guide,
    And all my steps attend;
    O keep me near Thy side,
    Be Thou my Friend.

3 Be Thou my Shield and Sun,
    My Saviour and my Guard;
    And when my work is done,
    My great Reward.
                        Unknown Author. 1863. ab.

DAWN. S. M.   Rev. Edwin Pond Parker. (1836—) 1871.

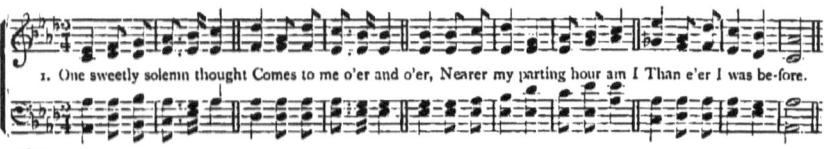

1. One sweetly solemn thought Comes to me o'er and o'er, Nearer my parting hour am I Than e'er I was be-fore.

368   *Nearing Home.*
2 Nearer my Father's house,
    Where many mansions be ;
    Nearer the throne where Jesus reigns,
    Nearer the crystal sea ;

3 Nearer my going home,
    Laying my burden down,
    Leaving my cross of heavy grief,
    Wearing my starry crown.

PILGRIM SONGS.

4 Nearer that hidden stream,
  Winding through shades of night,
  Rolling its cold, dark waves between
  Me and the world of light.

5 Jesus, to Thee I cling:
  Strengthen my arm of faith;
  Stay near me while my way-worn feet
  Press through the stream of death.
  Miss Phœbe Cary. (1825—1871.) 1852. ab. and alt.

OLMUTZ. S. M. Arr. by Lowell Mason. (1792—1872.) 1832.

1. YOUR harps, ye tremb-ling saints, Down from the wil-lows take; Loud to the praise of love di-vine Bid ev-ery string a-wake.

369 *Weak Believers encouraged.*

2 Though in a foreign land,
  We are not far from home;
  And nearer to our house above
  We every moment come.

3 His grace will to the end
  Stronger and brighter shine;
  Nor present things, nor things to come,
  Shall quench the spark divine.

4 When we in darkness walk,
  Nor feel the heavenly flame,
  Then is the time to trust our God,
  And rest upon His name.

5 Soon shall our doubts and fears
  Subside at His control;
  His loving-kindness shall break through
  The midnight of the soul.

6 Blest is the man, O God,
  That stays himself on Thee;

Who wait for Thy salvation, Lord,
  Shall Thy salvation see.
Rev. Augustus Montague Toplady. (1740—1778.) 1772. ab.

370 *Through the Sea.*
  Ps. cvii. 24.

1 WE'RE bound for yonder land,
  Where Jesus reigns supreme;
  We leave the shore at His command,
  Forsaking all for Him.

2 The Lord Himself will keep
  His people safe from harm;
  Will hold the helm, and guide the ship,
  With His almighty arm.

3 Then let the tempests roar,
  The billows heave and swell;
  We trust to reach the peaceful shore,
  Where all the ransomed dwell.

4 And when we gain the land,
  How happy shall we be!
  How shall we bless the mighty Hand
  That led us through the sea!
Rev. Thomas Kelly. (1769—1855.) 1809. ab.

HOMEWARD BOUND.

HOMEWARD BOUND. 10, 4. Calvin Sears Harrington. 1853.

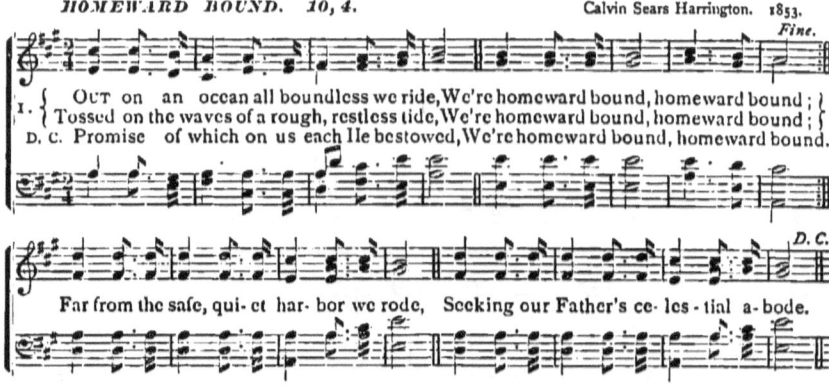

1. { Out on an ocean all boundless we ride, We're homeward bound, homeward bound; }
   { Tossed on the waves of a rough, restless tide, We're homeward bound, homeward bound; }
   D. C. Promise of which on us each He bestowed, We're homeward bound, homeward bound.

Far from the safe, qui-et har-bor we rode, Seeking our Father's ce-les-tial a-bode.

371 *Homeward bound.*

2 Wildly the storm sweeps us on as it
  We're homeward bound;   [roars;
  Look! yonder lie the bright heavenly
  We're homeward bound;   [shores;
  Steady! O pilot, stand firm at the wheel,
  Steady! we soon shall outweather the
      gale;   [sail;
  O how we fly 'neath the loud-creaking
  We're homeward bound.

3 Into the harbor of heaven we now
      glide,
  We're home at last;
  Softly we drift on its bright silver tide,
  We're home at last;
  Glory to God! all our dangers are o'er;
  We stand secure on the glorified shore;
  Glory to God! we will shout evermore,
  We're home at last.

Anonymous. 1853.

SHINING SHORE. 8, 7. D. George Frederick Root. (1820—) 1856.

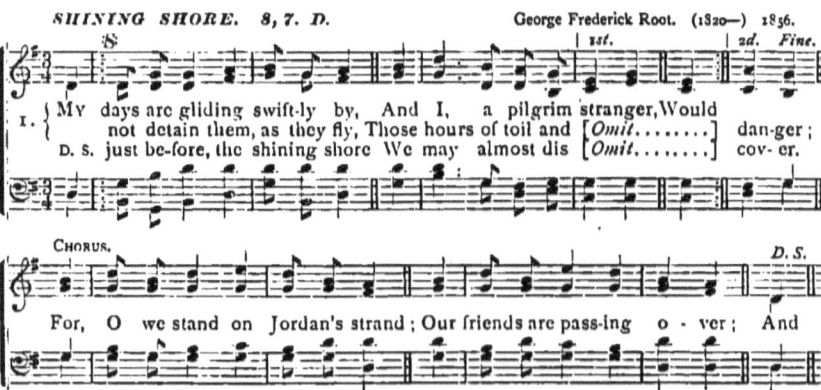

1. { My days are gliding swift-ly by, And I, a pilgrim stranger, Would
     not detain them, as they fly, Those hours of toil and [*Omit*........] dan-ger;
   D. S. just be-fore, the shining shore We may almost dis [*Omit*........] cov-er.

CHORUS.

For, O we stand on Jordan's strand; Our friends are pass-ing o-ver; And

HOMEWARD BOUND. 169

372 *Jordan's Strand.*

2 We'll gird our loins, my brethren dear,
  Our heavenly home discerning;
  Our absent Lord has left us word,
  "Let every lamp be burning:" *Cho.*

3 Should coming days be cold and dark,
  We need not cease our singing;
  That perfect rest nought can molest,
  Where golden harps are ringing: *Cho.*

4 Let sorrow's rudest tempest blow,
  Each cord on earth to sever;
  Our King says, "Come!" and there's our home,
  Forever, O forever: *Cho.*

  Rev. David Nelson. (1793—1844.) 1835.

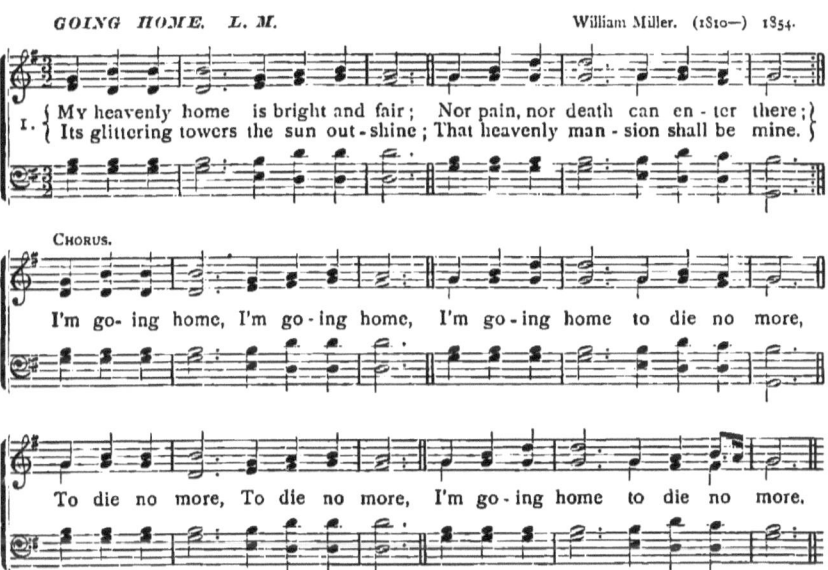

GOING HOME. L. M.   William Miller. (1810—) 1854.

1. My heavenly home is bright and fair; Nor pain, nor death can en-ter there;
   Its glittering towers the sun out-shine; That heavenly man-sion shall be mine.

CHORUS.
I'm go-ing home, I'm go-ing home, I'm go-ing home to die no more,
To die no more, To die no more, I'm go-ing home to die no more.

373 "*My heavenly Home is bright and fair.*"

2 My Father's house is built on high,
  Far, far above the starry sky;
  When from this earthly prison free,
  That heavenly mansion mine shall be.

3 While here, a stranger far from home,
  Affliction's waves may round me foam;
  And, tho' like Lazarus, sick and poor,
  My heavenly mansion is secure.

4 Let others seek a home below,
  Which flames devour, or waves o'er-
  Be mine a happier lot to own,   [flow,
  A heavenly mansion near the throne.

5 Then fail the earth, let stars decline,
  And sun and moon refuse to shine,
  All nature sink and cease to be,
  That heavenly mansion stands for me.

  Rev. William Hunter. (1811—) 1843.

NEARER, YET NEARER.

BETHANY. 6, 4.   Arr. by Lowell Mason. (1792—1872.) 1859.

1. Near-er, my God, to Thee, Near-er to Thee: E'en though it be a cross That rais-eth me;
Still all my song shall be, Near-er, my God, to Thee, Near-er, my God, to Thee, Near-er to Thee.

374   *"Nearer, my God, to Thee."*
         Gen. xxviii. 10—12.

2 Though like the wanderer,
     The sun gone down,
Darkness be over me,
     My rest a stone;
Yet in my dreams I'd be
Nearer, my God, to Thee,
     Nearer to Thee.

3 There let the way appear
     Steps unto heaven;
All that Thou send'st to me,
     In mercy given;
Angels to beckon me
Nearer, my God, to Thee,
     Nearer to Thee.

4 Then with my waking thoughts
     Bright with Thy praise,
Out of my stony griefs
     Bethel I'll raise;
So by my woes to be
Nearer, my God, to Thee,
     Nearer to Thee.

5 Or if on joyful wing
     Cleaving the sky,
Sun, moon, and stars forgot,
     Upwards I fly,
Still all my song shall be,
Nearer, my God, to Thee,
     Nearer to Thee.
      Mrs. Sarah Flower Adams. (1805—1848.) 1840.

375   *"Jesus is mine."*

1 FADE, fade, each earthly joy;
     Jesus is mine.
Break, every tender tie;
     Jesus is mine.
Dark is the wilderness,
Earth has no resting-place,
Jesus alone can bless;
     Jesus is mine.

2 Farewell, ye dreams of night;
     Jesus is mine.
Lost in this dawning bright,
     Jesus is mine.
All that my soul has tried,
Left but a dismal void;
Jesus has satisfied;
     Jesus is mine.
      Mrs. Horatius Bonar. 1845. ab.

NEARER, YET NEARER.

OAK. 6, 4.   Lowell Mason. 1854.

1. More love to Thee, O Christ, More love to Thee! Hear Thou the prayer I make, On bend-ed knee; This is my earn-est plea, More love, O Christ, to Thee, More love, O Christ, to Thee, More love to Thee!

376   "*More Love to Thee!*"
       John xxi. 17.

2 Once earthly joy I craved,
   Sought peace and rest;
   Now Thee alone I seek,
   Give what is best:
   This all my prayer shall be,
   More love, O Christ, to Thee,
   More love to Thee!

3 Let sorrow do its work,
   Send grief and pain;
   Sweet are Thy messengers,
   Sweet their refrain,
   When they can sing with me,
   More love, O Christ, to Thee,
   More love to Thee!

4 Then shall my latest breath
   Whisper Thy praise;
   This be the parting cry
   My heart shall raise,
   This still its prayer shall be,
   More love, O Christ, to Thee,
   More love to Thee!

Mrs. Elizabeth Payson Prentiss. (1819—) 1869.

377   "*Jesus is mine.*"

1 Now I have found a Friend,
   Jesus is mine;
   His love shall never end,
   Jesus is mine:
   Though earthly joys decrease,
   Though earthly friendships cease,
   Now I have lasting peace;
   Jesus is mine.

2 Though I grow poor and old,
   Jesus is mine;
   Though I grow faint and cold,
   Jesus is mine:
   He shall my wants supply;
   His precious blood is nigh,
   Naught can my hope destroy;
   Jesus is mine.

3 When earth shall pass away,
   Jesus is mine;
   In the great judgment day,
   Jesus is mine:
   O what a glorious thing,
   Then to behold my King,
   On tuneful harp to sing,
   Jesus is mine.

Henry Joy McCracken Hope. (1809—1872.) 1852. ab.

FOLLOWING ON.

378 "*I will fear no evil.*"
Ps. xxiii. 4.

2 Through the valley and shadow of death though I stray,
Since Thou art my Guardian, no evil I fear;
Thy rod shall defend me, Thy staff be my stay;
No harm can befall, with my Comforter near.

3 In the midst of affliction my table is spread;
With blessings unmeasured my cup runneth o'er;
With perfume and oil Thou anointest my head;
O what shall I ask of Thy providence more?

4 Let goodness and mercy, my bountiful God,
Still follow my steps till I meet Thee above;
I seek, by the path which my forefathers trod,
Through the land of their sojourn, Thy kingdom of love.

James Montgomery. (1771—1854.) 1822.

379 "*Faint, yet pursuing.*"

1 Though faint, yet pursuing, we go on our way;
The Lord is our Leader, His Word is our stay;
Though suffering, and sorrow, and trial be near,
The Lord is our Refuge, and whom can we fear?

2 He raiseth the fallen, He cheereth the faint;
The weak and oppressed, He will hear their complaint;
The way may be weary, and thorny the road,
But how can we falter? our help is in God.

Unknown Author. 1858. ab.

UPHELD, GUIDED, DEFENDED.

PORTUGUESE HYMN. 11.   John Reading. (1690—1766.) 1760.

1. How firm a foun-da-tion, ye saints of the Lord, Is laid for your faith in His ex-cellent word! What more can He say than to you He hath said, You who un-to Je-sus for ref-uge have fled? You who un-to Je-sus for ref-uge have fled?

380   *"Exceeding great and precious Promises."*
             2 Pet. i. 4.

2 "Fear not, I am with thee, O be not dismayed,
For I am thy God, and will still give thee aid;
I'll strengthen thee, help thee, and cause thee to stand,
Upheld by My righteous, omnipotent hand.

3 "When through the deep waters I call thee to go,
The rivers of woe shall not thee overflow;
For I will be with thee thy trouble to bless,
And sanctify to thee thy deepest distress.

4 "E'en down to old age, all My people shall prove
My sovereign, eternal, unchangeable love;
And when hoary hairs shall their temples adorn,
Like lambs they shall still in My bosom be borne.

5 "The soul that on Jesus hath leaned for repose
I will not, I will not desert to his foes;
That soul, though all hell should endeavor to shake,
I'll never, no never, no never forsake."

                                  George Keith. 1787. ab.

THE GOOD FIGHT OF FAITH.

MENDON. L. M.   German. Arr. by Lowell Mason. (1792—1872.) 1830.

1. Stand up, my soul, shake off thy fears, And gird the gospel armor on; March to the gates of endless joy, Where Jesus thy great Captain's gone.

381   *The Christian Warfare.*

2 Hell and thy sins resist thy course,
But hell and sin are vanquished foes;
Thy Jesus nailed them to the cross,
And sung the triumph when He rose.

3 Then let my soul march boldly on,
Press forward to the heavenly gate:
There peace and joy eternal reign,
And glittering robes for conquerors wait.

4 There shall I wear a starry crown,
And triumph in almighty grace;
While all the armies of the skies
Join in my glorious Leader's praise.
    Rev. Isaac Watts. (1674—1748.) 1709. ab. and alt.

382   *"The good Fight."*
     1 Tim. vi. 12.

1 Fight the good fight with all thy might,
Christ is thy strength, and Christ thy right;
Lay hold on life, and it shall be
Thy joy and crown eternally.

2 Run the straight race through God's good grace,
Lift up thine eyes, and seek His face;
Life with its way before us lies,
Christ is the path, and Christ the prize.

3 Cast care aside, upon thy Guide
Lean, and His mercy will provide;
Lean, and the trusting soul shall prove
Christ is its life, and Christ its love.

4 Faint not nor fear, His arms are near,
He changeth not, and thou art dear:
Only believe, and thou shalt see
That Christ is All in all to thee.
    Rev. John Samuel Bewley Monsell. (1811—) 1863.

383   *The Call to Vigilance.*

1 Awake, my soul, lift up thine eyes:
See where thy foes against thee rise,
In long array, a numerous host:
Awake, my soul, or thou art lost.

2 Thou tread'st upon enchanted ground,
Perils and snares beset thee round;
Beware of all, guard every part,
But most, the traitor in thy heart.

3 Come, then, my soul, now learn to wield
The weight of thine immortal shield;
Put on the armor from above
Of heavenly truth, and heavenly love.

4 The terror and the charm repel,
The powers of earth, and powers of hell;
The Man of Calvary triumphed here:
Why should His faithful followers fear?
    Mrs. Anna Lætitia Barbauld. (1743—1825.) 1773. ab.

THE RACE AND THE JOURNEY. 175

MISSIONARY CHANT. L. M.   Charles Zeuner. (1795—1857.) 1832.

1. A-WAKE, our souls, away our fears, Let ev-ery trembling thought be gone;
A-wake, and run the heavenly race, And put a cheer-ful cour-age on.

384   *The Christian Race.*
     Is. xl. 28—31.

2 True, 'tis a straight and thorny road,
And mortal spirits tire and faint;
But they forget the mighty God,
Who feeds the strength of every saint.

3 The mighty God, whose matchless
Is ever new, and ever young: [power,
And firm endures, while endless years
Their everlasting circles run.

4 From Thee, the overflowing spring,
Our souls shall drink a full supply;
While such as trust their native strength,
Shall melt away, and droop, and die.

5 Swift as an eagle cuts the air,
We'll mount aloft to Thine abode;
On wings of love our souls shall fly,
Nor tire amidst the heavenly road.
         Rev. Isaac Watts. 1709.

385   *Walking by Faith.*

1 'Tis by the faith of joys to come,
We walk thro' deserts dark as night;
Till we arrive at heaven, our home,
Faith is our guide, and faith our light.

2 The want of sight she well supplies;
She makes the pearly gates appear;
Far into distant worlds she pries,
And brings eternal glories near.

3 Cheerful we tread the desert through,
While faith inspires a heavenly ray;
Though lions roar and tempests blow,
And rocks and dangers fill the way.

4 So Abr'am, by divine command,
Left his own house to walk with God;
His faith beheld the promised land,
And fired his zeal along the road.
         Rev. Isaac Watts. 1709.

386   *The City yet to come.*
     Heb. xiii. 14.

1 "WE'VE no abiding city here,"
We seek a city out of sight,
Zion its name, the Lord is there,
It shines with everlasting light.

2 Zion! Jehovah is her strength!
Secure she smiles at all her foes;
And weary travellers at length
Within her sacred walls repose.

3 O sweet abode of peace and love,
Where pilgrims freed from toil are
    blest:
Had I the pinions of the dove,
I'd fly to thee, and be at rest.
     Rev. Thomas Kelly. (1769—1855.) 1812, 1853. ab.

LABAN. S. M. Lowell Mason. (1792—1872.) 1830.

1. Soldiers of Christ, arise, And put your armor on, Strong in the strength which God supplies Through His eternal Son.

387 *"The whole Armor."*
Eph. vi. 11—18.

2 Strong in the Lord of hosts,
And in His mighty power,
Who in the strength of Jesus trusts,
Is more than conqueror.

3 Stand, then, in His great might,
With all His strength endued,
And take, to arm you for the fight,
The panoply of God ;

4 That, having all things done,
And all your conflicts past,
Ye may o'ercome thro' Christ alone,
And stand entire at last.
Rev. Charles Wesley. (1708—1788.) 1749. ab.

388 *"Be on thy Guard."*

1 My soul, be on thy guard ;
Ten thousand foes arise,
And hosts of sins are pressing hard
To draw thee from the skies.

2 O watch, and fight, and pray,
The battle ne'er give o'er ;
Renew it boldly every day,
And help divine implore.

3 Ne'er think the victory won,
Nor once at ease sit down;
Thine arduous work will not be done
Till thou receive thy crown.

4 Fight on, my soul, till death
Shall bring thee to thy God ;
He'll take thee at thy parting breath,
To His divine abode.
George Heath. 1781.

389 *"Watch and pray."*
Eph. v. 14.

1 Gracious Redeemer, shake
This slumber from my soul ;
Say to me now, " Awake, awake !
And Christ shall make thee whole."

2 Give me on Thee to call,
Always to watch and pray,
Lest I into temptation fall,
And cast my shield away.

3 For each assault prepared
And ready may I be ;
Forever standing on my guard,
And looking up to Thee.

4 Myself I cannot save ;
Myself I cannot keep ;
But strength in Thee I surely have,
Whose eyelids never sleep.
Rev. Charles Wesley. 1749. ab.

FAITHFUL AND EARNEST. 177

KENTUCKY. S. M. Jeremiah Ingalls. (1764—1838.) 1805.

1. A CHARGE to keep I have, A God to glo-ri-fy, A nev-er-dy-ing soul to save, And fit it for the sky;

390   *"Keep the Charge of the Lord."* Lev. viii. 35

2 To serve the present age,
  My calling to fulfil:
  O may it all my powers engage
  To do my Master's will.

3 Arm me with jealous care,
  As in Thy sight to live,
  And O Thy servant, Lord, prepare
  A strict account to give.

4 Help me to watch and pray,
  And on Thyself rely,
  Assured, if I my trust betray,
  I shall forever die.
                  Rev. Charles Wesley. 1762.

391   *"Weigh not thy Life."*

1 MY soul, weigh not thy life
  Against thy heavenly crown,
  Nor suffer Satan's deadliest strife
  To beat thy courage down.

2 With prayer and crying strong,
  Hold on the fearful fight,
  And let the breaking day prolong
  The wrestling of the night.

3 The battle soon will yield,
  If thou thy part fulfil:

For strong as is the hostile shield,
  Thy sword is stronger still.

4 Thine armor is divine,
  Thy feet with victory shod;
  And on thy head shall quickly shine
  The diadem of God.
                  Unknown Author.

392   *God in All.*

1 TEACH me, my God and King,
  In all things Thee to see,
  And what I do in anything,
  To do it as for Thee;

2 To scorn the senses' sway,
  While still to Thee I tend;
  In all I do be Thou the Way,
  In all be Thou the End.

3 All may of Thee partake;
  Nothing so small can be
  But draws, when acted for Thy sake,
  Greatness and worth from Thee.

4 If done to obey Thy laws,
  E'en servile labors shine;
  Hallowed is toil, if this the cause,
  The meanest work, divine.
            Rev. George Herbert. (1593—1632.) 1635. ab.

COURAGE.

WEBB. 7, 6, D.   George James Webb. (1803–) 1830.

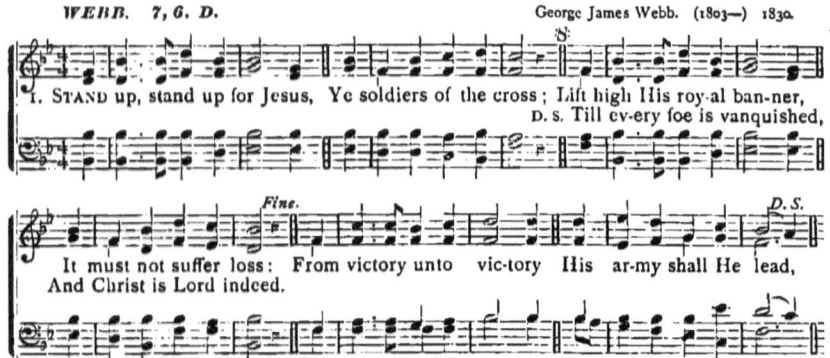

1. Stand up, stand up for Jesus, Ye soldiers of the cross; Lift high His royal banner,
D. s. Till every foe is vanquished,
It must not suffer loss: From victory unto victory His army shall He lead,
And Christ is Lord indeed.

393   *"Stand up, stand up for Jesus."*
2 Stand up, stand up for Jesus,
    The trumpet call obey;
    Forth to the mighty conflict,
    In this His glorious day;
    "Ye that are men, now serve Him"
    Against unnumbered foes;
    Let courage rise with danger,
    And strength to strength oppose.

3 Stand up, stand up for Jesus,
    Stand in His strength alone;
    The arm of flesh will fail you,
    Ye dare not trust your own;
    Put on the gospel armor,
    Each piece put on with prayer;
    Where duty calls, or danger,
    Be never wanting there.

4 Stand up, stand up for Jesus,
    The strife will not be long;
    This day the noise of battle,
    The next the victor's song:
    To him that overcometh,
    A crown of life shall be;
    He with the King of Glory
    Shall reign eternally.
         Rev. George Duffield, Jr. (1818–) 1858. ab.

394   *"Go forward, Christian Soldier."*
1 Go forward, Christian soldier,
    Beneath His banner true:
    The Lord Himself, thy Leader,
    Shall all thy foes subdue.
    Trust only Christ, thy Captain,
    Cease not to watch and pray;
    Heed not the treach'rous voices,
    That lure thy soul astray.

2 Go forward, Christian soldier,
    Nor dream of peaceful rest,
    Till Satan's host is vanquished,
    And heaven is all possest;
    Till Christ Himself shall call thee
    To lay thine armor by,
    And wear, in endless glory,
    The crown of victory.

3 Go forward, Christian soldier,
    Fear not the gathering night;
    The Lord has been thy shelter,
    The Lord will be thy light;
    When morn His face revealeth,
    Thy dangers all are past;
    O pray that faith and virtue
    May keep thee to the last.
         Rev. Lawrence Tuttiett. (1825–) 1866. ab

COURAGE AND TRUST.

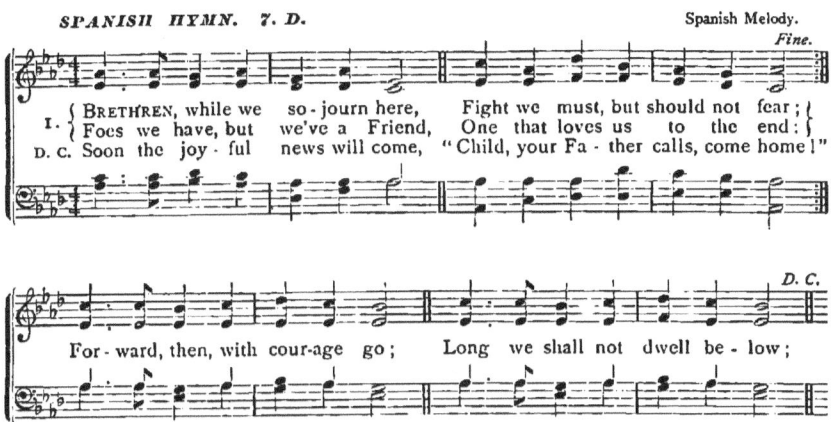

SPANISH HYMN. 7. D.   Spanish Melody.

1. Brethren, while we sojourn here,
Foes we have, but we've a Friend,
Fight we must, but should not fear;
One that loves us to the end:
Forward, then, with courage go;
Long we shall not dwell below;
Soon the joyful news will come,
"Child, your Father calls, come home!"

395   *The Conflict soon over.*

2 In the way a thousand snares
Lie, to take us unawares;
Satan, with malicious art,
Watches each unguarded part:
But, from Satan's malice free,
Saints shall soon victorious be;
Soon the joyful news will come,
"Child, your Father calls, come home!"

3 But of all the foes we meet,
None so oft mislead our feet,
None betray us into sin,
Like the foes that dwell within;
Yet let nothing spoil our peace,
Christ shall also conquer these;
Soon the joyful news will come,
"Child, your Father calls, come home!"
Rev. Joseph Swain. (1761—1796.) 1792.

396   *"Was von aussen und von innen."*

1 Lord, Thou art my Rock of strength,
And my home is in Thine arms;
Thou wilt send me help at length,
And I feel no wild alarms.
Sin nor death can pierce the shield
Thy defence has o'er me thrown;
Up to Thee myself I yield,
And my sorrows are Thine own.

2 When my trials tarry long,
Unto Thee I look and wait,
Knowing none, though keen and strong,
Can my trust in Thee abate.
And this faith I long have nursed
Comes alone, O God, from Thee;
Thou my heart didst open first,
Thou didst set this hope in me.

3 Let Thy mercy's wings be spread
O'er me, keep me close to Thee;
In the peace Thy love doth shed,
Let me dwell eternally.
Be my All; in all I do,
Let me only seek Thy will.
Where the heart to Thee is true,
All is peaceful, calm and still.
Rev. August Hermann Franke. (1663—1727.) 1711.
Tr. by Miss Catherine Winkworth. (1829--) 1855. ab.

ENDURING HARDNESS.

CHRISTMAS. C. M. — George Frederick Handel. (1685—1759.)

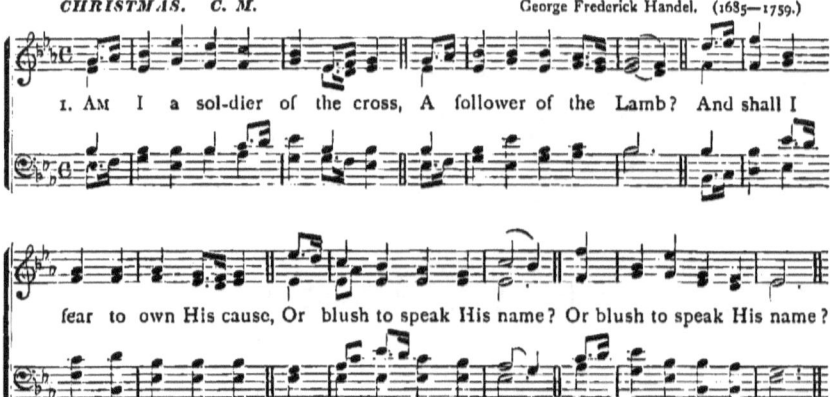

1. Am I a sol-dier of the cross, A follower of the Lamb? And shall I fear to own His cause, Or blush to speak His name? Or blush to speak His name?

397   *"Quit you like Men."*   1 Cor. xvi. 13.

2 Must I be carried to the skies
   On flowery beds of ease,
While others fought to win the prize,
   And sailed through bloody seas?

3 Are there no foes for me to face?
   Must I not stem the flood?
Is this vile world a friend to grace,
   To help me on to God?

4 Sure I must fight, if I would reign;
   Increase my courage, Lord;
I'll bear the toil, endure the pain,
   Supported by Thy word.

5 Thy saints, in all this glorious war,
   Shall conquer though they die;
They view the triumph from afar,
   And seize it with their eye.

6 When that illustrious day shall rise,
   And all Thine armies shine
In robes of victory through the skies,
   The glory shall be Thine.
       Rev. Isaac Watts. (1674—1748.) 1720.

398   *Pressing on.*   Phil. iii. 12—14.

1 Awake, my soul, stretch every nerve,
   And press with vigor on;
A heavenly race demands thy zeal,
   And an immortal crown.

2 A cloud of witnesses around
   Hold thee in full survey:
Forget the steps already trod,
   And onward urge thy way.

3 'Tis God's all-animating voice
   That calls thee from on high;
'Tis His own hand presents the prize
   To thine aspiring eye:—

4 That prize with peerless glories bright,
   Which shall new lustre boast,
When victors' wreaths and monarchs' gems
   Shall blend in common dust.

5 Blest Saviour, introduced by Thee,
   Have I my race begun;
And, crowned with victory, at Thy feet
   I'll lay my honors down.
       Rev. Philip Doddridge. (1702—1751.) 1755.

CROSS AND CROWN. 181

MAITLAND. C. M. — Aaron Chapin. c. 1820.

1. Must Jesus bear the cross alone, And all the world go free?
No, there's a cross for every one, And there's a cross for me.

399 *No Cross, no Crown.*

2 How happy are the saints above,
  Who once went sorrowing here!
  But now they taste unmingled love,
  And joy without a tear.

3 The consecrated cross I'll bear,
  Till death shall set me free;
  And then go home my crown to wear,
  For there's a crown for me.

4 Upon the crystal pavement, down
  At Jesus' piercéd feet,
  Joyful I'll cast my golden crown,
  And His dear Name repeat.

5 And palms shall wave, and harps shall ring,
  Beneath heaven's arches high;
  The Lord that lives, the ransomed sing,
  That lives, no more to die.

6 O precious cross! O glorious crown!
  O resurrection day!

Ye angels, from the stars come down,
And bear my soul away.
G. N. Allen. vs. 1–3. 1849. alt.

400 *"I am not ashamed."*
2 Tim. i. 12.

1 I'm not ashamed to own my Lord,
  Or to defend His cause,
  Maintain the honor of His word,
  The glory of His cross.

2 Jesus, my God! I know His Name,
  His Name is all my trust;
  Nor will He put my soul to shame,
  Nor let my hope be lost.

3 Firm as His throne His promise stands,
  And He can well secure
  What I've committed to His hands,
  Till the decisive hour.

4 Then will He own my worthless name
  Before His Father's face,
  And in the New Jerusalem
  Appoint my soul a place.
  Rev. Isaac Watts. 1709.

GLORYING IN THE CROSS.

RATHBUN. 8, 7. Ithamar Conkey. (1815—1867.) 1851.

1. In the cross of Christ I glory, Towering o'er the wrecks of time;
All the light of sa-cred sto-ry Gath-ers round its head su-blime.

401 *Glorying in the Cross.*
Gal. vi. 14.

2 When the woes of life o'ertake me,
Hopes deceive, and fears annoy,
Never shall the cross forsake me;
Lo, it glows with peace and joy.

3 When the sun of bliss is beaming
Light and love upon my way,
From the cross the radiance streaming
Adds more lustre to the day.

4 Bane and blessing, pain and pleasure,
By the cross are sanctified;
Peace is there, that knows no measure,
Joys that through all time abide.

5 In the cross of Christ I glory,
Towering o'er the wrecks of time;
All the light of sacred story
Gathers round its head sublime.
Sir John Bowring. (1792—1872.) 1825.

402 *"God is Love."*
1 John iv. 8.

1 God is love: His mercy brightens
All the path in which we rove;
Bliss He wakes, and woe He lightens:
God is wisdom, God is love.

2 Chance and change are busy ever;
Man decays, and ages move;
But His mercy waneth never:
God is wisdom, God is love.

3 E'en the hour that darkest seemeth
Will His changeless goodness prove;
From the mist His brightness stream- [eth:
God is wisdom, God is love.

4 He with earthly cares entwineth
Hope and comfort from above;
Everywhere His glory shineth:
God is wisdom, God is love.
Sir John Bowring. 1825.

403 *"I would love Thee."*

1 I would love Thee, God and Father,
My Redeemer and my King:
I would love Thee; for, without Thee,
Life is but a bitter thing.

2 I would love Thee: look upon me,
Ever guide me with Thine eye;
I would love Thee: if not nourished
By Thy love, my soul would die.

3 I would love Thee: may Thy bright-
Dazzle my rejoicing eyes; [ness
I would love Thee: may Thy goodness
Watch from heaven o'er all I prize.

4 I would love Thee, I have vowed it:
On Thy love my heart is set;
While I love Thee, I will never
My Redeemer's blood forget.
Madame Jeanne M. B. de la M. Guyon. (1648—1717.) 1710.

CROSS-BEARING.

ELLESDIE. 8, 7. D. Arr. from Johann C. W. A. Mozart, (1756—1791.)

1. Jesus, I my cross have taken, All to leave, and follow Thee;
Destitute, despised, forsaken, Thou, from hence, my all shalt be:
Perish, every fond ambition, All I've sought, and hoped, and known;
Yet how rich is my condition, God and heaven are still my own!

404 *"We have left all."* Mark x. 28.

2 Let the world despise and leave me,
They have left my Saviour, too;
Human hearts and looks deceive me;
Thou art not, like man, untrue;
And while Thou shalt smile upon me,
God of wisdom, love, and might,
Foes may hate, and friends may shun me,
Show Thy face and all is bright.

3 Go then, earthly fame and treasure;
Come disaster, scorn, and pain!
In Thy service, pain is pleasure;
With Thy favor, loss is gain.
I have called Thee, Abba, Father;
I have stayed my heart on Thee:
Storms may howl, and clouds may gather,
All must work for good to me.

4 Man may trouble and distress me,
'Twill but drive me to Thy breast;
Life with trials hard may press me,
Heaven will bring me sweeter rest.
O 'tis not in grief to harm me,
While Thy love is left to me;
O 'twere not in joy to charm me,
Were that joy unmixed with Thee.

Rev. Henry Francis Lyte. (1793—1847.) 1825.

405 *Dismission.*

Lord, dismiss us with Thy blessing,
Bid us now depart in peace;
Still on heavenly manna feeding,
Let our faith and love increase:
Fill each breast with consolation;
Up to Thee our hearts we raise;
When we reach our blissful station,
Then we'll give Thee nobler praise.

Unknown Author. 1775.

NOT ASHAMED.

HAMBURG. (GREGORIAN.) L. M.   Arr. by Lowell Mason. (1792—1872.) 1825.

1. JE - SUS, and shall it ev - er be, A mor-tal man a - shamed of Thee?
A-shamed of Thee, whom an-gels praise, Whose glories shine thro' end-less days?

406 *Not ashamed of Jesus.*
Rom. i. 16. Heb. ii. 11.

2 Ashamed of Jesus, that dear Friend
On whom my hopes of heaven depend!
No, when I blush, be this my shame,
That I no more revere His name.

3 Ashamed of Jesus! yes, I may,
When I've no guilt to wash away,
No tear to wipe, no good to crave,
No fear to quell, no soul to save.

4 Till then, nor is my boasting vain,
Till then I boast a Saviour slain ;
And O, may this my glory be,
That Christ is not ashamed of me.
Rev. Joseph Grigg. (—1768.) 1765. ab. and alt.
Rev. Benjamin Francis. (1734—1799.) 1787.

407 *Bearing the Cross for Christ.*

1 My precious Lord, for Thy dear Name
I bear the cross, despise the shame ;
Nor do I faint, while Thou art near ;
I lean on Thee ; how can I fear?

2 No other name but Thine is given
To cheer my soul, in earth or heaven;
No other wealth will I require ;
No other friend can I desire.

3 Yea, into nothing would I fall
For Thee alone, my All in all ;
To feel Thy love, my only joy,
To tell Thy love, my sole employ.
Moravian Collection. 1754. ab.

408 *All in all.*
Col. iii. 11.

1 IN Christ I've all my soul's desire ;
His spirit does my heart inspire
With boundless wishes large and high ;
And Christ will all my wants supply.

2 Christ is my Hope, my Strength, and
Guide ;   [died ;
For me He bled, and groaned, and
He is my Sun, to give me light,
He is my soul's supreme Delight.

3 Christ is the source of all my bliss ;
My wisdom and my righteousness ;
My Saviour, Brother, and my Friend ;
On Him alone I now depend.

4 Christ is my King, to rule and bless,
And all my troubles to redress ;
He's my Salvation and my All,
Whate'er on earth shall me befall.
John Dobell's (1757—1840) Collection. 1806.

CONFIDENCE.

ASAPH. L. M.   Felix Mendelssohn-Bartholdy. (1809—1847.)

1. O Thou, to whose all-searching sight The darkness shin-eth as the light, Search, prove my heart, it pants for Thee; O burst these bonds, and set it free.

409 *"Seelenbräutigam, o Du Gottes-Lamm."*

2 Wash out its stains, refine its dross;
Nail my affections to the cross;
Hallow each thought; let all within
Be clean, as Thou, my Lord, art clean.

3 If in this darksome wild I stray,
Be Thou my light, be Thou my way;
No foes, no violence I fear,
No fraud, while Thou, my God, art near.

4 When rising floods my soul o'erflow,
When sinks my heart in waves of woe,
Jesus, Thy timely aid impart, [heart.
And raise my head, and cheer my

5 Saviour, where'er Thy steps I see,
Dauntless, untired, I follow Thee;
O let Thy hand support me still,
And lead me to Thy holy hill.
        Gerhard Tersteegen. (1697—1769.)
Tr. by Rev. John Wesley (1703—1791.) 1738. ab.

SOLID ROCK. L. M. 6 l.   William Batchelder Bradbury. (1816—1868.) 1865.

1. My hope is built on nothing less Than Je-sus' blood and righteousness;
I dare not trust the sweetest frame, But wholly lean on Je-sus' name. On Christ, the sol-id rock, I stand; All oth-er ground is sink-ing sand, All oth-er ground is sink-ing sand.

410 *The solid Rock.*

2 When darkness seems to vail His face,
I rest on His unchanging grace;
In every high and stormy gale,
My anchor holds within the vail:
On Christ, the solid rock, I stand;
All other ground is sinking sand.

3 His oath, His covenant, and blood,
Support me in the whelming flood:
When all around my soul gives way,
He then is all my hope and stay:
On Christ, the solid rock, I stand;
All other ground is sinking sand.
        Rev. Edward Mote. 1865.

IN THE DEPTHS.

MESSIAH. 7. D.
Louis Joseph Ferdinand Herold. (1791—1833.) 1830.
Arr. by George Kingsley. (1811—) 1838.

1. JE-sus, Lov-er of my soul, Let me to Thy bo-som fly, While the nearer waters roll, While the tempest still is high; Hide me, O my Sav-iour, hide, Till the storm of life is past; Safe in-to the ha-ven guide; O receive my soul at last.

411 *"Jesus, Lover of my Soul."*

2 Other refuge have I none ;
 Hangs my helpless soul on Thee ;
 Leave, ah leave me not alone,
  Still support and comfort me.
 All my trust on Thee is stayed,
 All my help from Thee I bring ;
 Cover my defenceless head
  With the shadow of Thy wing.

3 Wilt Thou not regard my call ?
 Wilt Thou not accept my prayer ?
 Lo, I sink, I faint, I fall ;
 Lo, on Thee I cast my care ;
 Reach me out Thy gracious hand,
 While I of Thy strength receive,
 Hoping against hope I stand,
 Dying, and behold I live !
  Rev. Charles Wesley. (1708—1788.) 1740.

MARTYN. 7. D.

412 *"All I want."*

1 THOU, O Christ, art all I want ;
 More than all in Thee I find :
 Raise the fallen, cheer the faint,
 Heal the sick, and lead the blind.
 Just and holy is Thy Name ;
 I am all unrighteousness ;
 False and full of sin I am,
 Thou art full of truth and grace.

2 Plenteous grace with Thee is found,
 Grace to cover all my sin :
 Let the healing streams abound,
 Make and keep me pure within.
 Thou of Life the Fountain art ;
 Freely let me take of Thee ;
 Spring Thou up within my heart,
 Rise to all eternity.
  Rev. Charles Wesley. 1740.

Simeon Butler Marsh. (1798—) 1834.

TRUSTING THE LOVE OF CHRIST.

HENDON. 7. Rev. Cæsar Henri Abraham Malan. (1787—1864.) 1830.

1. Hark, my soul, it is the Lord; 'Tis thy Saviour, hear His word; Jesus speaks, and

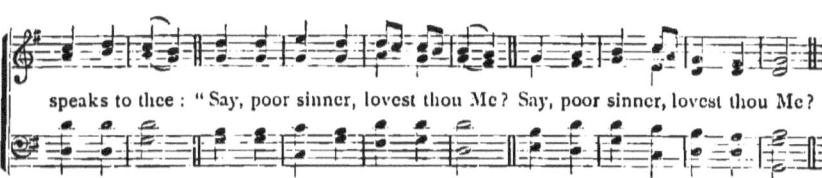

speaks to thee: "Say, poor sinner, lovest thou Me? Say, poor sinner, lovest thou Me?

413 *"Lovest thou Me?"*

2 "I delivered thee, when bound,
And, when wounded, healed Thy wound;
Sought thee wandering, set thee right,
Turned thy darkness into light.

3 "Can a woman's tender care
Cease towards the child she bare?
Yes, she may forgetful be,
Yet will I remember thee.

4 "Mine is an unchanging love,
Higher than the heights above,
Deeper than the depths beneath,
Free and faithful, strong as death.

5 "Thou shalt see My glory soon,
When the work of grace is done;
Partner of My throne shalt be;
Say, poor sinner, lovest thou Me?"

6 Lord, it is my chief complaint,
That my love is weak and faint;
Yet I love Thee, and adore;
O for grace to love Thee more.

William Cowper. (1731—1800.) 1779.

414 *"Loving Him who first loved me."*

1 Saviour, teach me, day by day,
Love's sweet lesson to obey;
Sweeter lesson cannot be,
Loving Him who first loved me.

2 Teach me all Thy steps to trace,
Strong to follow in Thy grace:
Learning how to love from Thee,
Loving Him who first loved me.

Unknown Author. 1854. ab.

415 *"Cast thy Burden upon the Lord."*
Ps. lv. 22.

1 Cast thy burden on the Lord,
Only lean upon His word;
Thou shalt soon have cause to bless,
His eternal faithfulness.

2 Ever in the raging storm,
Thou shalt see His cheering form,
Hear His pledge of coming aid:
"It is I, be not afraid."

3 Cast thy burden at His feet;
Linger at His mercy-seat:
He will lead thee by the hand
Gently to the better land.

Rev. Rowland Hill. (1744—1833.) 1783, v. 1.
George Rawson. (1807—) 1857. ab. and much alt.

SPIRITUAL DEJECTION.

ELIZABETHTOWN. C. M.   George Kingsley. (1811—) 1838.

1. O for a clos-er walk with God, A calm and heavenly frame,

A light to shine up-on the road That leads me to the Lamb!

416   *"A closer Walk."* Gen. v. 24. 1 John ii. 6.

2 Where is the blessedness I knew
    When first I saw the Lord?
  Where is the soul-refreshing view
    Of Jesus and His word?

3 What peaceful hours I once enjoyed,
    How sweet their memory still!
  But they have left an aching void
    The world can never fill.

4 Return, O Holy Dove, return,
    Sweet messenger of rest:
  I hate the sins that made Thee mourn,
    And drove Thee from my breast.

5 The dearest idol I have known,
    Whate'er that idol be;
  Help me to tear it from Thy throne,
    And worship only Thee.

6 So shall my walk be close with God,
    Calm and serene my frame;
  So purer light shall mark the road
    That leads me to the Lamb.
        William Cowper. (1731—1800.) 1779.

417   *Breathing after the Holy Spirit.*

1 Come, Holy Spirit, Heavenly Dove,
    With all Thy quickening powers,
  Kindle a flame of sacred love
    In these cold hearts of ours.

2 Look how we grovel here below,
    Fond of these trifling toys:
  Our souls can neither fly nor go
    To reach eternal joys.

3 In vain we tune our formal songs,
    In vain we strive to rise;
  Hosannas languish on our tongues,
    And our devotion dies.

4 Dear Lord, and shall we ever live
    At this poor dying rate,
  Our love so faint, so cold to Thee,
    And Thine to us so great?

5 Come, Holy Spirit, Heavenly Dove,
    With all Thy quickening powers,
  Come, shed abroad a Saviour's love,
    And that shall kindle ours.
        Rev. Isaac Watts. (1674—1748.) 1709.

418   *"Let us return."* Hos. vi. 1-4.

1 Come, let us to the Lord our God
    With contrite hearts return;
  Our God is gracious, nor will leave
    The desolate to mourn.

PANTING AFTER GOD. 189

2 Long hath the night of sorrow reigned;
The dawn shall bring us light:
God shall appear, and we shall rise
With gladness in His sight.

3 Our hearts, if God we seek to know,
Shall know Him and rejoice;
His coming like the morn shall be,
Like morning songs His voice.

4 As dew upon the tender herb,
Diffusing fragrance round;
As showers that usher in the spring,
And cheer the thirsty ground;

5 So shall His presence bless our souls,
And shed a joyful light;
That hallowed morn shall chase away
The sorrows of the night.

Rev. John Morrison. (1749—1798.) 1781. ab.

HEATH. C. M.
Lowell Mason. (1792—1872.) 1835.

1. As pants the hart for cool-ing streams, When heat-ed in the chase,
So pants my soul, O Lord, for Thee, And Thy re-fresh-ing grace.

419 *Panting for God.*
Ps. xlii.

2 For Thee, the Lord, the living Lord,
My thirsty soul doth pine:
O when shall I behold Thy face,
Thou Majesty Divine?

3 I sigh to think of happier days,
When Thou, O Lord, wert nigh;
When every heart was tuned to praise,
And none so blest as I.

4 Why restless, why cast down, my soul?
Trust God, and thou shalt sing
His praise again, and find Him still
Thy health's eternal spring.

Tate and Brady. 1696. alt.
Rev. Henry Francis Lyte. (1793—1847.) 1834.

420 *"O that I were as in Months past!"*
Job xxix. 2.

1 SWEET was the time when first I felt
The Saviour's pardoning blood
Applied to cleanse my soul from
guilt,
And bring me home to God.

2 Soon as the morn the light revealed,
His praises tuned my tongue;
And when the evening shades pre-
vailed,
His love was all my song.

3 But now, when evening shade prevails,
My soul in darkness mourns;
And when the morn the light reveals,
No light to me returns.

4 Rise, Saviour, help me to prevail,
And make my soul Thy care;
I know Thy mercy cannot fail:
Let me that mercy share.

Rev. John Newton. (1725—1807.) 1779. ab. and alt.

STORM AND STRUGGLE.

SESSIONS. L. M. Luther Orlando Emerson. (1820—) 1847.

1. The bil-lows swell, the winds are high, Clouds o-ver-cast my win-try sky;

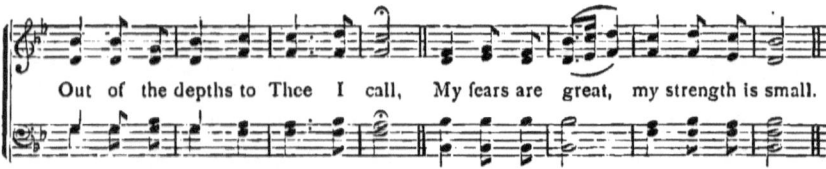

Out of the depths to Thee I call, My fears are great, my strength is small.

421 *Storm and Tempest.*

2 O Lord, the pilot's part perform,
And guard and guide me through the storm;
Defend me from each threatening ill,
Control the waves, say, "Peace, be still!"

3 Amidst the roaring of the sea
My soul still hangs her hope on Thee;
Thy constant love, Thy faithful care,
Is all that saves me from despair.

4 Dangers of every shape and name
Attend the followers of the Lamb,
Who leave the world's deceitful shore,
And leave it to return no more.

5 Though tempest-tost and half a wreck,
My Saviour through the floods I seek:
Let neither winds nor stormy main
Force back my shattered bark again.
William Cowper. (1731—1800.) 1779.

422 *Looking upwards.*

1 God of my life, to Thee I call,
Afflicted, at Thy feet I fall;
When the great water-floods prevail,
Leave not my trembling heart to fail.

2 Friend of the friendless and the faint,
Where should I lodge my deep complaint?
Where, but with Thee, whose open door
Invites the helpless and the poor?

3 Did ever mourner plead with Thee,
And Thou refuse that mourner's plea?
Does not the word still fixed remain,
That none shall seek Thy face in vain?

4 That were a grief I could not bear,
Didst Thou not hear and answer prayer;
But a prayer-hearing, answering God
Supports me under every load.

5 Poor though I am, despised, forgot,
Yet God, my God, forgets me not;
And he is safe, and must succeed,
For whom the Lord vouchsafes to plead.
William Cowper. 1779. ab.

SEEKING THE REFUGE.

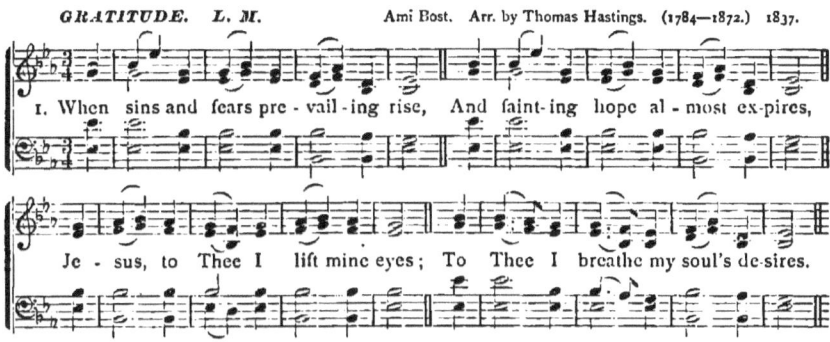

GRATITUDE. L. M. Ami Bost. Arr. by Thomas Hastings. (1784—1872.) 1837.

1. When sins and fears pre-vail-ing rise, And faint-ing hope al-most ex-pires, Je-sus, to Thee I lift mine eyes; To Thee I breathe my soul's de-sires.

423 *"Ye shall live also."*
John xiv. 19.

2 Art Thou not mine, my Living Lord?
And can my hope, my comfort die?
Fixed on Thine everlasting word,
That word which built the earth and sky?

3 If my Immortal Saviour lives,
Then my immortal life is sure;
His word a firm foundation gives;
Here let me build, and rest secure.

4 Here, O my soul, thy trust repose;
If Jesus is forever mine,
Not death itself, that last of foes,
Shall break a union so divine.
Miss Anne Steele. (1717—1778.) 1760. ab.

424 *Restoring and preserving Grace.*
Ps. cxxxviii.

1 To God I cried when troubles rose;
He heard me, and subdued my foes;
He did my rising fears control, [soul.
And strength diffused through all my

2 The God of heaven maintains His state,
Frowns on the proud, and scorns the great;
But from His throne descends to see
The sons of humble poverty.

3 Amid a thousand snares, I stand
Upheld and guarded by Thy hand;

Thy words my fainting soul revive,
And keep my dying faith alive.

4 Grace will complete what grace begins,
To save from sorrows and from sins;
The work that wisdom undertakes,
Eternal mercy ne'er forsakes.
Rev. Isaac Watts. (1674—1748.) 1719. ab.

425 *Christ all-sufficient.*

1 FOUNTAIN of grace, rich, full, and free,
What need I, that is not in Thee?
Full pardon, strength to meet the day,
And peace which none can take away.

2 Doth sickness fill my heart with fear?
'Tis sweet to know that Thou art near;
Am I with dread of justice tried?
'Tis sweet to know that Christ hath died.

3 In life, Thy promises of aid
Forbid my heart to be afraid;
In death, peace gently veils the eyes;
Christ rose, and I shall surely rise.

4 O all-sufficient Saviour, be
This all-sufficiency to me; [harm
Nor pain, nor sin, nor death can
The weakest shielded by Thine arm.
James Edmeston. (1791—1867.) 1844.

DELIVERANCE.

1. Oft when the waves of passion rise, And storms of life conceal the skies, And o'er the ocean sweep, Tossed in the long tempestuous night, We feel no ray of heavenly light To cheer the lonely deep.

426 *The Tempest.*

2 But lo, in our extremity,
The Saviour walking on the sea!
E'en now He passes by!
He silences our clamorous fear,
And mildly says, "Be of good cheer,
Be not afraid, 'tis I."

3 Ah, Lord, if it be Thou indeed,
So near us in our time of need,
So good, so strong to save,
Speak the kind word of power to me,
Bid me believe, and come to Thee,
Swift walking on the wave.

4 He bids me come! His voice I know,
And boldly on the waters go,
And brave the tempest's shock:
O'er rude temptations now I bound,
The billows yield a solid ground,
The wave is firm as rock.

5 Come in, come in, Thou Prince of Peace,
And all the storms of sin shall cease,
And fall, no more to rise;
O, if Thy Spirit still remain,
Our rest on distant shores we gain,
Our haven in the skies.

Rev. Charles Wesley. (1708—1788.) 1749. ab. and alt.

427 *"Verzage nicht, du Häuflein klein."*

1 Fear not, O little flock, the foe
Who madly seeks your overthrow,
Dread not his rage and power:
What though your courage sometimes faints,
His seeming triumph o'er God's saints
Lasts but a little hour.

2 As true as God's own word is true,
Not earth nor hell with all their crew
Against us shall prevail.
A jest and byword are they grown:
God is with us; we are His own;
Our victory cannot fail.

3 Amen, Lord Jesus, grant our prayer!
Great Captain, now Thine arm make bare;
Fight for us once again!
So shall Thy saints and martyrs raise
A mighty chorus to Thy praise,
World without end.

Gustavus Adolphus. (1594—1632.) 1631. in prose.
Rev. Jacob Fabricius. (1593—1654.) 1631. in verse.
Tr. by Miss Catherine Winkworth. (1829—) 1855. ab. and alt.

ALL IS WELL.

WALES. 8, 4.   Lowell Mason. (1792—1872.) 1858.

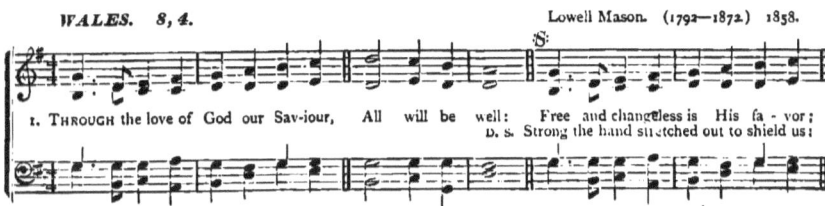

1. Through the love of God our Sav-iour, All will be well: Free and changeless is His fa-vor;
D. S. Strong the hand stretched out to shield us:

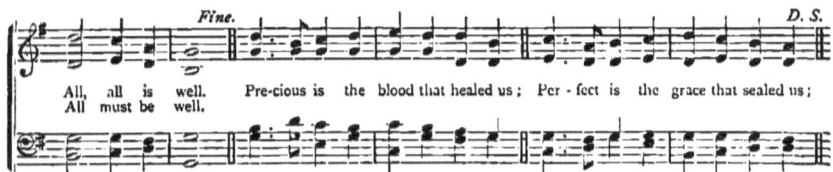

All, all is well. Pre-cious is the blood that healed us; Per-fect is the grace that sealed us;
All must be well.

428   *"All is well."*

2 Though we pass through tribulation,
    All will be well:
Ours is such a full salvation;
    All, all is well.
Happy, still in God confiding,
Fruitful, if in Christ abiding,
Holy, through the Spirit's guiding,
    All must be well.

3 We expect a bright to-morrow;
    All will be well;
Faith can sing through days of sorrow,
    All, all is well.
On our Father's love relying,
Jesus every need supplying,
Or in living, or in dying,
    All must be well.
        Mrs. Mary Bowly Peters. (—1856.) 1847.

429   *"A Friend above all others."*

1 There's a Friend above all others;
    O how He loves!
His is love beyond a brother's;
    O how He loves!
Earthly friends may fail and leave us,
This day kind, the next bereave us,
But this Friend will ne'er deceive us;
    O how He loves!

2 All thy sins shall be forgiven;
    O how He loves!
Backward all thy foes be driven;
    O how He loves!
Best of blessings He'll provide thee;
Naught but good shall e'er betide
    thee;
Safe to glory He will guide thee;
    O how He loves!

3 Pause, my soul, adore and wonder;
    O how He loves!
Nought can cleave this love asunder;
    O how He loves!
Neither trial, nor temptation,
Doubt, nor fear, nor tribulation,
Can bereave us of salvation;
    O how He loves!
       Rev. John Newton. (1725—1807.) 1779. alt.
         Miss Marianne Nunn. (1779—1847.)

CRYING FROM THE DEPTHS.

STATE STREET. S. M.   Jonathan C. Woodman. 1844.

1. Je - sus, my Strength, my Hope, On Thee I cast my care,
With hum-ble con - fi - dence look up, And know Thou hear'st my prayer.

430   *Watching and Praying.*
      Luke xviii. 1. Phil. iv. 13.

2 Give me on Thee to wait,
   Till I can all things do;
  On Thee, Almighty to create,
   Almighty to renew.

3 I want a sober mind,
   A self-renouncing will,
  That tramples down, and casts behind
   The baits of pleasing ill;

4 A soul inured to pain,
   To hardship, grief, and loss,
  Bold to take up, firm to sustain
   The consecrated cross.

5 I want a godly fear,
   A quick-discerning eye,
  That looks to Thee when sin is near,
   And sees the Tempter fly;

6 A spirit still prepared,
   And armed with jealous care,
  Forever standing on its guard,
   And watching unto prayer.
      Rev. Charles Wesley. (1708—1788.) 1742. ab.

431   *"Out of the Depths."*
      Ps. cxxx.

1 Out of the depths of woe,
   To Thee, O Lord, I cry;
  Darkness surrounds me, but I know
   That Thou art ever nigh.

2 I cast my hope on Thee;
   Thou canst, Thou wilt forgive;
  Wert Thou to mark iniquity,
   Who in Thy sight could live?

3 Humbly I wait on Thee,
   Confessing all my sin;
  Lord, I am knocking at Thy gate;
   Open, and take me in.

4 Glory to God above!
   The waters soon will cease;
  For lo, the swift-returning Dove
   Brings home the sign of peace.

5 Though storms His face obscure,
   And dangers threaten loud,
  Jehovah's covenant is sure,
   His bow is in the cloud.
      James Montgomery. (1771—1854.) 1822. ab.

CRYING FROM THE DEPTHS. 195

GOLDEN HILL. S. M. — Annanias Davisson. 1817.

1. Have mer-cy, Lord, on me, As Thou wert ev-er kind; Let me, op-pressed with loads of guilt, Thy wont-ed mer-cy find.

432 "*Have Mercy.*"
Ps. li.
2 Wash off my foul offence,
And cleanse me from my sin;
For I confess my crime, and see
How great my guilt has been.
3 Against Thee, Lord, alone,
And only in Thy sight,
Have I transgressed, and, though condemned,
Must own Thy judgment right.
Tate and Brady. 1696. ab.

433 "*Out of the Depths.*"
Ps. cxxx.
1 Out of the deep I call
To Thee, O Lord, to Thee,
Before Thy throne of grace I fall,
Be merciful to me.
2 Out of the deep I cry,
The woful deep of sin,
Of evil done in days gone by,
Of evil now within.
3 Out of the deep of fear,
And dread of coming shame,
From morning watch till night is near
I plead the Precious Name.
4 Lord, there is mercy now,
As ever was, with Thee;

Before Thy throne of grace I bow,
Be merciful to me.
Rev. Sir Henry Williams Baker. (1821–) 1868.

434 *Prayer for perfect Peace.*
1 Jesus, my Lord, attend
Thy fallen creature's cry,
And show Thyself the sinner's Friend,
And set me up on high.
2 From hell's oppressive power,
From earth and sin release,
And to Thy Father's grace restore,
And to Thy perfect peace.
3 Thy blood and righteousness
I make my only plea;
My present and eternal peace
Are both derived from Thee.
4 O then, impute, impart,
To me Thy righteousness;
And let me taste how good Thou art,
How full of truth and grace.
5 That Thou canst here forgive,
Grant me to testify;
And justified by faith to live,
And in that faith to die.
Rev. Charles Wesley. 1747. ab.

HUNGERING FOR RIGHTEOUSNESS.

DENFIELD. (AZMON.) C. M. Carl Gotthilf Gläser. (1784—1829.) 1828.
Arr. by Lowell Mason. (1792—1872.) 1839.

1. O for a heart to praise my God,
A heart from sin set free;
A heart that al-ways feels Thy blood
So free-ly spilt for me!

435 *"Make me a clean Heart."* Ps. li. 10.

2 A heart resigned, submissive, meek,
My dear Redeemer's throne;
Where only Christ is heard to speak,
Where Jesus reigns alone.

3 A humble, lowly, contrite heart,
Believing, true, and clean;
Which neither life nor death can part
From Him that dwells within.

4 A heart in every thought renewed,
And full of love divine;
Perfect, and right, and pure, and good,
A copy, Lord, of Thine.

5 Thy nature, dearest Lord, impart;
Come quickly from above;
Write Thy new Name upon my heart,
Thy new, best Name of Love.
    Rev. Charles Wesley. (1708—1788.) 1742. ab.

436 *Spiritual Freedom.*

1 O Lord, impart Thyself to me,
No other good I need;
When Thou, the Son, shalt make me free,
I shall be free indeed. [free,

2 I cannot rest till in Thy blood
I full redemption have;
But Thou, thro' whom I come to God,
Canst to the utmost save.

3 From sin, the guilt, the power, the pain,
Thou wilt redeem my soul:
Lord, I believe, and not in vain;
My faith shall make me whole.

4 I too with Thee shall walk in white;
With all Thy saints shall prove
The length, and depth, and breadth,
    and height
Of everlasting love.
    Rev. Charles Wesley. 1740. ab. and alt.

437 *For a tender Conscience.*

1 I want a principle within
Of jealous, godly fear;
A sensibility of sin,
A pain to feel it near.

2 From Thee that I no more may part,
No more Thy goodness grieve,
The filial awe, the fleshly heart,
The tender conscience give.

3 Quick as the apple of an eye,
O God, my conscience make;
Awake my soul when sin is nigh,
And keep it still awake.

HUNGERING FOR RIGHTEOUSNESS. 197

4 If to the right or left I stray,
   That moment, Lord, reprove;
   And let me weep my life away
   For having grieved Thy love.

5 O may the least omission pain
   My well-instructed soul,
   And drive me to the blood again
   Which makes the wounded whole.
                  Rev. Charles Wesley. 1749. ab.

PETERBOROUGH. C. M.   Rev. Ralph Harrison. (1748—1810.) 1786.

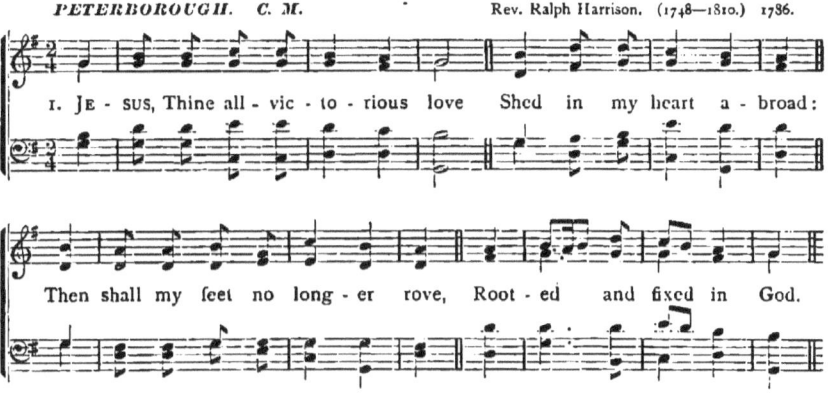

1. Jesus, Thine all-victorious love
   Shed in my heart abroad:
   Then shall my feet no longer rove,
   Rooted and fixed in God.

438 *The refining Fire of the Holy Spirit.*

2 O that in me the sacred fire
   Might now begin to glow;
   Burn up the dross of base desire,
   And make the mountains flow.

3 O that it now from heaven might fall,
   And all my sins consume:
   Come, Holy Ghost, for Thee I call;
   Spirit of burning, come.

4 Refining fire, go through my heart;
   Illuminate my soul;
   Scatter Thy life through every part,
   And sanctify the whole.

5 My steadfast soul, from falling free,
   Shall then no longer move;
   While Christ is all the world to me,
   And all my heart is love.
        Rev. Charles Wesley. 1740. ab. and alt.

439 *Breathing after Holiness.*
     Ps. cxix. 5, 131, 176, 35.

1 O THAT the Lord would guide my ways,
   To keep His statutes still;
   O that my God would grant me grace,
   To know and do His will!

2 Order my footsteps by Thy word,
   And make my heart sincere;
   Let sin have no dominion, Lord,
   But keep my conscience clear.

3 My soul hath gone too far astray,
   My feet too often slip:
   Yet since I've not forgot Thy way,
   Restore Thy wandering sheep.

4 Make me to walk in Thy commands,
   'Tis a delightful road;
   Nor let my head, or heart, or hands,
   Offend against my God.
        Rev. Isaac Watts. (1674—1748.) 1719.

198 ASPIRATIONS.

AUTUMN. 8, 7. D.   Spanish Melody. From Marechio.

1. Love Divine, all love excelling, Joy of heaven, to earth come down;
Fix in us Thy humble dwelling, All Thy faithful mercies crown:
D. S. Visit us with Thy salvation, Enter every trembling heart.
Jesus, Thou art all compassion, Pure, unbounded love Thou art;

440   *"Love Divine."*

2 Breathe, O breathe, Thy loving
    Spirit
Into every troubled breast;
Let us all in Thee inherit,
Let us find that second rest;
Take away our power of sinning,
Alpha and Omega be;
End of faith, as its beginning,
Set our hearts at liberty.

3 Come, almighty to deliver,
Let us all Thy life receive;
Suddenly return, and never,
Never more Thy temples leave.
Thee we would be always blessing,
Serve Thee as Thy hosts above,
Pray, and praise Thee without ceasing,
Glory in Thy perfect love.

Rev. Charles Wesley. (1708—1788.) 1747. ab. and sl. alt.

441   *Joy.*

1 Take, my soul, thy full salvation,
Rise o'er sin, and fear, and care;
Joy to find in every station
Something still to do or bear.
Think what Spirit dwells within thee;
What a Father's smile is thine;
What a Saviour died to win thee:
Child of heaven, shouldst thou repine?

2 Haste thee on from grace to glory,
Armed by faith, and winged by prayer;
Heaven's eternal day's before thee,
God's own hand shall guide thee there.
Soon shall close thy earthly mission,
Swift shall pass thy pilgrim days,
Hope soon change to glad fruition,
Faith to sight, and prayer to praise.

Rev. Henry Francis Lyte. (1793—1847.) 1833.

HALLELUJAH TO THE LAMB. 199

EDINBURG. 11. Edward L. White. (—1851.)

1. I ONCE was a stranger to grace and to God, I knew not my dan-ger, and felt not my load; Tho' friends spoke in rapture of Christ on the tree, Je-ho-vah, my Sav-iour, seemed nothing to me. Hal-le-lu-jah to the Lamb, Hal-le-lu-jah to the Lamb. Hal-le-lu-jah, Hal-le-lu-jah, Hal-le-lu-jah, A-men.

442   *"The Lord our Righteousness."*

2 When free grace awoke me by light from on high,
Then legal fears shook me, I trembled to die;
No refuge, no safety, in self could I see;
Jehovah, Thou only my Saviour must be. *Cho.*

3 My terrors all vanished before His sweet name;
My guilty fears banished, with boldness I came
To drink at the fountain, so copious and free:
Jehovah, my Saviour, is all things to me. *Cho.*

4 Jehovah, the Lord, is my treasure and boast;
Jehovah, my Saviour, I ne'er can be lost;
In Thee I shall conquer, by flood and by field,
Jehovah my anchor, Jehovah my shield! *Cho.*

5 E'en treading the valley, the shadow of death,
This watchword shall rally my faltering breath;
For while from life's fever my God sets me free,
Jehovah, my Saviour, my death-song shall be. *Cho.*

Rev. Robert Murray McCheyne. (1813—1843.) 1834. ab. and alt.

REJOICING IN GOD.

OAKSVILLE. C. M.   Charles Zeuner. (1795—1857.) 1839.

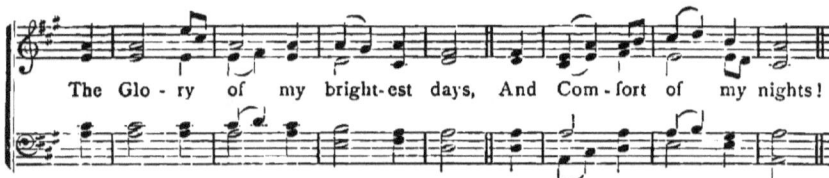

1. My God, the Spring of all my joys, The Life of my de-lights, The Glo-ry of my bright-est days, And Com-fort of my nights!

443   *Light in Darkness.*

2 In darkest shades if He appear,
   My dawning is begun ;
He is my soul's sweet Morning Star,
   And He my Rising Sun.

3 The opening heavens around me shine
   With beams of sacred bliss,
While Jesus shows His heart is mine,
   And whispers, I am His.

4 My soul would leave this heavy clay
   At that transporting word ;
Run up with joy the shining way,
   T' embrace my dearest Lord.

5 Fearless of hell and ghastly death,
   I'd break through every foe ;
The wings of love and arms of faith
   Should bear me conqueror through.
         Rev. Isaac Watts. (1674—1748.) 1709.

444   *Happiness only in God.*
        Ps. lxxiii. 25.

1 My God, my Portion, and my Love,
   My everlasting All,
I've none but Thee in heaven above,
   Or on this earthly ball.

2 In vain the bright, the burning sun
   Scatters his feeble light ;
'Tis Thy sweet beams create my noon ;
   If Thou withdraw, 'tis night.

3 To Thee we owe our wealth and friends,
   And health and safe abode ;
Thanks to Thy name for meaner things,
   But they are not my God.

4 Were I possessor of the earth,
   And called the stars my own,
Without Thy graces and Thyself,
   I were a wretch undone.

5 Let others stretch their arms like seas,
   And grasp in all the shore,
Grant me the visits of Thy face,
   And I desire no more.
        Rev. Isaac Watts. 1709. ab.

GOD OUR PORTION.

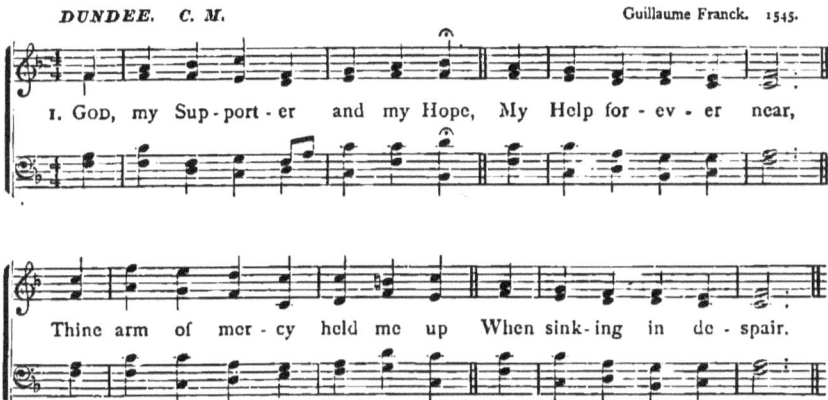

DUNDEE. C. M.   Guillaume Franck. 1545.

1. God, my Sup-port-er and my Hope, My Help for-ev-er near,
Thine arm of mer-cy held me up When sink-ing in de-spair.

445 *God our Portion here and hereafter.*
Ps. lxxiii. 23-28.

2 Thy counsels, Lord, shall guide my feet
Through this dark wilderness;
Thy hand conduct me near Thy seat,
To dwell before Thy face.

3 Were I in heaven without my God,
'Twould be no joy to me;
And while this earth is my abode,
I long for none but Thee.

4 What if the springs of life were broke,
And flesh and heart should faint?
God is my soul's eternal Rock,
The Strength of every saint.

5 But to draw near to Thee, my God,
Shall be my sweet employ:
My tongue shall sound Thy works abroad,
And tell the world my joy.
        Rev. Isaac Watts. 1719. ab.

446 *Christ our Strength and Righteousness.*
Ps. lxxi

1 My Saviour, my Almighty Friend,
When I begin Thy praise,
Where will the growing numbers end,
The numbers of Thy grace?

2 Thou art my everlasting trust,
Thy goodness I adore;
And since I knew Thy graces first,
I speak Thy glories more.

3 My feet shall travel all the length
Of the celestial road,
And march with courage in Thy strength
To see my Father, God.

4 When I am filled with sore distress
For some surprising sin,
I'll plead Thy perfect righteousness,
And mention none but Thine.

5 How will my lips rejoice to tell
The victories of my King!
My soul, redeemed from sin and hell,
Shall Thy salvation sing.
        Rev. Isaac Watts. 1719. ab.

PRAISE FOR DELIVERANCE.

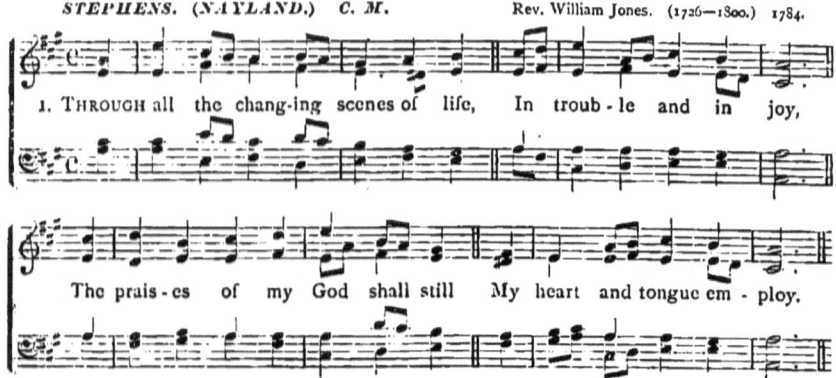

STEPHENS. (NAYLAND.) C. M.   Rev. William Jones. (1726—1800.) 1784.

1. Through all the chang-ing scenes of life, In troub-le and in joy, The prais-es of my God shall still My heart and tongue em-ploy.

447 *Safety in God.*
Ps. xxxiv.

2 Of His deliverance I will boast,
  Till all that are distressed
  From my example comfort take,
  And charm their griefs to rest.

3 O magnify the Lord with me,
  With me exalt His name:
  When in distress to Him I called,
  He to my rescue came.

4 The hosts of God encamp around
  The dwellings of the just;
  Deliverance He affords to all
  Who on His succor trust.

5 O make but trial of His love
  Experience will decide
  How blest are they, and only they,
  Who in His truth confide.

6 Fear Him, ye saints, and you will then
  Have nothing else to fear;
  Make you His service your delight,
  Your wants shall be His care.
  Tate and Brady. 1696. ab.

448 *Great Things done for us.*
Ps. cxxvi.

1 When God revealed His gracious name,
  And changed my mournful state,
  My rapture seemed a pleasing dream,
  The grace appeared so great.

2 The world beheld the glorious change,
  And did Thy hand confess;
  My tongue broke out in unknown strains,
  And sung surprising grace.

3 "Great is the work," my neighbors cried,
  And owned the power divine;
  "Great is the work," my heart replied,
  "And be the glory Thine."

4 The Lord can clear the darkest skies,
  Can give us day for night;
  Make drops of sacred sorrow rise
  To rivers of delight.

5 Let those who sow in sadness, wait
  Till the fair harvest come;
  They shall confess their sheaves are great,
  And shout the blessings home.
  Rev. Isaac Watts. (1674—1748.) 1719. ab.

FEAR, LOVE, PEACE.

ELIZABETHTOWN. C. M. George Kingsley. (1811—) 1838.

1. My God, how won-der-ful Thou art, Thy maj-es-ty how bright,

How beau-ti-ful Thy mer-cy-seat In depths of burn-ing light.

449   *Our Heavenly Father.*

2 How dread are Thine eternal years,
    O Everlasting Lord;
  By prostrate spirits day and night
    Incessantly adored.

3 O how I fear Thee, Living God,
    With deepest, tenderest fears,
  And worship Thee with trembling hope,
    And penitential tears.

4 Yet I may love Thee too, O Lord,
    Almighty as Thou art;
  For Thou hast stooped to ask of me
    The love of my poor heart.

5 No earthly father loves like Thee,
    No mother half so mild
  Bears and forbears, as Thou hast done
    With me, Thy sinful child.

6 Father of Jesus, love's reward,
    What rapture will it be,
  Prostrate before Thy throne to lie,
    And gaze, and gaze on Thee.

Rev. Frederick William Faber. (1814—1863.) 1849. ab.

450   *The inner Calm.*

1 CALM me, my God, and keep me calm,
    Soft resting on Thy breast;
  Soothe me with holy hymn and psalm,
    And bid my spirit rest.

2 Calm me, my God, and keep me calm;
    Let Thine outstretched wing
  Be like the shade of Elim's palm,
    Beside her desert spring.

3 Yes, keep me calm, tho' loud and rude
    The sounds my ear that greet;
  Calm in the closet's solitude,
    Calm in the bustling street;

4 Calm in the hour of buoyant health,
    Calm in my hour of pain;
  Calm in my poverty or wealth,
    Calm in my loss or gain;

5 Calm in the sufferance of wrong,
    Like Him who bore my shame,
  Calm 'mid the threatening, taunting throng
  Who hate Thy holy Name.

Rev. Horatius Bonar. (1808—) 1857. ab.

REJOICING IN LOVE AND HOPE.

GLORY. S. M. — Rev. Ralph Harrison. (1748–1810.) 1786.

1. Come, we that love the Lord, And let our joys be known; Join in a song of sweet ac-cord, And thus sur-round the throne.

451 *Heavenly Joy on Earth.*

2 Let those refuse to sing
That never knew our God;
But favorites of the heavenly King
May speak their joys abroad.

3 The men of grace have found
Glory begun below;
Celestial fruits on earthly ground
From faith and hope may grow.

4 The hill of Zion yields
A thousand sacred sweets
Before we reach the heavenly fields,
Or walk the golden streets.

5 Then let our songs abound,
And every tear be dry;
We're marching through Immanuel's ground
To fairer worlds on high.
    Rev. Isaac Watts. (1674—1748.) 1709. ab.

452 *"All in all."*
    Ps. lxxiii. 25.

1 My God, my Life, my Love,
To Thee, to Thee I call;
I cannot live if Thou remove,
For Thou art All in all.

2 To Thee, and Thee alone,
The angels owe their bliss;

They sit around Thy gracious throne,
And dwell where Jesus is.

3 Not all the harps above
Can make a heavenly place,
If God His residence remove,
Or but conceal His face.

4 Nor earth, nor all the sky,
Can one delight afford;
No, not a drop of real joy,
Without Thy presence, Lord.

5 Thou art the sea of love,
Where all my pleasures roll;
The circle where my passions move,
And centre of my soul.
    Rev. Isaac Watts. 1709. ab.

453 *"Our Captain leads us on."*

1 Our Captain leads us on;
He beckons from the skies;
He reaches out a starry crown,
And bids us take the prize.

2 "Be faithful unto death,
Partake My victory,
And thou shalt wear this glorious wreath,
And thou shalt reign with Me:

REJOICING IN LOVE AND HOPE.   205

3 'Tis thus the righteous Lord
   To every soldier saith,
   Eternal life is the reward
   Of all-victorious faith.

4 Who conquer in His might
   The victor's meed receive;
   They claim a kingdom in His right,
   Which God will freely give.
   Rev. Charles Wesley. (1708—1788.) 1749. ab. and sl. alt.

THATCHER.   S. M.   George Frederick Handel. (1685—1759.) 1732.

1. BE-HOLD what won-drous grace The Fa-ther hath be-stowed
On sin-ners of a mor-tal race, To call them sons of God!

454   *Adoption.*   1 John iii. 1. Gal. vi. 6.

2 Nor doth it yet appear
   How great we must be made;
   But when we see our Saviour here,
   We shall be like our Head.

3 A hope so much divine
   May trials well endure,   [sin,
   May purge our souls from sense and
   As Christ the Lord is pure.

4 If in my Father's love
   I share a filial part,
   Send down Thy Spirit, like a dove,
   To rest upon my heart.

5 We would no longer lie
   Like slaves beneath the throne;
   Our faith shall Abba, Father! cry,
   And Thou the kindred own.
   Rev. Isaac Watts. 1709. ab.

455   *Our House above.*

1 WE have a house above,
   Not made with mortal hands;
   And firm as our Redeemer's love,
   That heavenly fabric stands.

2 It stands securely high,
   Indissolubly sure;
   Our glorious mansion in the sky
   Shall evermore endure.

3 Beneath our earthly load
   We labor now and groan,
   And hasten toward that house of God,
   And struggle to be gone.

4 Full of immortal hope,
   We urge the restless strife,
   And hasten to be swallowed up
   Of everlasting life.

5 Thy grace with glory crown,
   Who hast the earnest given,
   And then triumphantly come down
   And take us up to heaven.
   Rev. Charles Wesley. 1759. ab. and sl. alt.

REJOICING IN LOVE AND HOPE.

EWING. 7, 6. D.   Bp. Alexander Ewing. (—1873.) 1861.

1. In heavenly love a-bid-ing, No change my heart shall fear; And safe is such con-fid-ing, For noth-ing changes here. The storm may roar without me, My heart may low be laid, But God is round a-bout me, And can I be dis-mayed?

456   *"I will fear no Evil."*
        Ps. xxiii. 4.

2 Wherever He may guide me,
   No want shall turn me back;
  My Shepherd is beside me,
   And nothing can I lack.
  His wisdom ever waketh,
   His sight is never dim,
  He knows the way He taketh,
   And I will walk with Him.

3 Green pastures are before me,
   Which yet I have not seen;
  Bright skies will soon be o'er me,
   Where darkest clouds have been.
  My hope I cannot measure,
   My path to life is free,
  My Saviour has my treasure,
   And He will walk with me.

      Miss Anna Laetitia Waring. 1850. sl. alt.

457   *"O Jesu, meine Sonne."*

1 I KNOW no life divided,
   O Lord of life, from Thee:
  In Thee is life provided
   For all mankind and me;
  I know no death, O Jesus,
   Because I live in Thee:
  Thy death it is which frees us
   From death eternally.

2 If, while on earth I wander,
   My heart is light and blest,
  Ah, what shall I be yonder,
   In perfect peace and rest?
  O blessèd thought in dying,
   We go to meet the Lord,
  Where there shall be no sighing,
   A kingdom our reward.

Rev. Carl Johann Philipp Spitta. (1801—1859.) 1833.
      Tr. by Richard Massie. 1860. ab.

JOYFUL TRUST. 207

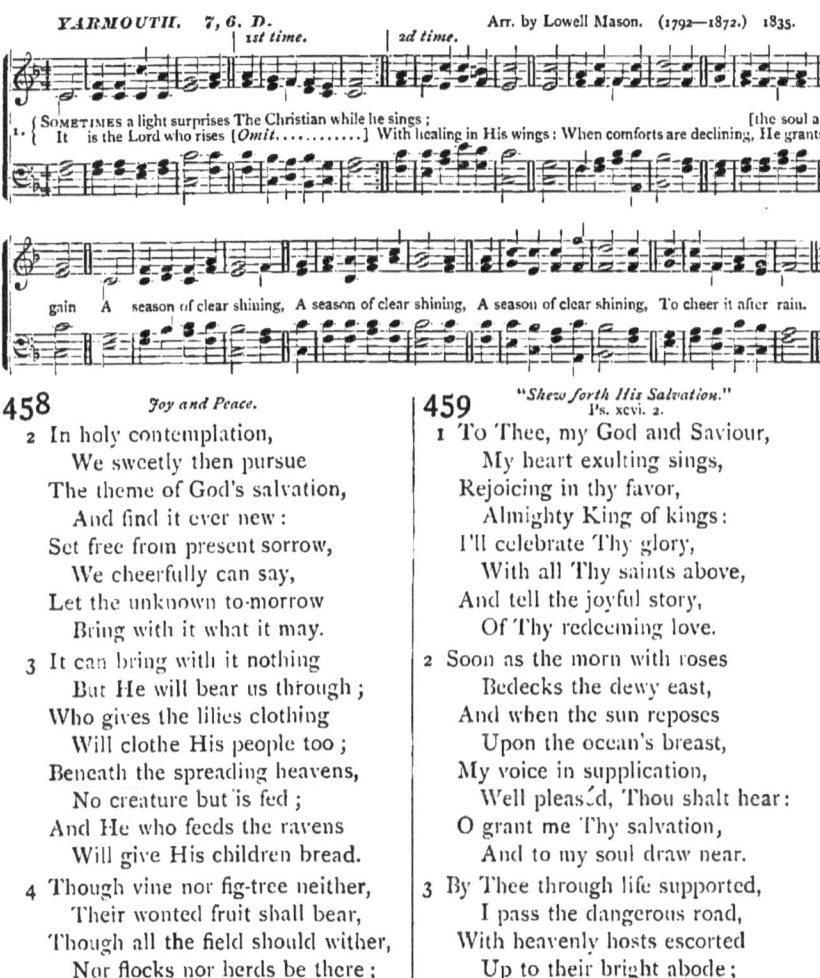

YARMOUTH. 7, 6. D.   Arr. by Lowell Mason. (1792—1872.) 1835.

1. SOMETIMES a light surprises The Christian while he sings;
It is the Lord who rises [Omit............] With healing in His wings: When comforts are declining, He grants [the soul a-gain] A season of clear shining, A season of clear shining, A season of clear shining, To cheer it after rain.

458   *Joy and Peace.*

2 In holy contemplation,
  We sweetly then pursue
The theme of God's salvation,
  And find it ever new:
Set free from present sorrow,
  We cheerfully can say,
Let the unknown to-morrow
  Bring with it what it may.

3 It can bring with it nothing
  But He will bear us through;
Who gives the lilies clothing
  Will clothe His people too;
Beneath the spreading heavens,
  No creature but is fed;
And He who feeds the ravens
  Will give His children bread.

4 Though vine nor fig-tree neither,
  Their wonted fruit shall bear,
Though all the field should wither,
  Nor flocks nor herds be there;
Yet God the same abiding,
  His praise shall tune my voice,
For, while in Him confiding,
  I cannot but rejoice.
      William Cowper. (1731—1800.) 1779.

459   *"Shew forth His Salvation."* Ps. xcvi. 2.

1 To Thee, my God and Saviour,
  My heart exulting sings,
Rejoicing in thy favor,
  Almighty King of kings:
I'll celebrate Thy glory,
  With all Thy saints above,
And tell the joyful story,
  Of Thy redeeming love.

2 Soon as the morn with roses
  Bedecks the dewy east,
And when the sun reposes
  Upon the ocean's breast,
My voice in supplication,
  Well pleas'd, Thou shalt hear:
O grant me Thy salvation,
  And to my soul draw near.

3 By Thee through life supported,
  I pass the dangerous road,
With heavenly hosts escorted
  Up to their bright abode;
There cast my crown before Thee;
  Now all my conflicts o'er,
And day and night adore Thee:
  What can an angel more?
      Rev. Thomas Haweis. (1732—1820.) 1792.

JOYFUL TRUST.

DENNIS. S. M.
Hans Georg Naegeli. (1773—1836.) 1832.
Arr. by William Batchelder Bradbury. (1816—1868.) 1849.

1. The Lord my Shep-herd is; I shall be well sup-plied: Since He is mine, and I am His, What can I want be-side?

460 *The Lord our Shepherd.*
Ps. xxiii.

2 He leads me to the place
 Where heavenly pasture grows;
 Where living waters gently pass,
 And full salvation flows.

3 If e'er I go astray,
 He doth my soul reclaim;
 And guides me, in His own right way,
 For His most holy name.

4 While He affords His aid,
 I cannot yield to fear;
 Though I should walk through death's dark shade,
 My Shepherd's with me there.

5 In spite of all my foes,
 Thou dost my table spread;
 My cup with blessings overflows,
 And joy exalts my head.

6 The bounties of Thy love
 Shall crown my following days;
 Nor from Thy house will I remove,
 Nor cease to speak Thy praise.
  Rev. Isaac Watts. (1674—1748.) 1719.

461 *Praise for temporal and spiritual Mercies.*
Ps. ciii. 1-7.

1 O bless the Lord, my soul;
 Let all within me join,
 And aid my tongue to bless His name,
 Whose favors are divine.

2 O bless the Lord, my soul,
 Nor let His mercies lie
 Forgotten in unthankfulness,
 And without praises die.

3 'Tis He forgives thy sins,
 'Tis He relieves thy pain,
 'Tis He that heals thy sicknesses,
 And makes thee young again.

4 He crowns thy life with love,
 When ransomed from the grave;
 He that redeemed my soul from hell,
 Hath sovereign power to save.

5 His wondrous works and ways
 He made by Moses known;
 But sent the world His truth and grace
 By His belovéd Son.
  Rev. Isaac Watts. 1719. ab.

TRUSTING, SERVING, ADORING. 209

VARINA. C. M. 6 l.
Christian Heinrich Rink. (1770—1846.)
Arr. by George Frederick Root. (1820—) 1849.

1. FA - THER, I know that all my life Is portioned out for me;
The chang-es that will sure - ly come I do not fear to see:
I ask Thee for a pres - ent mind, In - tent on pleas - ing Thee.

462 *"My Times are in Thy Hand."*
Ps. xxxi. 15.

2 I ask Thee for a thoughtful love,
Through constant watching wise,
To meet the glad with joyful smiles,
And wipe the weeping eyes;
A heart at leisure from itself,
To soothe and sympathize.

3 I would not have the restless will
That hurries to and fro,
Seeking for some great thing to do,
Or secret thing to know:
I would be treated as a child,
And guided where I go.

4 In service which Thy will appoints
There are no bonds for me;
My inmost heart is taught the truth
That makes Thy children free;
A life of self-renouncing love
Is one of liberty.

Miss Anna Laetitia Waring. 1850. ab. and alt.

463 *Far off, yet near.*

1 BEYOND, beyond that boundless sea,
Above that dome of sky,
Further than thought itself can flee,
Thy dwelling is on high:
Yet dear the awful thought to me,
That Thou, my God, art nigh.

2 We hear Thy voice when thunders roll
Through the wide fields of air;
The waves obey Thy dread control;
But still, Thou art not there:
Where shall I find Him, O my soul,
Who yet is everywhere?

3 O not in circling depth or height,
But in the conscious breast,
Present to faith, tho' vailed from sight,
There doth His Spirit rest:
O come, Thou Presence Infinite,
And make Thy creature blest.

Josiah Conder. (1789—1855.) 1822.

NAOMI. C. M. Hans Georg Naegeli. (1768—1836.) 1832.
Arr. by Lowell Mason. (1792—1872.) 1836.

1. FA - THER, what-e'er of earth-ly bliss Thy sovereign will de - nies,
Ac - cept - ed at Thy throne of grace, Let this pe - ti - tion rise:—

464 *"A calm, a thankful Heart."*

2 Give me a calm, a thankful heart,
From every murmur free ;
The blessings of Thy grace impart,
And make me live to Thee.

3 Let the sweet hope that Thou art mine
My life and death attend ;
Thy presence through my journey shine,
And crown my journey's end.
Miss Anne Steele. (1717—1778.) 1760. ab.

465 *"Sweet Will of God."*

1 I WORSHIP Thee, sweet Will of God,
And all Thy ways adore ;
And every day I live, I seem
To love Thee more and more.

2 I love to kiss each print where Thou
Hast set Thine unseen feet :
I cannot fear Thee, blessèd Will,
Thine empire is so sweet.

3 I have no cares, O blessèd Will,
For all my cares are Thine ;
I live in triumph, Lord, for Thou
Hast made Thy triumphs mine.

4 He always wins who sides with God,
To him no chance is lost ;
God's will is sweetest to him when
It triumphs at his cost.

5 Ill that He blesses is our good,
And unblest good is ill ;
And all is right that seems most
wrong,
If it be His sweet will.
Rev. Frederick William Faber. (1814—1863.) 1849. ab.

466 *The Mysteries of Providence.*

1 GOD moves in a mysterious way
His wonders to perform ;
He plants His footsteps in the sea,
And rides upon the storm.

2 Deep in unfathomable mines
Of never-failing skill,
He treasures up His bright designs,
And works His sovereign will.

3 Ye fearful saints, fresh courage take ;
The clouds ye so much dread
Are big with mercy, and shall break
In blessings on your head.

4 Judge not the Lord by feeble sense,
But trust Him for His grace ;
Behind a frowning providence
He hides a smiling face.

THY WILL BE DONE.

5 His purposes will ripen fast,
 Unfolding every hour;
 The bud may have a bitter taste,
 But sweet will be the flower.

6 Blind unbelief is sure to err,
 And scan His work in vain:
 God is His own Interpreter,
 And He will make it plain.
   William Cowper. (1731—1800.) 1779.

BRATTLE STREET. C. M. D.
Ignace Pleyel. (1757—1831.) 1791.
Arr. by Nahum Mitchell. (1770—1853.) 1812.

1. While Thee I seek, pro-tect-ing Power, Be my vain wish-es stilled; And may this con - se-
crat-ed hour With bet-ter hopes be filled. Thy love the powers of thought be-stowed, To
Thee my thoughts would soar; Thy mer-cy o'er my life has flowed, That mer-cy I a-dore.

467   *Habitual Devotion.*
2 In each event of life, how clear
  Thy ruling hand I see:
  Each blessing to my soul more dear,
  Because conferred by Thee.
  In every joy that crowns my days,
  In every pain I bear,
  My heart shall find delight in praise,
  Or seek relief in prayer.

3 When gladness wings my favored hour,
  Thy love my thoughts shall fill;
  Resigned, when storms of sorrow lower,
  My soul shall meet Thy will.
  My lifted eye, without a tear,
  The lowering storm shall see;
  My steadfast heart shall know no fear,
  That heart will rest on Thee.
   Miss Helen Maria Williams. (1762—1827.) 1786.

468   *Humble Reliance.*
1 My God, my Father, blissful Name,
  O may I call Thee mine?
  May I with sweet assurance claim
  A portion so divine?
  This only can my fears control,
  And bid my sorrows fly;
  What harm can ever reach my soul
  Beneath my Father's eye?

2 Whate'er Thy providence denies,
  I calmly would resign,
  For Thou art good and just and wise:
  O bend my will to Thine.
  Whate'er Thy sacred will ordains,
  O give me strength to bear;
  And let me know my Father reigns,
  And trust His tender care.
   Miss Anne Steele. 1760. ab.

GOD OUR REFUGE.

WARD. L. M. Old Scotch Melody. Arr. by Lowell Mason. (1792—1872.) 1830.

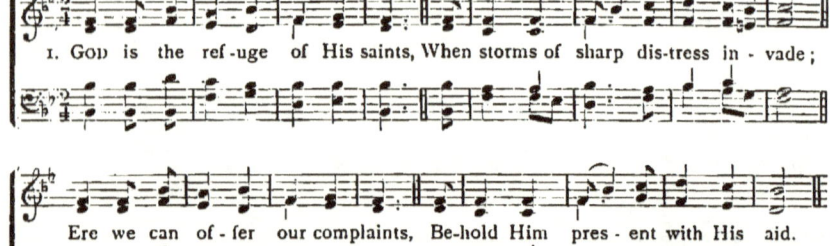

1. God is the ref-uge of His saints, When storms of sharp dis-tress in-vade;
Ere we can of-fer our complaints, Be-hold Him pres-ent with His aid.

469 *Safety and Triumph of God's People.*
Ps. xlvi.

2 Let mountains from their seats be
    hurled
Down to the deep, and buried there,
Convulsions shake the solid world;
Our faith shall never yield to fear.

3 Loud may the troubled ocean roar;
In sacred peace our souls abide,
While every nation, every shore,
Trembles, and dreads the swelling tide.

4 There is a stream, whose gentle flow
Supplies the City of our God,
Life, love, and joy, still gliding thro',
And watering our divine abode.

5 That sacred stream, Thine holy word,
Our grief allays, our fear controls;
Sweet peace Thy promises afford,
And give new strength to fainting
    souls.

6 Zion enjoys her Monarch's love,
Secure against a threatening hour;
Nor can her firm foundations move,
Built on His truth, and armed with
    power.
            Rev. Isaac Watts. (1674—1748.) 1719. alt.

470 *Divine Protection.*
Ps. cxxi.

1 Up to the hills I lift mine eyes,
Th' eternal hills beyond the skies:
Thence all her help my soul derives,
There my Almighty Refuge lives.

2 He lives, the everlasting God,
That built the world, that spread the
    flood;
The heavens with all their hosts He
    made,
And the dark regions of the dead.

3 He guides our feet, He guards our
    way;
His morning smiles bless all the day;
He spreads the evening veil, and keeps
The silent hours while Israel sleeps.

4 Israel, a name divinely blest,
May rise secure, securely rest;
Thy holy Guardian's wakeful eyes
Admit no slumber, nor surprise.

5 On thee foul spirits have no power;
And, in thy last departing hour,
Angels, that trace the airy road,
Shall bear thee homeward to thy God.
            Rev. Isaac Watts. 1719. ab.

THY WILL BE DONE. 213

GILEAD. L. M. Etienne Henri Mehul. (1763—1817.)

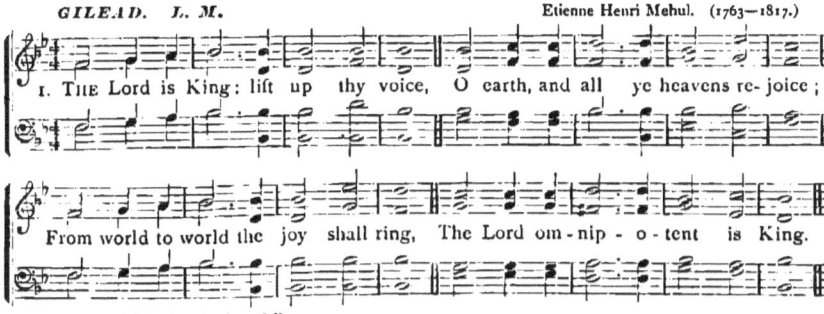

1. The Lord is King: lift up thy voice, O earth, and all ye heavens rejoice;
From world to world the joy shall ring, The Lord om-nip-o-tent is King.

471 *"The Lord reigneth."* Ps. xcvii.

2 The Lord is King: who then shall dare
Resist His will, distrust His care,
Or murmur at His wise decrees,
Or doubt His royal promises?

3 The Lord is King: child of the dust,
The Judge of all the earth is just;
Holy and true are all His ways:
Let every creature speak His praise.

4 O when His wisdom can mistake,
His might decay, His love forsake,
Then may His children cease to sing,
The Lord Omnipotent is King.
Josiah Conder. (1789—1855.) 1824. ab.

472 *Praising God forever.* Ps. cxlvi.

1 God of my life, through all its days
My grateful powers shall sound Thy praise;
The song shall wake with opening light,
And warble to the silent night.

2 When anxious cares would break my rest,
And griefs would tear my throbbing breast,
Thy tuneful praises, raised on high,
Shall check the murmur and the sigh.

3 When death or nature shall prevail,
And all its powers of language fail,

Joy through my swimming eyes shall break,
And mean the thanks I cannot speak.

4 But O, when that last conflict's o'er,
And I am chained to flesh no more,
With what glad accents shall I rise,
To join the music of the skies!

5 Soon shall I learn the exalted strains
Which echo o'er the heavenly plains;
And emulate, with joy unknown,
The glowing seraphs round Thy throne.
Rev. Philip Doddridge. (1702—1751.) 1755.

473 *"Be still, and know that I am God."*

1 Wait, O my soul, thy Maker's will!
Tumultuous passions, all be still;
Nor let a murm'ring thought arise:
His ways are just, His counsels wise.

2 He in the thickest darkness dwells,
Performs His work, the cause conceals;
And, tho' His footsteps are unknown,
Judgment and truth support His throne.

3 In heaven, and earth, and air, and seas,
He executes His firm decrees;
And by His saints it stands confessed,
That what He does is ever best.
Rev. Benjamin Beddome. (1717—1795.) 1818. ab.

FEAR NOT—HOPE IN GOD.

FRANKLIN SQUARE. S. M. Sylvanus Billings Pond. (1815—1871.) Before 1850.

1. Give to the wind thy fears; Hope, and be un-dis-mayed: God hears thy sighs, and counts thy tears; God shall lift up thy head.

474 *"Befiehl du deine Wege."*

2 Through waves and clouds and storms,
    He gently clears thy way:
  Wait thou His time, so shall this night
    Soon end in joyous day.

3 What though thou rulest not,
    Yet heaven and earth and hell
  Proclaim, God sitteth on the throne,
    And ruleth all things well.

4 Far, far above thy thought
    His counsel shall appear,
  When fully He the work hath wrought
    That caused thy needless fear.

  Rev. Paul Gerhardt. (1606—1676.) 1659.
  Tr. by Rev. John Wesley. (1703—1791.) 1739. ab.

475 *Trust in Providence.*
  Matt. vi. 25. 1 Pet. v. 7.

1 Commit thou all thy griefs
    And ways into His hands,
  To His sure truth and tender care,
    Who earth and heaven commands.

2 Who points the clouds their course,
    Whom wind and seas obey,
  He shall direct thy wandering feet,
    He shall prepare thy way.

3 Thou on the Lord rely,
    So safe shalt thou go on;
  Fix on His work thy steadfast eye,
    So shall thy work be done.

4 No profit canst thou gain
    By self-consuming care;
  To Him commend thy cause; His ear
    Attends the softest prayer.

  Rev. Paul Gerhardt. 1659.
  Tr. by Rev. John Wesley. 1739. ab.

476 *Sailing on.*

1 If, through unruffled seas,
    Toward heaven we calmly sail,
  With grateful hearts, O God, to Thee,
    We'll own the favoring gale.

2 But should the surges rise,
    And rest delay to come,
  Blest be the sorrow, kind the storm,
    Which drives us nearer home.

3 Soon shall our doubts and fears
    All yield to Thy control:
  Thy tender mercies shall illume
    The midnight of the soul.

4 Teach us, in every state,
    To make Thy will our own;
  And when the joys of sense depart,
    To live by faith alone.

  Rev. Augustus Montague Toplady. (1740—1778.) 1772. ab.
  and much alt.

FEAR NOT—REST IN GOD. 215

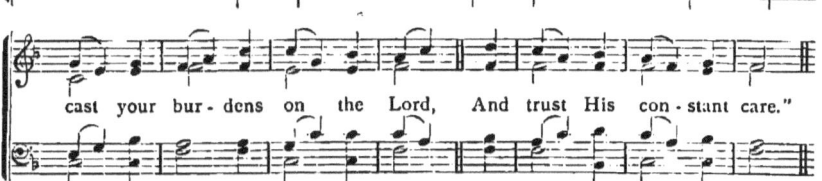

1. How gentle God's commands! How kind His precepts are! "Come, cast your burdens on the Lord, And trust His constant care."

477 *God's Care a Remedy for ours.*
1 Pet. v. 7.

2 While Providence supports,
Let saints securely dwell;
That hand, which bears all nature up,
Shall guide His children well.

3 Why should this anxious load
Press down your weary mind?
Haste to your heavenly Father's throne,
And sweet refreshment find.

4 His goodness stands approved,
Down to the present day;
I'll drop my burden at His feet,
And bear a song away.
Rev. Philip Doddridge. (1702—1751.) 1755.

478 *Safety in God.*
Ps. xxxi.

1 My spirit, on Thy care,
Blest Saviour, I recline:
Thou wilt not leave me to despair,
For Thou art Love Divine.

2 In Thee I place my trust,
On Thee I calmly rest;
I know Thee good, I know Thee just,
And count Thy choice the best.

3 Whate'er events betide,
Thy will they all perform;

Safe in Thy breast my head I hide,
Nor fear the coming storm.

4 Let good or ill befall,
It must be good for me;
Secure of having Thee in all,
Of having all in Thee.
Rev. Henry Francis Lyte. (1793—1847.) 1834.

479 *Importunity in Prayer.*
Luke xviii. 1–7.

1 Our Lord, who knows full well
The heart of every saint,
Invites us all our griefs to tell,
To pray, and never faint.

2 He bows His gracious ear,
We never plead in vain;
Yet we must wait till He appear,
And pray, and pray again.

3 Jesus, the Lord, will hear
His chosen when they cry;
Yes, though He may a while forbear,
He'll help them from on high.

4 Then let us earnest be,
And never faint in prayer;
He loves our importunity,
And makes our cause His care.
Rev. John Newton. (1725—1807.) 1779. ab. and alt.

THY WILL, NOT MINE.

ST. JUDE. G. D. Carl Maria Von Weber. (1786—1826.) 1820.

1. My Jesus, as Thou wilt: O may Thy will be mine; Into Thy hand of love I would my all resign. Through sorrow or through joy, Conduct me as Thine own, And help me still to say, My Lord, Thy will be done.

480 "*Mein Jesu, wie Du willst.*"

2 My Jesus, as Thou wilt:
　If needy here and poor,
　Give me Thy people's bread,
　Their portion rich and sure.
　The manna of Thy word
　Let my soul feed upon ;
　And if all else should fail,
　My Lord, Thy will be done.

3 My Jesus, as Thou wilt:
　Though seen through many a tear,
　Let not my star of hope
　Grow dim or disappear.
　Since Thou on earth hast wept
　And sorrowed oft alone,
　If I must weep with Thee,
　My Lord, Thy will be done.

4 My Jesus, as Thou wilt:
　All shall be well for me ;
　Each changing future scene
　I gladly trust with Thee.
　Straight to my home above,
　I travel calmly on,
　And sing in life or death,
　My Lord, Thy will be done.
　　Rev. Benjamin Schmolke. (1672—1737.) 1716.
　　Tr. by Miss Jane Borthwick. 1853. ab.

481 "*Thy Way, not mine.*"

1 THY way, not mine, O Lord,
　However dark it be !
　Lead me by Thine own hand ;
　Choose out the path for me.
　I dare not choose my lot ;
　I would not, if I might ;
　Choose Thou for me, my God,
　So shall I walk aright.

2 Choose Thou for me my friends,
　My sickness or my health,
　Choose Thou my cares for me,
　My poverty or wealth.
　Not mine, not mine the choice,
　In things or great or small ;
　Be Thou my Guide, my Strength,
　My Wisdom, and my All.
　　Rev. Horatius Bonar. (1808—) 1857. ab.

I NEED THEE. 217

AURELIA. 7, 6. D. Samuel Sebastian Wesley. 1868.

1. I need Thee, precious Jesus, For I am full of sin; My soul is dark and guilt-y, My heart is dead with-in; I need the cleans-ing fount-ain Where I can al-ways flee, The blood of Christ most pre-cious, The sin-ner's per-fect plea.

482 "*He is precious.*" 1 Pet. ii. 7.

2 I need Thee, precious Jesus,
  For I am very poor;
  A stranger and a pilgrim,
  I have no earthly store;
  I need the love of Jesus
  To cheer me on my way,
  To guide my doubting footsteps,
  To be my strength and stay.

3 I need Thee, precious Jesus,
  I need a friend like Thee,
  A friend to soothe and pity,
  A friend to care for me.
  I need the heart of Jesus
  To feel each anxious care,
  To tell my every trouble,
  And all my sorrows share.

4 I need Thee, precious Jesus,
  And hope to see Thee soon,
  Encircled with the rainbow,
  And seated on Thy throne:

There, with Thy blood-bought children,
  My joy shall ever be,
  To sing Thy praises, Jesus,
  To gaze, my Lord, on Thee.

Rev. Frederick Whitfield. (1829—) 1859. ab. and sl. alt.

483 "*Still keep me.*"

1 O Lamb of God, still keep me
  Near to Thy wounded side;
  'Tis only there in safety
  And peace I can abide.
  What foes and snares surround me,
  What doubts and fears within!
  The grace that sought and found me,
  Alone can keep me clean.

2 Soon shall my eyes behold Thee
  With rapture face to face;
  One half hath not been told me
  Of all Thy power and grace;
  Thy beauty, Lord, and glory,
  The wonders of Thy love,
  Shall be the endless story
  Of all Thy saints above.

James George Deck. 1857. ab.

BAPTISM.

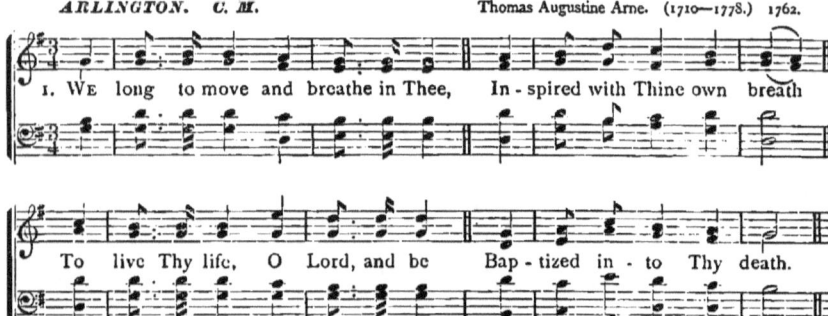

ARLINGTON. C. M. Thomas Augustine Arne. (1710—1778.) 1762.

1. We long to move and breathe in Thee,
In-spired with Thine own breath
To live Thy life, O Lord, and be
Bap-tized in-to Thy death.

484 *Baptism of Adults.*

2 Thy death to sin we die below,
But we shall rise in love;
We here are planted in Thy woe,
But we shall bloom above.

3 Above we shall Thy glory share,
As we Thy cross have borne;
E'en we shall crowns of honor wear,
When we the thorns have worn.

4 Thy crown of thorns is all our boast,
While now we fall before
The Father, Son, and Holy Ghost,
And tremble, love, adore.
Unknown Author.

485 *Profession and Covenant.*

1 Witness, ye men and angels, now,
Before the Lord we speak;
To Him we make our solemn vow,
A vow we dare not break:—

2 That long as life itself shall last,
Ourselves to Christ we yield;
Nor from His cause will we depart,
Or ever quit the field.

3 We trust not in our native strength
But on His grace rely,

That, with returning wants, the Lord
Will all our need supply.

4 O guide our doubtful feet aright,
And keep us in Thy ways;
And, while we turn our vows to prayers,
Turn Thou our prayers to praise.
Rev. Benjamin Beddome. (1717—1795.) 1818.

486 *Christ's Regard for Children.*
Mark x. 13-16.

1 See, Israel's gentle Shepherd stands,
With all-engaging charms;
Hark, how He calls the tender lambs,
And folds them in His arms!

2 "Permit them to approach," He cries,
"Nor scorn their humble name;
For 'twas to bless such souls as these,
The Lord of angels came."

3 We bring them, Lord, in thankful hands,
And yield them up to Thee;
Joyful that we ourselves are Thine,
Thine let our offspring be.
Rev. Philip Doddridge. (1702—1751.) 1755. ab.

487 *The Token of the Covenant.*

1 In token that thou shalt not fear
Christ crucified to own,
We print the cross upon thee here,
And stamp thee His alone.

BAPTISM. 219

2 In token that thou shalt not blush
   To glory in His Name,
   We blazon here upon thy front
   His glory and His shame.

3 In token that thou shalt not flinch
   Christ's quarrel to maintain,
   But 'neath His banner manfully
   Firm at thy post remain;

4 In token that thou too shalt tread
   The path He travelled by,
   Endure the cross, despise the shame,
   And sit thee down on high;

5 Thus, outwardly and visibly,
   We seal thee for His own;
   And may the brow, that wears His cross,
   Hereafter share His crown.
   Rev. Henry Alford. (1810—1871.) 1832.

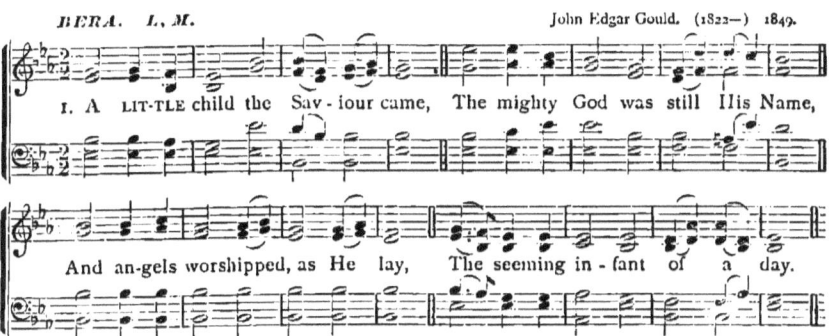

BERA. L., M.   John Edgar Gould. (1822—) 1849.

1. A LIT-TLE child the Sav-iour came, The mighty God was still His Name,
And an-gels worshipped, as He lay, The seeming in-fant of a day.

488 *"Let little Children come to Me."*

2 He who, a little child, began
  The life divine to show to man, [free,
  Proclaims from heaven the message
  "Let little children come to Me."

3 We bring them, Lord, and with the sign
  Of sprinkled water name them Thine:
  Their souls with saving grace endow,
  Baptize them with Thy Spirit now.

4 O give Thine angels charge, good Lord,
  Them safely in Thy way to guard;
  Thy blessing on their lives command,
  And write their names upon Thy hand.
  Rev. William Robertson. (—1743.) 1751. ab.

489 *Prayer for the Children of the Church.*

1 DEAR Saviour, if these lambs should
    stray
  From Thy secure enclosure's bound,

And, lured by worldly joys away,
  Among the thoughtless crowd be
    found;

2 Remember still that they are Thine,
  That Thy dear sacred name they bear;
  Think that the seal of love divine,
  The sign of covenant grace, they wear.

3 In all their erring, sinful years,
  O let them ne'er forgotten be;
  Remember all the prayers and tears
  Which made them consecrate to Thee.

4 And when these lips no more can pray,
  These eyes can weep for them no
    more,
  Turn Thou their feet from folly's way,
  The wanderers to Thy fold restore.
  Mrs. Ann Bradley Hyde. (—1872.) 1824.

CONFESSION OF FAITH.

HAPPY DAY. L. M.   Arr. from Edward Francis Rimbault. (1816—)

1. { O HAP- PY day that fixed my choice On Thee, my Sav - iour and my God! }
   { Well may this glow - ing heart re - joice And tell its rap - tures all a - broad. }

Hap - py day, hap - py day, When Je - sus washed my sins a - way.

He taught me how to watch and pray, And live re - joic - ing ev - ery day.

490   *The happy Bond.*
2 Chron. xv. 15.

2 O happy bond, that seals my vows
To Him who merits all my love:
Let cheerful anthems fill His house,
While to that sacred shrine I move.

3 'Tis done; the great transaction's done:
I am my Lord's, and He is mine;
He drew me, and I followed on,
Charmed to confess the voice divine.

4 Now rest, my long divided heart,
Fixed on this blissful centre, rest;
With ashes who would grudge to part,
When called on angels' bread to feast?

5 High heaven, that heard the solemn vow,
That vow renewed shall daily hear,
Till in life's latest hour I bow,
And bless in death a bond so dear.

         Rev. Philip Doddridge. (1702—1751.) 1755.

491   *Trusting the Merits of Christ.*
Phil. iii. 7–9.

1 No more, my God, I boast no more
Of all the duties I have done;
I quit the hopes I held before,
To trust the merits of Thy Son.

2 Now for the love I bear His name,
What was my gain I count my loss;
My former pride I call my shame,
And nail my glory to His cross.

3 Yes, and I must and will esteem
All things but loss for Jesus' sake;
O may my soul be found in Him,
And of His righteousness partake.

4 The best obedience of my hands
Dares not appear before Thy throne;
But faith can answer Thy demands,
By pleading what my Lord has done.

         Rev. Isaac Watts. (1674—1748.) 1709.

CONFESSION OF FAITH.

MESSIAH. 7. D.
Louis Joseph Ferdinand Herold. (1791—1833.) 1830.
Arr. by George Kingsley. (1311—) 1838.

1. PEOPLE of the living God, I have sought the world around, Paths of sin and sorrow trod, Peace and comfort nowhere found. Now to you my spir-it turns, Turns, a fu-gi-tive unblest; Brethren, where your al-tar burns, O receive me in-to rest!

492 *Choosing the Portion of God's Heritage.*
Ruth i. 16, 17.

2 Lonely I no longer roam,
   Like the cloud, the wind, the wave;
Where you dwell shall be my home,
   Where you die shall be my grave;
Mine the God whom you adore,
   Your Redeemer shall be mine;
Earth can fill my heart no more,
   Every idol I resign.
James Montgomery. (1771—1854.) 1819, 1853. ab.

493 *The burdened Pilgrim welcomed.*

1 PILGRIM, burdened with thy sin,
   Come the way to Zion's gate:
There, till mercy lets thee in,
   Knock, and weep, and watch, and wait.
Knock—He knows the sinner's cry;
Weep—He loves the mourner's tears;
Watch, for saving grace is nigh;
Wait, till heavenly light appears.

2 Hark, it is the Bridegroom's voice:
   "Welcome, pilgrim, to thy rest!"
Now within the gate rejoice,
   Safe, and sealed, and bought, and blest:
Safe, from all the lures of vice;
Sealed, by signs the chosen know;
Bought by love, and life the price;
Blest, the mighty debt to owe.
Rev. George Crabbe. (1754—1832.) 1807. ab.

494 *"Thine for ever!"*

1 THINE for ever!—God of love,
   Hear us from Thy throne above;
Thine for ever may we be,
   Here and in eternity.
Thine for ever!—Lord of life,
   Shield us through our earthly strife;
Thou, the Life, the Truth, the Way,
   Guide us to the realms of day.

2 Thine for ever!—Saviour, keep
   These Thy frail and trembling sheep;
Safe alone beneath Thy care,
   Let us all Thy goodness share.
Thine for ever!—Thou our Guide,
   All our wants by Thee supplied,
All our sins by Thee forgiven,
   Lead us, Lord, from earth to heaven.
Mrs. Mary Fawler Maude. 1848. ab.

UXBRIDGE. L. M. 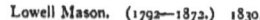Lowell Mason. (1792—1872.) 1830.

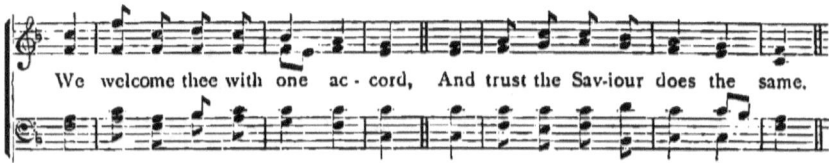

495 *"Come in!"*

2 Those joys, which earth cannot afford,
We'll seek in fellowship to prove;
Joined in one spirit to our Lord,
Together bound by mutual love.

3 And, while we pass this vale of tears,
We'll make our joys and sorrows known, [fears,
We'll share each other's hopes and
And count a brother's case our own.
    Rev. Thomas Kelly. (1769—1855.) 1812. ab.

496 *Glorying in the Cross.*

1 At Thy command, our dearest Lord,
Here we attend Thy dying feast;
Thy blood, like wine, adorns Thy board,
And Thine own flesh feeds every guest.

2 Our faith adores Thy bleeding love,
And trusts for life in One that died;
We hope for heavenly crowns above,
From a Redeemer crucified.

3 Let the vain world pronounce it shame,
And fling their scandals on Thy cause;
We come to boast our Saviour's name,
And make our triumphs in His cross.

4 With joy we tell the scoffing age,
He that was dead has left His tomb;
He lives above their utmost rage,
And we are waiting till He come.
    Rev. Isaac Watts. (1674—1748.) 1709.

497 *The Table spread.*

1 My God, and is Thy table spread,
And does Thy cup with love o'erflow?
Thither be all Thy children led,
And let them Thy sweet mercies know.

2 Hail, sacred feast, which Jesus makes,
Rich banquet of His flesh and blood:
Thrice happy he who here partakes
That sacred stream, that heavenly food!

3 Why are its bounties all in vain
Before unwilling hearts displayed?
Was not for you the Victim slain?
Are you forbid the children's bread?

4 O let Thy table honored be,
And furnished well with joyful guests;
And may each soul salvation see,
That here its holy pledges tastes.
    Rev. Philip Doddridge. (1702—1751.) 1755. ab. and alt.

LORD'S SUPPER. 223

HEBRON. L. M. Lowell Mason. 1830.

1. Je-sus, Thou Joy of lov-ing hearts, Thou Fount of life, Thou light of men,
From the best bliss that earth im-parts, We turn un-filled to Thee a-gain.

498 "*Jesu, Dulcedo cordium.*"

2 Thy truth unchanged hath ever stood;
Thou savest those that on Thee call;
To them that seek Thee, Thou art good,
To them that find Thee, All in all.

3 We taste Thee, O thou living Bread,
And long to feast upon Thee still;
We drink of Thee, the Fountain Head,
And thirst, our souls from Thee to fill.

4 O Jesus, ever with us stay;
Make all our moments calm and bright;
Chase the dark night of sin away;
Shed o'er the world Thy holy light.

Bernard of Clairvaux. (1091—1153.) 1140.
Tr. by Rev. Ray Palmer. (1808—) 1858. ab.

499 *The sweet Wonders of the Cross.*

1 O THE sweet wonders of that cross
Where my Redeemer loved and died:
Her noblest life my spirit draws
From His dear wounds, and bleeding side.

2 I would forever speak His name
In sounds to mortal ears unknown;
With angels join to praise the Lamb,
And worship at His Father's throne.

Rev. Isaac Watts. 1709. ab.

500 "*Christi Blut und Gerechtigkeit.*"

1 JESUS, Thy blood and righteousness
My beauty are, my glorious dress;
'Mid flaming worlds, in these arrayed,
With joy shall I lift up my head.

2 When from the dust of death I rise,
To take my mansion in the skies,
E'en then shall this be all my plea:
"Jesus hath lived, and died for me."

3 Bold shall I stand in that great day;
For who aught to my charge shall lay?
While, through Thy blood, absolved I am
From sin's tremendous curse and shame.

4 This spotless robe the same appears
When ruined nature sinks in years;
No age can change its glorious hue;
The robe of Christ is ever new.

5 O let the dead now hear Thy voice;
Bid, Lord, Thy banished ones rejoice;
Their beauty this, their glorious dress,
Jesus, the Lord, our Righteousness.

Count Nikolaus Ludwig Zinzendorf. (1700—1760.) 1739.
Tr. by Rev. John Wesley. (1703—1791.) 1740. ab.

LORD'S SUPPER.

ELIZABETHTOWN. C. M. — George Kingsley. (1811—) 1838.

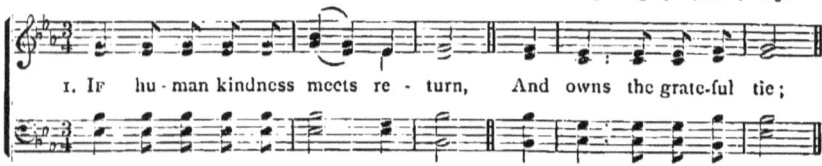

1. If human kindness meets return, And owns the grateful tie;

If tender thoughts within us burn, To feel a friend is nigh;

501 *Grateful and tender Remembrance.*

2 O shall not warmer accents tell
   The gratitude we owe
 To Him, who died, our fears to quell,
   Our more than orphan's woe?

3 While yet His anguished soul surveyed
   Those pangs He would not flee,
 What love His latest words displayed
   "Meet, and remember Me."

4 Remember Thee, Thy death, Thy shame,
   Our sinful hearts to share!
 O memory, leave no other name
   But His recorded there.

Hon. and Rev. Gerard Thomas Noel. (1782—1851.) 1813.

502 *Remembrance pledged.*

1 ACCORDING to Thy gracious word,
   In meek humility,
 This will I do, my dying Lord,
   I will remember Thee.

2 Thy body, broken for my sake,
   My bread from heaven shall be;
 Thy testamental cup I take,
   And thus remember Thee.

3 Gethsemane can I forget?
   Or there Thy conflict see,
 Thine agony and bloody sweat,
   And not remember Thee?

4 When to the cross I turn mine eyes,
   And rest on Calvary,
 O Lamb of God, my sacrifice,
   I must remember Thee:

5 Remember Thee and all Thy pains,
   And all Thy love to me;
 Yea, while a breath, a pulse remains,
   Will I remember Thee.

6 And when these failing lips grow dumb,
   And mind and memory flee,
 When Thou shalt in Thy kingdom come,
   Jesus, remember me.

James Montgomery. (1771—1854.) 1825.

LORD'S SUPPER.

BALERMA. C. M. Scotch Melody. Hugh Wilson. 1768.
Arr. by Lowell Mason. (1792—1872.) 1836.

1. How sweet and awful is the place,
With Christ within the doors,
While everlasting love displays
The choicest of her stores.

503 *At the Table.*

2 While all our hearts, and all our songs,
Join to admire the feast,
Each of us cry, with thankful tongues,
"Lord, why was I a guest?"

3 "Why was I made to hear Thy voice,
And enter while there's room,
When thousands make a wretched choice,
And rather starve than come?"

4 'Twas the same love that spread the feast,
That sweetly forced us in;
Else we had still refused to taste,
And perished in our sin.

5 Pity the nations, O our God;
Constrain the earth to come;
Send Thy victorious word abroad,
And bring the strangers home.
Rev. Isaac Watts. (1674—1748.) 1709.

504 *The Sacrament a Pledge of Heaven.*

1 HAPPY the souls to Jesus joined,
And saved by grace alone;
Walking in all Thy ways, we find
Our heaven on earth begun.

2 The Church triumphant in Thy love,
Their mighty joys we know;
They sing the Lamb in hymns above,
And we in hymns below.

3 Thee, in Thy glorious realm, they praise,
And bow before Thy throne;
We, in the kingdom of Thy grace:
The kingdoms are but one.

4 The holy to the holiest leads;
From hence our spirits rise;
And he that in Thy statutes treads
Shall meet Thee in the skies.
Rev. Charles Wesley. (1708—1788.) 1745.

505 *"Worthy the Lamb."*

1 "WORTHY the Lamb for sinners slain,"
Cry the redeemed above,
"Blessing and honor to obtain,
And everlasting love."

2 "Worthy the Lamb," on earth we sing,
"Who died our souls to save;
Henceforth, O Death, where is thy sting?
Thy victory, O Grave?"
James Montgomery. 1825, 1853. ab.

COMMUNION OF SAINTS.

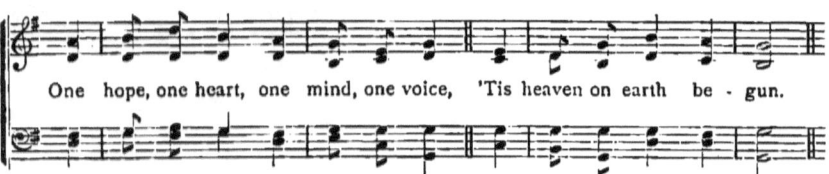

MELODY. (CHELMSFORD.) C. M.   Aaron Chapin. 1813.

1. Our souls, by love together knit, Cemented, mixed in one, One hope, one heart, one mind, one voice, 'Tis heaven on earth begun.

506   *"Knit together in Love."* Col. ii. 2.

2 Our hearts have often burned within,
    And glowed with sacred fire,
While Jesus spoke and fed and blessed,
    And filled th' enlarged desire.

3 The little cloud increases still,
    The heavens are big with rain;
We haste to catch the teeming shower,
    And all its moisture drain.

4 A rill, a stream, a torrent flows;
    But pour a mighty flood:
O sweep the nations, shake the earth,
    Till all proclaim Thee God.

5 And when Thou mak'st Thy jewels up,
    And sett'st Thy starry crown,
When all Thy sparkling gems shall shine,
    Proclaimed by Thee Thine own;

6 May we, a little band of love,
    We sinners, saved by grace,
From glory unto glory changed,
    Behold Thee face to face.

    Rev. William Edward Miller. (1766—1839.) 1800.

507   *Resting in Hope.*

1 My Lord, my Love, was crucified,
    He all the pains did bear;
But in the sweetness of His rest
    He makes His servants share.

2 How sweetly rest Thy saints above
    Which in Thy bosom lie;
The Church below doth rest in hope
    Of that felicity.

    Rev. John Mason. 1683. ab.

508   *At Parting.*

1 Blest be the dear, uniting love,
    That will not let us part;
Our bodies may far off remove,
    We still are joined in heart.

2 Joined in one spirit to our Head,
    Where He appoints we go,
And still in Jesus' footsteps tread,
    And do His work below.

3 Partakers of the Saviour's grace,
    The same in mind and heart,
Nor joy, nor grief, nor time, nor place,
    Nor life, nor death, can part.

    Rev. Charles Wesley. (1708—1788.) 1742. ab.

COMMUNION OF SAINTS.

CHRISTMAS. C. M. George Frederick Handel. (1685—1759.)

1. Come, let us join our friends above That have obtained the prize, And on the eagle wings of love, To joy celestial rise, To joy celestial rise.

509 *One Church, one Army.*

2 Let saints below in concert sing
  With those to glory gone;
  For all the servants of our King
  In earth and heaven are one.

3 One family, we dwell in Him,
  One Church above, beneath,
  Though now divided by the stream,
  The narrow stream of death.

4 One army of the living God,
  To His command we bow;
  Part of the host have crossed the flood,
  And part are crossing now.

5 E'en now to their eternal home
  Some happy spirits fly;
  And we are to the margin come,
  And soon expect to die.

6 Dear Saviour, be our constant Guide;
  Then, when the word is given,
  Bid Jordan's narrow stream divide,
  And land us safe in heaven.
  Rev. Charles Wesley. 1759. ab. and alt.

510 *"The Saints above."*

1 Give me the wings of faith, to rise
  Within the veil, and see
  The saints above, how great their joys,
  How bright their glories be.

2 Once they were mourning here below,
  And wet their couch with tears;
  They wrestled hard, as we do now,
  With sins, and doubts, and fears.

3 I ask them, whence their victory came?
  They, with united breath,
  Ascribe their conquest to the Lamb,
  Their triumph to His death.

4 They marked the footsteps that He trod:
  His zeal inspired their breast;
  And following their incarnate God,
  Possess the promised rest.

5 Our glorious Leader claims our praise
  For His own pattern given,
  While the long cloud of witnesses
  Show the same path to heaven.
  Rev. Isaac Watts. (1674—1748.) 1709.

COMMUNION OF SAINTS.

SWEET HOME. 11.   Sir Henry Rowley Bishop. (1780—1855.) 1829.

1. 'Mid scenes of con-fu-sion and creature complaints, How sweet to the soul is com-mu-nion with saints; To find at the ban-quet of mer-cy there's room, And feel in the presence of Je-sus at home. Home, home, sweet, sweet home;

D. S. Pre-pare me, dear Sav-iour, for glo-ry, my home.

511 *"In Glory, at Home."*

2 Sweet bonds that unite all the children of peace!
And thrice precious Jesus, whose love cannot cease!
Though oft from Thy presence in sadness I roam,
I long to behold Thee in glory, at home.

3 While here in the valley of conflict I stay,
O give me submission, and strength as my day;
In all my afflictions to Thee would I come,
Rejoicing in hope of my glorious home.

4 Whate'er Thou deniest, O give me Thy grace,
The Spirit's sure witness, and smiles of Thy face;
Endue me with patience to wait at Thy throne,
And find, even now, a sweet foretaste of home.

5 I long, dearest Lord, in Thy beauties to shine;
No more as an exile in sorrow to pine;
And in Thy dear image arise from the tomb,
With glorified millions to praise Thee at home.

Rev. David Denham. 1837. ab.

COMMUNION OF SAINTS. 229

VOX ANGELICA. 11, 10. Rev. John Bacchus Dykes. 1861.

1. Hark, hark, my soul: an-gel-ic songs are swell-ing O'er earth's green fields and ocean's wave-beat shore:
How sweet the truth those blessèd strains are tell-ing Of that new life when sin shall be no more.

CHORUS.
An-gels of Je-sus, An-gels of light, Sing-ing to wel-come the pil-grims of the night.

512   "*Pilgrims of the Night.*"

2 Onward we go, for still we hear them singing,
   "Come, weary souls, for Jesus bids you come;"
And through the dark, its echoes sweetly ringing,
   The music of the Gospel leads us home. *Cho.*

3 Far, far away, like bells at evening pealing,
   The voice of Jesus sounds o'er land and sea;
And laden souls, by thousands meekly stealing,
   Kind Shepherd, turn their weary steps to Thee. *Cho.*

4 Rest comes at length; though life be long and dreary,
   The day must dawn, and darksome night be past;
Life's journey ends in welcome to the weary,
   And heaven, the heart's true home, will come at last. *Cho.*

5 Angels, sing on: your faithful watches keeping,
   Sing us sweet fragments of the songs above;
Till morning's joy shall end the night of weeping,
   And life's long shadows break in cloudless love. *Cho.*

Rev. Frederick William Faber. (1814—1863.) 1849. ab. and alt.

COMMUNION OF SAINTS.

BOYLSTON. S. M.   Lowell Mason. (1792—1872.) 1832.

1. Blest be the tie that binds Our hearts in Chris-tian love: The

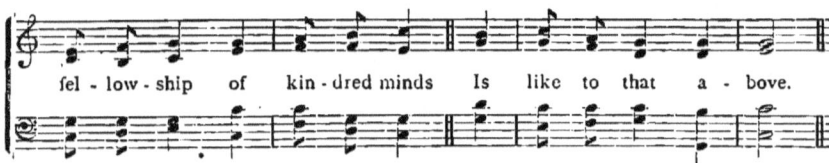

fel - low - ship of kin - dred minds Is like to that a - bove.

513   *Brotherly Love.*

2 Before our Father's throne
  We pour our ardent prayers;
Our fears, our hopes, our aims are one,
  Our comforts and our cares.

3 We share our mutual woes;
  Our mutual burdens bear;
And often for each other flows
  The sympathizing tear.

4 When we asunder part,
  It gives us inward pain;
But we shall still be joined in heart,
  And hope to meet again.

5 This glorious hope revives
  Our courage by the way;
While each in expectation lives,
  And longs to see the day.

6 From sorrow, toil, and pain,
  And sin we shall be free;
And perfect love and friendship reign
  Through all eternity.

      Rev. John Fawcett. (1739—1817.) 1772.

514   *Cross and Crown.*

1 O what, if we are Christ's,
  Is earthly shame or loss?
Bright shall the crown of glory be,
  When we have borne the cross.

2 Keen was the trial once,
  Bitter the cup of woe,
When martyred saints, baptized in blood,
  Christ's sufferings shared below.

3 Bright is their glory now,
  Boundless their joy above,
Where, on the bosom of their God,
  They rest in perfect love.

4 Lord, may that grace be ours,
  Like them in faith to bear
All that of sorrow, grief, or pain
  May be our portion here.

5 Enough, if Thou at last
  The word of blessing give,
And let us rest beneath Thy feet,
  Where saints and angels live.

      Rev. Sir Henry Williams Baker. (1821—) 1852.

COMMUNION OF SAINTS.

BADEA. S. M.   German Melody.

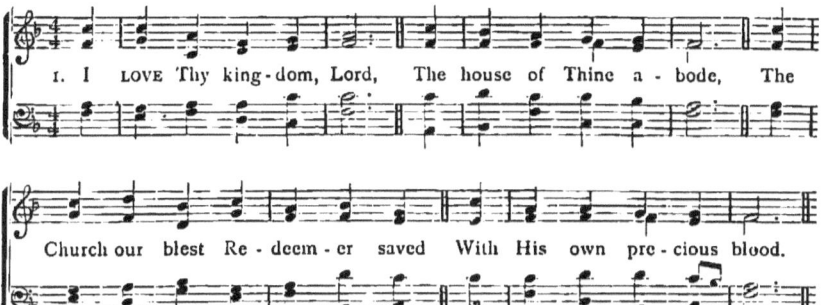

1. I love Thy kingdom, Lord, The house of Thine abode, The Church our blest Redeemer saved With His own precious blood.

515   *Love to the Church.*
Ps. cxxxvii.

2 I love Thy Church, O God:
Her walls before Thee stand,
Dear as the apple of Thine eye,
And graven on Thy hand.

3 For her my tears shall fall,
For her my prayers ascend;
To her my cares and toils be given,
Till toils and cares shall end.

4 Beyond my highest joy
I prize her heavenly ways,
Her sweet communion, solemn vows,
Her hymns of love and praise.

5 Jesus, Thou Friend Divine,
Our Saviour and our King,
Thy hand from every snare and foe
Shall great deliverance bring.

6 Sure as Thy truth shall last,
To Zion shall be given
The brightest glories earth can yield,
And brighter bliss of heaven.
Rev. Timothy Dwight. (1752—1817.) 1800. ab.

516   *The Blessedness of Gospel-times.*
Is. lii. 7—9. Matt. xiii. 16, 17.

1 How beauteous are their feet
Who stand on Zion's hill!
Who bring salvation on their tongues,
And words of peace reveal.

2 How charming is their voice,
How sweet the tidings are!
"Zion, behold thy Saviour King;
He reigns and triumphs here."

3 How happy are our ears,
That hear this joyful sound,
Which kings and prophets waited for,
And sought, but never found!

4 How blessèd are our eyes,
That see this heavenly light!
Prophets and kings desired it long,
But died without the sight.

5 The watchmen join their voice,
And tuneful notes employ;
Jerusalem breaks forth in songs,
And deserts learn the joy.

6 The Lord makes bare His arm
Through all the earth abroad;
Let every nation now behold
Their Saviour and their God.
Rev. Isaac Watts. (1674—1748.) 1709.

CHURCH-DEDICATION.

ST. MARTIN'S. C. M. William Tansur. (1699—1774.) 1735.

1. A-RISE, O King of grace, a-rise, And en-ter to Thy rest;
Lo, Thy Church waits with long-ing eyes, Thus to be owned and blest.

517 *Prayer of Dedication.*
Ps. cxxxii.

2 Enter with all Thy glorious train,
Thy Spirit and Thy word;
All that the ark did once contain
Could no such grace afford.

3 Here, mighty God, accept our vows,
Here let Thy praise be spread;
Bless the provisions of Thy house,
And fill Thy poor with bread.

4 Here let the Son of David reign,
Let God's Anointed shine,
Justice and truth His court maintain,
With love and power divine.

5 Here let Him hold a lasting throne,
And as His kingdom grows,
Fresh honors shall adorn His crown,
And shame confound His foes.

Rev. Isaac Watts. (1674—1748.) 1719.

518 *God's Blessing invoked.*

1 O THOU, whose own vast temple stands,
Built over earth and sea,
Accept the walls that human hands
Have raised to worship Thee.

2 Lord, from Thine inmost glory send,
Within these walls t' abide,
The peace that dwelleth without end
Serenely by Thy side.

3 May erring minds, that worship here,
Be taught the better way;
And they who mourn, and they who fear,
Be strengthened as they pray.

4 May faith grow firm, and love grow warm,
And pure devotion rise,
While round these hallowed walls the storm
Of earth-born passion dies.

William Cullen Bryant. (1794—) 1826.

519 *On opening a Place for Worship.* 7.
Tune, PLEYEL'S HYMN, p. 17.

1 LORD of hosts, to Thee we raise
Here a house of prayer and praise:
Thou Thy people's hearts prepare
Here to meet for praise and prayer.

2 Let the living here be fed
With Thy word, the heavenly bread;
Here in hope of glory blest,
May the dead be laid to rest.

CHURCH-DEDICATION. 233

3 Here to Thee a temple stand,
While the sea shall gird the land;
Hear reveal Thy mercy sure,
While the sun and moon endure.

4 Hallelujah! earth and sky
To the joyful sound reply;
Hallelujah! hence ascend
Prayer and praise till time shall end.
James Montgomery. (1771—1854.) 1825.

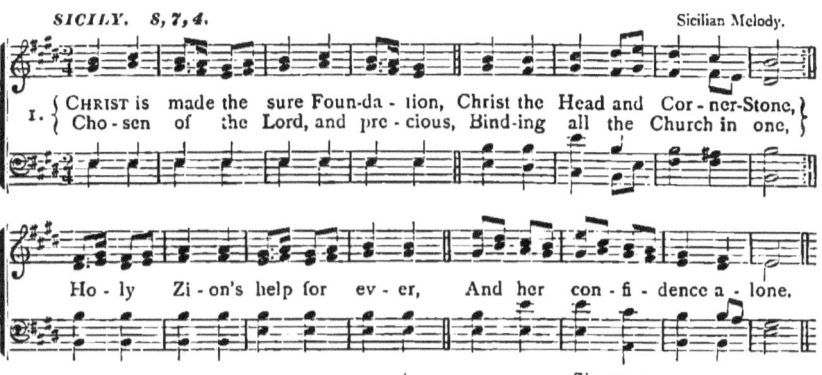

SICILY. 8, 7, 4.   Sicilian Melody.

1. { Christ is made the sure Foun-da - tion, Christ the Head and Cor - ner-Stone,
  Cho - sen of the Lord, and pre - cious, Bind-ing all the Church in one,

Ho - ly Zi - on's help for ev - er, And her con - fi - dence a - lone.

520   *"Angulare Fundamentum."*

2 All that dedicated city,
 Dearly loved of God on high,
 In exultant jubilation
 Pours perpetual melody;
 God the One in Three adoring
 In glad hymns eternally.

3 To this temple, where we call Thee,
 Come, O Lord of hosts, to-day:
 With Thy wonted loving-kindness,
 Hear Thy servants as they pray;
 And Thy fullest benediction
 Shed within its walls alway.

4 Here vouchsafe to all Thy servants
 What they ask of Thee to gain,
 What they gain from Thee forever
 With the blessèd to retain,
 And hereafter in Thy glory
 Evermore with Thee to reign.
  Unknown Author of the 8th century.
Tr. by Rev. John Mason Neale. (1818—1866.) 1851. ab.
          and alt.

521   *Zion secure.*
   Ps. cxxv. 2.

1 Zion stands by hills surrounded,
 Zion kept by power divine:
 All her foes shall be confounded,
 Though the world in arms combine.
  Happy Zion!
 What a favored lot is thine!

2 Every human tie may perish;
 Friend to friend unfaithful prove;
 Mothers cease their own to cherish;
 Heaven and earth at last remove;
  But no changes
 Can attend Jehovah's love.

3 In the furnace God may prove thee,
 Thence to bring Thee forth more
  bright,
 But can never cease to love Thee;
 Thou art precious in His sight:
  God is with thee,
 God, thine everlasting Light.
  Rev. Thomas Kelly. (1769—1855.) 1806. ab.

234 FOR THOSE AT SEA.

PILGRIM. 8, 7. D. George Kingsley. (1811—) 1853.

1. Tossed up-on life's rag-ing bil-low, Sweet it is, O Lord, to know, Thou didst press a sail-or's pil-low, And canst feel a sail-or's woe. Nev-er slumb'ring, nev-er sleep-ing, Though the night be dark and drear, Thou the faith-ful watch art keep-ing, "All, all's well," Thy constant cheer.

522 *Christ on the Lake of Galilee.*
Mark iv. 35.

2 And though loud the wind is howling,
  Fierce tho' flash the lightnings red;
 Darkly tho' the storm-cloud's scowling
  O'er the sailor's anxious head;
 Thou canst calm the raging ocean,
  All its noise and tumult still,
 Hush the tempest's wild commotion,
  At the bidding of Thy will.

3 Thus my heart the hope will cherish,
  While to Thee I lift mine eye;
 Thou wilt save me ere I perish,
  Thou wilt hear the sailor's cry,
 And though mast and sail be riven,
  Life's short voyage will soon be o'er;
 Safely moored in Heaven's wide haven,
  Storm and tempest vex no more.

Rev. George Washington Bethune. (1805—1862.) 1847. alt.

523 *"Rocked in the Cradle of the Deep."* L. M.
Tune, AMES, p. 35.

1 ROCKED in the cradle of the deep,
  I lay me down in peace to sleep;
  Secure I rest upon the wave,
  For Thou, O Lord, hast power to save.

2 I know Thou wilt not slight my call,
  For Thou dost mark the sparrow's fall;
  And calm and peaceful is my sleep,
  Rocked in the cradle of the deep.

3 And such the trust that still were mine,
  Tho' stormy winds swept o'er the brine,
  Or though the tempest's fiery breath
  Roused me from sleep to wreck and death.

4 In ocean cave still safe with Thee,
  The germ of immortality;
  And calm and peaceful is my sleep,
  Rocked in the cradle of the deep.

Mrs. Emma C. Willard. (1787—1870.) 1830.

FOR THOSE AT SEA. 235

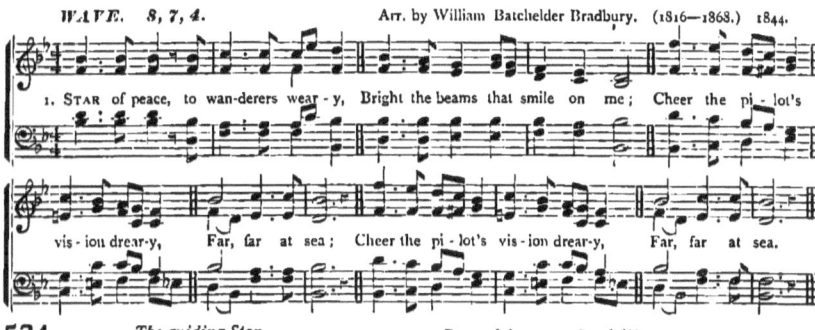

524 *The guiding Star.*
2 Star of hope, gleam on the billow,
   Bless the soul that sighs for thee ;
   Bless the sailor's lonely pillow,
     Far, far at sea.
3 Star of faith, when winds are mocking
   All his toil, he flies to thee ;

   Save him on the billows rocking,
     Far, far at sea.
4 Star divine, O safely guide him,
   Bring the wanderer home to thee :
   Sore temptations long have tried him,
     Far, far at sea.
        Mrs. Jane Bell Cross Simpson. 1830. ab.

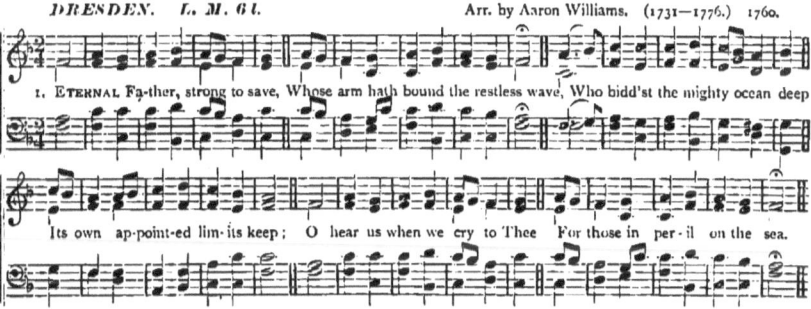

525 *"For those in Peril on the Sea."*
2 O Saviour, whose almighty word
   The winds and waves submissive heard,
   Who walkedst in the foaming deep,
   And calm amid its rage didst sleep ;
   O hear us when we cry to Thee
   For those in peril on the sea.
3 O Sacred Spirit, who didst brood
   Upon the chaos dark and rude,
   Who bad'st its angry tumult cease,

   And gavest light, and life, and peace ;
   O hear us when we cry to Thee
   For those in peril on the sea.
4 O Trinity of love and power,
   Our brethren shield in danger's hour ;
   From rock and tempest, fire and foe,
   Protect them wheresoe'er they go ;
   And ever let there rise to Thee
   Glad hymns of praise from land and sea.
        William Whiting. (1825—). 1860.

236   THE CITY OF GOD.

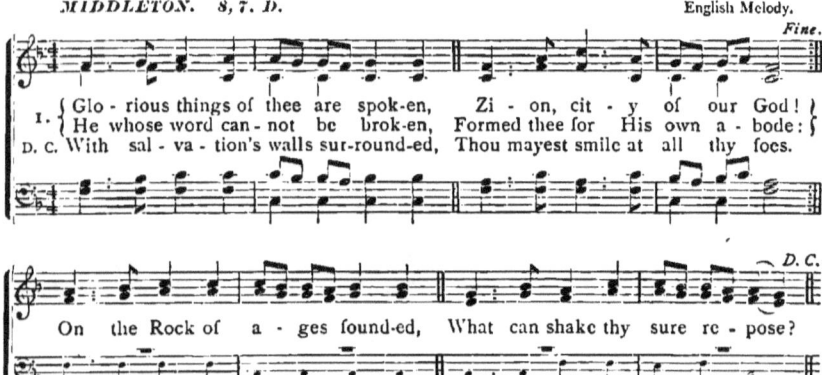

MIDDLETON. 8, 7. D.   English Melody.

1. Glorious things of thee are spoken, Zion, city of our God!
   He whose word cannot be broken, Formed thee for His own abode:
D.C. With salvation's walls surrounded, Thou mayest smile at all thy foes.
   On the Rock of ages founded, What can shake thy sure repose?

526 *The City of God.*
Is. xxxiii. 20, 21.

2 See, the streams of living waters,
   Springing from eternal love,
   Well supply thy sons and daughters,
   And all fear of want remove:
   Who can faint, while such a river
   Ever flows their thirst t' assuage?
   Grace, which, like the Lord, the Giver,
   Never fails from age to age.

3 Round each habitation hovering,
   See the cloud and fire appear,
   For a glory and a covering,
   Showing that the Lord is near:
   Thus deriving from their banner
   Light by night, and shade by day,
   Safe they feed upon the manna
   Which He gives them when they pray.
   Rev. John Newton. (1725—1807). 1779.

527 *"Igjennem Nat og Traengsel."*

1 Thro' the night of doubt and sorrow,
   Onward goes the pilgrim band,
   Singing songs of expectation,
   Marching to the Promised Land.
   And before us through the darkness
   Gleaming clear the guiding Light;
   Brother clasps the hand of brother,
   And steps fearless through the night.

2 One the light of God's dear presence,
   Never in its work to fail,
   Which illumes the wild rough places
   Of this gloomy haunted vale.
   One the object of our journey,
   One the faith which never tires,
   One the earnest looking forward,
   One the hope our God inspires.

3 One the strain which mouths of thousands
   Lift as from the heart of one;
   One the conflict, one the peril,
   One the march in God begun,
   One the gladness of rejoicing
   On the Resurrection shore,
   With One Father o'er us shining
   In His love for evermore.
   Bernhardt Severin Ingemann. (1789—1862.
   Tr. by Rev. Sabine Baring Gould. (1834—) 1867. ab.)

GLAD TIDINGS TO ZION. 237

ZION. 8, 7, 4. Thomas Hastings. (1784—1872.) 1830.

1. On the mountain's top appearing, Lo, the sacred herald stands, Welcome news to Zion bearing, Zion long in hostile lands: Mourning captive, God Himself will loose thy bands; Mourning captive, God Himself will loose thy bands.

528 *Good Tidings to Zion.*
Is. lii. 7.

2 Has thy night been long and mournful?
Have thy friends unfaithful proved?
Have thy foes been proud and scornful,
By thy sighs and tears unmoved?
Cease thy mourning;
Zion still is well beloved.

3 God, thy God, will now restore thee;
He Himself appears thy Friend;
All thy foes shall flee before thee;
Here their boasts and triumphs end:
Great deliverance
Zion's King vouchsafes to send.

4 Enemies no more shall trouble;
All thy wrongs shall be redressed;
For Thy shame thou shalt have double,
In thy Maker's favor blessed;
All thy conflicts
End in everlasting rest.
Rev. Thomas Kelly. (1769—1855.) 1806.

529 *Light in the Darkness.*
Matt. iv. 16.

1 O'er the gloomy hills of darkness,
Look, my soul, be still and gaze;
Sun of Righteousness, arising,
Bring the bright, the glorious day:
Send the Gospel
To the earth's remotest bound.

2 Kingdoms wide that sit in darkness,
Grant them, Lord, Thy glorious light,
And from eastern coast to western
May the morning chase the night;
And redemption,
Freely purchased, win the day.

3 Fly abroad, thou mighty Gospel,
Win and conquer, never cease:
May thy lasting wide dominions
Multiply, and still increase;
Sway Thy sceptre,
Saviour, all the world around.
Rev. William Williams. (1717—1791.) 1772. ab. and alt.

THE CHURCH'S FUTURE.

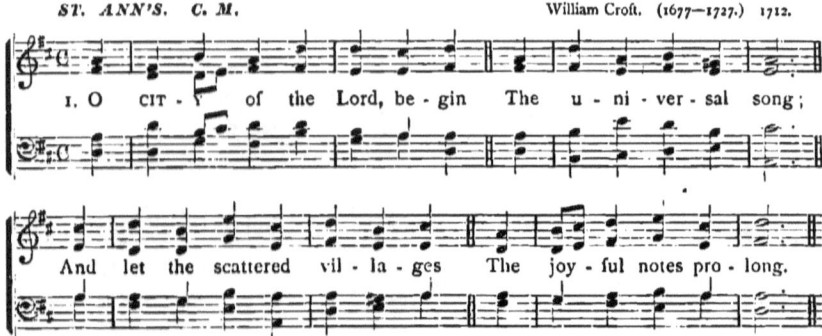

ST. ANN'S. C. M. — William Croft. (1677—1727.) 1712.

1. O city of the Lord, begin
The universal song;
And let the scattered villages
The joyful notes prolong.

530 *God praised for His Gospel.*
Is. xlii. 10-12.

2 Let Kedar's wilderness afar
Lift up the lonely voice;
And let the tenants of the rock,
With accent rude, rejoice.

3 O from the streams of distant lands,
Unto Jehovah sing;
And joyful from the mountain-tops
Shout to the Lord, the King.

4 Let all combined, with one accord,
The Saviour's glories raise,
Till, in the earth's remotest bounds,
The nations sound His praise.
Michael Bruce. (1746—1767.) 1781. ab.

531 *The immovable Kingdom.*

1 O WHERE are kings and empires now
Of old that went and came?
But, Lord, Thy Church is praying yet,
A thousand years the same.

2 We mark her goodly battlements,
And her foundations strong;
We hear within the solemn voice
Of her unending song.

3 For not like kingdoms of the world
Thy holy Church, O God!
Though earthquake shocks are threatening her,
And tempests are abroad;

4 Unshaken as eternal hills,
Immovable she stands,
A mountain that shall fill the earth,
A house not made by hands.
Bp. Arthur Cleveland Coxe. (1818—) 1833. alt.

532 *The Millennium.*
Micah iv. 1, 2. Is. ii. 1-4.

1 BEHOLD, the Mountain of the Lord
In latter days shall rise,
Above the mountains and the hills,
And draw the wondering eyes.

2 To this the joyful nations round,
All tribes and tongues, shall flow;
Up to the hill of God they'll say,
And to His house, we'll go.

3 The beam that shines on Zion's hill
Shall lighten every land;
The King who reigns in Zion's towers
Shall all the world command.

4 No strife shall vex Messiah's reign,
Or mar the peaceful years;
To ploughshares soon they beat their swords,
To pruning-hooks their spears.

THE CHURCH'S FUTURE.   239

5 No longer hosts encoutering hosts
    Their millions slain deplore ;
    They hang the trumpet in the hall,
    And study war no more.

6 Come, then, O come from every land,
    To worship at His shrine ;
    And, walking in the light of God,
    With holy beauties shine.
                                Michael Bruce. 1781.

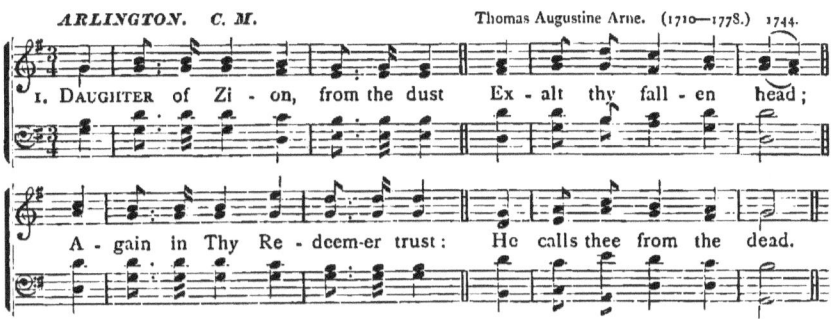

ARLINGTON.   C. M.   Thomas Augustine Arne. (1710—1778.) 1744.

1. Daughter of Zion, from the dust Exalt thy fallen head ;
   Again in Thy Redeemer trust :   He calls thee from the dead.

533   *The Restoration of Israel.*

2 Awake, awake, put on thy strength,
    Thy beautiful array ;
    The day of freedom dawns at length,
    The Lord's appointed day.

3 Rebuild thy walls, thy bounds enlarge,
    And send thy heralds forth ;
    Say to the South, " Give up thy charge,
    And keep not back, O North."

4 They come, they come : thine exiled
        bands,
    Where'er they rest or roam,
    Have heard Thy voice in distant lands,
    And hasten to their home.

5 Thus, though the universe shall burn,
    And God His works destroy,
    With songs the ransomed shall return,
    And everlasting joy.
            James Montgomery. (1771—1854.) 1825, 1853.

534   *The Spirit creating all Things new.*

1 Spirit of power and might, behold
    A world by sin destroyed ;
    Creator, Spirit, as of old,
    Move on the formless void.

2 Give Thou the word : that healing
        sound
    Shall quell the deadly strife,
    And earth again, like Eden crowned,
    Produce the tree of life.

3 If sang the morning stars for joy
    When nature rose to view,
    What strains will angel-harps employ
    When Thou shalt all renew !

4 And if the sons of God rejoice
    To hear a Saviour's name,
    How shall the ransomed raise their
        voice,
    To whom that Saviour came !

5 So every kindred, tongue, and tribe,
    Assembling round the throne,
    Thy new creation shall ascribe
    To sovereign love alone.
                    James Montgomery. 1825, 1853.

SPREAD OF THE GOSPEL.

HUMMEL. C. M. Charles Zeuner. (1795—1857.) 1832.

1. Great God, the nations of the earth
Are by creation Thine;
And in Thy works, by all beheld,
Thy radiant glories shine,

535 *The Gospel for all Nations.*
Mark xiii. 10.

2 But, Lord, Thy greater love has sent
Thy gospel to mankind,
Unveiling what rich stores of grace
Are treasured in Thy mind.

3 Lord, when shall these glad tidings
The spacious earth around, [spread
Till every tribe, and every soul,
Shall hear the joyful sound?

4 Smile, Lord, on each divine attempt
To spread the gospel's rays,
And build on sin's demolished throne
The temples of Thy praise.
Rev. Thomas Gibbons. (1720—1785.) 1769. ab. and alt.

536 *Prayer heard, and Zion restored.*
Ps. cii. 13-21.

1 Let Zion and her sons rejoice;
Behold the promised hour: [voice,
Her God hath heard her mourning
And comes t'exalt His power.

2 Her dust and ruins that remain
Are precious in our eyes;
Those ruins shall be built again,
And all that dust shall rise.

3 The Lord will raise Jerusalem,
And stand in glory there;

Nations shall bow before His name,
And kings attend with fear.

4 This shall be known when we are
And left on long record, [dead,
That ages yet unborn may read,
And trust and praise the Lord.
Rev. Isaac Watts. (1674—1748.) 1719. ab.

537 *Prayer for Home Missions.*

1 On Zion and on Lebanon,
On Carmel's blooming height,
On Sharon's fertile plains, once shone
The glory, pure and bright.

2 From thence its mild and cheering ray
Streamed forth from land to land;
And empires now behold its day;
And still its beams expand.

3 But ah, our deserts deep and wild
See not this heavenly light;
No sacred beams, no radiance mild,
Dispel their dreary night.

4 Thou, who didst lighten Zion's hill,
On Carmel who didst shine,
Our deserts let Thy glory fill,
Thy excellence divine.
Bp. Henry Ustick Onderdonk. (1789—1858.) 1826. ab.

SPREAD OF THE GOSPEL.

BEMINSTER. 7.   Bristol Collection.

1. Spread, O spread, thou might-y word, Spread the king-dom of the Lord,

Where-so-e'er His breath has given Life to be-ings meant for heaven.

538 *"Walte, walte nah und fern."*

2 Tell them how the Father's will
Made the world, and keeps it still;
How He sent His Son to save
All who help and comfort crave.

3 Tell of our Redeemer's love,
Who forever doth remove,
By His holy sacrifice,
All the guilt that on us lies.

4 Tell them of the Spirit given
Now, to guide us up to heaven,
Strong and holy, just and true,
Working both to will and do.

5 Word of life, most pure and strong,
Lo, for Thee the nations long:
Spread, till from its dreary night
All the world awakes to light.

6 Lord of harvest, let there be
Joy and strength to work for Thee:
Let the nations, far and near,
See Thy light, and learn Thy fear.

Rev. Jonathan Frederic Bahnmaier. (1774—1841.) 1823.
Tr. by Miss Catherine Winkworth. (1829—) 1858. ab.

539 *Honoring the Lord with our Substance.* 8, 7.
Prov. iii. 9.

1 With my substance I will honor
My Redeemer and my Lord;
Were ten thousand worlds my manor,
All were nothing to His word.

2 While the heralds of salvation,
His abounding grace proclaim,
Let His friends of every station
Gladly join to spread His fame.

Rev. Benjamin Francis. (1734—1799.) 1787. ab.

540 *Christ's universal Reign.*

1 Wake the song of jubilee;
Let it echo o'er the sea:
Now is come the promised hour;
Jesus reigns with glorious power.

2 All ye nations, join and sing,
Praise your Saviour, praise your King;
Let it sound from shore to shore,
"Jesus reigns for evermore!"

3 Hark, the desert lands rejoice;
And the islands join their voice:
Joy! the whole creation sings,
"Jesus is the King of kings!"

Rev. Leonard Bacon. (1802—) 1833.

THE GLORY OF THE KINGDOM.

MISSIONARY CHANT. L. M. Charles Zeuner. (1795—1857.) 1832.

1. Ye Christian heralds, go, proclaim
Salvation thro' Immanuel's name;
To distant climes the tidings bear,
And plant the Rose of Sharon there.

541 *"Go ye into all the World."*
Mark xvi. 15.

2 He'll shield you with a wall of fire,
With flaming zeal your breast inspire,
Bid raging winds their fury cease,
And hush the tempest into peace.

3 And when our labors all are o'er,
Then we shall meet to part no more,
Meet, with the blood-bought throng to fall,
And crown our Jesus Lord of all.

Mrs. Voke. 1816.

542 *The Spirit accompanying the Word.*

1 O Spirit of the living God,
In all Thy plenitude of grace,
Where'er the foot of man hath trod,
Descend on our apostate race.

2 Give tongues of fire, and hearts of love,
To preach the reconciling word;
Give power and unction from above,
Whene'er the joyful sound is heard.

3 Be darkness, at Thy coming, light,
Confusion, order in Thy path;
Souls without strength inspire with might;
Bid mercy triumph over wrath.

4 Baptize the nations; far and nigh
The triumphs of the cross record;
The name of Jesus glorify,
Till every kindred call Him Lord.

James Montgomery. (1771—1854.) 1825. ab.

543 *Light in Darkness.*
Is. ix. 2.

1 Though now the nations sit beneath
The darkness of o'erspreading death:
God will arise with light divine,
On Zion's holy towers to shine.

2 That light shall shine on distant lands,
And wandering tribes, in joyful bands,
Shall come Thy glory, Lord, to see,
And in Thy courts to worship Thee.

3 O light of Zion, now arise,
Let the glad morning bless our eyes:
Ye nations, catch the kindling ray,
And hail the splendors of the day.

Rev. Leonard Bacon. (1802—) 1845.

544 *For a Missionary Meeting.*

1 Assembled at Thy great command,
Before Thy face, dread King, we stand;
The voice that marshaled every star,
Has called Thy people from afar.

2 We meet, thro' distant lands to spread
The truth for which the martyrs bled;
Along the line, to either pole,
The thunder of Thy praise to roll.

THE GLORY OF THE KINGDOM. 243

3 Our prayers assist, accept our praise,
Our hopes revive, our courage raise,
Our counsels aid ; and, O impart
The single eye, the faithful heart.

4 Forth with Thy chosen heralds come,
Recall the wandering spirits home ;
From Zion's mount send forth the sound,
To spread the spacious earth around.

Rev. William Bengo Collyer. (1782—1854.) 1812. ab.

DUKE STREET. L. M. John Hatton. c. 1790.

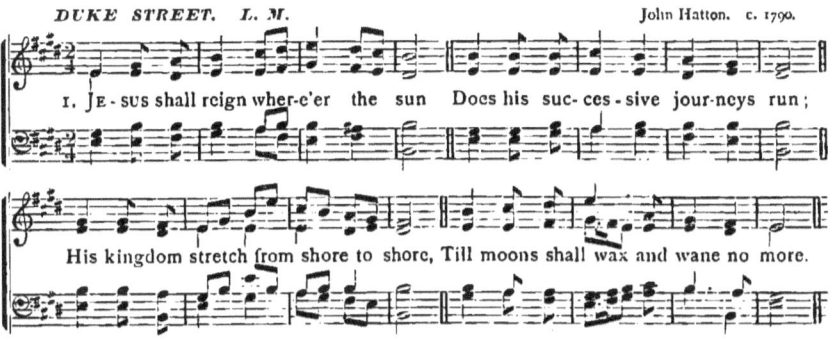

1. JE-SUS shall reign wher-e'er the sun Does his suc-ces-sive jour-neys run;
His kingdom stretch from shore to shore, Till moons shall wax and wane no more.

545 *Christ's Dominion.*
Ps. lxxii.

2 To Him shall endless prayer be made,
And praises throng to crown His head ;
His Name, like sweet perfume shall rise
With every morning sacrifice.

3 People and realms of every tongue
Dwell on His love with sweetest song ;
And infant voices shall proclaim
Their early blessings on His Name.

4 Blessings abound where'er He reigns ;
The prisoner leaps to loose his chains ;
The weary find eternal rest,
And all the sons of want are blest.

5 Where He displays His healing power,
Death and the curse are known no more ;
In Him the tribes of Adam boast
More blessings than their father lost.

6 Let every creature rise and bring
Peculiar honors to our King ;

Angels descend with songs again,
And earth repeat the loud Amen.

Rev. Isaac Watts. (1674—1748.) 1719. ab. and sl. alt.

546 *The holy City purified and guarded.*
Is. lii. 1, 2.

1 TRIUMPHANT Zion, lift thy head
From dust, and darkness, and the dead :
Tho' humbled long, awake at length,
And gird thee with thy Saviour's strength.

2 Put all thy beauteous garments on,
And let thy various charms be known :
The world thy glories shall confess,
Decked in the robes of righteousness.

3 No more shall foes unclean invade,
And fill thy hallow'd walls with dread :
No more shall hell's insulting host
Their victory and thy sorrows boast.

4 God from on high thy groans will hear ;
His hand thy ruins shall repair ;
Nor will thy watchful Monarch cease
To guard thee in eternal peace.

Rev. Philip Doddridge. (1702—1751.) 1755. ab. and sl. alt.

GO, TEACH ALL NATIONS.

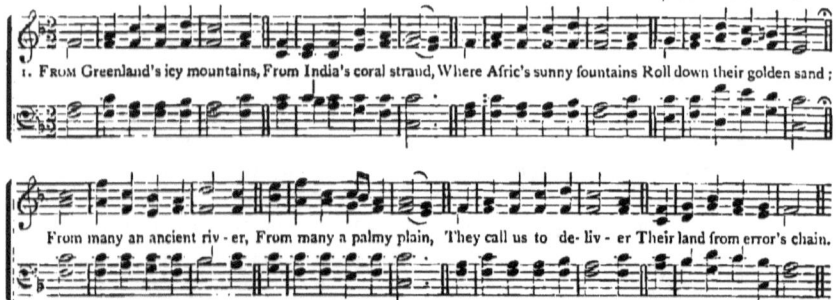

MISSIONARY HYMN. 7, 6. D.   Lowell Mason. (1792—1872.) 1823.

1. From Greenland's icy mountains, From India's coral strand, Where Afric's sunny fountains Roll down their golden sand; From many an ancient riv-er, From many a palmy plain, They call us to de-liv-er Their land from error's chain.

547   *"From Greenland's icy Mountains."*

2 What though the spicy breezes
    Blow soft o'er Ceylon's isle,
Though every prospect pleases,
    And only man is vile :
In vain with lavish kindness
    The gifts of God are strown,
The heathen in his blindness
    Bows down to wood and stone.

3 Can we, whose souls are lighted
    With wisdom from on high,
Can we to men benighted
    The lamp of life deny?
Salvation, O salvation!
    The joyful sound proclaim,
Till each remotest nation
    Has learnt Messiah's name.

4 Waft, waft, ye winds, His story,
    And you, ye waters, roll,
Till, like a sea of glory,
    It spreads from pole to pole;
Till o'er our ransomed nature,
    The Lamb for sinners slain,
Redeemer, King, Creator,
    In bliss returns to reign.
        Bp. Reginald Heber. (1783—1826.) 1819.

548   *The final Reign of Christ.*

1 When shall the voice of singing
    Flow joyfully along,
When hill and valley, ringing
    With one triumphant song,
Proclaim the contest ended,
    And Him, who once was slain,
Again to earth descended,
    In righteousness to reign?

2 Then from the craggy mountains
    The sacred shout shall fly;
And shady vales and fountains
    Shall echo the reply:
High tower and lowly dwelling
    Shall send the chorus round,
All hallelujah swelling
    In one eternal sound.
        James Edmeston. (1791—1867.) 1822. alt.

549   *"The Gospel Banner."*

1 Now be the Gospel banner
    In every land unfurled,
And be the shout, " Hosanna !"
    Re-echoed through the world :
Till every isle and nation,
    Till every tribe and tongue,
Receive the great salvation,
    And join the happy throng.

SPREAD OF THE GOSPEL. 245

Yes, Thou shalt reign forever,
O Jesus, King of kings:
Thy light, Thy love, Thy favor,
Each ransomed captive sings.

The isles for Thee are waiting,
The deserts learn Thy praise,
The hills and valleys greeting,
The song responsive raise.
Thomas Hastings. (1784—1872.) 1830. ab.

WEBB. 7, 6. D.   George James Webb. (1803—) 1830.

1. The morning light is breaking,
The darkness disappears;
The sons of earth are waking
To penitential tears:
Each breeze that sweeps the ocean
Brings tidings from afar,
Of nations in commotion,
Prepared for Zion's war.

550 *"The Morning Light is breaking."*

2 See heathen nations bending
Before the God we love,
And thousand hearts ascending,
In gratitude above;
While sinners, now confessing,
The gospel call obey,
And seek the Saviour's blessing,
A nation in a day.

3 Blest river of salvation,
Pursue thine onward way;
Flow thou to every nation,
Nor in thy riches stay:
Stay not, till all the lowly
Triumphant reach their home;
Stay not, till all the holy
Proclaim, "The Lord is come."
Rev. Samuel Francis Smith. (1808—) 1831. ab.

551 *"Hail to the Lord's Anointed!"*

1 HAIL to the Lord's Anointed,
Great David's greater Son;
Hail, in the time appointed,
His reign on earth begun!
He comes to break oppression,
To set the captive free,
To take away transgression,
And rule in equity.

2 He comes with succor speedy
To those who suffer wrong;
To help the poor and needy,
And bid the weak be strong;
To give them songs for sighing,
Their darkness turn to light,
Whose souls, condemned and dying,
Were precious in His sight.

3 For Him shall prayer unceasing
And daily vows ascend;
His kingdom still increasing,
A kingdom without end:
The tide of time shall never
His covenant remove;
His Name shall stand forever,
That Name to us is Love.
James Montgomery. (1771—1854.) 1822. ab.

246   SPREAD OF THE GOSPEL.

HERALD ANGELS. 7. D.   Felix Mendelssohn-Bartholdy. (1809—1847.) 1846.

1. Go, ye mes-sengers of God, Like the beams of morn-ing fly; Take the won-der-working rod,
Wave the ban-ner cross on high: { Where the loft-y min-a-ret
Gleams a-long the morning skies, } Wave it till the crescent set,
And the "Star of Ja-cob" rise; Wave it till the crescent set, And the "Star of Ja-cob" rise.

552   "*Go, ye Messengers of God.*"

2 Go to many a tropic isle,
   In the bosom of the deep,
Where the skies forever smile,
   And th' oppressed forever weep.
O'er the negro's night of care
   Pour the living light of heaven;
Chase away the fiend despair,
   Bid him hope to be forgiven.

3 Where the golden gates of day
   Open on the palmy East,
Wide the bleeding cross display,
   Spread the gospel's richest feast.
Bear the tidings round the ball,
   Visit every soil and sea;
Preach the cross of Christ to all,
   Christ, whose love is full and free.
           Rev. Joshua Marsden. 1812.

553   *The Victory anticipated.*
       Ps. lxxii.

1 HASTEN, Lord, the glorious time,
   When, beneath Messiah's sway,
Every nation, every clime,
   Shall the gospel call obey.
Mightiest kings His power shall own,
   Heathen tribes His name adore;
Satan and his host o'erthrown,
   Bound in chains, shall hurt no more

2 Then shall wars and tumults cease,
   Then be banished grief and pain;
Righteousness, and joy, and peace,
   Undisturbed shall ever reign.
Time shall sun and moon obscure,
   Seas be dried, and rocks be riven,
But His reign shall still endure,
   Endless as the days of Heaven.
      Miss Harriet Auber. (1773—1862.) 1829. ab.

MILLENNIAL JUBILEE. 247

BENEVENTO. 7. D. — Samuel Webbe. (1740—1816.) c. 1770.

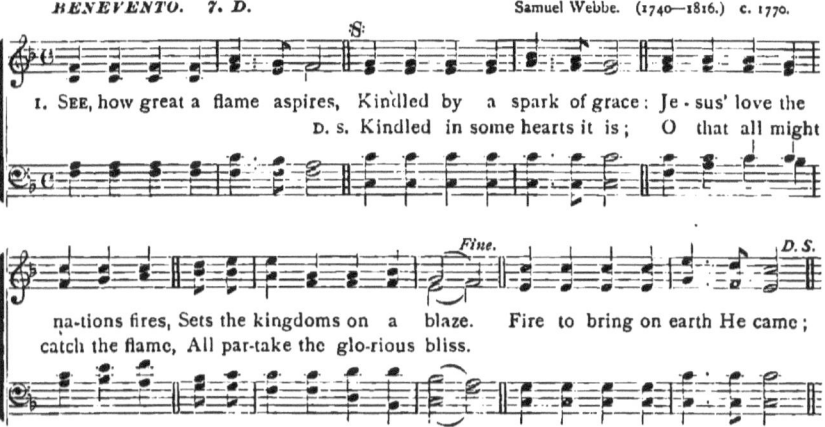

1. See, how great a flame aspires, Kindled by a spark of grace: Je-sus' love the
   D. s. Kindled in some hearts it is; O that all might
   na-tions fires, Sets the kingdoms on a blaze. Fire to bring on earth He came;
   catch the flame, All par-take the glo-rious bliss.

554 *"Jesus' Love the Nations fires."*

2 When He first the work begun,
   Small and feeble was His day;
Now the word doth swiftly run,
   Now it wins its widening way;
More and more it spreads and grows,
   Ever mighty to prevail;
Sin's strongholds it now o'erthrows,
   Shakes the trembling gates of hell.

3 Saw ye not the cloud arise,
   Little as a human hand?
Now it spreads along the skies,
   Hangs o'er all the thirsty land.
Lo, the promise of a shower,
   Drops already from above;
But the Lord shall shortly pour
   All the riches of His love.

Rev. Charles Wesley. (1708—1788.) 1749. ab. and sl. alt.

555 *"The Song of Jubilee."*

1 Hark, the song of jubilee,
   Loud as mighty thunders roar,
Or the fulness of the sea,
   When it breaks upon the shore:

Hallelujah! for the Lord
   God Omnipotent shall reign;
Hallelujah! let the word
   Echo round the earth and main.

2 Hallelujah! hark, the sound,
   From the centre to the skies,
Wakes above, beneath, around,
   All creation's harmonies.
See Jehovah's banners furled,
   Sheathed His sword: He speaks;
'tis done,
And the kingdoms of this world
   Are the kingdoms of His Son.

3 He shall reign from pole to pole
   With illimitable sway;
He shall reign, when like a scroll
   Yonder heavens have passed away.
Then the end; beneath His rod
   Man's last enemy shall fall:
Hallelujah! Christ in God,
   God in Christ, is All in all.

James Montgomery. (1771—1854.) 1819, 1825. 1717.

248 CHRISTIAN WORK.

HARK, THE VOICE. 8, 7. D.   Philip P. Van Arsdale. (1816—) 1869.

1. Hark, the voice of Jesus calling, Who will go and work to-day? Fields are white, and harvests waiting,
D. S. Who will answer, glad-ly saying,
Who will bear the sheaves away? Loud and long the Master calleth, Rich reward He offers free:
"Here am I, send me, send me?"

556   *Your Mission.*

2 If you can not cross the ocean,
   And the heathen lands explore,
   You can find the heathen nearer,
   You can help them at your door.
   If you can not give your thousands,
   You can give the widow's mite ;
   And the least you give for Jesus
   Will be precious in His sight.

3 If you can not speak like angels,
   If you can not preach like Paul,
   You can tell the love of Jesus,
   You can say He died for all ;
   If you can not rouse the wicked
   With the judgment's dread alarms,
   You can lead the little children
   To the Saviour's waiting arms.

4 While the souls of men are dying,
   And the Master calls for you,
   Let none hear you idly saying,
   "There is nothing I can do."
   Take the task He gives you gladly,
   Let His work your pleasure be ;
   Answer quickly, when He calleth,
   "Here am I, send me, send me."
         Rev. Daniel March. (1816—) 1869.

557   *"Come over and help us."* Acts xvi. 9.

1 Hark, what mean those lamentations,
   Rolling sadly through the sky?
   'Tis the cry of heathen nations,
   " Come and help us, or we die."
   Lost and helpless and desponding,
   Wrapt in error's night they lie ;
   To their cries your hearts responding,
   Haste to help them ere they die.

2 Hark, again those lamentations
   Rolling sadly through the sky;
   Louder cry the heathen nations,
   "Come and help us, or we die."
   Hear the heathen's sad complaining;
   Christians, hear their dying cry ;
   And the love of Christ constraining,
   Join to help them ere they die.
        Rev. John Cawood. (1775—1852.) 1819. alt.

558   *The Call to Service.*

1 We are living, we are dwelling,
   In a grand and awful time,
   In an age on ages telling ;
   To be living is sublime.
   Hark, the waking up of nations,
   Gog and Magog to the fray.
   Hark, what soundeth? is creation
   Groaning for its latter day?

PRAYING AND WORKING. 249

2 Worlds are charging, heaven beholding,
   Thou hast but an hour to fight ;
   Now the blazoned cross unfolding,
   On, right onward for the right !

On ! let all the soul within you
For the truth's sake go abroad.
Strike, let every nerve and sinew
Tell on ages, tell for God.
Bp. Arthur Cleveland Coxe. (1818—) 1840.

CRAWFORD. 8, 7. D.   Luther Orlando Emerson. (1820—) 1863.

1. { SAVIOUR, sprinkle many nations, Fruitful let Thy sorrows be ;
     By Thy pains and consolations, Draw the Gentiles unto Thee : }
D. C. Let them see Thee in Thy glory, And Thy mercy manifold.

Of Thy Cross the wondrous story, Be it to the nations told ;

559 "*So shall He sprinkle many Nations.*"
Is. lii. 15.

2 Far and wide, though all unknowing,
   Pants for Thee each mortal breast ;
   Human tears for Thee are flowing,
   Human hearts in Thee would rest,
   Thirsting, as for dews of even,
   As the new-mown grass for rain ;
   Thee, they seek, as God of heaven,
   Thee as Man for sinners slain.

3 Saviour, lo, the isles are waiting,
   Stretch'd the hand, and strained the sight,
   For Thy Spirit, new creating
   Love's pure flame and wisdom's light ;
   Give the word, and of the preacher
   Speed the foot, and touch the tongue,
   Till on earth by every creature
   Glory to the Lamb be sung.
   Bp. Arthur Cleveland Coxe. 1851.

560   *Sowing and Reaping.*

1 HE that goeth forth with weeping,
   Bearing precious seed in love,
   Never tiring, never sleeping,
   Findeth mercy from above :
   Soft descend the dews of heaven,
   Bright the rays celestial shine ;
   Precious fruits will thus be given,
   Through an influence all divine.

2 Sow thy seed, be never weary,
   Let no fears thy soul annoy ;
   Be the prospect ne'er so dreary,
   Thou shalt reap the fruits of joy.
   Lo, the scene of verdure brightening,
   See the rising grain appear ;
   Look again : the fields are whitening,
   For the harvest time is near.
   Thomas Hastings. (1784—1872.) 1836.

THE OLD, OLD STORY.

TELL THE STORY. 7, 6. D. William Gustavus Fischer. (1835—) 1869.

1. I LOVE to tell the sto-ry, Of un-seen things above, Of Je-sus and His glory, Of Je-sus and His love. I love to tell the sto-ry, Be-cause I know 'tis true; It sat-is-fies my longings, As nothing else can do.

CHORUS.
I love to tell the sto-ry, 'Twill be my theme in glory, To tell the old, old sto-ry Of Jesus and His love.

561 *"I love to tell the Story."*

2 I love to tell the story;
More wonderful it seems,
Than all the golden fancies
Of all our golden dreams.
I love to tell the story,
It did so much for me!
And that is just the reason
I tell it now to thee.

3 I love to tell the story;
'Tis pleasant to repeat,
What seems, each time I tell it,
More wonderfully sweet.
I love to tell the story,
For some have never heard
The message of salvation,
From God's own holy word.

4 I love to tell the story;
For those who know it best,
Seem hungering and thirsting
To hear it like the rest.

And when, in scenes of glory,
I sing the New, New Song,
'Twill be the Old, Old Story
That I have loved so long.
Miss Kate Hankey. 1865.

562 *"The Lord's Salvation."*
[Omitting the Chorus.]

1 O THAT the Lord's salvation
Were out of Zion come,
To heal His ancient nation,
To lead His outcasts home.
How long the holy City
Shall heathen feet profane?
Return, O Lord, in pity;
Rebuild her walls again.

2 Let fall Thy rod of terror,
Thy saving grace impart;
Roll back the veil of error,
Release the fettered heart.
Let Israel, home returning,
Her lost Messiah see;
Give oil of joy for mourning,
And bind Thy Church to Thee.
Rev. Henry Francis Lyte. (1793—1847.) 1834.

THE OLD, OLD STORY.

563 *"The blood-red Banner."*
[Omitting the Chorus.]

1 UPLIFT the blood-red banner,
  And shout, with trumpet's sound,
Deliverance to the captive,
  And freedom to the bound;
Earth's jubilee of glory,
  The year of full release:
O tell the wondrous story,
  Go forth and publish peace.

2 Go forth, Confessors, Martyrs,
  With zeal and love unpriced,
And preach the blood of sprinkling,
  And live, or die, for Christ;
For Christ claim every nation,
  Your banner wide unfurled;
Go forth and preach salvation,
  Salvation for the world.
          Benjamin Gough. (1805—) 1865. ab.

THE OLD, OLD STORY. 7, 6. D.   William Howard Doane. (1832—) 1869.

1. Tell me the old, old sto-ry Of unseen things a-bove, Of Je-sus and His glo-ry, Of
   D. S. For I am weak and wea-ry, And
Je-sus and His love. Tell me the sto-ry sim-ply, As to a lit-tle child, Tell me the old, old
help-less and de-filed.
sto-ry, Tell me the old, old sto-ry, Tell me the old, old sto-ry Of Je-sus and His love.

564 *"Tell me the old, old Story."*

2 Tell me the story slowly,
    That I may take it in—
  That wonderful redemption,
    God's remedy for sin.
  Tell me the story often,
    For I forget so soon!
  The "early dew" of morning
    Has passed away at noon.

3 Tell me the story softly,
    With earnest tones, and grave;
  Remember, I'm the sinner
    Whom Jesus came to save.

  Tell me that story always,
    If you would really be,
  In any time of trouble,
    A comforter to me.

4 Tell me the same old story,
    When you have cause to fear
  That this world's empty glory
    Is costing me too dear.
  Yes, and when that world's glory
    Is drawing on my soul,
  Tell me the old, old story:
    "Christ Jesus makes thee whole."
          Miss Kate Hankey. 1865.

CHRISTIAN WORKING.

LOUVAN. L. M. — Virgil Corydon Taylor. (1817–) 1847.

1. My gracious Lord, I own Thy right
To ev-ery ser-vice I can pay,
And call it my su-preme de-light
To hear Thy dic-tates and o-bey.

565 *Serving Christ.*
Phil. i. 22.

2 I would not breathe for worldly joy,
  Or to increase my worldly good;
  Nor future days nor powers employ
  To spread a sounding name abroad.

3 'Tis to my Saviour I would live,
  To Him who for my ransom died;
  Nor could the bowers of Eden give
  Such bliss as blossoms at His side.

4 His work my hoary age shall bless,
  When youthful vigor is no more;
  And my last hour of life confess
  His dying love, His saving power.
Rev. Philip Doddridge. (1702—1751.) 1755. ab. and alt.

566 *For Grace to surrender all.*

1 Jesus, our best belovéd Friend,
  Draw out our souls in pure desire;
  Jesus, in love to us descend,
  Baptize us with Thy Spirit's fire.

2 Our souls and bodies we resign,
  To fear and follow Thy commands;
  O take our hearts, our hearts are Thine,
  Accept the service of our hands.

3 Firm, faithful, watching unto prayer,
  May we Thy blesséd will obey;

Toil in Thy vineyard here, and bear
The heat and burden of the day.
James Montgomery. (1771—1854.) 1825. ab.

567 *The useful Life.*

1 Go, labor on; spend and be spent,
  Thy joy to do the Father's will:
  It is the way the Master went;
  Should not the servant tread it still?

2 Go, labor on; 'tis not for naught;
  Thine earthly loss is heavenly gain:
  Men heed thee, love thee, praise thee not;
  The Master praises,—what are men?

3 Go, labor on; enough, while here,
  If He shall praise thee, if He deign
  Thy willing heart to mark and cheer:
  No toil for Him shall be in vain.

4 Toil on, and in thy toil rejoice;
  For toil comes rest, for exile home;
  Soon shalt thou hear the Bridegroom's voice,
  The midnight peal: "Behold, I come!"
Rev. Horatius Bonar. (1808—) 1857. ab.

568 *Adorning the Doctrine.*
Titus ii. 10-13.

1 So let our lips and lives express
  The holy Gospel we profess;
  So let our works and virtues shine,
  To prove the doctrine all divine.

2 Thus shall we best proclaim abroad
    The honors of our Saviour God ;
    When His salvation reigns within,
    And grace subdues the power of sin.
3 Our flesh and sense must be denied,
    Passion and envy, lust and pride ;
    While justice, temperance, truth and
    Our inward piety approve.   [love,
4 Religion bears our spirits up,
    While we expect that blessèd hope,
    The bright appearance of the Lord,
    And faith stands leaning on His word.
          Rev. Isaac Watts. (1674—1748.) 1709. sl. alt.

569   *Grief for the Sins of Men.*
              Ps. cxix. 136, 158.

1 ARISE, my tenderest thoughts, arise ;
    To torrents melt, my streaming eyes ;
    And thou, my heart, with anguish feel
    Those evils which thou canst not heal.
2 See human nature sunk in shame ;
    See scandals poured on Jesus' name ;
    The Father wounded thro' the Son ;
    The world abused, the soul undone.
3 My God, I feel the mournful scene ;
    My spirit yearns o'er dying men ;
    And fain my pity would reclaim
    And snatch the firebrands from the
                                        flame.
4 But feeble my compassion proves,
    And can but weep where most it loves ;
    Thy own all-saving arm employ,
    And turn these drops of grief to joy.
          Rev. Philip Doddridge. 1755. ab. and alt.

570   *The Vision of dry Bones.*
              Ezek. xxxvii. 3.

1 LOOK down, O Lord, with pitying eye :
    See Adam's race in ruin lie ;
    Sin spreads its trophies o'er the ground,
    And scatters slaughtered heaps around.
2 And can these mouldering corpses live ?
    And can these perished bones revive ?
    That, mighty God, to Thee is known ;
    That wondrous work is all Thine own.

3 Thy ministers are sent in vain
    To prophesy upon the slain ;
    In vain they call, in vain they cry,
    Till Thine almighty aid is nigh.
4 But if Thy Spirit deign to breathe,
    Life spreads through all the realms of
                                        death :
    Dry bones obey Thy powerful voice ;
    They move, they waken, they rejoice.
5 So when Thy trumpet's awful sound
    Shall shake the heavens and rend the
                                        ground,
    Dead saints shall from their tombs arise,
    And spring to life beyond the skies.
          Rev. Philip Doddridge. 1755.

571   *"Come, Sacred Spirit !"*
              Ezek. xxxvi. 37.

1 COME, Sacred Spirit, from above,
    And fill the coldest heart with love ;
    Soften to flesh the rugged stone,
    And let Thy god-like power be known.
2 Speak Thou, and, from the haughtiest
                                        eyes,
    Shall floods of pious sorrow rise ;
    While all their glowing souls are borne
    To seek that grace, which now they
                                        scorn.
3 O let a holy flock await,
    Numerous around Thy temple-gate,
    Each pressing on with zeal to be
    A living sacrifice to Thee.
          Rev. Philip Doddridge. 1755. ab.

572   *Hoping for a Revival.*

1 WHILE I to grief my soul gave way,
    To see the work of God decline,
    Methought I heard the Saviour say,
    " Dismiss thy fears, the ark is Mine.
2 Though for a time I hide My face,
    Rely upon My love and power ;
    Still wrestle at a throne of grace,
    And wait for a reviving hour."
          Rev. John Newton. (1725—1807.) 1779. ab.

254. REVIVAL PRAYED FOR.

MIDDLETON. 8, 7. D. English Melody.

1. Sav-iour, vis-it Thy plan-ta-tion, Grant us, Lord, a gra-cious rain;
   All will come to des-o-la-tion, Un-less Thou re-turn a-gain.
   D. C. Lest, for want of Thine as-sist-ance, Ev-ery plant should droop and die.

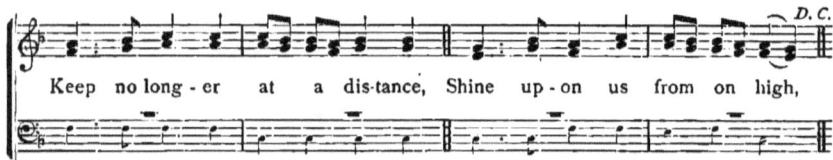

Keep no long-er at a dis-tance, Shine up-on us from on high,

---

573 *Prayer for Rain.*

2 Once, O Lord, Thy garden flourished;
  Every part looked gay and green;
  Then Thy word our spirits nourished:
  Happy seasons we have seen.
  But a drought has since succeeded,
  And a sad decline we see:
  Lord, Thy help is greatly needed,
  Help can only come from Thee.

3 Let our mutual love be fervent;
  Make us prevalent in prayer;
  Let each one esteemed Thy servant
  Shun the world's bewitching snare.
  Break the tempter's fatal power,
  Turn the stony heart to flesh,
  And begin from this good hour
  To revive Thy work afresh.
  Rev. John Newton. (1725–1807.) 1779. ab. and alt.

574 *Prayer for Light.*

1 LIGHT of those whose dreary dwelling
  Borders on the shades of death,
  Come, and by Thy love's revealing
  Dissipate the clouds beneath:
  The new heaven and earth's Creator,
  In our deepest darkness rise,
  Scattering all the night of nature,
  Pouring eye-sight on our eyes.

2 Still we wait for Thine appearing;
  Life and joy Thy beams impart,
  Chasing all our fears, and cheering
  Every poor benighted heart:
  Come, and manifest the favor
  God hath for our ransomed race;
  Come, Thou glorious God and Saviour,
  Come, and bring the gospel-grace.

3 Save us in Thy great compassion,
  O thou mild, pacific Prince,
  Give the knowledge of salvation,
  Give the pardon of our sins;
  By Thine all-restoring merit,
  Every burdened soul release,
  Every weary, wandering spirit
  Guide into Thy perfect peace.
  Rev. Charles Wesley. (1708–1788.) 1745

ALERTNESS AND DILIGENCE.

ST. MICHAEL. S. M.   Arr. from John Day's Psalter. 1562.

1. Ye servants of the Lord, Each in his office wait,

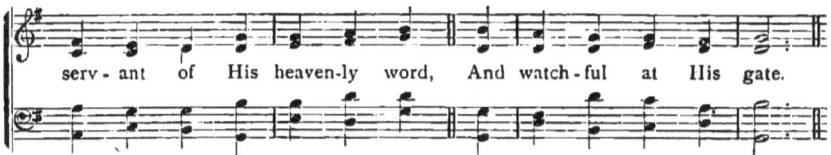

servant of His heavenly word, And watchful at His gate.

575   *The watchful Servant.*
Luke xii. 35-38.

2 Let all your lamps be bright,
   And trim the golden flame;
Gird up your loins as in His sight,
   For awful is His name.

3 Watch! 'tis your Lord's command;
   And while we speak, He's near:
Mark the first signal of His hand,
   And ready all appear.

4 O happy servant he,
   In such a posture found!
He shall his Lord with rapture see,
   And be with honor crowned.

5 Christ shall the banquet spread
   With His own royal hand,
And raise that faithful servant's head
   Amid the angelic band.
   Rev. Philip Doddridge. (1702—1751.) 1755. sl. alt.

576   *Sowing beside all Waters.*
Is. xxxii. 20.

1 Sow in the morn thy seed,
   At eve hold not thy hand;
To doubt and fear give thou no heed,
   Broadcast it o'er the land.

2 Beside all waters sow,
   The highway furrows stock,
Drop it where thorns and thistles grow,
   Scatter it on the rock.

3 The good, the fruitful ground
   Expect not here nor there;
O'er hill and dale alike 'tis found;
   Go forth, then, everywhere.

4 And duly shall appear,
   In verdure, beauty, strength,
The tender blade, the stalk, the ear,
   And the full corn at length.

5 Thou canst not toil in vain;
   Cold, heat, the moist and dry,
Shall foster and mature the grain
   For garners in the sky.

6 Then, when the glorious end,
   The day of God shall come,
The angel-reapers shall descend,
   And heaven sing, "Harvest home!"
   James Montgomery. (1771—1854.) 1825. ab.

CHRIST FOR THE WORLD.

OLIVET. 6, 4.   Lowell Mason. (1792—1872.) 1830.

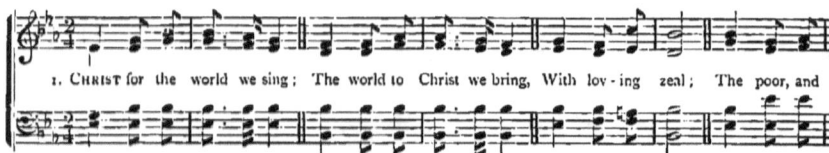

1. Christ for the world we sing; The world to Christ we bring, With lov-ing zeal; The poor, and

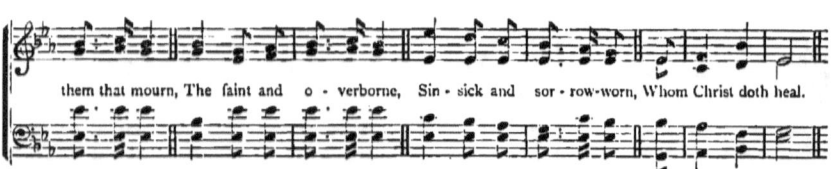

them that mourn, The faint and o-verborne, Sin-sick and sor-row-worn, Whom Christ doth heal.

577   *"Christ for the World."*

2 Christ for the world we sing;
   The world to Christ we bring,
     With fervent prayer:
   The wayward and the lost,
   By restless passion tossed,
   Redeemed, at countless cost,
     From dark despair.

3 Christ for the world we sing;
   The world to Christ we bring,
     With one accord;
   With us the work to share,
   With us reproach to dare,
   With us the cross to bear,
     For Christ our Lord.

4 Christ for the world we sing;
   The world to Christ we bring,
     With joyful song;
   The new-born souls, whose days,
   Reclaimed from error's ways,
   Inspired with hope and praise,
     To Christ belong.

           Rev. Samuel Wolcott. (1813—) 1869.

578   *"Speed on Thy Word."*

1 Lord of all power and might,
   Father of love and light,
     Speed on Thy word:
   O let the Gospel sound
   All the wide world around,
   Wherever man is found:
     God speed His word.

2 Hail, blessèd Jubilee:
   Thine, Lord, the glory be;
     Hallelujah!
   Thine was the mighty plan,
   From Thee the work began;
   Away with praise of man,
     Glory to God!

3 Onward shall be our course,
   Despite of fraud or force;
     God is before:
   His word ere long shall run
   Free as the noon-day sun;
   His purpose must be done:
     God bless His word.

     Rev. Hugh Stowell. (1799—1865.) 1854 ab. and sl. alt.

LET THERE BE LIGHT. 257

ITALIAN HYMN. 6, 4. Felice Giardini. (1716—1796.) 1760.

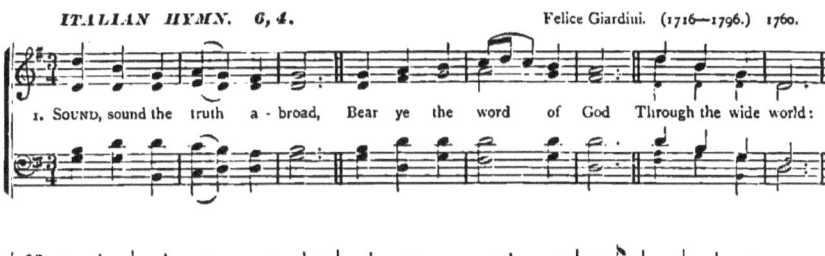

1. Sound, sound the truth abroad, Bear ye the word of God Through the wide world:

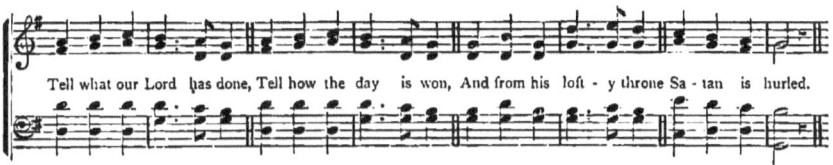

Tell what our Lord has done, Tell how the day is won, And from his loft-y throne Satan is hurled.

579 *Called to Missionary Work.*
Is. lviii. 1.

2 Far over sea and land,
'Tis our Lord's own command,
  Bear ye His name;
Bear it to every shore,
Regions unknown explore,
  Enter at every door;
    Silence is shame.

3 Speed on the wings of love,
Jesus, who reigns above,
  Bids us to fly;
They who His message bear
Should neither doubt nor fear,
He will their Friend appear,
    He will be nigh.
Rev. Thomas Kelly. (1769—1855.) 1820. ab.

580 *"Let there be Light!"*
Gen. i. 3. 2 Cor. iv. 6.

1 Thou, whose almighty Word
Chaos and darkness heard,
  And took their flight;
Hear us, we humbly pray,
And where the Gospel's day
Sheds not its glorious ray,
  "Let there be light!"

2 Thou, who didst come to bring
On Thy redeeming wing
  Healing and sight,
Health to the sick in mind,
Sight to the inly blind,
O, now to all mankind
  "Let there be light!"

3 Spirit of truth and love,
Life-giving, holy Dove,
  Speed forth Thy flight:
Move o'er the water's face,
Bearing the lamp of grace,
And in earth's darkest place
  "Let there be light!"

4 Blessèd and Holy Three,
Glorious Trinity,
  Wisdom, Love, Might;
Boundless as ocean's tide,
Rolling in fullest pride,
Through the world, far and wide,
  "Let there be light!"
Rev. John Marriott. (1780—1825.) 1813.

MARCHING ON

FAITHFUL. C. M. Samuel Parkman Tuckerman, (1818—) 1848.

1. Through sorrow's night and dan-ger's path, A - mid the deepening gloom,

We, soldiers of an in - jured King, Are marching to the tomb.

581 *"Marching to the Tomb."*

2 There, when the turmoil is no more,
    And all our powers decay,
    Our cold remains in solitude
    Shall sleep the years away.

3 Our labors done, securely laid
    In this our last retreat,
    Unheeded, o'er our silent dust
    The storms of life shall beat.

4 Yet not thus lifeless, thus inane,
    The vital spark shall lie ;
    For o'er life's wreck that spark shall rise
    To seek its kindred sky.

5 These ashes too, this little dust,
    Our Father's care shall keep,
    Till the last angel rise and break
    The long and dreary sleep.

6 Then love's soft dew o'er every eye
    Shall shed its mildest rays,

And the long-silent dust shall burst
    With shouts of endless praise.
        Henry Kirke White. (1785—1806.) 1806.

582 *The March to Canaan.*

1 Forth to the Land of Promise bound,
    Our desert path we tread ;
    God's fiery pillar for our guide,
    His Captain at our head.

2 E'en now we faintly trace the hills,
    And catch their distant blue ;
    And the bright city's gleaming spires
    Rise dimly on our view.

3 Soon, when the desert shall be crossed,
    The flood of death passed o'er,
    Our pilgrim hosts shall safely land
    On Canaan's peaceful shore.

4 There love shall have its perfect work,
    And prayer be lost in praise ;
    And all the servants of our God
    Their endless anthems raise.
        Rev. Henry Alford. (1810—1871.) 1828.

HEAVEN IN SIGHT.

AVON. (MARTYRDOM.) C. M.   Hugh Wilson. 1768.

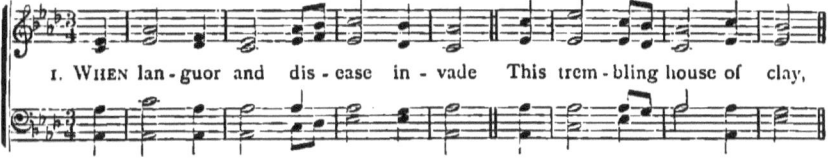

1. WHEN languor and disease invade This trembling house of clay,

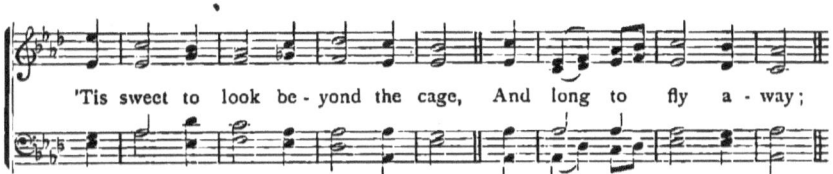

'Tis sweet to look beyond the cage, And long to fly away;

583   *In Sickness.*

2 Sweet to look inward, and attend
The whispers of His love;
Sweet to look upward to the place
Where Jesus pleads above;

3 Sweet to look back, and see my name
In life's fair book set down;
Sweet to look forward, and behold
Eternal joys my own;

4 Sweet on His faithfulness to rest,
Whose love can never end;
Sweet on His covenant of grace
For all things to depend;

5 Sweet, in the confidence of faith,
To trust His firm decrees;
Sweet to lie passive in His hands,
And know no will but His;

6 Sweet to rejoice in lively hope,
That, when my change shall come,
Angels will hover round my bed,
And waft my spirit home.

Rev. Augustus Montague Toplady. (1740—1778.) 1776. ab.

584   *Dying Hymn.*

1 EARTH, with its dark and dreadful ills,
Recedes and fades away:
Lift up your heads, ye heavenly hills.
Ye gates of death, give way.

2 My soul is full of whispered song,
My blindness is my sight;
The shadows that I feared so long
Are all alive with light.

3 The while my pulses faintly beat,
My faith doth so abound,
I feel grow firm beneath my feet
The green, immortal ground.

4 That faith to me a courage gives,
Low as the grave to go:
I know that my Redeemer lives,
That I shall live, I know.

5 The palace walls I almost see,
Where dwells my Lord and King:
O grave, where is thy victory,
O death, where is thy sting!

Miss Alice Cary. (1820—1871.) 1870.

SLEEPING IN JESUS.

REST. L. M. William Batchelder Bradbury. (1816—1868.) 1843.

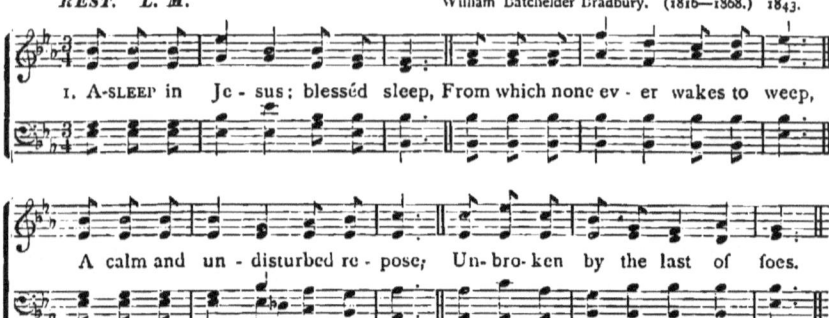

1. A-sleep in Je - sus: blessèd sleep, From which none ev - er wakes to weep,
A calm and un - disturbed re - pose; Un- bro- ken by the last of foes.

585 *"Asleep in Jesus."*

2 Asleep in Jesus: O how sweet
To be for such a slumber meet;
With holy confidence to sing,
That death hath lost his venomed sting.

3 Asleep in Jesus: peaceful rest,
Whose waking is supremely blest;
No fear, no woe, shall dim that hour
That manifests the Saviour's power.

4 Asleep in Jesus: O for me
May such a blissful refuge be;
Securely shall my ashes lie,
Waiting the summons from on high.

5 Asleep in Jesus: far from thee
Thy kindred and their graves may be;
But thine is still a blessèd sleep,
From which none ever wakes to weep.

Mrs. Margaret Mackay. 1832. ab.

586 *The Death of the Righteous.*
Num. xxiii. 10.

1 How blest the righteous, when he dies,
When sinks a weary soul to rest:
How mildly beam the closing eyes,
How gently heaves th' expiring breast.

2 So fades a summer cloud away;
So sinks the gale, when storms are o'er;
So gently shuts the eye of day;
So dies a wave along the shore.

3 A holy quiet reigns around,
A calm which life nor death destroys;
And naught disturbs that peace profound,
Which his unfettered soul enjoys.

4 Farewell, conflicting hopes and fears,
Where lights and shades alternate dwell:
How bright th' unchanging morn appears,
Farewell, inconstant world, farewell.

5 Life's labor done, as sinks the clay,
Light from its load the spirit flies;
While heaven and earth combine to say,
"How blest the righteous when he dies!"

Mrs. Anna Lætitia Barbauld. (1743—1825.) 1773. ab. and alt.

587 *At the Interment of a Body.*

1 Unveil thy bosom, faithful tomb;
Take this new treasure to thy trust,
And give these sacred relics room
To seek a slumber in the dust.

2 Nor pain, nor grief, nor anxious fear
Invade thy bounds. No mortal woes
Can reach the peaceful sleeper here,
While angels watch the soft repose.

DYING IN THE LORD. 261

3 So Jesus slept: God's dying Son
Pass'd thro' the grave, and blest the bed:
Rest here, blest saint, till from His throne
The morning break, and pierce the shade.

4 Break from His throne, illustrious morn;
Attend, O earth, His sovereign word;
Restore thy trust: a glorious form
Shall then ascend to meet the Lord.
Rev. Isaac Watts. (1674—1748.) 1734. alt.

ROSEDALE. L. M. George Frederick Root. (1820—) 1843.

1. Why should we start and fear to die? What timorous worms we mortals are:
Death is the gate of endless joy, And yet we dread to enter there.

588 *Christ's Presence makes Death easy.*
2 The pains, the groans, and dying strife
Fright our approaching souls away;
Still we shrink back again to life,
Fond of our prison and our clay.

3 O if my Lord would come and meet,
My soul should stretch her wings in haste,
Fly fearless through death's iron gate,
Nor feel the terrors as she passed.

4 Jesus can make a dying bed
Feel soft as downy pillows are,
While on His breast I lean my head,
And breathe my life out sweetly there.
Rev. Isaac Watts. 1709.

589 *Dying in the Lord.*
1 THE hour of my departure's come;
I hear the voice that calls me home:
At last, O Lord, let trouble cease,
And let Thy servant die in peace.

2 The race appointed I have run,
The combat's o'er, the prize is won,
And now my witness is on high,
And now my record's in the sky.

3 Not in mine innocence I trust;
I bow before Thee in the dust;
And through my Saviour's blood alone
I look for mercy at Thy throne.

4 I leave the world without a tear,
Save for the friends I held so dear;
To heal their sorrows, Lord, descend,
And to the friendless prove a Friend.

5 I come, I come, at Thy command,
I give my spirit to Thy hand;
Stretch forth Thine everlasting arms,
And shield me in the last alarms.

6 The hour of my departure's come;
I hear the voice that calls me home:
Now, O my God, let trouble cease;
Now let Thy servant die in peace.
Michael Bruce. (1746—1767.) 1781.

LIVING AND DYING.

MAGDALENE. 6, 5. Rev. John Bacchus Dykes. 1861.

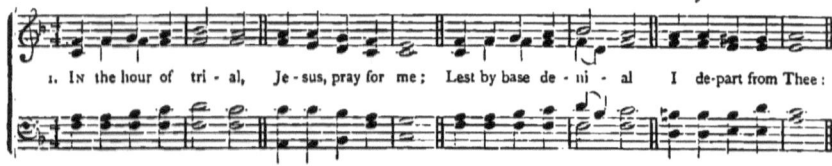

1. In the hour of tri - al, Je - sus, pray for me; Lest by base de - ni - al I de-part from Thee:

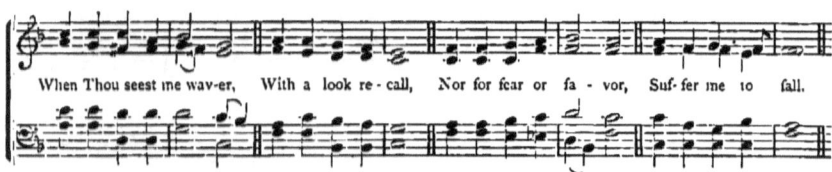

When Thou seest me wav-er, With a look re - call, Nor for fear or fa - vor, Suf- fer me to fall.

590 *The Hour of Trial.*

2 If with sore affliction
  Thou in love chastise,
  Pour Thy benediction
  On the sacrifice:
  Then, upon Thine altar
  Freely offered up,
  Though the flesh may falter,
  Faith shall drain the cup.

3 When in dust and ashes
  To the grave I sink,
  While heaven's glory flashes
  O'er the shelving brink,
  On Thy truth relying
  Through that mortal strife,
  Lord, receive me, dying,
  To eternal life.
  James Montgomery. (1771—1854.) 1853. ab.

591 *House set in Order.*

1 SET thy house in order,
  Thou shalt die, not live;
  May the voice to each one
  Solemn warning give:
  Pilgrims here and strangers,
  Weak and frail alike,
  Who can tell among us
  Where the blow may strike?

2 Set thy house in order,
  All its bulwarks tell;
  Try the ground beneath thee,
  Stir and delve it well:
  Soon shall break the tempest;
  Would'st thou bide the shock?
  Hearer be and doer,
  Founded on the rock.

3 Set thy house in order,
  Gather up thy stores,
  Every weapon brighten
  For thy Captain's wars
  Sort out all thy treasures,
  Earthly dross remove;
  Three alone are lasting,
  Faith, and hope, and love.
  Rev. Henry Alford. (1810—1871.) 1865. ab.

LIVING AND DYING. 263

592 *Journeying on.*

1 BRIGHTER still and brighter
  Glows the western sun,
  Shedding all its gladness
  O'er our work that's done.
  Time will soon be over,
  Toil and sorrow past,
  May we, blessèd Saviour,
  Find a rest at last.

2 Onward, ever onward,
  Journeying o'er the road
  Worn by saints before us,
  Journeying on to God;

Leaving all behind us,
May we hasten on,
Backward never looking
Till the prize is won.

3 Bliss, all bliss excelling,
  When the ransomed soul,
  Earthly toils forgetting,
  Finds its promised goal;
  Where in joys unheard of
  Saints with angels sing,
  Never weary raising
  Praises to their King.

  Rev. Godfrey Thring. (1823—) 1854. ab.

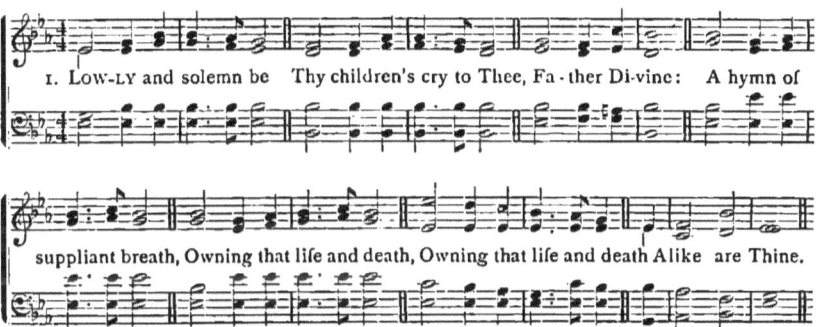

OLIVET. 6, 4. Lowell Mason. (1792—1872.) 1831.

1. Low-ly and solemn be Thy children's cry to Thee, Fa-ther Di-vine: A hymn of suppliant breath, Owning that life and death, Owning that life and death Alike are Thine.

593 *A Funeral Hymn.*

2 O Father, in that hour,
  When earth all succoring power
    Shall disavow;
  When spear, and shield, and crown,
  In faintness are cast down;
    Sustain us, Thou.

3 By Him who bowed to take
  The death-cup for our sake,
    The thorn, the rod;

From whom the last dismay
  Was not to pass away;
    Aid us, O God.

4 Tremblers beside the grave,
  We call on Thee to save,
    Father divine:
  Hear, hear our suppliant breath;
  Keep us in life and death,
    Thine, only Thine.

  Mrs. Felicia Dorothea Hemans. (1794—1835.) 1832. ab.

MOURNING IN HOPE.

CHINA. C. M. — Timothy Swan. (1758—1842.) 1800.

1. Why do we mourn departing friends, Or shake at death's alarms?
'Tis but the voice that Jesus sends, To call them to His arms.

594 *The Death and Burial of a Saint.*

2 Are we not tending upward, too,
   As fast as time can move?
Nor would we wish the hours more slow,
   To keep us from our love.

3 Why should we tremble to convey
   Their bodies to the tomb?
There the dear flesh of Jesus lay,
   And left a long perfume.

4 The graves of all His saints He blest,
   And softened every bed;
Where should the dying members rest
   But with the dying Head?

5 Thence He arose, ascending high,
   And showed our feet the way;
Up to the Lord our flesh shall fly,
   At the great rising-day.

6 Then let the last loud trumpet sound,
   And bid our kindred rise;
Awake, ye nations under ground;
   Ye saints, ascend the skies.

   Rev. Isaac Watts. (1674—1748.) 1709.

595 *Why should we weep?*

1 Why should our tears in sorrow flow,
   When God recalls His own,
And bids them leave a world of woe
   For an immortal crown?

2 Is not e'en death a gain to those
   Whose life to God was given?
Gladly to earth their eyes they close,
   To open them in heaven.

   Rev. John Rippon. (1751—1836.) 1787. ab.

596 *The Blessedness of dying Saints.*
Rev. xiv. 13.

1 Hear what the voice from heaven proclaims
   For all the pious dead;
Sweet is the savour of their names,
   And soft their sleeping bed.

2 They die in Jesus, and are blest;
   How kind their slumbers are:
From sufferings and from sins released,
   And freed from every snare.

3 Far from this world of toil and strife,
   They're present with the Lord;
The labors of their mortal life
   End in a large reward.

   Rev. Isaac Watts. 1709.

CONSOLATION. 265

597 *Death of an Infant.*

1 WITH joy I see a thousand charms
  Spread o'er the Saviour's face;
  While infants in His tender arms
  Receive His smiling grace.

2 "I take these little lambs," said He,
  "And lay them in my breast;
  Protection they shall find in Me,
  In Me be ever blest."

3 "Death may the bands of life unloose.
  But can't dissolve My love;
  Millions of infant souls compose
  The family above."

4 His words, ye happy parents, hear,
  And shout, with joys divine,
  "Dear Saviour, all we have and are
  Shall be forever Thine."

Rev. Philip Doddridge. (1702—1751.) 1755. ab.

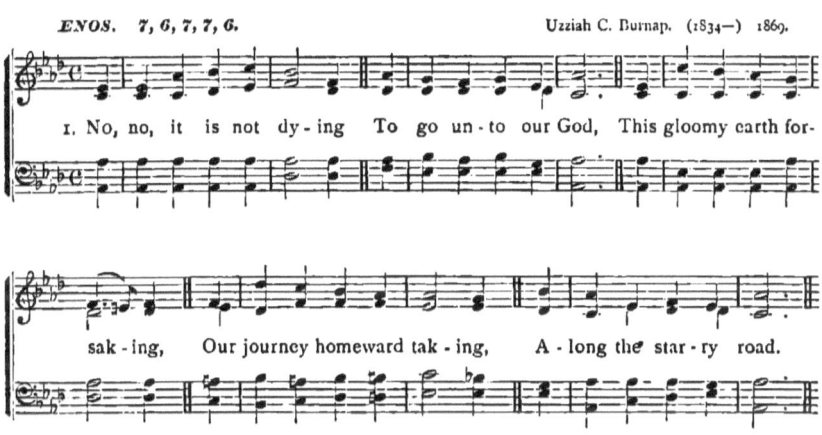

ENOS. 7, 6, 7, 7, 6.   Uzziah C. Burnap. (1834—) 1869.

1. No, no, it is not dy-ing To go un-to our God, This gloomy earth for-sak-ing, Our journey homeward tak-ing, A-long the star-ry road.

598 *"Non, ce n'est pas mourir."*

2 No, no, it is not dying
  To hear this gracious word,
  "Receive a Father's blessing,
  For evermore possessing
  The favor of Thy Lord."

3 No, no, it is not dying
  The Shepherd's voice to know;
  His sheep He ever leadeth,
  His peaceful flock He feedeth,
  Where living pastures grow.

4 No, no, it is not dying
  To wear a lordly crown;
  Among God's people dwelling,
  The glorious triumph swelling
  Of Him whose sway we own.

5 O no, this is not dying,
  Thou Saviour of mankind:
  There, streams of love are flowing,
  No hindrance ever knowing;
  Here, drops alone we find.

Rev. Cæsar Henri Abraham Malan. (1787—1864.) 1841.
Tr. by Prof. Robinson Potter Dunn. (1825—1867.) 1852.

DEATH ABOLISHED.

599 *"For ever with the Lord."*

2 Here in the body pent,
 Absent from Him I roam,
Yet nightly pitch my moving tent
 A day's march nearer home.

3 My Father's house on high,
 Home of my soul, how near,
At times, to faith's foreseeing eye,
 Thy golden gates appear.

4 Ah, then my spirit faints
 To reach the land I love,
The bright inheritance of saints,
 Jerusalem above.

5 " Forever with the Lord ;"
 Father, if 'tis Thy will,
The promise of that faithful word
 E'en here to me fulfil.
  James Montgomery. (1771—1854.) 1835. ab.

600 *"The Death of the Righteous."*

1 O for the death of those
 Who slumber in the Lord :
O be like theirs my last repose,
 Like theirs my last reward.

2 Their bodies in the ground,
 In silent hope, may lie,

Till the last trumpet's joyful sound
 Shall call them to the sky.

3 Their ransomed spirits soar,
 On wings of faith and love,
To meet the Saviour they adore,
 And reign with Him above.

4 With us their names shall live
 Through long-succeeding years,
Embalmed with all our hearts can give,
 Our praises and our tears.
  Rev. Samuel Francis Smith. (1808—) 1831.

601 *Resting in Hope.*

1 Rest for the toiling hand,
 Rest for the anxious brow,
Rest for the weary, way-sore feet,
 Rest from all labor now.

2 Rest for the fevered brain,
 Rest for the throbbing eye ;
Thro'these parched lips of thine no more
 Shall pass the moan or sigh.

3 Soon shall the trump of God
 Give out the welcome sound,
That shakes thy silent chamber-walls,
 And breaks the turf-sealed ground.

BETTER TO BE WITH CHRIST. 267

4 Ye dwellers in the dust,
   Awake, come forth and sing;
   Sharp has your frost of winter been,
   But bright shall be your spring.

5 'Twas sown in weakness here,
   'Twill then be raised in power:
   That which was sown an earthly seed,
   Shall rise a heavenly flower.
   Rev. Horatius Bonar. (1808–) 1857. ab.

GREENWOOD. S. M.   Joseph E. Sweetser. (1825–) 1849.

1. Far from my heaven-ly home, Far from my Fa-ther's breast,
Fainting I cry, "Blest Spir-it, come, And speed me to my rest."

602   *Far from Home.*
         Ps. cxxxvii.

2 Upon the willows long
   My harp has silent hung:
   How should I sing a cheerful song
   Till Thou inspire my tongue?

3 My spirit homeward turns,
   And fain would thither flee;
   My heart, O Zion, droops and yearns,
   When I remember thee.

4 To thee, to thee I press,
   A dark and toilsome road:
   When shall I pass the wilderness
   And reach the saint's abode?

5 God of my life, be near:
   On Thee my hopes I cast;
   O guide me through the desert here,
   And bring me home at last.
   Rev. Henry Francis Lyte. (1793—1847.) 1834.

603   *"Non, ce n'est pas mourir."*

1 It is not death to die,
   To leave this weary road,
   And, 'midst the brotherhood on high,
   To be at home with God.

2 It is not death to close
   The eye long dimmed by tears,
   And wake in glorious repose,
   To spend eternal years.

3 It is not death to bear
   The wrench that sets us free
   From dungeon-chain, to breathe the air
   Of boundless liberty.

4 It is not death to fling
   Aside this sinful dust,
   And rise, on strong exulting wing,
   To live among the just.

5 Jesus, Thou Prince of Life,
   Thy chosen cannot die;
   Like Thee, they conquer in the strife,
   To reign with Thee on high.
   Rev. Cæsar Henri Abraham Malan. (1787—1864.) 1841.
   Tr. by Rev. George Washington Bethune. (1805—1862.) 1847.

THE LORD COMETH.

PEARSALL. 7, 6. D. Katholisches Gesangbuch.

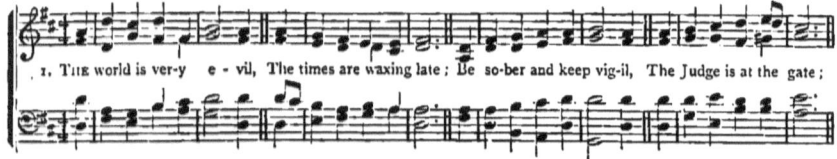

1. The world is ver-y e-vil, The times are waxing late; Be so-ber and keep vig-il, The Judge is at the gate;

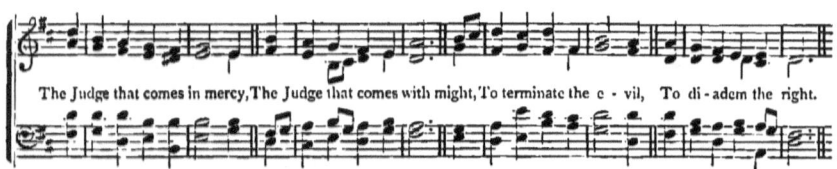

The Judge that comes in mercy, The Judge that comes with might, To terminate the e-vil, To di-adem the right.

604 *"Hora novissima."*

2 Arise, arise, good Christian,
   Let right to wrong succeed;
   Let penitential sorrow
     To heavenly gladness lead;
   To light that hath no evening,
     That knows no moon nor sun,
   The light so new and golden,
     The light that is but one.

3 O Home of fadeless splendor,
   Of flowers that fear no thorn,
   Where they shall dwell as children
     Who here as exiles mourn.
   'Midst power that knows no limit,
     Where wisdom has no bound,
   The beatific vision
     Shall glad the saints around.

Bernard of Cluny, c. 1145.
Tr. by Rev. John Mason Neale. (1818—1866.) 1858. ab. and sl. alt.

605 *"Ermuntert euch, ihr Frommen."*

1 REJOICE, rejoice, believers,
   And let your lights appear;
   The evening is advancing,
     And darker night is near.
The Bridegroom is arising,
   And soon He will draw nigh;
   Up, pray, and watch, and wrestle,
     At midnight comes the cry.

2 See that your lamps are burning,
   Replenish them with oil;
   Look now for your salvation,
     The end of sin and toil.
   The watchers on the mountain
     Proclaim the Bridegroom near,
   Go meet Him as He cometh,
     With hallelujahs clear.

3 Our hope and expectation,
   O Jesus, now appear;
   Arise, thou Sun so longed for,
     O'er this benighted sphere.
   With hearts and hands uplifted,
     We plead, O Lord, to see
   The day of earth's redemption,
     And ever be with Thee.

Laurentius Laurenti. (1660—1722.)
Tr. by Miss Jane Borthwick. 1853. ab. and sl. alt.

THE LORD COMETH.

606 *The Pilgrims of Jesus.*

1 O HAPPY band of pilgrims,
  If onward ye will tread,
With Jesus as your Fellow,
  To Jesus as your Head.
O happy, if ye labor
  As Jesus did for men;
O happy, if ye hunger
  As Jesus hungered then.

2 The cross that Jesus carried
  He carried as your due;
The crown that Jesus weareth,
  He weareth it for you.

The trials that beset you,
  The sorrows ye endure,
The manifold temptations
  That death alone can cure:

3 What are they, but His jewels,
  Of right celestial worth?
What are they but the ladder,
  Set up to heaven on earth?
O happy band of pilgrims,
  Look upward to the skies;
Where such a light affliction
  Shall win you such a prize.

Joseph of the Studium. (—883.)
Rev. John Mason Neale. (1818—1866.) 1862. ab. and sl. alt.

WARSAW. L. M.   Thomas Clark. 1804.

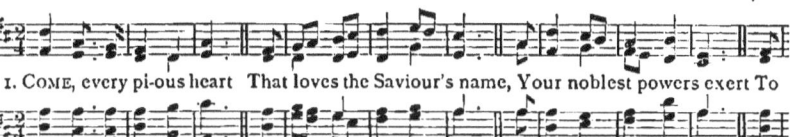

1. Come, every pi-ous heart That loves the Saviour's name, Your noblest powers exert To

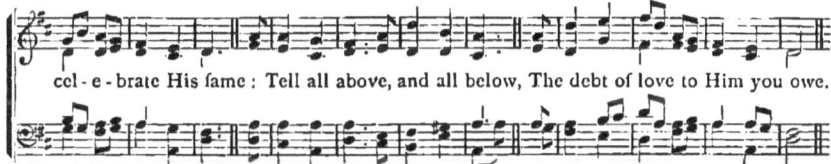

cel-e-brate His fame: Tell all above, and all below, The debt of love to Him you owe.

607 *The Lord will come.*

2 He left His starry crown,
  And laid His robes aside;
On wings of love came down,
  And wept, and bled, and died:
What He endured, O who can tell,—
To save our souls from death and hell!

3 From the dark grave He rose,
  The mansions of the dead;
And thence His mighty foes
  In glorious triumph led:
Up thro' the sky the Conqu'ror rode,
And reigns on high, the Saviour-God.

4 From thence He'll quickly come,
  His chariot will not stay,
And bear our spirits home
  To realms of endless day:
There shall we see His lovely face
And ever be in His embrace.

Rev. Samuel Stennett. (1727—1795.) 1787. ab.

CHRIST IN GLORY.

HARWELL. 8, 7. 6 l.   Lowell Mason. (1792—1872.) 1840.

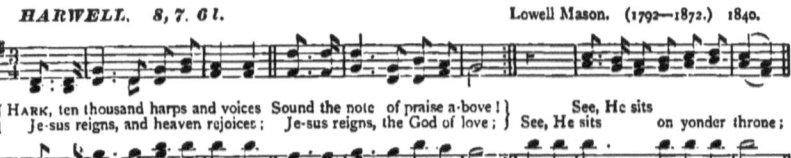

1. { Hark, ten thousand harps and voices Sound the note of praise a-bove! }
   { Je-sus reigns, and heaven rejoices; Jesus reigns, the God of love; } See, He sits See, He sits on yonder throne;

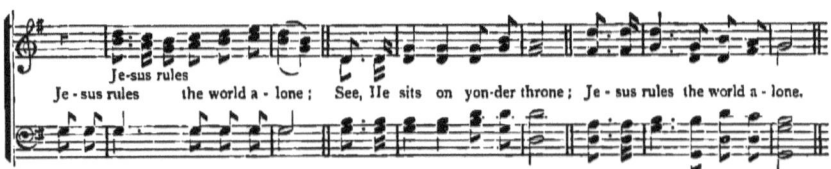

Je-sus rules Je-sus rules the world a-lone; See, He sits on yon-der throne; Je-sus rules the world a-lone.

608   *Worshipped of Angels.*
        Heb. i. 6.

2 King of glory, reign forever!
    Thine an everlasting crown;
   Nothing from Thy love shall sever
    Those whom Thou hast made Thine
   Happy objects of Thy grace, [own;
    Destined to behold Thy face.

3 Saviour, hasten Thine appearing;
    Bring, O bring the glorious day,
   When the awful summons hearing,
    Heaven and earth shall pass away:
   Then, with golden harps, we'll sing,
    "Glory, glory to our King!"
       Rev. Thomas Kelly. (1769—1855.) 1804. ab.

609   "*Wer sind die vor Gottes Throne?*"

1 Who are these like stars appearing,
    These, before God's throne who stand?
   Each a golden crown is wearing,
    Who are all this glorious band?
   Alleluia! hark, they sing,
   Praising loud their heavenly King.

2 These are they who have contended
    For their Saviour's honor long,
   Wrestling on till life was ended,
    Following not the sinful throng:
   These, who well the fight sustained,
   Triumph thro' the Lamb have gained.

3 These, like priests have watched and waited,
   Offering up to Christ their will,
   Soul and body consecrated,
    Day and night they serve Him still:
   Now, in God's most holy place,
   Blest they stand before His face.

4 Lo, the Lamb Himself now feeds them,
    On Mount Zion's pastures fair;
   From His central throne He leads them
    By the living fountain there:
   Lamb and Shepherd, Good Supreme,
   Free He gives the cooling stream.
       Rev. Heinrich Theodor Schenk. (—1727.)
      Tr. by Miss Frances Elizabeth Cox. 1841. ab.

COME, LORD JESUS. 271

TAMWORTH. 8, 7, 4. Charles Lockhart. (—1816.) c. 1790.

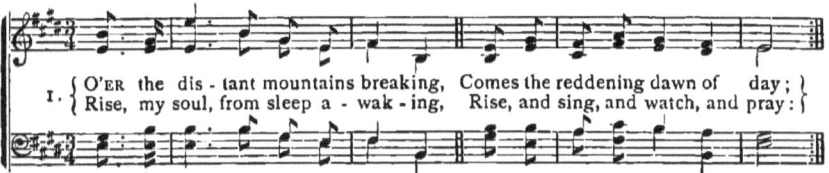

O'er the dis-tant mountains breaking, Comes the reddening dawn of day;
Rise, my soul, from sleep a-wak-ing, Rise, and sing, and watch, and pray:

'Tis thy Sav-iour, 'Tis thy Sav-iour, On His bright, re-turn-ing way.

610 *"Surely I come quickly."*
Rev. xxii. 20.

2 Long, too long, in sin and sadness,
  Far away from Thee I pine;
  When, O when, shall I the gladness
  Of Thy Spirit feel in mine?
    O my Saviour,
  When shall I be wholly Thine?

3 Nearer is my soul's salvation,
  Spent the night, the day at hand;
  Keep me in my lowly station,
  Watching for Thee, till I stand,
    O my Saviour,
  In Thy bright and promised land.

4 With my lamp well-trimmed and burning,
  Swift to hear, and slow to roam,
  Watching for Thy glad returning
  To restore me to my home,
    Come, my Saviour,
  O my Saviour, quickly come.
  Rev. John Samuel Bewley Monsell. (1811—) 1863. ab.

611 *Christ's Second Coming.*

1 Lo, He comes, with clouds descending,
  Once for favored sinners slain;
  Thousand thousand saints attending
  Swell the triumph of His train:
    Hallelujah!
  God appears on earth to reign.

2 Every eye shall now behold Him,
  Robed in dreadful majesty;
  Those who set at nought and sold Him,
  Pierced and nailed Him to the tree,
    Deeply wailing,
  Shall the true Messiah see.

3 Now redemption, long expected,
  See in solemn pomp appear:
  All His saints, by men rejected,
  Now shall meet Him in the air:
    Hallelujah!
  See the day of God appear.

4 Yea, amen; let all adore Thee,
  High on Thine eternal throne:
  Saviour, take the power and glory;
  Claim the kingdom for Thine own.
    O come quickly,
  Hallelujah! come, Lord, come.
  Rev. Charles Wesley. (1708—1788.) 1758.
  Rev. Martin Madan. (1726—1790.) 1760. ab.

LOOKING TO THE PROMISED LAND.

TAPPAN. C. M. George Kingsley. (1811—) 1838.

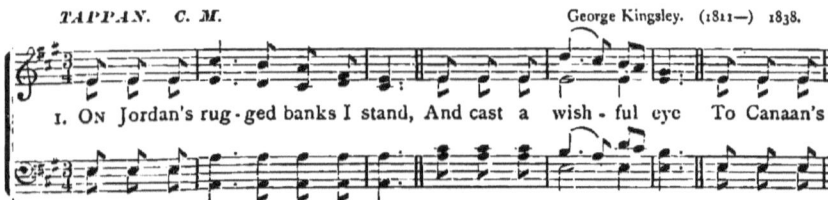

1. On Jordan's rug-ged banks I stand, And cast a wish-ful eye To Canaan's

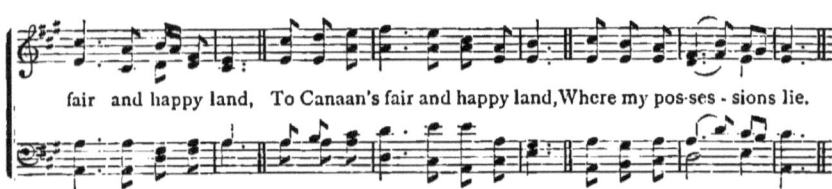

fair and happy land, To Canaan's fair and happy land, Where my pos-ses-sions lie.

612 *The Promised Land.*

2 O the transporting, rapturous scene
That rises to my sight:
Sweet fields arrayed in living green,
And rivers of delight.

3 All o'er those wide-extended plains
Shines one eternal day;
There God, the Son, forever reigns,
And scatters night away.

4 No chilling winds, or poisonous breath,
Can reach that healthful shore:
Sickness and sorrow, pain and death,
Are felt and feared no more.

5 When shall I reach that happy place,
And be for ever blest?
When shall I see my Father's face,
And in His bosom rest?

6 Filled with delight, my raptured soul
Can here no longer stay:

Though Jordan's waves around me roll,
Fearless I'd launch away.
Rev. Samuel Stennett. (1727—1795.) 1787. ab.

613 *Heavenly Hope.*

1 When I can read my title clear
To mansions in the skies,
I bid farewell to every fear,
And wipe my weeping eyes.

2 Should earth against my soul engage,
And hellish darts be hurled,
Then I can smile at Satan's rage,
And face a frowning world.

3 Let cares like a wild deluge come,
And storms of sorrow fall;
May I but safely reach my home,
My God, my heaven, my all;

4 There shall I bathe my weary soul
In seas of heavenly rest,
And not a wave of trouble roll
Across my peaceful breast.
Rev. Isaac Watts. (1674—1748.) 1709.

NEW JERUSALEM COMING DOWN.

NORTHFIELD. C. M. Jeremiah Ingalls. (1764—1838.) 1805.

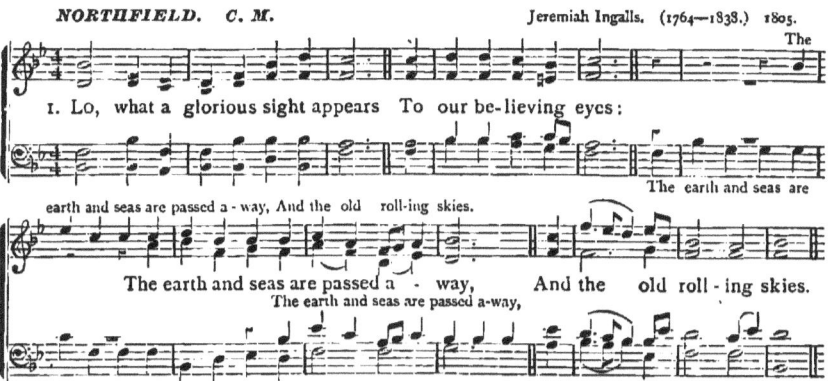

1. Lo, what a glorious sight appears To our be-lieving eyes: The earth and seas are passed a-way, And the old roll-ing skies.

614 *"A new Heaven and a new Earth."*
Rev. xxi. 1–4.

2 From the third heaven where God re-
 That holy, happy place, [sides,
 The New Jerusalem comes down,
 Adorned with shining grace.

3 Attending angels shout for joy,
 And the bright armies sing,
 "Mortals, behold the sacred seat
 Of your descending King.

4 "The God of glory down to men
 Removes His blest abode;
 Men, the dear objects of His grace,
 And He the loving God.

5 "His own soft hand shall wipe the
 From every weeping eye; [tears
 And pains, and groans, and griefs, and
 And death itself shall die." [fears,

6 How long, dear Saviour, O how long
 Shall this bright hour delay?
 Fly swifter round, ye wheels of time,
 And bring the welcome day.
 Rev. Isaac Watts. 1709.

615 *"Sweet Fields."*

1 THERE is a land of pure delight,
 Where saints immortal reign;
 Infinite day excludes the night,
 And pleasures banish pain.

2 There, everlasting spring abides,
 And never-withering flowers:
 Death, like a narrow sea, divides
 This heavenly land from ours.

3 Sweet fields beyond the swelling flood,
 Stand dressed in living green:
 So to the Jews old Canaan stood,
 While Jordan rolled between.

4 But timorous mortals start and shrink
 To cross this narrow sea,
 And linger shivering on the brink,
 And fear to launch away.

5 O could we make our doubts remove,
 Those gloomy doubts that rise,
 And see the Canaan that we love
 With unbeclouded eyes;

6 Could we but climb where Moses stood,
 And view the landscape o'er,
 Not Jordan's stream, nor death's cold
  flood,
 Should fright us from the shore.
 Rev. Isaac Watts. 1709.

JERUSALEM THE GOLDEN.

EWING. 7, 6. D. Bp. Alexander Ewing. (—1873.) 1861.

1. JE-RU-SA-LEM the gold-en, With milk and hon-ey blest, Be-neath thy con-tem-pla-tion Sink heart and voice op-prest: I know not, O I know not, What so-cial joys are there; What ra-dian-cy of glo-ry, What light be-yond compare.

616 "*Urbs Syon aurea.*"

2 They stand, those halls of Zion,
    All jubilant with song,
And bright with many an angel,
    And all the martyr throng:
The Prince is ever in them,
    The daylight is serene;
The pastures of the bless'd
    Are decked in glorious sheen.

3 There is the throne of David;
    And there, from care released,
The shout of them that triumph,
    The song of them that feast;
And they who, with their leader,
    Have conquered in the fight,
Forever, and forever,
    Are clad in robes of white.
        Bernard of Cluny. c. 1145.
Tr. by Rev. John Mason Neale. (1818—1866.) 1851. alt.

617 "*O bona Patria.*"

1 For thee, O dear, dear Country,
    Mine eyes their vigils keep;
For very love, beholding
    Thy happy name, they weep.
The mention of thy glory
    Is unction to the breast,
And medicine in sickness,
    And love, and life, and rest.

2 O one, O only Mansion,
    O Paradise of joy,
Where tears are ever banished,
    And smiles have no alloy;
The Lamb is all thy splendor,
    The Crucified thy praise;
His laud and benediction
    Thy ransomed people raise.

3 With jasper glow thy bulwarks,
    Thy streets with emerald blaze;
The sardius and the topaz
    Unite in thee their rays;
Thine ageless walls are bonded
    With amethyst unpriced;
The saints built up its fabric,
    And the Corner-stone is Christ.

JERUSALEM THE GLORIOUS.

4 Thou hast no shore, fair ocean ;
   Thou hast no time, bright day :
   Dear fountain of refreshment
    To pilgrims far away.
   Upon the Rock of Ages
   They raise thy holy tower ;
   Thine is the victor's laurel,
   And thine the golden dower.
        Bernard of Cluny. c. 1145.
    Tr. by Rev. John Mason Neale. 1851. alt.

618   *"Urbs Syon inclyta, Gloria."*

1 JERUSALEM the glorious,
   The home of the elect,
   O dear and future vision
   That eager hearts expect :
   E'en now by faith I see thee,
   E'en here thy walls discern ;
   To thee my thoughts are kindled,
   And strive and pant and yearn.

2 New mansion of new people,
   Whom God's own love and light
   Promote, increase, make holy,
   Identify, unite.
   And there the band of prophets
   United praise ascribes,
   And there the twelve-fold chorus
   Of Israel's ransomed tribes.

3 And there the Sole-Begotten
   Is Lord in regal state ;
   He, Judah's mystic Lion,
   He, Lamb immaculate.
   O fields that know no sorrow,
   O state that fears no strife,
   O princely bowers, O land of flowers,
   O realm and home of life.
        Bernard of Cluny. c. 1145.
    Tr. by Rev. John Mason Neale. 1851. alt.

619   *The Saints marching up.*

1 TEN thousand times ten thousand,
   In sparkling raiment bright,
   The armies of the ransomed saints
   Throng up the steeps of light :

   'Tis finished, all is finished,
   Their fight with death and sin :
   Fling open wide the golden gates,
   And let the victors in.

2 What rush of Hallelujahs
   Fills all the earth and sky ;
   What ringing of a thousand harps
   Bespeaks the triumph nigh.
   O day, for which Creation
   And all its tribes were made ;
   O joy, for all its former woes
   A thousand-fold repaid.

3 O then what raptured greetings
   On Canaan's happy shore ;
   What knitting severed friendships up,
   Where partings are no more.
   Then eyes with joy shall sparkle,
   That brimmed with tears of late :
   Orphans no longer fatherless,
   Nor widows desolate.
      Rev. Henry Alford. (1810—1871.) 1866.

620   *The Country beyond the Stars.*

1 MY soul, there is a country
   Afar beyond the stars,
   Where stands a wingèd sentry,
   All skilful in the wars.
   There, above noise and danger,
   Sweet Peace sits crowned with smiles,
   And One born in a manger
   Commands the beauteous files.

2 If thou canst get but thither,
   There grows the flower of peace,
   The rose that cannot wither,
   Thy fortress and thine ease.
   Leave then thy foolish ranges,
   For none can thee secure,
   But One, who never changes,
   Thy God, thy Life, thy Cure.
      Henry Vaughan. (1621—1695.) 1650.

LONGING FOR HEAVEN.

ST. ASAPH. C. M. D. Jean Maria Giornovichi. (1745—1804.)

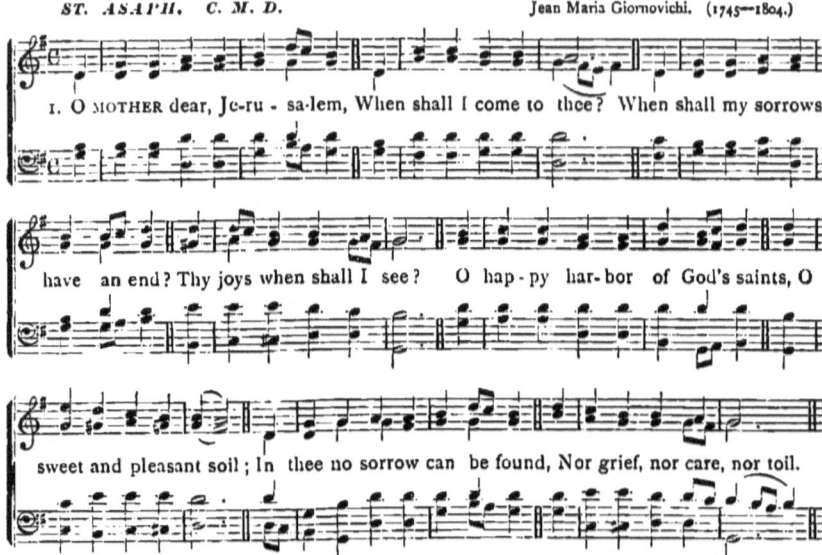

1. O MOTHER dear, Je-ru-sa-lem, When shall I come to thee? When shall my sorrows have an end? Thy joys when shall I see? O hap-py har-bor of God's saints, O sweet and pleasant soil; In thee no sorrow can be found, Nor grief, nor care, nor toil.

621 *"O Mother dear, Jerusalem."*

2 No dimming cloud o'ershadows thee,
   Nor gloom, nor darksome night;
   But every soul shines as the sun,
   For God Himself gives light.
   Thy walls are made of precious stone,
   Thy bulwarks diamond-square,
   Thy gates are all of orient pearl:
   O God, if I were there!

3 Right through thy streets with pleasing
        sound
   The flood of life doth flow,
   And on the banks, on either side,
   The trees of life do grow.
   Those trees each month yield ripened
        fruit;
   For evermore they spring,
   And all the nations of the earth
   To thee their honors bring.

4 There the blest souls that hardly 'scaped
     The snare of death and hell,
   Triumph in joy eternally,
     Whereof no tongue can tell.
   O mother dear, Jerusalem,
     When shall I come to thee?
   When shall my sorrows have an end?
     Thy joys when shall I see?
Rev. Francis Baker, 1616. alt.
Rev. David Dickson. (1583—1663.) 1649. ab.

622 *Resigned to Death.*

1 AND let this feeble body fail,
     And let it faint or die,
   My soul shall quit the mournful vale,
     And soar to worlds on high;
   Shall join the disembodied saints,
     And find its long-sought rest,
   That only bliss for which it pants,
     In my Redeemer's breast.

HAPPY HOME. 277

2 O what hath Jesus bought for me!
   Before my ravished eyes
Rivers of life divine I see,
   And trees of Paradise:
I see a world of spirits bright,
   Who reap the pleasures there;
They all are robed in spotless white,
   And conquering palms they bear.

3 O what are all my sufferings here,
   If, Lord, Thou count me meet
With that enraptured host to appear,
   And worship at Thy feet!
Give joy or grief, give ease or pain,
   Take life or friends away,
I come, to find them all again
   In that eternal day.
      Rev. Charles Wesley. (1708—1788.) 1759. ab.

RHINE. C. M.   Arr. from Friedrich Burgmüller. (1804—) c. 1840.

1. JE-RU-SA-LEM, my happy home, Name ever dear to me, When shall my labors have an end In joy, and peace, and thee? In joy, and peace, and thee?

623 *"Jerusalem, my happy Home."*

2 When shall these eyes thy heaven-built
     And pearly gates behold; [walls
   Thy bulwarks with salvation strong,
     And streets of shining gold?

3 O when, thou City of my God,
     Shall I thy courts ascend,
   Where congregations ne'er break up,
     And Sabbaths have no end?

4 There happier bowers than Eden's
     bloom,
   Nor sin nor sorrow know:

   Blest seats, through rude and stormy
     scenes
   I onward press to you.

5 Apostles, martyrs, prophets, there
     Around my Saviour stand;
   And soon my friends in Christ below
     Will join the glorious band.

6 Jerusalem, my happy home,
     My soul still pants for thee;
   Then shall my labors have an end
     When I thy joys shall see.
      Unknown. Williams and Boden's Collection. 1801. ab.

LONGING FOR HEAVEN.

CONTRAST. 8. D. Jonathan Edson. 1782.

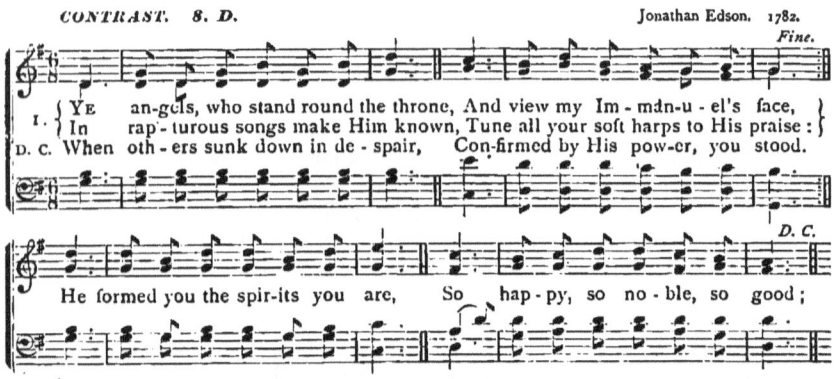

1. Ye an-gels, who stand round the throne, And view my Im-man-u-el's face,
   In rap-turous songs make Him known, Tune all your soft harps to His praise:
   D.C. When oth-ers sunk down in de-spair, Con-firmed by His pow-er, you stood.
   He formed you the spir-its you are, So hap-py, so no-ble, so good;

624   *Panting for Heaven.*

2 Ye saints, who stand nearer than they,
And cast your bright crowns at His feet,
His grace and His glory display,
And all His rich mercy repeat :
He snatched you from hell and the grave,
He ransomed from death and despair ;
For you He was mighty to save,
Almighty to bring you safe there.

3 O when will the period appear,
When I shall unite in your song ?
I'm weary of lingering here,
And I to your Saviour belong :
I'm fettered, and chained up in clay ;
I struggle, and pant to be free ;
I long to be soaring away,
My God and my Saviour to see.

4 I want to put on my attire,
Washed white in the blood of the Lamb ;
I want to be one of your choir,
And tune my sweet harp to His name ;
I want, O I want to be there,
Where sorrow and sin bid adieu,
Your joy and your friendship to share,
To wonder, and worship with you.

                Miss Maria De Fleury. 1791.

625   *"The King in His Beauty."* Is. xxxiii. 17, 24.

1 I LONG to behold Him arrayed
With glory and light from above,
The King in His beauty displayed,
His beauty of holiest love :
I languish and die to be there,
Where Jesus hath fixed His abode ;
O when shall we meet in the air,
And fly to the mountain of God !

2 With Him I on Zion shall stand,
For Jesus hath spoken the word ;
The breadth of Immanuel's land
Survey by the light of my Lord.
But when, on Thy bosom reclined,
Thy face I am strengthened to see,
My fulness of rapture I find,
My heaven of heavens in Thee.

3 How happy the people that dwell
Secure in the City above !
No pain the inhabitants feel,
No sickness or sorrow shall prove.
Physician of souls, unto me
Forgiveness and holiness give ;
And when from the body set free,
O then to the City receive.

         Rev. Charles Wesley. (1708—1788.) 1762. ab.

THE SAINTS IN LIGHT. 279

1. What are these in bright ar-ray, This in-num-er-a-ble throng, Round the al--tar night and day,
D. S. Wis-dom, rich-es to ob-tain,

Hymning one tri-um-phant song: "Worthy is the Lamb, once slain, Blessing, hon-or, glo-ry, power,
New do-min-ion ev-ery hour."

626 *The Song of the Sealed.*
Rev. vii. 9–16.

2 These through fiery trials trod;
These from great afflictions came;
Now, before the throne of God,
Sealed with His Almighty Name,
Clad in raiment pure and white,
Victor-palms in every hand,
Through their dear Redeemer's might,
More than conquerors they stand.

3 Hunger, thirst, disease unknown,
On immortal fruits they feed;
Them the Lamb amidst the throne,
Shall to living fountains lead;
Joy and gladness banish sighs,
Perfect love dispels all fear,
And forever from their eyes
God shall wipe away the tear.
James Montgomery. (1771—1854.) 1819, 1853.

627 *The happy Saints.*

1 High in yonder realms of light,
Dwell the raptured saints above,
Far beyond our feeble sight,
Happy in Immanuel's love:
Pilgrims in this vale of tears,
Once they knew, like us below,
Gloomy doubts, distressing fears,
Torturing pain, and heavy woe.

2 Mid the chorus of the skies,
Mid th' angelic lyres above,
Hark, their songs melodious rise,
Songs of praise to Jesus' love:
Happy spirits, ye are fled,
Where no grief can entrance find;
Lulled to rest the aching head,
Soothed the anguish of the mind.

3 All is tranquil and serene,
Calm and undisturbed repose,
There no cloud can intervene,
There no angry tempest blows:
Every tear is wiped away,
Sighs no more shall heave the breast,
Night is lost in endless day,
Sorrow, in eternal rest.
Rev. Thomas Raffles. (1788—1863.) 1812. ab. and alt.

WORK AND REST.

WORK, FOR THE NIGHT IS COMING. 7, 6, 7, 5. Lowell Mason. (1792—1872.)

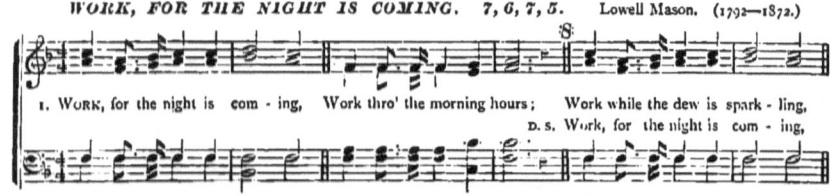

1. Work, for the night is com - ing, Work thro' the morning hours; Work while the dew is spark - ling,
D. S. Work, for the night is com - ing,

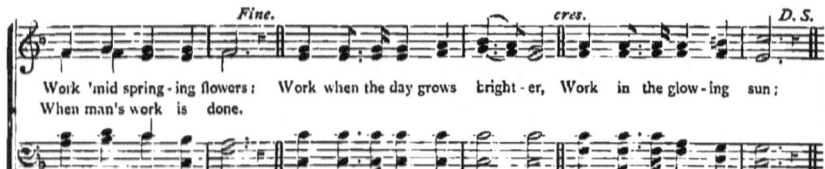

Work 'mid spring - ing flowers: Work when the day grows bright - er, Work in the glow - ing sun;
When man's work is done.

628 *Work.*

2 Work, for the night is coming,
 Under the sunset skies;
 Fill brightest hours with labor,
 Rest comes sure and soon.
 Give every flying minute
 Something to keep in store:
 Work, for the night is coming,
 When man works no more.

3 Work, for the night is coming,
 Under the sunset skies;
 While their bright tints are glowing,
 Work, for the daylight flies.
 Work till the last beam fadeth,
 Fadeth to shine no more;
 Work while the night is dark'ning,
 When man's work is o'er.
   Rev. Sidney Dyer.

WOODLAND. C. M. 5 l. Nathaniel D. Gould. (1781—1864.) 1832.

1. There is an hour of peaceful rest, To mourning wanderers given; There is a joy for souls distrest, A balm for ev - ery wounded breast, 'Tis found a - bove, in heaven.

BEYOND THE RIVER. 281

629 *The Heavenly Rest.*

2 There is a home for weary souls
  By sin and sorrow driven;
  When tossed on life's tempestuous shoals,
  Where storms arise, and ocean rolls,
  And all is drear but heaven.

3 There, faith lifts up her cheerful eye,
  To brighter prospects given;
  And views the tempest passing by,
  The evening shadows quickly fly,
  And all serene in heaven.

4 There, fragrant flowers, immortal, bloom,
  And joys supreme are given;
  There, rays divine disperse the gloom:
  Beyond the confines of the tomb
  Appears the dawn of heaven.
  Rev. William Bingham Tappan. (1794—1849.) 1822, 1846.
  ab.

WE SHALL MEET. 8, 6, 7, 7. 7, 6.   Hubert Platt Main. (1839—) 1867.

1. We shall meet beyond the riv-er, By-and-by, by-and-by; And the dark-ness shall be o-ver, By-and-by, by-and-by: With the toil-some jour-ney done, And the glo-rious bat-tle won, We shall shine forth as the sun, By-and-by, by-and-by.

630 *"We shall meet."*

2 We shall strike the harps of glory,
  By-and-by, by-and-by;
  We shall sing redemption's story,
  By-and-by, by-and-by;
  And the strains for evermore
  Shall resound in sweetness o'er
  Yonder everlasting shore,
  By-and-by, by-and-by.

3 We shall see and be like Jesus,
  By-and-by, by-and-by;
  Who a crown of life will give us,
  By-and-by, by-and-by;
  And the angels who fulfil
  All the mandates of His will,
  Shall attend, and love us still,
  By-and-by, by-and-by.

4 There our tears shall all cease flowing,
  By-and-by, by-and-by;
  And with sweetest rapture knowing,
  By-and-by, by-and-by;
  All the blest ones who have gone
  To the land of life and song,
  We with shoutings shall rejoin,
  By-and-by, by-and-by.
  Rev. John Atkinson. 1867.

REST AND GLORY.

REST FOR THE WEARY. 8, 7.   Rev. William McDonald. (1820—) 1858.

1. In the Christian's home in glory, There remains a land of rest; There my Saviour's gone before me, To fulfil my soul's request. { There is rest for the weary, On the other side of Jordan, There is rest for the weary, There is rest for the weary, There is rest for you. In the sweet fields of Eden, Where the tree of life is blooming, There is rest for you. }

631 "*Rest for the Weary.*"

2 He is fitting up my mansion,
   Which eternally shall stand,
For my stay shall not be transient
   In that holy, happy land. *Cho.*

3 Pain and sickness ne'er shall enter,
   Grief nor woe my lot shall share;
But in that celestial centre
   I a crown of life shall wear. *Cho.*

4 And the grave shall then be conquer'd,
   And the sting of death be lost;
And our bark, all safely anchored,
   Never more be tempest-tost. *Cho.*

5 Sing, O sing, ye heirs of glory;
   Shout your triumph as you go;
Zion's gate will ope before ye,
   You shall find an entrance thro'. *Ch.*
        Rev. Samuel Young Harmer. (1809—) 1856.

632 *The Multitude before the Throne.*
       [Omitting the Chorus.]

1 Hark the sound of holy voices,
   Chanting at the crystal sea,
Hallelujah, Hallelujah,
   Hallelujah! Lord to Thee.

2 Multitude, which none can number,
   Like the stars in glory stand,
Clothed in white apparel, holding
   Palms of victory in their hand.

3 They have come from tribulation,
   And have washed their robes in blood,
Washed them in the blood of Jesus;
   Tried they were, and firm they stood.

4 Gladly, Lord, with Thee they suffered,
   Gladly, Lord, with Thee they died;
And by death to life immortal
   They were born, and glorified.

THE RIVER OF LIFE. 283

5 Now they reign in heavenly glory,
   Now they walk in golden light,
   Now they drink, as from a river,
   Holy bliss and infinite.

6 Love and peace they taste forever,
   And all truth and knowledge see
   In the beatific vision
   Of the blessèd Trinity.
   Bp. Christopher Wordsworth. (1807—) 1863. ab.

BEAUTIFUL RIVER. 8, 7. Rev. Robert Lowry. (1826—) 1864.

1. Shall we gather at the river Where bright angel feet have trod; With its crystal tide forever Flowing by the throne of God?

Chorus. Yes, we'll gather at the river, The beautiful, the beautiful river; Gather with the saints at the river, That flows by the throne of God.

633 *The River of Life.*
   Rev. xxii. 1.

2 On the margin of the river,
   Washing up its silver spray,
   We will walk and worship ever,
   All the happy golden day. *Cho.*

3 On the bosom of the river,
   Where the Saviour-King we own,
   We shall meet, and sorrow never
   'Neath the glory of the throne. *Cho.*

4 Ere we reach the shining river,
   Lay we every burden down;
   Grace our spirits will deliver,
   And provide a robe and crown. *Cho.*

5 At the smiling of the river,
   Mirror of the Saviour's face,
   Saints whom death will never sever,
   Lift their songs of saving grace. *Cho.*

6 Soon we'll reach the silver river,
   Soon our pilgrimage will cease;
   Soon our happy hearts will quiver
   With the melody of peace. *Cho.*
   Rev. Robert Lowry. 1864.

THE NEW JERUSALEM.

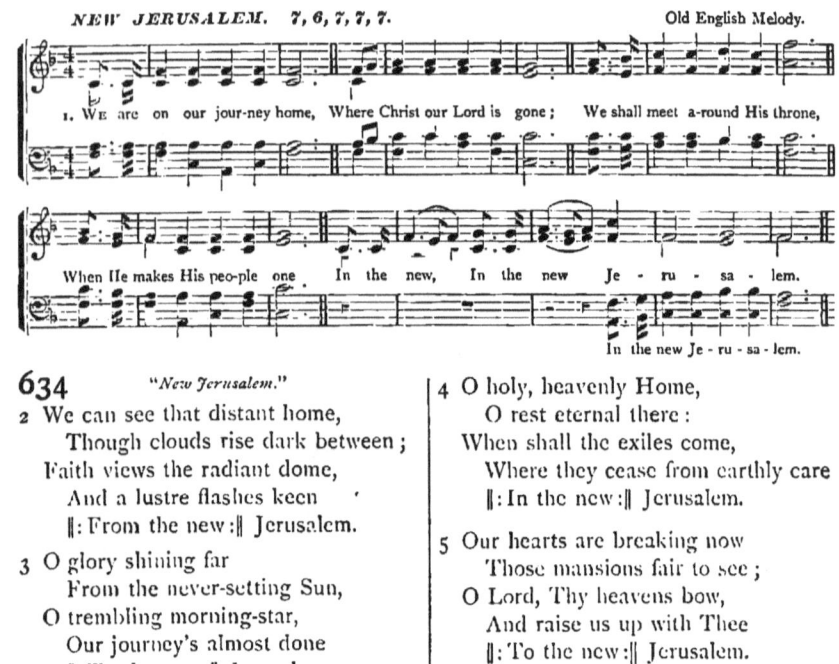

NEW JERUSALEM. 7, 6, 7, 7, 7. Old English Melody.

1. We are on our journey home, Where Christ our Lord is gone; We shall meet around His throne, When He makes His people one. In the new, In the new Jerusalem. In the new Jerusalem.

634 *"New Jerusalem."*

2 We can see that distant home,
  Though clouds rise dark between;
  Faith views the radiant dome,
  And a lustre flashes keen
  ‖: From the new :‖ Jerusalem.

3 O glory shining far
  From the never-setting Sun,
  O trembling morning-star,
  Our journey's almost done
  ‖: To the new :‖ Jerusalem.

4 O holy, heavenly Home,
  O rest eternal there:
  When shall the exiles come,
  Where they cease from earthly care
  ‖: In the new :‖ Jerusalem.

5 Our hearts are breaking now
  Those mansions fair to see;
  O Lord, Thy heavens bow,
  And raise us up with Thee
  ‖: To the new :‖ Jerusalem.

Rev. Charles Beecher. (1819—) 1857.

LISCHER. H. M. Friedrich Schneider. (1786—1853.) 1840.

1. { Safe Home, safe Home in port! Rent cordage, shattered deck, }
   { Torn sails, provisions short, And only not a wreck: } But O the joy upon the shore, To tell our voyage perils o'er! To tell.... our voyage perils o'er!

To tell our voyage, &c.

SAFE HOME. 285

635 *"Safe Home."*
2 No more the foe can harm:
 No more of leaguered camp,
 And cry of night-alarm,
 And need of ready lamp:
 And yet how nearly had he failed,
 How nearly had that foe prevailed!

3 The lamb is in the fold
 In perfect safety penned:
 The lion once had hold,
 And thought to make an end;
 But One came by with wounded side,
 And for the sheep the Shepherd died.

Joseph of the Studium. (—883.)
Rev. John Mason Neale. (1818—1866.) 1862. ab.

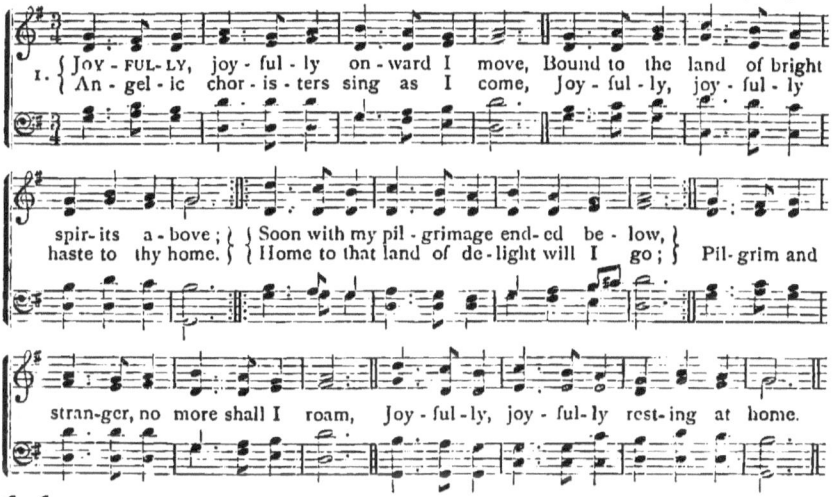

JOYFULLY. 10. D. Rev. Abraham Dow Merrill. (179/—) 1845.

1. Joy-ful-ly, joy-ful-ly on-ward I move, Bound to the land of bright spir-its a-bove;
 An-gel-ic chor-is-ters sing as I come, Joy-ful-ly, joy-ful-ly haste to thy home.
 Soon with my pil-grimage end-ed be-low, Home to that land of de-light will I go;
 Pil-grim and stran-ger, no more shall I roam, Joy-ful-ly, joy-ful-ly rest-ing at home.

636 *Moving onward.*
2 Friends, fondly cherished, have passed on before,
 Waiting, they watch me approaching the shore;
 Singing to cheer me through death's chilling gloom,
 Joyfully, joyfully haste to thy home.
 Sounds of sweet melody fall on my ear;
 Harps of the blessèd, your voices I hear;
 Rings with the harmony heaven's high dome,
 Joyfully, joyfully haste to thy home.

3 Death, with thy weapons of war, lay me low,
 Strike, king of terrors, I fear not the blow;
 Jesus hath broken the bars of the tomb;
 Joyfully, joyfully will I go home.
 Bright will the morn of eternity dawn,
 Death shall be banished, his sceptre be gone;
 Joyfully, then, shall I witness his doom,
 Joyfully, joyfully, safely at home.

Rev. William Hunter. (1811—) 1843.

TIMES AND SEASONS.

BENEVENTO. 7. D. Samuel Webbe. (1740—1816.) c. 1770.

1. While with ceaseless course the sun Hasted through the former year,
   Many souls their race have run, Never-more to meet us here:
   Fixed in an eternal state, They have done with all below;
   We a little longer wait, But how little, none can know.

637 *The new Year.*

2 As the wingèd arrow flies
  Speedily the mark to find;
As the lightning from the skies
  Darts and leaves no trace behind;
Swiftly thus our fleeting days
  Bear us down life's rapid stream:
Upward, Lord, our spirits raise,
  All below is but a dream.

3 Thanks for mercies past receive;
  Pardon of our sins renew;
Teach us henceforth how to live
  With eternity in view:
Bless Thy word to young and old;
  Fill us with a Saviour's love;
And when life's short tale is told,
  May we dwell with Thee above.
  Rev. John Newton. (1725—1807). 1779.

638 *The old Year.*

1 Thou who roll'st the year around,
    Crowned with mercies large and free,
  Rich Thy gifts to us abound,
    Warm our thanks shall rise to Thee:
  Kindly to our worship bow,
    While our grateful praises swell,
  That, sustained by Thee, we now
    Bid the parting year farewell.

2 All its numbered days are sped,
    All its busy scenes are o'er,
  All its joys for ever fled,
    All its sorrows felt no more:
  Mingled with th' eternal past,
    Its remembrance shall decay;
  Yet to be revived at last
    At the solemn judgment-day.

3 All our follies, Lord, forgive;
    Cleanse each heart and make us Thine;
  Let Thy grace within us live,
    As our future suns decline;
  Then, when life's last eve shall come,
    Happy spirits, let us fly
  To our everlasting home,
    To our Father's house on high.
    Rev. Ray Palmer. (1808—) 1832.

TIMES AND SEASONS.   287

639   *For New Year's Eve.*

1 FOR Thy mercy and Thy grace,
Faithful through another year,
Hear our songs of thankfulness,
Father and Redeemer, hear.
In our weakness and distress,
Rock of strength, be Thou our stay;
In the pathless wilderness
Be our true and living way.

2 Who of us death's awful road
In the coming year shall tread?
With Thy rod and staff, O God,
Comfort Thou his dying bed.
Keep us faithful, keep us pure,
Keep us evermore Thine own;
Help Thy servants to endure,
Fit us for the promised crown.
Rev. Henry Downton. (1818—) 1839. ab.

COME, LET US ANEW. 11,5.   Samuel Webbe. c. 1770.

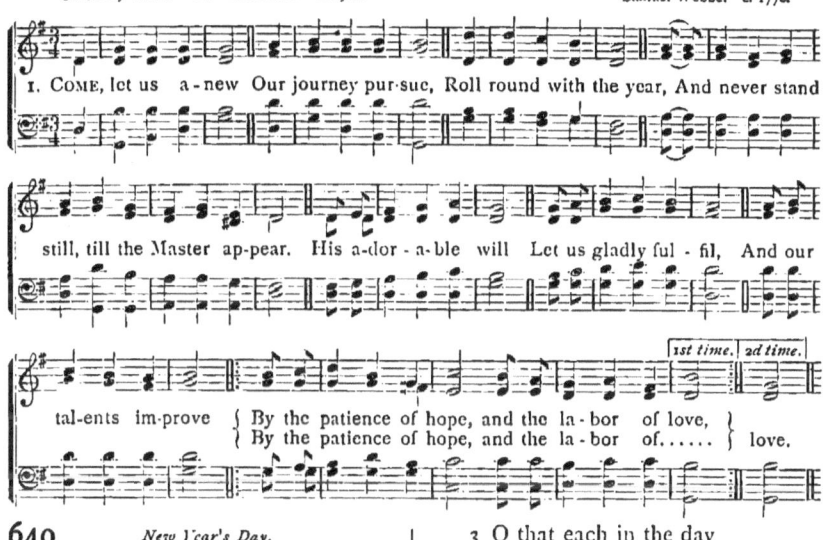

1. Come, let us a-new Our journey pursue, Roll round with the year, And never stand still, till the Master appear. His a-dor-a-ble will Let us gladly ful-fil, And our tal-ents im-prove { By the patience of hope, and the la-bor of love, } { By the patience of hope, and the la-bor of...... } love.

640   *New Year's Day.*

2 Our life is a dream,
Our time, as a stream,
Glides swiftly away,
And the fugitive moment refuses to stay.
The arrow is flown,
The moment is gone,
The millennial year
Rushes on to our view, and eternity's here.

3 O that each in the day
Of His coming might say,
"I have fought my way through,
"I have finished the work Thou didst give me to do."
O that each from his Lord
May receive the glad word,
"Well and faithfully done,
"Enter into My joy, and sit down on My throne."
Rev. Charles Wesley. (1708—1788.) 1750.

TIMES AND SEASONS.

DUNDEE. C. M. — Guillaume Franck. 1545.

1. Our God, our help in a-ges past, Our hope for years to come,

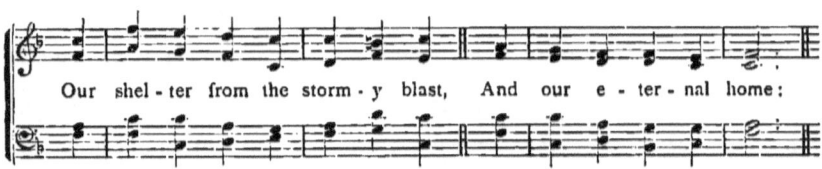

Our shel-ter from the storm-y blast, And our e-ter-nal home:

641 *Man frail, and God eternal.*
Ps. xc.

2 Under the shadow of Thy throne,
   Thy saints have dwelt secure;
Sufficient is Thine arm alone,
   And our defence is sure.

3 Before the hills in order stood,
   Or earth received her frame,
From everlasting Thou art God,
   To endless years the same.

4 A thousand ages, in Thy sight,
   Are like an evening gone;
Short as the watch that ends the night,
   Before the rising sun.

5 Time, like an ever-rolling stream,
   Bears all its sons away;
They fly, forgotten, as a dream
   Dies at the opening day.

6 Our God, our help in ages past,
   Our hope for years to come,
Be Thou our guard while troubles last,
   And our eternal home.
      Rev. Isaac Watts. (1674—1748.) 1719. ab.

642 *God's eternal Dominion.*

1 Great God, how infinite art Thou,
   What worthless worms are we:
Let the whole race of creatures bow,
   And pay their praise to Thee.

2 Thy throne eternal ages stood,
   Ere seas or stars were made;
Thou art the ever-living God,
   Were all the nations dead.

3 Eternity, with all its years,
   Stands present in Thy view;
To Thee there's nothing old appears,
   Great God, there's nothing new.

4 Our lives through various scenes are drawn,
   And vexed with trifling cares;
While Thine eternal thought moves on
   Thine undisturbed affairs.

5 Great God, how infinite art Thou,
   What worthless worms are we;
Let the whole race of creatures bow,
   And pay their praise to Thee.
      Rev. Isaac Watts. 1709. ab.

MERCIES AND DELIVERANCES. 289

DOWNS. C. M. Lowell Mason. (1792—1872.) 1832.

1. When all Thy mer-cies, O my God, My ris-ing soul sur-veys,

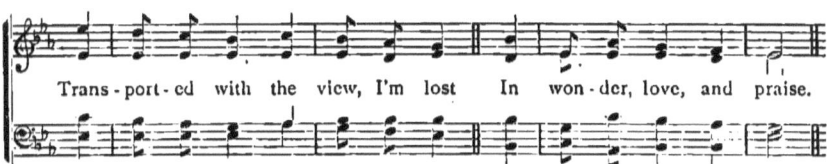

Trans-port-ed with the view, I'm lost In won-der, love, and praise.

643 *Mercies of God recounted.*

2 Unnumbered comforts to my soul
Thy tender care bestowed,
Before my infant heart conceived
From whom those comforts flowed.

3 When worn with sickness, oft hast Thou
With health renewed my face;
And, when in sins and sorrows sunk,
Revived my soul with grace.

4 Ten thousand thousand precious gifts
My daily thanks employ;
Nor is the least a cheerful heart
That tastes those gifts with joy.

5 Through every period of my life
Thy goodness I'll pursue;
And after death, in distant worlds,
The glorious theme renew.

6 Through all eternity to Thee
A joyful song I'll raise;
For O, eternity's too short
To utter all Thy praise.
    Joseph Addison. (1672—1719.) 1712. ab.

644 *Thanksgiving for Preservation of Life.*
    Ps. cvii.

1 How are Thy servants blest, O Lord,
How sure is their defence!
Eternal Wisdom is their guide,
Their help, Omnipotence.

2 In foreign realms and lands remote,
Supported by Thy care,
Through burning climes they pass unhurt,
And breathe in tainted air.

3 When by the dreadful tempest borne
High on the broken wave,
They know Thou art not slow to hear,
Nor impotent to save.

4 The storm is laid, the winds retire,
Obedient to Thy will;
The sea, that roars at Thy command,
At Thy command is still.

5 In midst of dangers, fears, and deaths.
Thy goodness we'll adore;
We'll praise Thee for Thy mercies past,
And humbly hope for more.
    Joseph Addison. 1712. ab. and alt.

TIMES AND SEASONS.

LÜTZEN. C. M. Nicholaus Hermann. (—1561.) 1554.

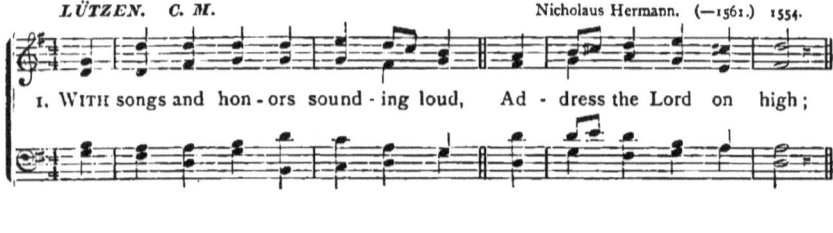

1. With songs and hon-ors sound-ing loud, Ad-dress the Lord on high;

O-ver the heavens He spreads His cloud, And wa-ters veil the sky.

645 *The revolving Seasons.*
Ps. cxlvii.

2 He sends His showers of blessings down,
  To cheer the plains below;
  He makes the grass the mountains crown,
  And corn in valleys grow.

3 His steady counsels change the face
  Of the declining year;
  He bids the sun cut short his race,
  And wintry days appear.

4 His hoary frost, His fleecy snow,
  Descend and clothe the ground;
  The liquid streams forbear to flow,
  In icy fetters bound.

5 He sends His word and melts the snow,
  The fields no longer mourn;
  He calls the warmer gales to blow,
  And bids the spring return.

6 The changing wind, the flying cloud,
  Obey His mighty word:
  With songs and honors sounding loud,
  Praise ye the sovereign Lord.
  Rev. Isaac Watts. (1674—1748.) 1719. ab.

646 *"The Voice of Praise."*
Ps. lxvi.

1 Lift up to God the voice of praise,
  Whose breath our souls inspired;
  Loud and more loud the anthem raise,
  With grateful ardor fired.

2 Lift up to God the voice of praise,
  Whose goodness, passing thought,
  Loads every moment, as it flies,
  With benefits unsought.

3 Lift up to God the voice of praise,
  From whom salvation flows;
  Who sent His Son our souls to save
  From everlasting woes.

4 Lift up to God the voice of praise,
  For hope's transporting ray,
  Which lights through darkest shades of death,
  To realms of endless day.
  Rev. Ralph Wardlaw. (1779—1853.) 1803. ab.

THE OLD AND NEW YEAR.

SHAWMUT. S. M.   Lowell Mason. (1792—1872.) 1833.

1. A few more years shall roll, A few more seasons come,

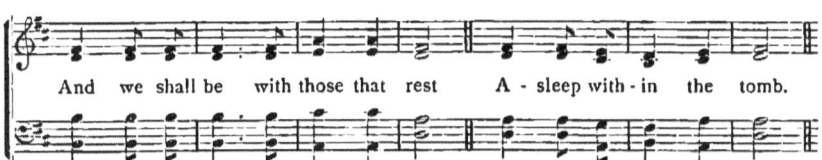

And we shall be with those that rest Asleep with-in the tomb.

647   *"A few more Years."*

2 A few more suns shall set
   O'er these dark hills of time ;
And we shall be where suns are not,
   A far serener clime.

3 A few more storms shall beat
   On this wild rocky shore ;
And we shall be where tempests cease,
And surges swell no more.

4 A few more struggles here,
   A few more partings o'er,
A few more toils, a few more tears,
   And we shall weep no more.

5 A few more Sabbaths here
   Shall cheer us on our way ;
And we shall reach the endless rest,
   The eternal Sabbath day.

6 'Tis but a little while,
   And He shall come again,
Who died that we might live, who lives
That we with Him may reign.

7 Then, O my Lord, prepare
   My soul for that glad day ;
O wash me in Thy precious blood,
   And take my sins away.
    Rev. Horatius Bonar. (1808—) 1857. ab.

648   *Our Fathers.*
    Zech. i. 5.

1 How swift the torrent rolls
   That bears us to the sea ;
The tide that hurries thoughtless souls
   To vast eternity.

2 Our fathers, where are they,
   With all they called their own ?
Their joys and griefs, and hopes, and cares,
   And wealth and honor gone.

3 God of our fathers, hear,
   Thou everlasting Friend,
While we, as on life's utmost verge,
   Our souls to Thee commend.

4 Of all the pious dead
   May we the footsteps trace,
Till with them, in the land of light,
   We dwell before Thy face.
Rev. Philip Doddridge. (1702—1751.) 1755. ab. and alt.

TIMES AND SEASONS.

ST. PAUL'S. L. M.   Johann Friedrich Lampe. (—1750.) 1745.

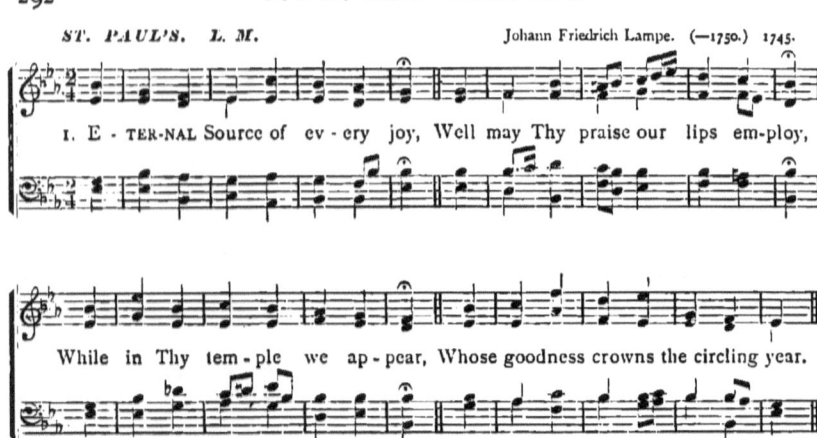

1. E-TER-NAL Source of ev-ery joy, Well may Thy praise our lips em-ploy, While in Thy tem-ple we ap-pear, Whose goodness crowns the circling year.

649   *For New Year's Day.*
Ps. lxv. 11.

2 Wide as the wheels of nature roll,
Thy hand supports and guides the whole:
The sun is taught by Thee to rise,
And darkness when to veil the skies.

3 The flowery spring, at Thy command,
Perfumes the air and paints the land;
The summer rays with vigor shine,
To raise the corn and cheer the vine.

4 Thy hand in autumn richly pours
Through all our coasts redundant stores;
And winters, softened by Thy care,
No more a face of horror wear.

5 Seasons, and months, and weeks, and days,
Demand successive songs of praise;
And be the grateful homage paid,
With morning light and evening shade.

6 Here in Thy house let incense rise,
And circling sabbaths bless our eyes;

Till to those lofty heights we soar,
Where days and years revolve no more.
Rev. Philip Doddridge. (1702—1751.) 1755. ab. and alt.

650   *For the opening and closing Year.*

1 GREAT God, we sing that mighty hand
By which supported still we stand:
The opening year Thy mercy shows;
Let mercy crown it till it close.

2 By day, by night, at home, abroad,
Still we are guided by our God;
By His incessant bounty fed,
By His unerring counsel led.

3 With grateful hearts the past we own;
The future, all to us unknown,
We to Thy guardian care commit,
And peaceful leave before Thy feet.

4 In scenes exalted or deprest,
Be Thou our joy, and Thou our rest;
Thy goodness all our hopes shall raise,
Adored through all our changing days.
Rev. Philip Doddridge. 1755. ab. and alt.

FASTS AND FESTIVALS.

FEDERAL STREET. L. M.   Henry Kemble Oliver. (1800—) 1832.

1. While o'er our guilt-y land, O Lord, We view the ter-rors of Thy sword, O whither shall the help-less fly? To whom but Thee di-rect their cry?

651 *Deliverance from national Judgments implored.*

2 On Thee, our Guardian God, we call;
Before Thy throne of grace we fall;
And is there no deliverance there?
And must we perish in despair?

3 See, we repent, we weep, we mourn;
To our forsaken God we turn;
O spare our guilty country, spare
The Church which Thou hast planted here.

4 We plead Thy grace, indulgent God,
We plead Thy Son's atoning blood,
We plead Thy gracious promises;
And are they unavailing pleas?

5 These pleas, presented at Thy throne,
Have brought ten thousand blessings
On guilty lands in helpless woe; [down
Let them prevail and help us too.
Rev. Samuel Davies. (1724—1761.) 1769.

652 *Humble Confession of Sin.*

1 In prayer together let us fall,
And cry for mercy, one and all,
And weep before the Judge, and say,
O turn from us Thy wrath away.

2 Thy grace have we offended sore
By sins, O God, which we deplore;

Pour down upon us from above
The riches of Thy pardoning love.

3 Forgive the sin that we have wrought,
Increase the good that we have sought;
That we at length, our wanderings o'er,
May please Thee here and evermore.
Rev. John Mason Neale. (1818—1866.) 1851. alt.
Rev. Sir Henry Williams Baker. (1821—) 1861. ab.

653 *Forefathers' Day.*

1 O God, beneath Thy guiding hand,
Our exiled fathers crossed the sea;
And when they trod the wintry strand,
With prayer and psalm they worshipped Thee.

2 Thou heard'st, well pleased, the song, the prayer:
Thy blessing came, and still its power
Shall onward through all ages bear
The memory of that holy hour.

3 Laws, freedom, truth, and faith in God
Came with those exiles o'er the waves;
And where their pilgrim feet have trod,
The God they trusted guards their graves.

4 And here Thy name, O God of love,
Their children's children shall adore,
Till these eternal hills remove,
And spring adorns the earth no more.
Rev. Leonard Bacon. (1802—) 1838, 1845. ab.

FESTIVALS AND FASTS.

NUREMBURG. 7.   Johann Rudolph Ahle. (1625—1673.) 1664.

1. Praise to God, im-mor-tal praise,
For the love that crowns our days!
Boun-teous Source of ev-ery joy,
Let Thy praise our tongues em-ploy.

654 *Thanksgiving.*
Ps. lxv.

2 For the blessings of the field,
For the stores the gardens yield;
For the fruits in full supply,
Ripened 'neath the summer sky;

3 Flocks that whiten all the plain;
Yellow sheaves of ripened grain;
Clouds that drop their fattening dews;
Suns that temperate warmth diffuse;

4 All that spring with bounteous hand
Scatters o'er the smiling land;
All that liberal autumn pours
From her rich o'erflowing stores:

5 These to Thee, my God, we owe,
Source whence all our blessings flow;
And for these my soul shall raise
Grateful vows and solemn praise.
Mrs. Anna Lætitia Barbauld. (1743—1825.) 1773. ab. and alt.

655 *Thanksgiving or Fast.*

1 God of nations, King of kings,
Head of all created things,
Pleading at Thy throne we stand,
Save Thy people, bless our land.

2 On our fields of grass and grain
Drop, O Lord, the kindly rain;
O'er our wide and goodly land
Crown the labors of each hand.

3 Let Thy kind protection be
O'er our commerce on the sea;
Open, Lord, Thy bounteous hand,
Bless Thy people, bless our land.

4 Let our rulers ever be
Men that love and honor Thee;
Let the powers by Thee ordained,
Be in righteousness maintained.

5 In the people's hearts increase
Love of piety and peace;
Thus, united we shall stand,
One wide, free, and happy land.
Rev. Henry Harbaugh. (1818—1867.) 1860. ab. and alt.

656 *Exhortation to Praise.*
Ps. cl.

1 Praise the Lord, His glories show,
Saints within His courts below,
Angels round His throne above,
Praise Him, all that share His love.

2 Earth, to heaven exalt the strain,
Send it, heaven, to earth again;
Age to age, and shore to shore,
Praise Him, praise Him, evermore.

FESTIVALS AND FASTS. 295

3 Praise the Lord, His goodness trace,
All the wonders of His grace;
All that He hath borne and done,
All He sends us through His Son.

4 Strings and voices, hands and hearts,
In the concert bear your parts;
All that breathe, your Lord adore,
Praise Him, praise Him, evermore.
Rev. Henry Francis Lyte. (1793—1847.) 1834, 1841.

ST. MARTIN'S. C. M. William Tansur. (1699—1774.) 1735.

1. Let chil-dren hear the might-y deeds, Which God per-formed of old;
Which in our young-er years we saw, And which our fa-thers told.

657 *The Story handed down.*
Ps. lxxviii.

2 He bids us make His glories known,
His works of power and grace;
And we'll convey His wonders down
Through every rising race.

3 Our lips shall tell them to our sons,
And they again to theirs,
That generations yet unborn
May teach them to their heirs.

4 Thus shall they learn, in God alone
Their hope securely stands;
That they may ne'er forget His works,
But practice His commands.
Rev. Isaac Watts. (1674—1748.) 1719.

658 *God's Dealings with our Fathers.*
Ps. xliv.

1 O Lord, our fathers oft have told,
In our attentive ears,

Thy wonders in their days performed,
And elder times than theirs.

2 For not their courage, not their sword,
To them salvation gave;
Nor strength that from unequal force
Their fainting troops could save.

3 But Thy right hand and powerful arm,
Whose succor they implored;
Thy presence with the chosen race,
Who Thy great name adored.

4 As Thee their God our fathers owned,
Thou art our sovereign King:
O therefore, as Thou didst to them,
To us deliverance bring.

5 To Thee the triumph we ascribe,
From whom the conquest came;
In God we will rejoice all day,
And ever bless Thy name.
Tate and Brady. 1696. ab. and alt.

AMERICA. 6, 4.　　　　　　　　　　　　John Bull? (1563—1628.) 1605.
　　　　　　　　　　　　　　　　　　　Henry Carey. (1693—1743.)

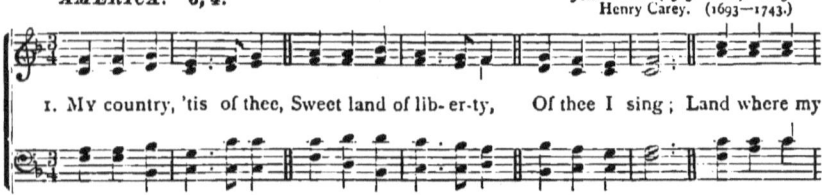

1. My country, 'tis of thee, Sweet land of lib-er-ty, Of thee I sing; Land where my

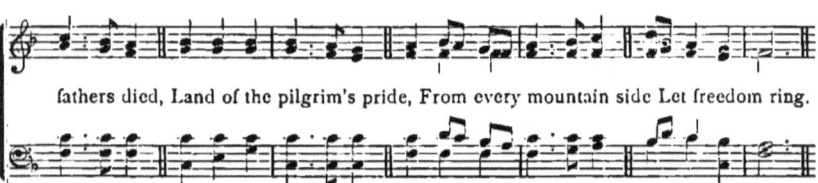

fathers died, Land of the pilgrim's pride, From every mountain side Let freedom ring.

659 *National Hymn.*

2 My native country, thee,
　Land of the noble, free,
　　Thy name I love;
　I love thy rocks and rills,
　Thy woods and templed hills;
　My heart with rapture thrills
　　Like that above.

3 Let music swell the breeze,
　And ring from all the trees
　　Sweet freedom's song:
　Let mortal tongues awake,
　Let all that breathe partake,
　Let rocks their silence break,
　　The sound prolong.

4 Our fathers' God, to Thee,
　Author of liberty,
　　To Thee we sing;
　Long may our land be bright
　With freedom's holy light;
　Protect us by Thy might,
　　Great God, our King.
　　　Rev. Samuel Francis Smith. (1808—) 1832.

660 *"God save the State."*

1 GOD bless our native land;
　Firm may she ever stand,
　　Through storm and night;
　When the wild tempests rave,
　Ruler of wind and wave,
　Do Thou our country save
　　By Thy great might.

2 For her our prayer shall rise
　To God, above the skies;
　　On Him we wait;
　Thou who art ever nigh,
　Guarding with watchful eye,
　To Thee aloud we cry,
　　God save the State.
　　　Rev. John Sullivan Dwight. (1812—) 1844.

DOXOLOGIES.

1 *C. M.*
To Father, Son, and Holy Ghost,
The God whom we adore,
Be glory, as it was, is now,
And shall be evermore.
Tate and Brady. 1696.

2 *S. M.*
To God the Father, Son,
And Spirit, One and Three,
Be glory, as it was, is now,
And shall forever be.
Rev. John Wesley. (1703—1791.) 1741.

3 *L. M.*
PRAISE God, from whom all blessings flow;
Praise Him, all creatures here below;
Praise Him above, ye heavenly host;
Praise Father, Son, and Holy Ghost.
Bp. Thomas Ken. (1637—1711.) 1697.

4 *L. M.*
To God the Father, God the Son,
And God the Spirit, Three in One,
Be honor, praise, and glory given,
By all on earth, and all in heaven.
Rev. Isaac Watts. (1674—1748.) 1709.

5 *L. M. 6 l.*
To God the Father, God the Son,
And God the Spirit, Three in One,
Be honor, praise, and glory given,
By all on earth, and all in heaven;
As was through ages heretofore,
Is now, and shall be evermore.
Rev. Isaac Watts. 1709. First 4 lines.

6 *C. P. M.*
To Father, Son, and Holy Ghost,
The God whom heaven's triumphant
    And saints on earth adore;   [host
Be glory as in ages past,
As now it is, and so shall last,
When time shall be no more.
Tate and Brady. 1696. alt.

7 *L. P. M.*
Now to the great and sacred Three,
The Father, Son, and Spirit, be
Eternal praise and glory given,
Through all the worlds where God is
    known,
By all the angels near the throne,
And all the saints in earth and
    heaven.
Rev. Isaac Watts. 1719.

8 *H. M.*
O GOD, for ever blest,
    To Thee all praise be given;
Thy Name Triune confest
    By all in earth and heaven;
As heretofore it was, is now,
And shall be so forevermore.
Rev. Edward Henry Bickersteth. (1825—) 1870.

9 *8, 7.*
PRAISE the Father, earth and heaven,
Praise the Son, the Spirit praise,
As it was, and is, be given
Glory through eternal days.
Unknown Author. 1827.

10 *8, 7. D.*
WORSHIP, honor, glory, blessing,
    Lord, we offer to Thy name:
Young and old their praise expressing,
    Join Thy goodness to proclaim.
As the saints in heaven adore Thee,
    We would bow before Thy throne;
As the angels serve before Thee,
    So on earth Thy will be done!
Edward Osler. (1798—1863.) 1836.

11 *8, 7, 4.*
GLORY be to God the Father,
    Glory be to God the Son,
Glory be to God the Spirit,
    Great Jehovah, Three in One:
        Glory, glory,
    While eternal ages run.
Rev. Horatius Bonar. (1808—) 1866.

DOXOLOGIES.

12 *7, 6. D.*
Father, Son, and Holy Ghost,
 One God whom we adore,
Join we with the heavenly host,
 To praise Thee evermore:
Live, by heaven and earth adored,
 Three in One, and One in Three,
Holy, holy, holy Lord,
 All glory be to Thee.
Rev. Charles Wesley. (1708—1788.) 1746. alt.

13 *7.*
Sing we to our God above
Praise eternal as His love:
Praise Him, all ye heavenly host,
Father, Son, and Holy Ghost.
Rev. Charles Wesley. 1740.

14 *7. 6 l.*
Praise the Name of God most high,
Praise Him, all below the sky,
Praise Him, all ye heavenly host,
Father, Son, and Holy Ghost;
As through countless ages past,
Evermore His praise shall last.
Unknown Author. 1827.

15 *7. 6 l.*
God the Father, God of grace,
Saviour, born of mortal race,
Comforter, our Life and Light,
One in essence, love and might;
Thee whom all in heaven adore,
We would worship evermore.
Rev. Ray Palmer. (1808—) 1873.

16 *7. D.*
Praise our glorious King and Lord,
Angels waiting on His word,
Saints that walk with Him in white,
Pilgrims walking in His light:
Glory to the Eternal One,
Glory to His Only Son,
Glory to the Spirit be
Now, and through eternity.
Rev. Alexander Ramsay Thompson. (1822—) 1869.

17 *6, 4.*
To the great One in Three
 The highest praises be,
  Hence evermore;
His sovereign majesty
May we in glory see,
And to eternity
 Love and adore.
Rev. Charles Wesley. 1757.

18 *6, 4.*
To God the Father, Son,
And Spirit, Three in One,
 All praise be given:
Crown Him in every song;
To Him your hearts belong,
Let all His praise prolong
 On earth, in heaven.
Rev. Edwin Francis Hatfield. (1807—). 1843.

19 *10.*
To Father, Son, and Spirit, ever blest,
Eternal praise and worship be addrest;
From age to age, ye saints, His name adore,
And spread His fame, till time shall be no more.
Rev. Simon Browne. (1680—1732.) 1720. alt.

20 *10, 11.*
All glory to God, the Father and Son,
And Spirit of grace, the great Three in One;
Let highest ascriptions forever be given
By all the creation on earth and in heaven.
Rippon's Collection. 1778.

21 *11.*
O Father Almighty, to Thee be addrest, [ever blest,
With Christ and the Spirit, One God
All glory and worship, from earth and from heaven, [given.
As was, and is now, and shall ever be
Unknown Author.

THE APOSTLES' CREED.

I BELIEVE in GOD THE FATHER Almighty, Maker of heaven and earth: And in JESUS CHRIST His only Son our Lord; who was conceived by the Holy Ghost; born of the Virgin Mary; suffered under Pontius Pilate; was crucified, dead, and buried; He descended into hell; the third day He rose again from the dead; He ascended into heaven; and sitteth on the right hand of God the Father Almighty; from thence He shall come to judge the quick and the dead.

I believe in the HOLY GHOST; the holy Catholic Church; the Communion of Saints; the Forgiveness of sins; the Resurrection of the body; and the Life everlasting. Amen.

CHANTS.

300 CHANTS.

BEATUS VIR.   Gregorian. Arr. by Thomas Tallis. (1529—1585.) 1565.

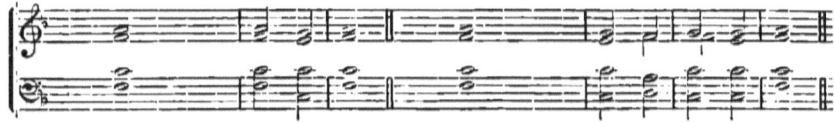

3
Ps. i.

1 BLESSÈD is the man that walketh not in the counsel | of the ·· un- | godly, ‖ Nor standeth in the way of sinners, nor sitteth in the | seat — | of the | scornful.

2 But his delight is in the | law ·· of the | Lord ; ‖ And in His law doth he | medi - tate | day and | night.

3 And he shall be like a tree planted by the | rivers ·· of | water, ‖ That bringeth forth his | fruit — | in his | season ;

4 His leaf also | shall not | wither ; ‖ And whatso- | ever ·· he | doeth ·· shall | prosper.

5 The ungodly | are not | so : ‖ But are like the chaff which the | wind — | driveth ·· a- | way.

6 Therefore the ungodly shall not | stand ·· in the | judgment, ‖ Nor sinners in the congre- | gation | of the | righteous.

7 For the Lord knoweth the | way ·· of the | righteous : ‖ But the way of the un- | godly | shall — | perish.

DOMINUS REGIT ME.

4
Ps. xxiii.

1 THE Lord is my Shepherd ; I | shall not | want. ‖ He maketh me to lie down in green pastures ; He leadeth me beside the | still — | waters.

2 He restoreth my soul ; He leadeth me in paths of righteousness for His | Name's — | sake. ‖ Yea, though I walk through the valley of the shadow of death, I will fear no evil : for Thou art with me ; Thy rod and Thy staff they — | comfort me.

3 Thou preparest a table before me in the presence of mine enemies, Thou

CHANTS. 301

anointest my head with oil : my | cup ··runneth | over. ‖ Surely goodness and mercy shall follow me all the days of my life ; and I will dwell in the house of the | Lord, for | ever. ‖ A- | men.

GLORIA PATRI. Henry Purcell. (1658—1695.)

5
GLORY be to the Father, and | to the | Son, ‖ And | to the | Holy | Ghost.
As it was in the beginning, is now, and | ever ··shall | be, ‖ World without | end. A- | men, A- | men.

DEUS MISEREATUR. Richard Langdon. (—1798.)

6
Ps. lxvii.
1 GOD be merciful unto us, and | bless — | us, ‖ And cause His | face to | shine up- | on us,
2 That Thy way may be known up- | on — | earth, ‖ Thy saving | health a- | mong all | nations.
3 Let the people praise | Thee, O | God ! ‖ Let all the | people | praise — | Thee.
4 O let the nations be glad and | sing for | joy, ‖ For Thou shalt judge the people righteously, and govern the | na - tions up- | on — | earth.
5 Let the people praise | Thee, O | God ! ‖ Let all the | people | praise — | Thee.
6 Then shall the earth | yield her | increase, ‖ And God, even our own | God, shall | bless — | us.
7 God shall | bless — | us, ‖ And all the ends of the | earth shall | fear — | Him.
8 God shall | bless — | us, ‖ And all the ends of the | earth shall | fear — | Him.

302 CHANTS.

QUAM DILECTA.   Thomas Saunders Dupuis. (1733—1796.)

7   Ps. lxxxiv.

1 How amiable are Thy | taber- | nacles ‖ O | Lord — | of — | hosts!
2 My soul longeth, yea even fainteth for the | courts··of the | Lord ‖ My heart and my flesh crieth out | for the | living | God.
3 Yea, the sparrow hath found her an house, and the swallow a nest for herself, where she may | lay her | young ‖ Even Thine altars, O Lord of hosts, my | King — | and my | God.
4 Blessèd are they that | dwell in··Thy | house ‖ They will be | still — | praising | Thee.
5 Blessèd is the man whose | strength··is in | Thee ‖ In whose heart | are the | ways of | them.
6 Who passing through the valley of Baca | make··it a | well ‖ The rain | also | filleth··the | pools.
7 They go from | strength to | strength ‖ Every one of them in Zion ap- | pear- eth··be- | fore — | God.
8 O Lord God of hosts, | hear my | prayer ‖ Give ear, | O — | God of | Jacob.
9 Behold, O | God our | shield ‖ And look upon the | face of | Thine an- | ointed.
10 For a day in Thy courts is better | than a | thousand ‖ I had rather be a door-keeper in the house of my God, than to dwell in the | tents of | wicked- | ness.
11 For the Lord God is a | sun and | shield ‖ The Lord will give grace and glory; no good thing will He withhold from | them that | walk up- | rightly.
12 O | Lord of | hosts ‖ Blessèd is the | man that | trusteth··in | Thee.

VENITE, EXULTEMUS.

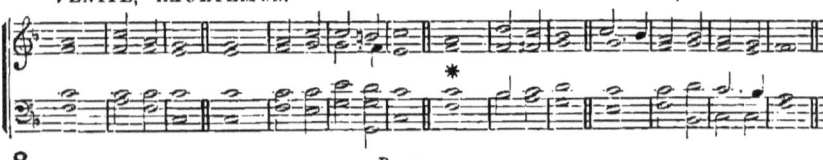

8   Ps. xcv.

1 O come, let us | sing··unto the | Lord ‖ Let us heartily rejoice in the | strength of | our sal- | vation.

CHANTS. 303

2 Let us come before His presence with | thanks- — | giving ‖ And show our- selves | glad in | Him with | psalms.
3 For the Lord is a | great — | God ‖ And a great | King a- | bove all | gods.
4 In His hands are all the corners | of the | earth ‖ And the strength of the | hills is | His — | also.
5 The sea is His | and He | made it ‖ And His hands pre- | pared·· the | dry — | land.
6 O come, let us worship | and fall | down ‖ And kneel be- | fore the | Lord our | Maker.
7 For He is the | Lord our | God ‖ And we are the people of His pasture, | and the | sheep··of His | hand.
8 O worship the Lord in the | beauty··of | holiness ‖ Let the whole earth | stand in | awe of | Him.
*9 For He cometh, for He cometh to | judge the | earth ‖ And with righteousness to judge the world, and the | people | with His | truth.

CANTATE DOMINO.

9
Ps. xcviii.

1 O SING unto the Lord a new song: for He hath done | marvel··ous | things ; ‖ His right hand and His holy arm hath | gotten | Him the | victory.
2 The Lord hath made known | His sal- | vation ; ‖ His righteousness hath He openly showed | in the | sight··of the | heathen.
3 He hath remembered His mercy and truth toward the | house of | Israel ; ‖ All the ends of the earth have seen the sal- | vation | of our | God.
4 Make a joyful noise unto the Lord, | all the | earth ‖ Make a loud noise, and re- | joice and | sing — | praise.
5 Sing unto the Lord | with the | harp, ‖ With the harp, | and the | voice··of a | psalm.
6 With trumpets and | sound of | cornet ‖ Make a joyful noise be- | fore the | Lord the | King.
7 Let the sea roar, and the | fulness··there- | of ; ‖ The world, and | they that | dwell there- | in.
8 Let the floods | clap their | hands, ‖ Let the|hills be | joyful··to- | gether
*9 Before the Lord ; for He cometh to | judge the | earth ; ‖ With righteousness shall He judge the world, | and the | people··with | equity.

JUBILATE DEO.
Gregorian.

10 Ps. c.

1 MAKE a joyful noise unto the Lord, | all ye | lands ‖ Serve the Lord with glad- ness ; come before His | presence | with — | singing.
2 Know ye that the Lord | He is | God ‖ It is He that hath made us, and not we ourselves ; we are His people, | and the | sheep of·· His | pasture.
3 Enter into His gates with thanksgiving, and into His | courts with | praise ‖ Be thankful unto Him, | and — | bless His | name.
4 For the Lord is good ; His mercy is | ever- | lasting ‖ And His truth endureth to | all — | gene- | rations.

BENEDIC ANIMA MEA.
Charles Norris. (1740—1790.)

11 Ps. ciii.

1 PRAISE the Lord, | O my | soul ; ‖ And all that is within me, | praise His | holy | name.
2 Praise the Lord, | O my | soul ; ‖ And for- | get not | all His | benefits.
3 Who forgiveth | all Thy | sin, ‖ And | healeth·· all | thine in- | firmities.
4 Who saveth thy | life·· from de- | struction ; ‖ And crowneth thee with | mercy ·· and | loving- | kindness.
5 O praise the Lord, ye angels of His, ye that ex- | cel in | strength ; ‖ Ye that fulfil His commandment, and hearken unto the | voice of | His — | word.
6 O praise the Lord, | all·· ye His | hosts ; ‖ Ye servants of | His that | do His | pleasure.
*7 O speak good of the Lord, all ye works of His, in all places of | His do- | min- ion. ‖ Praise thou the | Lord, O | — my | soul.

LEVAVI OCULOS.

CHANTS.

12   Ps. cxxi.

1 I WILL lift up mine eyes | unto the | hills ‖ From whence | cometh | my — | help.
2 My help cometh | from the | Lord ‖ Which | made — | heaven·· and | earth.
3 He will not suffer thy | foot·· to be | moved; ‖ He that | keepeth·· thee | will not | slumber.
4 Behold, He that | keepeth | Israel ‖ Shall neither | slumber | nor — | sleep.
5 The Lord | is thy | keeper; ‖ The Lord is thy shade up- | on thy | right — | hand.
6 The sun shall not | smite thee·· by | day, ‖ Nor the | moon — | by — | night.
'7 The Lord shall preserve thee from | all — | evil; ‖ He | shall pre- | serve thy | soul.
8 The Lord shall preserve thy going out and thy | coming | in ‖ From this time forth, and | even·· for | ever- | more.

LÆTATUS SUM.

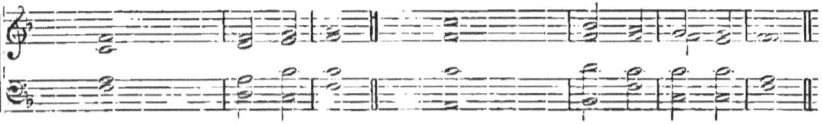

13   Ps. cxxii.

1 I WAS glad when they said | unto | me, ‖ Let us go in- | to the | house·· of the | Lord.
2 Our feet shall stand with- | in thy | gates, ‖ O | — Je- | rusa- | lem.
3 Jerusalem is builded | as a | city ‖ That | is com- | pact to- | gether:
4 Whither the tribes go up, the | tribes·· of the | Lord, ‖ Unto the testimony of Israel, to give thanks un- | to the | name·· of the | Lord.
5 For there are set | thrones of | judgment, ‖ The thrones | of the | house of | David.
6 Pray for the peace of Je- | rusa- | lem; ‖ They shall | prosper·· that | love — | thee.
7 Peace be with- | in thy | walls ‖ And prosperi- | ty with- | in thy | palaces.
8 For my brethren and com- | panions' | sakes ‖ I will now say, | Peace — | be with· | in thee.
9 Because of the house of the | Lord our | God ‖ I will | seek — | thy — | good.

CHANTS.

LAUDATE DOMINUM.

14   Ps. cl.

1 Praise ye the Lord. Praise God | in His | sanctuary: ‖ Praise him in the | firma - ment | of His | power.

2 Praise Him for His | mighty | acts: ‖ Praise Him ac- | cording··to His | excel - lent | greatness.

3 Praise Him with the | sound··of the | trumpet: ‖ Praise Him | with the | psaltery··and | harp.

4 Praise.Him with the | timbrel ·and | dance: ‖ Praise Him with | stringed·· instru- | ments and | organs.

5 Praise Him upon the | loud — | cymbals: ‖ Praise Him upon the | high — | sounding | cymbals.

6 Let every thing that | hath — | breath, ‖ Praise the | Lord. Praise | ye the | Lord.

DESPECTUM ET NOVISSIMUM.   Flintoft.

15   Isaiah liii.

1 He is despised and rejected of men; A man of sorrows and ac- | quainted·· with | grief: ‖ And we hid as it were our faces from Him; He was despised and | we es- | teemed Him | not.

2 Surely He hath borne our griefs, and | carried··our | sorrows: ‖ Yet we did esteem Him stricken, smitten of | God, — | and af- | flicted.

3 But He was wounded for our transgressions, He was bruised for | our in- | iquities; ‖ The chastisement of our peace was upon Him, and | with His | stripes··we are | healed.

4 All we like sheep have gone astray; we have turned every one to | his own | way; ‖ And the Lord hath laid on Him the in- | iquity | of us | all.

5 He was oppressed and | He··was af- | flicted; ‖ Yet He | open - ed | not his | mouth.

CHANTS. 307

6 He is brought as a | lamb·· to the | slaughter, ‖ And as a sheep before her shearers is dumb, so He | open - eth | not His | mouth.
7 Yet it pleased the Lord to bruise Him ; yea, He hath | put·· Him to | grief, ‖ When Thou shalt make His soul an offering for sin, He shall see His seed, He | shall pro- | long His | days.
8 And the pleasure of the Lord shall prosper | in His | hand, ‖ He shall see of the travail of His soul, | and — | shall be | satisfied.

QUAM PULCHRI SUPER MONTES.

16 Isaiah lii. 7–9.
1 How beautiful up- | on the | mountains ‖ Are the feet of him that bringeth good | tidings,·· that | publish - eth | peace ;
2 That bringeth good tidings of good, that publisheth | sal- — | vation : ‖ That saith unto Zion, | thy — | God — | reigneth!
3 Thy watchmen shall lift | up the | voice ; | With the voice to- | gether | shall they | sing :
4 For they shall see | eye to | eye, ‖ When the Lord shall | bring a- | gain — Zion.
5 Break forth | into | joy, ‖ Sing together, ye waste places | of Je- | rusa- | lem.
6 For the Lord hath comforted | His — | people, ‖ He hath re- | deemed·· Je- | rusa- | lem.
*7 The Lord hath made bare His holy arm in the eyes of | all the | nations ; ‖ And all the ends of the earth shall see the sal- | vation | of our | God.

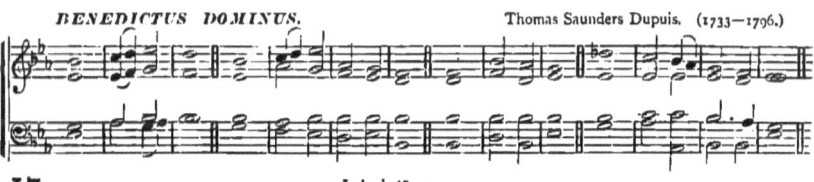

BENEDICTUS DOMINUS.   Thomas Saunders Dupuis. (1733—1796.)

17 Luke i. 68–71.
1 BLESSED be the Lord God of | Isra- | el, ‖ For He hath visited | and re- | deemed·· His | people ;
2 And hath raised up a mighty sal- | vation | for us ‖ In the house | of His | servant | David.

3 As He spake by the mouth of His | holy | prophets, ‖ Which have been | since the | world be- | gan;

4 That we should be saved | from our | enemies, ‖ And from the | hand of | all that | hate us.

ET PASTORES ERANT. Gregorian.

18
Luke ii. 8–14.

1 AND there were in the same country shepherds abiding | in the | field, ‖ Keeping watch | over··their | flocks by | night.

2 And, lo! the angel of the Lord came upon them, and the glory of the Lord shone | round a-| bout them; ‖ And | they were | sore a- | fraid.

3 And the angel said unto them, | Fear — | not; ‖ For, behold! I bring you tidings of great joy, which | shall be | to all | people.

4 For unto you is born this day, in the city of | David,··a | Saviour, ‖ Which | is — | Christ the | Lord.

5 And this shall be a | sign··unto | you: ‖ Ye shall find the babe wrapped in swaddling-clothes, | lying | in a | manger.

6 And suddenly there was | with the | angel ‖ A multitude of the heavenly host, | praising | God, and | saying,

7 Glory to God | in the | highest, ‖ And on earth | peace, good- | will to | men.

MAGNIFICAT. Rev. Samuel Wesley. (1662—1735.)

19
Luke i. 46–55.

1 My soul doth magni- | fy the | Lord, ‖ And my spirit hath re- | joiced in | God my | Saviour.

CHANTS. 309

2 For He hath regarded the low estate of | His hand- | maiden ; ‖ For behold, from henceforth all gener- | ations··shall | call me | blessed.
3 For He that is mighty hath done to | me great | things, ‖ And | holy | is His | Name.
4 And His mercy is on | them that | fear Him, ‖ From gener- | ation··to | gener- | ation.
5 He hath showed strength | with His | arm, ‖ He hath scattered the proud in the imagi- | nation | of their | hearts.
6 He hath put down the mighty | from their | seats, ‖ And exalted | them of | low de- | gree.
7 He hath filled the hungry | with good | things, ‖ And the rich He | hath sent | empty··a- | way.
8 He hath holpen his servant | Isra- | el, ‖ In re- | membrance | of His | mercy.
*9 As He spake to our fathers, to | Abra- | ham, ‖ And | to his | seed for- | ever.

PATER NOSTER.

20
1 Our Father who art in heaven, | hallow - ed | be Thy | name ; ‖ Thy kingdom come, Thy will be done on | earth··as it | is in | heaven.
2 Give us this | day our | daily | bread ; ‖ And forgive us our trespasses, as we forgive them that | trespass··a- | gainst — | us.
3 And lead us not into temptation, but de- | liver | us from | evil ; ‖ For Thine is the kingdom, and the power, and the glory, for ever. | A- — | — | men.

VENITE AD ME.   Philip Hayes. (1739—1797.)

21   Matt. xi. 28-30.
1 Come unto Me, all ye that labor, and are | heavy | laden, ‖ And | I will | give you | rest.
2 Take My yoke upon you, and learn of Me ; for I am meek and | lowly··in | heart, ‖ And ye shall find | rest — | unto··your | souls.
3 For My | yoke is | easy ‖ And | My — | burden··is | light.

GLORIA IN EXCELSIS.

22

1 GLORY be to | God on | high, ‖ And on earth | peace, good- | will ·· towards | men.

2 We praise Thee, we bless Thee, we | worship | Thee, ‖ We glorify Thee, we give thanks to | Thee for | Thy great | glory.

3 O Lord God, | heavenly | King, ‖ God the | Father | Al- — | mighty.

4 O Lord, the only begotten Son, | Jesus | Christ ; ‖ O Lord God, Lamb of | God, Son | of the | Father,

5 That takest away the | sins ·· of the | world, ‖ Have mercy | upon | us.
6 Thou that takest away the | sins ·· of the | world, ‖ Have mercy | upon | us.
7 Thou that takest away the | sins ·· of the | world, ‖ Re- | ceive our | prayer.
8 Thou that sittest at the right hand of | God the | Father, ‖ Have mercy | upon | us.

9 For Thou | only ·· art | holy : ‖ Thou | only | art the | Lord :
10 Thou only, O Christ, with the | Holy | Ghost, ‖ Art most high in the | glory ·· of | God the | Father. ‖ A- | men.

CHANTS.

GLORIA PATRI.
Ludwig Spohr. (1784—1859.)

23 Glory be to the Father, and | to | the | Son: ‖ And | to | the | Ho - ly | Ghost:

As it was in the beginning, is now, and | ev - er | shall be, ‖ World | with - out | end. A- | men.

TE DEUM LAUDAMUS.
William Crotch. (1775—1847.)

24

1 WE praise Thee, | O — | God ; ‖ we acknowledge | Thee to | be the | Lord. ‖ All the earth doth | worship | Thee, ‖ the Father | ever- | last- — | ing.

2 To Thee all Angels | cry a- | loud ; ‖ the Heavens, and | all the | powers·· there- | in. ‖ To Thee Cherubim, and | Sera- | phim ‖ con- | tin - ual- | ly do | cry,

3 Holy, | Holy, | Holy, ‖ Lord | God of | Saba- | oth ; ‖ Heaven and earth are full of the | Majes- | ty ‖ of | Thy — | glo- — | ry.

4 The glorious company | of the | Apostles ‖ praise | — — | — — | Thee ; ‖ The goodly fellowship | of the | Prophets ‖ praise | — — | — — | Thee.

5 The noble army | of — | Martyrs ‖ praise | — — | — — | Thee. ‖ The holy Church throughout | all the | world ‖ doth | — ac- | knowledge | Thee,

6 The | Fa- — | ther ‖ of an | in - finite | Majes- | ty ; ‖ Thine a- | dora - ble, | true, ‖ and | on- — | ly — | Son ;

7 Also the | Holy | Ghost, ‖ the | Com- — | — fort- | er. ‖ Thou art the | King of | Glory, ‖ O | — — | — — | Christ.

8 Thou art the ever- | lasting | Son ‖ of | — the | Fa- — | ther. ‖ When Thou tookest upon Thee to de- | liver | man, ‖ Thou didst humble Thyself to be | born — | of a | Virgin.

9 When Thou hadst overcome the | sharpness ·· of | death, ‖ Thou didst open the Kingdom of Heaven to | all be- | liev- — | ers. ‖ Thou sittest at the right hand | of — | God ‖ in the glory | of the | Fa- — | ther.

10 We believe that | Thou shalt | come ‖ to | be — | our — | Judge. ‖ We therefore pray Thee, | help Thy | servants, ‖ whom Thou hast redeemed | with Thy | precious | blood.

11 Make them to be numbered | with Thy | saints ‖ in glory | ever- | last- — | ing. ‖ O Lord, | save Thy | people, ‖ and | bless Thine | heri- | tage.

12 Gov- | — ern | them ‖ and | lift them | up for- | ever. ‖ Day | by — | day ‖ we | magni- | fy — | Thee.

13 And we worship | Thy — | Name, ‖ ever, | world with- | out — | end. ‖ Vouchsafe, | O — | Lord, ‖ to keep us | this day | without | sin.

14 O Lord, have mercy up- | on — | us, ‖ have | mercy ·· up- | on — | us. ‖ O Lord, let Thy mercy be up- | on — | us, ‖ as our | trust — | is in | Thee.

*15 O Lord, in Thee | have I | trusted, ‖ let me never | be con- | found- — | ed.

CHANTS. 313

26 *Before the Administration.*
Ps. ciii. 17, 18.

1 THE mercy of the Lord is from everlasting to everlasting upon | them that | fear Him, ‖ And His righteousness | unto | children's | children.

2 To such as keep His | cove- | nant; ‖ And to those that remember His com- | mand - ments to | do — | them.

BAPTISMAL CHANT.

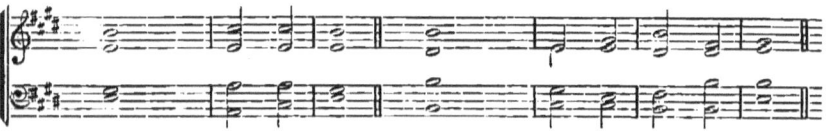

27 Mark x. 14.

1 SUFFER little children to come unto Me, and for- | bid them | not: ‖ For of | such ·· is the | kingdom ·· of | heaven.

Acts ii. 39.

2 For the promise is unto you, and | to your | children; ‖ And to all that are afar off, even as many as the | Lord our | God shall | call.

BAPTISMAL CHANT.

28 *After the Administration.*
Ezek. xxxvi. 25, 26.

1 THEN will I sprinkle clean | water ·· up- | on you, ‖ And | ye shall | be — | clean :

2 A new heart also | will I | give you, ‖ And a new spirit | will I | put with- | in · you,

3 And I will take away the stony heart | out of ·· your | flesh, ‖ And I will | give ·· you a | heart of | flesh.

Is. xliv. 3, 4.

4 I will pour my Spirit up- | on thy | seed, ‖ And my | blessing ·· up- | on thine | offspring :

5 And they shall spring up as a- | mong the | grass, ‖ As | willows ·· by the | water- | courses.

314   CHANTS.

PASCHA NOSTRUM.   William Hayes. (1708—1779.)

29   1 Cor. v. 7, 8. Rom. vi. 9-11.

1 CHRIST our passover is sacri- | ficed | for us, ‖ Therefore | let us | keep the | feast.
2 Not with the old leaven, neither with the leaven of | malice ·· and | wicked - ness, ‖ But with the unleavened bread of sin- | ceri - ty | and — | truth.
3 Christ, being raised from the dead, | dieth ·· no | more ; ‖ Death hath no more do- | minion | over | Him.
4 For in that He died, He died unto | sin — | once : ‖ But in that He liveth, He | liveth | unto | God.
5 Likewise reckon ye also yourselves to be dead indeed | unto | sin, ‖ But alive unto God through | Jesus | Christ our | Lord.
6 Now is Christ risen | from the | dead, ‖ And become the first- | fruits of | them that | slept.
7 For since by | man came | death, ‖ By man came also the resur- | rection | of the | dead.
8 For as in Adam | all — | die, ‖ Even so in Christ shall | all be | made a- | live.

AUDIVI VOCEM.

30   Rev. xiv. 13 ; xx. 6 ; i. 5, 6.

1 I HEARD a voice from heaven, saying | unto ·· me, | Write, ‖ Blessed are the dead, who die | in the | Lord from | henceforth :
2 Yea, saith the Spirit, that they may rest | from their | labors, ‖ And their | works do | follow | them.
3 Blessed and holy is he that hath part in the first | resur- | rection ; ‖ On such the | second ·· death | hath no | power ;

CHANTS. 315

4 But they shall be priests of God | and of | Christ, ‖ And shall reign with | Him a | thousand | years.

5 Unto Him that | loved | us, ‖ And washed us from our sins | in His | own — | blood,

6 And hath made us kings and priests to God | and His | Father ; ‖ To Him be glory and do- | minion·· for | ever·· and | ever.

FROM THE RECESSES.

31

1 FROM the recesses of a lowly spirit
   Our humble prayer ascends. O | Father! | hear it ;
   Borne on the trembling wings of | fear and | meekness,
            For- | give its | weakness.

2 We see Thy hand—it leads us, it supports us :—
   We hear Thy voice—it | counsels·· and it | courts us :—
   And then we turn away!—yet | still Thy | kindness
            For- | gives our | blindness.

3 Who can resist Thy gentle call,—appealing
   To every generous thought and | grateful | feeling?—
   O who can hear the accents | of Thy | mercy,
            And | never | love Thee?

4 Kind Benefactor! plant within this bosom
   The | seeds of | holiness,— ‖ and let them blossom
   In fragrance,—and in beauty | bright and | vernal,—
            And | spring e- | ternal.

5 Then place them in those everlasting gardens
   Where angels walk—and | seraphs·· are the | wardens ;—
   Where every flower, brought safe through | death's dark | portal,
            Be- | comes im- | mortal.

                          Sir John Bowring. (1792—1872.) 1825. ab.

CHANTS.

"THY WILL BE DONE." — Lowell Mason. (1792—1872.)

32

1 "Thý will be | done!" ‖ In devious way
   The hurrying stream of | life may | run ; ‖
   Yet still our grateful hearts shall say, | .
      "Thy will be | done."

2 "Thy will be | done!" ‖ If o'er us shine
   A gladdening and a | prosperous | sun, ‖
   This prayer will make it more divine— |
      "Thy will be | done!"

3 "Thy will be | done!" ‖ Though shrouded o'er
   Our | path with | gloom, ‖ one comfort—one
   Is ours:—to breathe, while we adore, |
      "Thy will be | done."

Sir John Bowring. (1792—1872.) 1825. ab.

AVISON. 11, 11, 12, 11. — Charles Avison. (1710—1770.)

Shout the glad tidings, ex-ult-ing-ly sing,..... Je-ru-sa-lem triumphs, Mes-si-ah is King! si-ah is King, Mes-si-ah is King, Mes-si-ah is King!

1. Zi-on the mar-vel-ous sto-ry be tell-ing, The Son of the

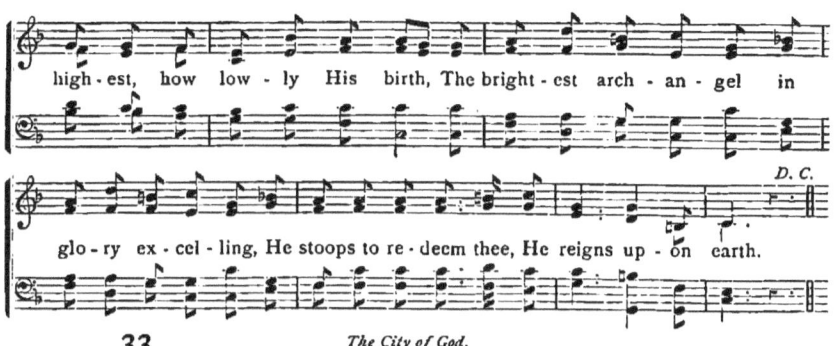

high-est, how low-ly His birth, The bright-est arch-an-gel in glo-ry ex-cel-ling, He stoops to re-deem thee, He reigns up-on earth.

33 *The City of God.*

2 Tell how He cometh ; from nation to nation,
  The heart-cheering news, let the earth echo round ;
  How free to the faithful He offers salvation,
  How His people with joy everlasting are crowned.
    Shout the glad tidings, etc.

3 Mortals, your homage be gratefully bringing,
  And sweet let the gladsome hosanna arise ;
  Ye angels the full hallelujah be singing;
  One chorus resound through the earth and the skies.
    Shout the glad tidings, etc.
            Rev. William Augustus Muhlenburg. (1796—) 1823.

34 *Miriam's Song.*

1 SOUND the loud timbrel o'er Egypt's dark sea,
  Jehovah has triumphed, His people are free.
  Sing, for the pride of the tyrant is broken,
  His chariots, his horsemen, all splendid and brave ;
  How vain was their boasting! the Lord hath but spoken,
  And chariots and horsemen are sunk in the wave.
    Sound the loud timbrel, etc.

2 Praise to the Conqueror, praise to the Lord ;
  His word was our arrow, His breath was our sword.
  Who shall return to tell Egypt the story
  Of those she sent forth in the hour of her pride?
  For the Lord hath looked out from His pillar of glory,
  And all her brave thousands are dashed in the tide.
    Sound the loud timbrel, etc.
            Thomas Moore. (1779—1852.) 1816. sl. alt.

ALPHABETICAL INDEX OF TUNES.

A.
	PAGE
Adrian	24
Ahira (Leighton)	30
Aletta	16, 124
Alexander	91
All to Christ I owe	135
Alvan	32
America	296
Ames	85
(Amor) Jesu Bone Pastor	139
Amsterdam	162
Antioch	65
Ariel	150
Arlington	218, 230
Asaph	185
Athens	137
Aurelia	217
Autumn	10, 95, 198
Ava	119
Avison	316
Avon (Martyrdom)	79, 259
(Azmon) Denfield	196

B.
Baden	231
Balerma	56, 149, 225
Bartimeus	130
Bavaria	104
Beautiful River	283
Belmont	104
Bemerton	40
Beminster	241
Benevento	247, 286
Bera	219
Bethany	170
Bethlehem	67
Beulah	279
Boardman	148
Boylston	230
Braden	116, 144
Bradford	93
Brattle Street	211
Brest	82
Brown	92
Brownell	41
Byefield	22

C.
Capello	68
Carol	72
(Chelmsford) Melody	286
Chesterfield	58
China	264

| PAGE |
Christmas	180, 227
Collins	145
Come, let us anew	287
Come, ye disconsolate	107
Comfort	181
Contrast	154, 278
Coronation	96
Cowper	134
Crawford	138, 249
Crucifix	78

D.
Dallas	21
Dalston	47
Darwell	4
Dawn	163
Dedham	147
Denfield (Azmon)	196
Dennis	208, 215
Dormance (Talmar)	126
Dort	90
Downs	55, 289
Dresden	235
Duke Street	57, 243
Dundee	201, 288

E.
Edinburgh	100
Elizabethtown	188, 203, 224
Ellesdie	141, 183
El Paran	34
Enos	205
Ernan	6, 13
Evening Hymn	26
Even Me	123
Eventide	81
Ewing	206, 274
Expostulation	102

F.
Faithful	258
Federal Street	80, 293
Finney	71
Folsom	60
Forest	19
Franklin Square	214

G.
Ganges	115
Gilead	213
Glory	204
Going Home	169

| PAGE |
Golden Hill	117, 195
Gorton	111, 266
Goshen	172
Gratitude	191
Greenville	105
Greenwood	297
(Gregorian) Hamburg	74, 184
Guide	163

H.
Haddam	45
Halle	30
Hamburg (Gregorian)	74, 184
Happy Day	220
Hark, the voice	248
Harwell	3, 99, 270
Hastings	87
He leadeth me	158
Heath	189
Heber	165
Hebron	142, 233
Hendon	42, 187
Henley	102
Henry	60
Herald Angels	89, 246
Hermon	122
Homeward Bound	108
Horton	108
Hummel	52, 290
Hursley	12, 27

I.
I do believe	131
I'm a Pilgrim	150
Immanuel	135
Italian Hymn	1, 11, 257

J.
Jesu, Bone Pastor (Amor)	139
Jesus, Guide	163
Joyfully	285

K.
Kentucky	177

L.
Laban	176
Lanesboro'	36
Lebanon	130
(Leighton) Ahira	30
Lenox	98
Lisbon	38
Lischer	44, 284
Louvan	121, 252

ALPHABETICAL INDEX OF TUNES.

	PAGE
Loving-kindness	152
Lützen	240
Lyons	48

M.

	PAGE
Magdalene	263
Maitland	181
Manoah	73
Marlow	100
Martyn	100, 186
(Martyrdom) Avon	79, 259
Mear	37
Meinhold	83
Melody (Chelmsford)	226
Meudebras	43
Mendon	174
Meribah	103, 114
Messiah	2, 186, 221
Middleton	236, 254
Migdol	85
Miles' Lane	97
Missionary Chant	50, 175, 242
Missionary Hymn	244
Morning Star	63
Mornington	9
Mozart	88

N.

	PAGE
Naomi	210
Nashville	51
(Nayland) Stephens	202
Nearer my Home	166
Nettleton	140
New Haven	20
New Jerusalem	234
Nicæa	5
Northfield	273
Nuremburg	156, 264

O.

	PAGE
Oak	171
Oaksville	200
Old Hundred	43
Oliphant	160
Olive's Brow	76
Olivet	120, 256, 263
Olmutz	8, 167
Olney	110
Ortonville	146

P.

	PAGE
Park Street	84
Pass me not	123
Pearsall	268
Penitence	132
Penuel	144
Peterborough	197
Pilgrim	234
Pleyel's Hymn	17
Portuguese Hymn	173

R.

	PAGE
Rathbun	183
Redhead	77
Renovation	25
Rest	260
Rest for the Weary	252
Retreat	14
Revive us again	154
Rhine	277
Rock of Ages	128
Rockingham	7

	PAGE
Rosedale	261
Rosefield	15, 109

S.

	PAGE
Sabbath	33
Salvation	59
Scotland	101
Sessions	106, 190
Shawmut	131, 291
Shepherd	161
Shining Shore	168
Sicily	233
Siloam	94
Silver Street	62, 157
Solid Rock	18
Song	153
Spanish Hymn	149
St. Ann's	288
St. Asaph	276
St. Gervais	49
St. Jude	216
St. Martin's	232, 295
St. Michael	255
St. Paul's	292
St. Thomas	63
State Street	194
Stephanos	113
Stephens (Nayland)	202
Stockwell	28
Stow	86
Stracathro	164
Sweet Home	228
Sweet Hour of Prayer	18

T.

	PAGE
(Talmar) Dorrnance	126
Tamworth	271
Tappan	272
Tell the Story	250
Tennessee	125
Thatcher	53, 205
The Lord will provide	150
The old, old Story	251
The sweetest Name	152
To-day	195
Toplady	128
Truro	54
Trusting	136

U.

	PAGE
Uxbridge	222

V.

	PAGE
Valentia	61
Varina	75, 209
Vespers	29
Vox Angelica	229

W.

	PAGE
Wales	109
Ward	212
Warner	119
Warsaw	98, 230
Wave	235
We shall meet	241
Webb	178, 215
Willoughby	192
Wilmot	70
Windham	118
Woodland	125, 230
Woodstock	23
Woodworth	120, 197

	PAGE
Work, for the Night	280

Y.

	PAGE
Yarmouth	207

Z.

	PAGE
Zebulon	151
Zephyr	112
Zerah	64
Zion	237

INDEX TO CHANTS.

A.

	PAGE
Audivi Vocem	314

B.

	PAGE
Baptismal Chant	312, 313
Beatus Vir	300
Benedic Anima Mea	304
Benedictus Dominus	307

C.

	PAGE
Cantate Domino	303

D.

	PAGE
Despectum et Novissimum	306
Deus Misereatur	301
Dominus Regit Me	300

E.

	PAGE
Et Pastores Erant	308

F.

	PAGE
From the Recesses	315

G.

	PAGE
Gloria in Excelsis	310
Gloria Patri	301, 311, 312

J.

	PAGE
Jesus, Guide	163
Jubilate Deo	304

L.

	PAGE
Lætatus Sum	305
Laudate Dominum	306
Levavi Oculos	304

M.

	PAGE
Magnificat	308

P.

	PAGE
Pascha Nostrum	314
Pater Noster	309

Q.

	PAGE
Quam Dilecta	302
Quam Pulchri	307

T.

	PAGE
Te Deum Laudamus	311
The Ten Commandments	299
Thy Will be done	316

V.

	PAGE
Venite ad Me	309
Venite, Exultemus	302

METRICAL INDEX OF TUNES.

C. M.

	PAGE
Antioch	65
Arlington	218, 239
Athens, 81	137
Avon (Martyrdom)	79, 239
(Azmon) Denfield	196
Balerma	56, 149, 225
Bemerton	40
Boardman	122
Bradford	93
Brattle Street, 81	211
Brown	92
Byefield	22
Carol, 81	72
(Chelmsford) Melody	226
Chesterfield	58
China	264
Christmas	180, 227
Coronation	96
Cowper	134
Dedham	147
Denfield (Azmon)	196
Downs	55, 239
Dundee	201, 288
Elizabethtown	188, 203, 224
Faithful	238
Heath	189
Heber	165
Henry	60
Hermon	122
Hummel	52, 293
I do believe	131
Immanuel	185
Lanesboro'	36
Lützen	240
Maitland	131
Manoah	73
Marlow	100
(Martyrdom) Avon	79, 239
Mear	37
Melody (Chelmsford)	226
Miles' Lane	97
Naomi	210
(Nayland) Stephens	202
Northfield	273
Oakesville	200
Ortonville	146
Peterborough	197
Rhine	277
Siloam	94
St. Ann's	238
St. Asaph, 81	276
St. Martin's	232, 295
Stephens (Nayland)	202

	PAGE
Stracathro	164
Tappan	272
Tennessee	125
Valentia	61
Varina, 6 or 81	75, 209
Woodland, 51	125, 280
Woodstock	23
Zephyr	112
Zerah, 61	64

L. M.

	PAGE
Ames	35
Asaph	185
Bera	219
Brownell, 61	41
Capello	68
Collins, 81	115
Dresden, 61	235
Duke Street	57, 243
El Paran	34
Ernan	6, 13
Evening Hymn	26
Federal Street	80, 293
Forest	19
Gilead	213
Going Home	169
Gratitude	191
(Gregorian) Hamburg	74, 184
Hamburg (Gregorian)	74, 184
Happy Day	220
He leadeth me	158
Hebron	142, 223
Hursley	12, 27
Lonvan	121, 252
Loving-kindness	152
Mendon	174
Migdol	85
Missionary Chant	50, 175, 242
Old Hundred	46
Olive's Brow	76
Park Street	84
Rest	260
Retreat	14
Rockingham	7
Rosedale	261
Sessions	106, 190
Solid Rock, 61	187
St. Paul's	292
Sweet Hour of Prayer, 81	18
Truro	54
Uxbridge	222
Ward	212
Warner	119

	PAGE
Windham	118
Woodworth	120, 127

S. M.

	PAGE
Adrian	24
Ahira (Leighton)	39
Alexander	91
Badea	231
Boylston	230
Braden	116, 144
Dawn	166
Dennis	208, 215
Franklin Square	214
Glory	204
Golden Hill	117, 195
Gorton	111, 266
Greenwood	267
Kentucky	177
Laban	176
Lebanon, 81	136
(Leighton) Ahira	39
Lisbon	28
Mornington	9
Olmutz	8, 167
Olney	110
Renovation	25
Shawmut	133, 291
Silver Street	62, 157
St. Michael	235
St. Thomas	63
State Street	104
Thatcher	53, 205

C. P. M.

	PAGE
Ariel	150
Ganges	115
Meribah	103, 114
Willoughby	192

L. P. M.

	PAGE
Nashville	51

S. P. M.

	PAGE
Dalston	47

C. L. M.

	PAGE
Hastings	87

H. M.

	PAGE
Darwell	4
Haddam	45
Lenox	96
Lischer	44, 234

METRICAL INDEX OF TUNES.

	PAGE
Slow	86
Warsaw	98, 269
Zebulon	151

5, 5, 6, 5.
	PAGE
Lyons	48

5, 8.
	PAGE
Guide	163

6.
	PAGE
All to Christ I owe	155
St. Jude, 8l	216

6, 4.
	PAGE
America	206
Bethany	170
Dort	90
Italian Hymn	1, 11, 257
New Haven	20
Oak	171
Olivet	129, 256, 233
To-day	107

6, 4, 6, 4, 4, 4.
	PAGE
Ava	113

6, 5.
	PAGE
Magdalene	262

6, 6, 6, 4.
	PAGE
Nearer my Home	166

6, 9.
	PAGE
Comfort	131

7.
	PAGE
Aletta	16, 124
Beminster	241
Benevento, 8l	217, 286
Bethlehem, 6l	67
Beulah, 8l	279
Dallas	21
Halle, 6l	30
Hendon	42, 187
Herald Angels, 8l	89, 216
Horton	103
Martyn, 8l	109, 186
Meinhold, 6l	83
Messiah, 8l	2, 186, 221
Morning Star, 8l	63
Mozart	88
Nuremburg	156, 294
Pleyel's Hymn	17
Redhead, 6l	77
Rock of Ages, 6l	124
Rosefield, 6l	15, 109
Sabbath, 6l	33
Spanish Hymn, 8l	179
St. Gervais	49
Toplady, 6l	128
Trusting	136

7, 6.
	PAGE
Amsterdam	162
Aurelia	217
Crucifix	78
Ewing	206, 274
Mendebras	43
Missionary Hymn	241
Pearsall	268
Penitence	132
Salvation	59
Tell the Story	250
The old, old Story	251
Webb	178, 215
Yarmouth	207

7, 6, 7, 5.
	PAGE
Work, for the Night	280

7, 6. 7, 7, 6.
	PAGE
Enos	265

7. 6, 7, 7, 7.
	PAGE
New Jerusalem	284

8.
	PAGE
Contrast, 8l	154, 278
Penuel, 6l	141

8, 4.
	PAGE
Wales	193

8, 5.
	PAGE
Pass me not	123
Song	133

8, 5, 8, 3.
	PAGE
Stephanos	113

8, 6; 7, 7, 7, 6.
	PAGE
We shall meet	281

8, 7.
	PAGE
(Amor) Jesu Bone Pastor, 8l	139
Autumn, 8l	10, 95, 198
Bartimeus	130
Bavaria, 6l	104
Beautiful River	243
Crawford, 8l	138, 249
Dorrnance (Talmar)	126
Ellesdie, 8l	141, 183
Even Me	123
Hark, the voice, 8l	248
Harwell, 6 or 8l	3, 99, 270
Jesu, Bone Pastor (Amor), 8l	139
Middleton, 8l	236, 254
Nettleton, 8l	140
Pilgrim, 6l	70
Rathbun	182
Rest for the Weary	282
Shining Shore, 8l	168
Stockwell	28
(Talmar) Dorrnance	126

	PAGE
The sweetest Name	152
Vespers	29
Wilmot	70

8, 7, 4.
	PAGE
Alvan	22
Belmont	104
Brest	82
Finney	71
Greenville	105
Oliphant	160
Shepherd	161
Sicily	253
Tamworth	271
Wave	235
Zion	267

9, 11, 10, 10.
	PAGE
I'm a Pilgrim	159

10.
	PAGE
Eventide	31
Joyfully	285

10, 4.
	PAGE
Homeward Bound	168

10, 8.
	PAGE
Jesus, Guide	163

10, 11; 11, 11, 12, 11.
	PAGE
Avison	316

11.
	PAGE
Edinburgh	199
Expostulation	102
Goshen	174
Portuguese Hymn	173
Sweet Home	228

11, 5.
	PAGE
Come, let us anew	287

11, 6, 5.
	PAGE
The Lord will provide	159

11, 10.
	PAGE
Come, ye disconsolate	107
Folsom	69
Henley	102
Vox Angelica	229

11, 12.
	PAGE
Revive us again	154

11, 12, 12, 10.
	PAGE
Nicæa	5

12, 11.
	PAGE
Scotland	101

INDEX OF SCRIPTURE TEXTS.

Genesis.

	HYMN
1 : 2	534
1 : 3	580
2 : 2, 3	76
5 : 24	416
19 : 17	236
22 : 8, 14	553
24 : 31	405
24 : 53	505
27 : 31	376, 377
28 : 1-15	574
24 : 23-33	333
32 : 21	521

Exodus.

20 : 11	76
25 : 23	2.)

Leviticus.

8 : 35	390

Numbers.

10 : 33	354, 357
11 : 9	395
21 : 17	523
24 : 17-19	553

Deuteronomy.

31 : 1-4	612, 615

Joshua.

14 : 8	437

Judges.

8 : 4	379

Ruth.

1 : 16, 17	491

1st Samuel.

3 : 10	72
7 : 12	311

1st Kings.

3 : 5	17, 35
8	518, 519
18 : 44	554

2d Kings.

4 : 26	438
20 : 1	591

2d Chronicles.

15 : 15	490

Nehemiah.

	HYMN
9 : 5	87

Esther.

4 : 16	281

Job.

3 : 17	629, 631
19 : 25	195
29 : 2	420
38	116

Psalms.

2	551
4	61, 63
5	84
14	562
16	130
19	54, 125, 129
23	300, 378, 455
24 : 2, 3	350
23 : 1-4	436
24	194, 296
26 : 2	310
27 : 5	411
29	55
31	478
31 : 3	369, 361
31 : 15	125, 462, 467
34	447
35 : 5-9	121
41 : 1-3	137, 320
41 : 3	317
42	419
45 : 2	325
46	439
46 : 10	473, 474
48 : 14	354
51	264, 255, 484
51 : 1	262
51 : 10	435
51 : 17	263
55 : 22	415
62	396
63	83, 536, 597
65	654
65 : 2	255
65 : 11	649, 650
66	646
66 : 2	334, 410
68 : 18	197
69 : 15	422
71	446, 466, 643
72	545, 519, 553

	HYMN
72 : 15	551
73 : 23-28	445
73 : 24	355
73 : 25	343, 444, 452
77 : 19	466
78	657
78 : 53	355
80	573
83 : 1	356, 357
84	79, 100
85 : 6	348
88	237
90	641
90 : 5, 6	359, 617
91	64, 67
92	56, 78
93	101
95 : 1-6	89
96	151, 439
96 : 2	459
97	101, 431, 471
98	150
99	90
100	103, 104
102 : 13-21	536
103	122, 312
103 : 1-7	461
103 : 8-12	119
103 : 13-18	120
104	108
107	644
107 : 24	370
109 : 20	144
110 : 4	364
117	59, 105
118	85
118 : 6	395
118 : 24	97
119	131, 439
119 : 105	128, 130, 132
119 : 130	127
119 : 136, 158	560
119 : 176	303
121	102, 470
122	82, 106, 545
125	526, 591
125 : 2	521
126	448, 560
127	68
130	421, 131, 433
132	517, 520
135 : 2	213
136	95
137	515, 602

	HYMN
137 : 2	369
138	424
139	124, 400
146	115, 472
147	645
148	4, 111
150	656

Proverbs.

1 : 20-23	209
3 : 9	529
8 : 4	260
18 : 24	314, 420

Ecclesiastes.

9 : 10	287, 266

Canticles.

2 : 16	375, 377, 443
5 : 2	179, 250
5 : 10-16	325

Isaiah.

2 : 1-4	532
4 : 6	411
6 : 1-3	5
6 : 3	2, 8, 20, 111
6 : 8	556
9 : 1-7	147
9 : 2	549
9 : 6	154
21 : 11	152
26 : 3	424
26 : 4	287
27 : 13	221
32 : 1	548
32 : 20	516
33 : 17, 24	625
31 : 30, 21	596
35 : 8-10	346, 366
38 : 1	591
40 : 9	544
40 : 28-31	381
42 : 7	529
42 : 10-12	530, 549
43 : 6	583
49 : 15	419
52 : 1, 2	546
52 : 7-9	516, 528
52 : 15	559
53 : 1	234, 523
53 : 4, 5, 12	190
55 : 1, 2	251, 224, 233
55 : 4	360

INDEX OF SCRIPTURE TEXTS. 323

	HYMN
57:15	468
58:1	579
61:1,2	112, 140, 316
61:13	441
63:1	135
63:7	333

Jeremiah.

3:12, 14, 22	251
9:1	550
23:6	143, 500
20:13	35
31:3	579
31:18-20	251

Ezekiel.

11:19	261
18:31	241
36:26	251
33:11	241
36:37	571
37:3	570

Daniel.

2:44	531

Hosea.

6:1-4	413
11:8	273

Micah.

4:1,2	532
6:6	207

Habakkuk.

3:2	18
3:17	458

Haggai.

2:7	161, 210

Zechariah.

1:8	643
13:1	223, 232, 302

Matthew.

1:21	290, 300, 328, 332
	349
2:1-10	136, 137, 150
2:10	135
3:7	259
4:1-11	169
4:16	520
6:25	464, 473
7:7	35
8:23-27	421, 532, 535
9:35	170
10:40-42	495
11:19	314
11:28	267, 271, 380
11:28-30	223, 239, 240
12:20	212
13:1-8	576
13:16, 17	516
13:46	299
14:35, 36	172
14:27	426
18:20	11
19:13, 14	486, 488, 597
2):1-12	566
21:28	556

	HYMN
25:1-13	372, 605
25:21	649
25:31-46	254, 256
26:26-30	490, 497, 503
26:36	173, 1,6, 177
26:41	328
27:...175, 176, 183, 184, 205	
27:46	180
28:	224
24:1-6	193
28:19	511, 552

Mark.

1:12, 13	160
1:32	40
4:24	576
4:38	522, 525
4:39	421
6:50	426
8:33	406
10:13-16	486, 488, 597
10:28	404
10:47	283, 291
10:51, 52	263
13:10	505
13:33	388
13:37	390
11:1-3	613
14:22-25	496, 497
14:32-35	173, 176
14:36	410
15	176, 183, 184, 215
16:6	190, 200
16:15	541, 552

Luke.

2:7-15..113, 158, 162, 163	
2:13	110
2:11	100, 165, 106
2:29	549
2:32	520
3:7	259
4:1-13	160
4:18	112, 153
4:18,19	149, 521
7:34	311
7:47	307, 313
8:22-35	421, 522, 525
9:23	263, 399, 404
10:20	397
10:30	319, 335
12:32	316, 427
12:35-38	575, 605
14:16-24	235, 508
14:27	236
15:18	251
16:19-31	272
18:1	430
18:7	479
18:13	273
18:16	486, 488
18:37, 38	276, 277
19:41	260
22:19	501, 502
22:19, 20	496, 497, 503
23	176, 182, 184, 275
23:13	282, 430
23:55 } 24:1 }	193
24:1	76
24:29	57, 62, 65, 71

	HYMN
24:34	196
24:44, 45	180

John.

1:9, 14, 17	124
1:16	305
3:7	237
3:16	145, 225
4:34	567
4:35	536
6:35, 51, 53-57	498
6:37	265
7:37	140, 242
8:36	436
9:4	319, 633
10:3, 4	350, 356
12:41	5
14:2	373, 599
11:6	138, 815
14:16	48
14:19	423
18:1	173, 176
19	176, 182, 184, 275
19:2	170
19:5	337
19:30	183, 188
19:34	113, 227
21:15	390, 449
21:17	346

Acts.

1:9	267
2:1-3	15
2:4	542
2:30	469
2:47	465
9:6	231
9:11	49
10:33	564
10:36	217
10:38	167, 170
10:44	53
11:23	494
13:47	547
16:9	547, 557
26:29	659

Romans.

1:16	406
2:4	261
6:3	484
8:14, 16	50
8:31	395
10:1	560
10:10	495
10:21	260
12:5	508, 513
12:12	211
13:11	368
14:11	542

1st Corinthians.

1:23-29	141
1:30	146
2:2	295
5:7	215
10:31	392
11:23-26	496, 497, 503
11:24	501, 502
15:19, 20	507
15:43	601

	HYMN
15:47, 49	213
15:55	584
15:53	567
16:13	333, 391, 397

2d Corinthians.

1:12	437
1:22	46, 50
4:4	127
4:6	500
5:1	455
5:7	355
5:14	168, 535
5:17	391
5:21	431
6:2	248, 252
13:11	29
15:15	430

Galatians.

3:22	271
6:6	434
6:14	182, 401

Ephesians.

1:13, 14	50
2:5	143
2:8	206
2:19	815
3:15	509
3:16	42
4:4-6	509, 513, 527
4:8	197
4:25	508
4:30	249, 230
5:14	389
6:11-13	388, 393
6:11-18	387
6:13	392
6:14	381

Philippians.

1:21	189
1:22	481, 565
1:23	624
2:9	336
2:10	309, 542
3:7-9	491, 515
3:12-14	398
4:11	464, 463
4:13	430

Colossians.

2:2	505
3:11	408, 412, 45..
3:23	392
4:2	41

1st Thessalonians.

4:14	585
4:17	599
4:18	504, 505

1st Timothy.

6:12	382

2d Timothy.

1:12	400
2:3, 4	394
3:16	126, 198
4:6	647

INDEX OF SCRIPTURE TEXTS.

Titus.
	HYMN
2 : 12	31
2 : 10-13	568

Hebrews.
	HYMN
1 : 6	608
2 : 10	208
2 : 11	406
4 : 7	239
4 : 9	75, 77, 81
4 : 14, 15	187, 220
4 : 16	17, 18, 212, 238
5 : 6	564
5 : 17	212
6 : 6	191
6 : 19	324
6 : 20	363
7 : 25	193, 195
9 : 14	437
10 : 4, 12	297
10 : 20-22	198
10 : 29	278
11 : 13	353, 358
11 : 14	348, 380
12 : 1, 2	398
12 : 2	440
13 : 5	380
13 : 13	407
13 : 14	386

James.
	HYMN
1 : 12	381, 388, 394, 899
4 : 13-15	246, 637
5 : 8, 9	604

1st Peter.
	HYMN
1 : 8	310, 331
2 : 7	326, 334, 382
2 : 21	168, 171
5 : 4	367
5 : 7	415, 475, 477

2d Peter.
	HYMN
1 : 4	380
1 : 19	55

1st John.
	HYMN
1 : 3	118
2 : 1	209
2 : 6	416
3 : 1	434
4 : 8	402
4 : 19	290, 414

Jude.
	HYMN
24, 25	89

Revelations.
	HYMN
1 : 7	186, 604, 611
1 : 18	222
2 : 10	453
3 : 11	514
3 : 12	644
3 : 20	179, 250
4 : 8	8
4 : 11	21, 180
5 : 6-12	219
5 : 11	619
5 : 12	185, 203, 204, 205, 215, 218
5 : 13	3, 216, 505

	HYMN
7 : 9	510
7 : 9-12	109
7 : 9-17	609, 622, 626, 627, 632
7 : 14	399
7 : 15-17	81
11 : 15	555
13 : 8	223
14 : 13	596, 600
15 : 3	143, 341
19 : 11	548
20 : 8	558
21	616, 617, 618, 621, 623
21 : 1-4	614
21 : 22-25	81
22	621, 631
22 : 12	567
22 : 16	443
22 : 17-20	244
22 : 20	610

CHANTS.

Psalms.
	CHANT
1	3
23	4
67	6
84	7
95	8
98	9
100	10
103	11
103 : 17, 18	26
121	12

	CHANT
122	13
150	14

Isaiah.
	CHANT
41 : 3, 4	28
52 : 7-9	16
53	15

Ezekiel.
	CHANT
36 : 25, 26	28

Matthew.
	CHANT
6 : 9-13	20
11 : 28-30	21

Mark.
	CHANT
10 : 14	27

Luke.
	CHANT
1 : 46-55	19
1 : 68-71	17
2 : 8-14	18

Acts.
	CHANT
2 : 39	27

Romans.
	CHANT
6 : 9-11	29

1st Corinthians.
	CHANT
5 : 7, 8	29

Revelations.
	CHANT
1 : 5, 6	30
14 : 13	30
20 : 6	30

INDEX OF SUBJECTS.

The figures refer to the numbers of the hymns.

ABBA, FATHER.
454 Behold what wondrous
404 Jesus, I my cross
ABRAHAMIC COVENANT.
489 Dear Saviour, if these lambs
ACCEPTED TIME.
248 Now is the accepted time
249 To-day the Saviour calls
247 While life prolongs its
ACCESS TO GOD.
347 Arise, my soul, arise
17 Behold the throne of grace
209 Come, let us lift our joyful
118 Our heavenly Father calls
ACTIVITY—See *Christian Activity.*
ADOPTION.
454 Behold what wondrous
33 Blessed are the sons of God
468 My God, my Father
ADORATION—See *Christ, God, Holy Spirit,* and *Trinity.*
ADVENT—See *Christ, Advent of*
ADVOCATE—See *Christ.*
AFFLICTIONS:
BLESSINGS OF.
466 God moves in a mysterious
399 Must Jesus bear the cross
125 Since all the varying scenes
458 Sometimes a light surprises
626 What are these in bright
COMFORT UNDER.
238 Come, ye disconsolate,
445 My supporter and my
512 Hark, hark, my soul, angelic
350 He leadeth me, O blessed
380 How firm a foundation
629 There is an hour of peaceful
428 Through the love of God
504 Why do we mourn departing
505 Why should our tears in
COURAGE IN.
647 A few more years shall roll
307 Am I a soldier of the cross
415 Cast thy burden on the
475 Commit thou all thy griefs
441 Take, my soul, thy full
378 The Lord is my Shepherd
PRAYER IN.
450 Calm me, my God, and keep
23 Gently, Lord, O gently lead
422 God of my life, to Thee
590 In the hour of trial
289 My faith looks up to Thee
499 O Thou, to whose all-search
431 Out of the depths of woe

AFFLICTIONS:
REFUGE IN.
67 Call Jehovah thy salvation
224 Come unto me when
425 Fountain of grace, rich
29 From every stormy wind
469 God is the refuge of His
380 How firm a foundation
477 How gentle God's commands
411 Jesus, Lover of my soul
290 Jesus, Thy name I love
306 Lord, Thou art my Rock
434 To God I cried when
583 When languor and disease
187 Where high the heavenly
270 With tearful eyes I look
REJOICING IN.
303 I heard the voice of Jesus
641 In the Christian's home in
683 Joyfully, joyfully, onward I
119 My soul, repeat the praise
514 O what, if we are Christ's
411 The Lord is King, lift up
370 We're bound for yonder
626 What are these in bright
467 While Thee I seek
SUBMISSION UNDER.
462 Father, I know that all my
464 Father, whate'er of earthly
465 I worship Thee, sweet Will
468 My God, my Father
480 My Jesus, as Thou wilt
481 Thy way, not mine
473 Wait, O my soul, Thy
ALARM.
257 Awaked by Sinai's awful
254 Lo, on a narrow neck
239 My former hopes are fled
258 O where shall rest be found
237 While life prolongs its
ALL IN ALL—See *Christ* and *God.*
ALL IS WELL.
428 Through the love of God
ALMS—See *Charity.*
ANGELS:
AT CORONATION OF CHRIST.
217 All hail the power of Jesus'
218 Come, let us join our
AT RESURRECTION OF CHRIST.
201 Christ, the Lord, is risen
196 Yes, the Redeemer rose
JOY OF.
624 Ye angels, who stand round
MINISTRY OF.
512 Hark, hark, my soul

ANGELS:
64 Saviour, breathe an evening
SONG OF.
166 Calm on the listening ear
153 Hark, the herald angels
160 Hark, what mean those
165 It came upon the midnight
158 When Jordan hushed his
148 While shepherds watched
ASCENSION OF CHRIST—See *Christ.*
ASHAMED OF JESUS.
400 I'm not ashamed to own
466 Jesus, and shall it ever be
ASLEEP IN JESUS—See *Death.*
ASPIRATIONS:
FOR CHRIST.
354 Guide me, O Thou great
482 I need Thee, precious Jesus
376 More love to Thee, O Christ
335 O Love Divine, how sweet
319 O that I could for ever
62 Sun of my soul
FOR DIVINE GRACE.
42 Come, dearest Lord, descend
430 Jesus, my strength, my
435 O for a heart to praise
FOR FIDELITY.
437 I want a principle
483 O Lamb of God, still keep
439 O that the Lord would guide
FOR GOD.
419 As pants the hart for
403 I would love Thee, God
408 My God, my Father
374 Nearer, my God, to Thee
284 Take me, O my Father
FOR HEAVEN.
351 As when the weary traveller
602 Far from my heavenly
625 I long to behold Him
623 Jerusalem, my happy home
511 'Mid scenes of confusion
621 O mother dear, Jerusalem
610 O'er the distant mountains
358 Rise, my soul, and stretch
624 Ye angels, who stand round
FOR HOLINESS.
462 Father, I know that all
280 My faith looks up to Thee
416 O for a closer walk
436 O Lord, impart Thyself
409 O Thou whose all-search
484 We long to move and

INDEX OF SUBJECTS

ASPIRATIONS:
 FOR THE HOLY SPIRIT.
  44 Come, Holy Ghost, in love
  47 Holy Ghost, with light
  277 Lord, I hear of showers
 FOR PEACE AND REST.
  431 Jesus, my Lord, attend
  362 O God of Bethel, by whose
  267 O that my load of sins
 OF FAITH—See *Faith*.
 OF HOPE—See *Hope*.
ASSURANCE:
 DECLARED.
  316 Children of the heavenly
  195 I know that my Redeemer
  211 I know that my Redeemer
  435 In heavenly love abiding
  377 Now I have found a Friend
 DESIRED.
  337 Arise, my soul, arise
  423 When sins and fears
  50 Why should the children of
  369 Your harps, ye trembling
ATONEMENT:
 COMPLETED.
  224 Blow ye the trumpet
  200 Christ, the Lord, is risen
  201 Christ, the Lord, is risen
  235 Come, happy souls
  209 Come, let us lift our
  235 Come, sinners, to the
  198 Done is the work that saves
  188 Hark, the voice of love
  190 Surely Christ thy griefs
  197 The happy morn is come
  183 "'Tis finished," so the
 NEEDED.
  283 Come, ye faithful, raise
  141 Dearest of all the names
  146 How heavy is the night
  264 Lord, I am vile, conceived
  297 Not all the blood of beasts
  237 Rock of ages, cleft for me
 SUFFICIENT.
  233 Come, ye sinners, poor
  242 From the cross uplifted
  215 Hail, Thou once despised
  193 He lives, the great
  224 Let every mortal ear
  324 Now I have found the
  178 O sacred Head, now
  234 Sinners, will you scorn
  225 The voice of free grace
  133 Thou art the Way

BACKSLIDING—See *Declension*.
BAPTISM:
 ADULT.
  447 In token that thou shalt
  434 We long to move and
 INFANT.
  483 A little child the Saviour
  489 Dear Saviour, if thou hast
  486 See Israel's gentle Shepherd
 OF HOLY SPIRIT.
  512 O Spirit of the living God
BEING OF GOD—See *God*.
BELIEVERS—See *Christians* and *Saints*.
BENEVOLENCE—See *Charity*.
BEREAVEMENT—See *Afflictions*, *Death*, and *Funeral Hymns*.
BIBLE—See *Word of God*.

BLIND BARTIMEUS.
  291 Mercy, O Thou Son of
  292 Lord, I know Thy grace
BLOOD OF CHRIST—See *Atonement* and *Christ*.
BREVITY OF LIFE—See *Life*.
BROTHERLY LOVE—See *Communion of Saints*.
BURIAL—See *Funeral Hymns*.

CALVARY.
  242 Come to Calvary's holy
  176 Go to dark Gethsemane
  Also see *Christ, crucified*.
CHANGE OF HEART—See *Conversion*.
CHARITY.
  536 Hark, the voice of Jesus
  539 With my substance I will
  Also see *Communion of Saints*.
CHASTENINGS—See *Afflictions*.
CHILDREN.
  356 Saviour, like a Shepherd
  486 See Israel's gentle Shepherd
  23 Shepherd of tender youth
CHRIST:
 ABIDING WITH BELIEVERS.
  57 The day, O Lord, is spent
  62 Sun of my soul
 ADORATION OF.
  219 Behold the glories of the
  162 Brightness of the Father's
  205 Come, all ye saints of God
  218 Come, let us join our
  209 Come, let us lift our joyful
  204 Glory to God on high
  215 Hail, thou once despised
  603 Hark, ten thousand harps
  210 Infinite excellence is Thine
  323 Jesus, my Lord, my God
  32) Jesus, the very thought
  230 Jesus, Thy name I love
 ADVENT, FIRST.
  163 Angels from the realms of
  154 Bright and joyful is the
  151 Brightest and best of the
  161 Come, Thou long-expected
  149 Hark, the glad sound, the
  153 Hark, the herald angels
  160 Hark, what mean those
  150 Joy to the world, the
  151 Sing to the world, ye distant
  147 The race that long in
  158 When Jordan hushed his
  148 While shepherds watched
  Also see *Star of Bethlehem*.
 ADVENT, SECOND — See *Second Coming of*.
 ADVOCATE
  209 Come, let us lift our joyful
  193 He lives, the great Redeemer
  282 Jesus, Thou art the sinner's
 AGONY.
  180 Alas, and did my Saviour
  176 Go to dark Gethsemane
  275 I see the crowd in Pilate's
  177 Lord, in this Thy mercy
  173 'Tis midnight; and on
 ALL IN ALL.
  344 I hear the Saviour say
  408 In Christ I've my all
  412 Thou, O Christ, art all I
  345 Thy tears, not mine

CHRIST:
 ALPHA AND OMEGA.
  440 Love Divine, all love
 ANNUNCIATION OF.
  166 Calm on the listening ear
  165 It came upon the midnight
  Also see *Advent of* and *Angels, Song of*.
 ASCENSION OF.
  242 Hail the day that sees Him
  194 Our Lord is risen from
  206 Rise, glorious Conqueror
  207 The Lord on high ascends
 ATONEMENT OF.
  180 Alas! and did my Saviour
  337 Arise, my soul, arise
  215 Hail, Thou once despised
  297 Not all the blood of beasts
  181 O Jesus, sweet the tears I
  199 Surely Christ thy griefs
  554 Tell me the old, old story
  345 Thy tears, not mine
  Also see *Atonement*.
 BEAUTY OF.
  625 I long to behold Him
  325 Majestic sweetness sits
 BENEVOLENCE OF.
  170 When, like a stranger, on
 BIRTH OF—See *Advent*.
 BLOOD OF.
  232 Come to Calvary's holy
  274 In evil long I took delight
  174 Ye that pass by, behold
 CAPTAIN.
  427 Fear not, O little flock
  453 Our Captain leads us on
  381 Stand up, my soul, shake off
 CHARACTER OF.
  167 Behold, where in a mortal
  171 How beauteous were the
  168 My dear Redeemer, and
  108 O worship the King
 COMING TO— See *Conversion*.
 COMMUNION WITH—See *Communion*.
 COMPASSION OF—See *Love of*.
  212 With joy we meditate the
 CONDESCENSION OF—See *Incarnate*.
 CONQUEROR.
  93 Again the Lord of life
  195 He comes in blood-stained
  194 Our Lord is risen from
  206 Rise, glorious Conqueror
  203 Sons of Zion, raise your
  207 The Lord on high ascends
 CORNER-STONE.
  520 Christ is made the sure
 CORONATION OF.
  217 All hail the power of Jesus'
  203 Sons of Zion, raise your
 CROSS OF—See *Cross*.
 CRUCIFIXION OF—See *Sacrifice* and *Passion*.
 DAY-STAR.
  55 We lift our hearts to Thee.
  158 When Jordan hushed his
 DEATH OF—See *Atonement* and *Passion of*.
 DELIGHT IN.
  301 Let worldly minds the
  328 Oh, for a thousand tongues
  624 Ye angels, who stand round

INDEX OF SUBJECTS.

CHRIST:
DESIRE OF NATIONS.
151 Come, Thou long-expected
153 Hark, the herald angels
210 Infinite excellence is Thine
DIVINITY OF.
134 Bright and joyful is the
173 O, where is He that trod
EXALTED.
217 All hail the power of Jesus'
219 Behold the glories of the
233 Come, ye faithful, raise
2 2 Rejoice, the Lord is King
208 The head that once was
EXAMPLE.
177 Behold, where, in a mortal
176 Go to dark Gethsemane
168 My dear Redeemer, and
EXCELLENCY OF.
210 Infinite excellence is Thine.
331 O could I speak the
FAITH IN—See *Faith.*
237 Not all the blood of beasts
FINISHED WORK OF.
214 Blow ye the trumpet
194 Done is the work that
184 Hark, the voice of love and
134 Thou art the Way; to Thee
183 "'Tis finished," so the
FORERUNNER.
333 Our journey is a thorny
FOUNTAIN.
232 Come to Calvary's holy
425 Fountain of grace, rich, full
305 I heard the voice of Jesus
302 There is a fountain filled
FRIEND.
193 He lives, the great Redeemer
432 I need Thee, precious Jesus
377 Now I have found a Friend
314 One there is, above all
429 There's a Friend above
FRIEND OF SINNERS.
324 Come, O Thou Traveller
271 Jesus, the sinner's Friend
242 Jesus, Thou art the sinner's
FULLNESS OF.
425 Fountain of grace, rich, full
305 I heard the voice of Jesus
135 I know that my Redeemer
299 I've found the pearl of
412 Thou, O Christ, art all I
424 Ye angels, who stand round
GLORYING IN.
400 I'm not ashamed to own
401 In the cross of Christ I
406 Jesus, and shall it ever
407 My precious Lord, for Thy
GLORY OF.
219 Behold the glories of the
149 Glory, glory everlasting
215 Hail, thou once despiséd
603 Hark, ten thousand harps
611 Lo, He comes, with clouds
204 The head that once was
GRACE OF.
336 Amazing grace, how sweet
142 Grace, 'tis a charming
143 How heavy is the night
835 Majestic sweetness sits
137 Salvation, O the joyful
213 With joy we meditate
GRATITUDE TO—See *Gratitude.*

CHRIST:
HIDING-PLACE.
411 Jesus, Lover of my soul
483 O Lamb of God, still keep
HIGH PRIEST.
337 Arise, my soul, arise
214 Come, let us join in songs
198 Done is the work that
211 I know that my Redeemer
223 Now let our cheerful eyes
186 Now to the Lord, who
187 Where high the heavenly
212 With joy we meditate
HOPE OF HIS PEOPLE.
141 Dearest of all the names
423 When sins and fears
HUMANITY OF.
139 Awhile in spirit, Lord, with
167 Behold, where, in a mortal
214 Come, let us join in songs
141 Dearest of all the names
171 How beauteous were the
163 My dear Redeemer, and
213 O mean may seem this
170 When, like a stranger on
187 Where high the heavenly
212 With joy we meditate the
HUMILITY OF
171 How beauteous were the
IMMANUEL.
141 Dearest of all the names
213 O mean may seem this
INCARNATE—See *Humanity of.*
134 O Word of God Incarnate
INCOMPARABLE.
309 Jesus is the Name we
325 Majestic sweetness sits
IN GETHSEMANE.
176 Go to dark Gethsemane
177 Lord, in this Thy mercy's
173 'Tis midnight; and on
INTERCESSION OF.
337 Arise, my soul, arise
203 Hail the day that sees Him
193 He lives, the great
INVITATION OF.
249 Come, said Jesus' sacred
243 From the cross uplifted
305 I heard the voice of Jesus
241 Sinners, turn, why will ye
140 The Saviour calls, let
270 With tearful eyes I look
JUDGE.
611 Lo, He comes, with clouds
254 Lo, on a narrow neck of
236 When Thou, my righteous
KING OF GLORY.
200 Christ, the Lord, is risen
603 Hark, ten thousand harps
159 Joy to the world, the Lord
194 Our Lord is risen from the
293 Sons of Zion, raise your
KING OF SAINTS.
108 O worship the King
103 Ye servants of God
KING, SOVEREIGN
336 Join all the glorious names
327 O Jesus, King most
222 Rejoice, the Lord is King
KNOCKING.
250 Behold, a stranger's at the
179 O Jesus, Thou art standing

CHRIST:
LAMB OF GOD.
219 Behold the glories of the
205 Come, all ye saints of God
218 Come, let us join our
185 Come, let us sing the song
204 Glory to God on high
215 Hail, Thou once despiséd
237 Not all the blood of
LEADER.
234 Go forward, Christian
3 0 He leadeth me : O blessed
881 Stand up, my soul, shake
361 The way is dark; I cannot
LIFE.
205 I heard the voice of Jesus
316 Lord, I was blind, I could
LIFE OF—See *Ministry of.*
LIGHT.
305 I heard the voice of Jesus
316 Lord, I was blind, I could
443 My God, the Spring of all
LONG-SUFFERING OF.
149 O Jesus, Thou art standing
LORD.
217 All hail the power of Jesus'
299 Jesus, Thy Name I love
208 The head that once was
LOVE OF.
278 Depth of mercy, can there
214 Come, let us join in songs
149 Glory, glory everlasting
413 Hark, my soul, it is the
135 He comes in blood-stained
454 Love Divine, all love
347 Now begin the heavenly
335 O Love divine, how sweet
314 One there is, above all others
137 Plunged in a gulf of dark
564 Tell me the old, old story
LOVELINESS OF.
331 Jesus, these eyes have never
339 Jesus, the very thought
325 Majestic sweetness sits
327 O Jesus, King most
364 Thou dear Redeemer, dying
LOVING-KINDNESS OF.
338 Awake, my soul, to joyful
MAN OF SORROWS.
190 Surely Christ thy griefs
MEDIATOR—See *Intercession of.*
214 Come, let us join in songs
MEEKNESS OF.
167 Behold, where, in a mortal
171 How beauteous were the
168 My dear Redeemer, and
MERCY OF.
324 Now I have found the
145 Roll o your triumphant
144 Sweet is Thy mercy, Lord
MINISTRY OF.
167 Behold, where, in a mortal
163 My dear Redeemer, and
172 O where is He that trod
170 When, like a stranger,
MIRACLES OF—See *Ministry of.*
MISSION OF.
167 Behold, where, in a mortal
235 Come, happy souls,
149 Hark, the glad sound, the
159 Joy to the world, the Lord
580 Thou, whose almighty

INDEX OF SUBJECTS.

CHRIST:
MORNING-STAR.
  443 My God, the Spring of all
NAME OF.
  141 Dearest of all the names
  332 How sweet the name of
  345 Jesus, I love Thy charming
  301 Jesus is the Name we
  250 Jesus, Thy Name I love
  325 O for a thousand tongues
  310 There is no name so sweet
NAMES OF.
  154 Bright and joyful is the
  335 Join all the glorious names
  147 The race that long is in
NATIVITY—See *Advent.*
OFFICES OF.
  337 Hail, my ever-blessed Jesus
  342 Join all the glorious names
ONLY PLEA.
  271 Jesus, the sinner's Friend
  245 Just as I am, without one
  205 Vain, delusive world, adieu
OUR PASSOVER.
  291 Christ, the Lord, is risen
  215 Hail, thou once despised.
PASSION.
  11 Alas! and did my Saviour
  115 Go to dark Gethsemane
  131 Heart of stone, relent
  215 In evil long I took
  275 I see the crowd in Pilate's
  177 Lord, in this Thy mercy's
  175 Lord Jesus, when we stand
  184 O come, and mourn with
  174 O sacred Head, now
  104 O worship the King
  1.0 Surely Christ Thy griefs
  113 The royal banners forward
  107 'Tis Heaven begun below
  149 When I survey the
  171 Ye that pass by, behold
  100 Ye servants of God
PATTERN—See *Example.*
PHYSICIAN.
  293 Lord, I know Thy grace
  241 Mercy, O Thou Son of
  170 When, like a stranger on
POWER OF—See *Divinity of.*
PRECIOUS.
  312 How sweet the name of
  433 I need Thee, precious
  345 Jesus, I love Thy charming
  311 Jesus, these eyes have
  313 Jesus, the very thought of
  443 My God, the Spring of all
  331 O could I speak the
  364 Thou dear Redeemer, dying
PRESENCE OF.
  312 How tedious and tasteless
  14 Jesus, where'er Thy people
  11 Where two or three, with
PRIEST.
  211 Blow ye the trumpet, blow
  214 Come, let us join in songs
  336 Join all the glorious names
  186 Now to the Lord, who
  212 With joy we meditate the
PRINCE OF PEACE.
  153 Watchman, tell us of the
PROPHET.
  214 Come, let us join in songs
  160 Hark, what mean those

CHRIST:
  336 Join all the glorious names
  186 Now to the Lord, who
RANSOM.
  162 Brightness of the Father's
  223 Come, ye faithful, raise
REDEEMER.
  219 Behold the glories of the
  149 Glory, glory everlasting
  195, 211 I know that my
REFUGE.
  411 Jesus, Lover of my soul
  393 Lord, Thou art my Rock
  483 O Lamb of God, still keep
REIGNING.
  192 He dies, the Friend of
  531 Hail to the Lord's anointed
  664 Hark, ten thousand harps
  555 Hark, the song of jubilee
  538 Hasten, Lord, the glorious
  1.0 Joy to the world, the Lord
  222 Rejoice, the Lord is King
  200 Rise, glorious Conqueror
  151 Sing to the Lord, ye distant
  203 Sons of Zion, raise your
  208 The head that once was
  207 The Lord on high ascends
  540 Wake the song of jubilee
  518 When shall the voice of
  109 Ye servants of God
RESURRECTION OF.
  291 Christ, the Lord, is risen aga
  200 Christ, the Lord, is risen to-
  202 Hail the day that sees Him
  192 He dies, the Friend of
  193 He lives, the great Redeemer
  199 How ca'm and beautiful
  195 I know that my Redeemer
  194 Our Lord is risen from
  197 The happy morn is come
  196 Yes, the Redeemer rose
RIGHTEOUSNESS OF.
  146 How heavy is the night
  434 Jesus, my Lord, attend
  540 Jesus, Thy blood and
  410 My hope is built on nothing
  446 My Saviour, my almighty
  401 No more, my God, I boast
ROCK.
  536 Glorious things of thee are
  410 My hope is built on nothing
  287 Rock of ages, cleft for me
SACRIFICE—See *Passion of.*
  140 Alas! and did my Saviour
  337 Arise, my soul, arise
  207 Not all the blood of beasts
  181 O Jesus, sweet the tears I
  313 Sweet the moments, rich
SAVIOUR, THE.
  413 I once was a stranger to
  177 Lord, in this Thy mercy's
  334 O could I speak the
  178 O sacred Head, now wounded
  Also see *Passion* and *Sacrifice of.*
SECOND COMING OF.
  607 Come, every pious heart
  164 Jesus came, the heavens
  611 Lo, He comes, with clouds
  251 Lo, on a narrow neck
  614 Lo, what a glorious sight
  610 O'er the distant mountains
  3 See the ransomed millions

CHRIST:
  256 When Thou, my righteous
SHEPHERD.
  475 In heavenly love abiding
  303 I was a wandering sheep
  356 Saviour, like a shepherd
  23 Shepherd of tender youth
  378 The Lord is my shepherd
  400 The Lord my shepherd is
SONG OF SONGS.
  341 Saints in glory, we
SUN OF RIGHTEOUSNESS.
  529 O'er the gloomy hills of
SURETY.
  337 Arise, my soul, arise
SYMPATHY OF.
  220 Now let our cheerful eyes
  187 Where high the heavenly
  212 With joy we meditate
TEMPTATION OF.
  109 Awhile in spirit, Lord
TRUST IN—See *Trust.*
VICTORIOUS—See *Conqueror.*
WAY, TRUTH, AND LIFE.
  315 Jesus, my All, to Heaven
  188 Thou art the Way; to Thee
WEEPING.
  260 Did Christ o'er sinners weep
WORD OF GOD.
  194 O Word of God, Incarnate
CHRIST'S GRACE EXTOLLED.
  366 Amazing grace, how sweet
  141 Awake, and sing the song
  451 Come, we that love the
  142 Grace, 'tis a charming
  305 I heard the voice of Jesus
  561 I love to tell the story
  313 Sweet the moments, rich
  448 When God revealed His
CHRISTIANS—See *Saints.*
CHRIST, THE LIFE OF
  375 Fade, fade, each earthly
  423 When sins and fears
CONFLICTS OF.
  419 As pants the hart for
  472 God of my life, through all
  411 Jesus, Lover of my soul
  434 Jesus, my Lord, attend
  416 O for a closer walk
  450 Sweet was the time when
CONQUERORS THROUGH CHRIST.
  338 Awake, my soul, stretch
  363 Our journey is a thorny
  Also see *Warfare.*
DUTIES OF.
  399 A charge to keep I have
  567 Go, labor on; spend and
  568 So let our lips and lives
ENCOURAGEMENTS OF.
  384 Awake, our souls, away
  346 Children of the heavenly
  427 Fear not, O little flock
  343 How firm a foundation
  456 In heavenly love abiding
  381 Stand up, my soul, shake
  378 The Lord is my Shepherd
  428 Through the love of God
  360 Your harps, ye trembling
EXAMPLE OF.
  510 Give me the wings of faith
  568 So let our lips and lives
FELLOWSHIP OF—See *Communion.*

INDEX OF SUBJECTS. 329

CHRISTIANS:
GRACES OF.
　450 Calm me, my God, and
　464 Father, whate'er of earthly
　437 I want a principle
　430 Jesus, my Strength, my
　445 O for a heart to praise
　568 So let our lips and lives
　Also see *Faith, Hope,* and *Love.*
CHRISTIAN ACTIVITY.
CALLS TO.
　567 Go, labor on; spend and
　556 Hark, the voice of Jesus
　383 Stand up, stand up for
　554 We are living, we are
　623 Work, for the night is
DUTY OF.
　390 A charge to keep I have
　397 Am I a soldier of the cross
　566 Jesus, our best beloved
　565 My gracious Lord, I own
　564 So let our lips and lives
　392 Teach me, my God, and
ENCOURAGEMENT IN.
　641 Come, let us anew
　382 Fight the good fight with
　555 He that goeth forth with
　391 My soul, weigh not thy
　319 This is the day of toil
　575 Sow in the morn thy seed
CHRISTIAN MINISTRY — See *Ministry.*
CHRISTMAS—See *Angels, Song of,* and *Christ, Advent of.*
CHURCH:
BELOVED OF GOD.
　526 Glorious things of thee are
　528 On the mountain's top
　521 Zion stands by hills
BELOVED OF SAINTS.
　82 How did my heart rejoice
　515 I love Thy kingdom, Lord
　492 People of the living God
GLORY OF.
　541 Daughter of Zion, from the
　526 Glorious things of thee are
　611 Lo, what a glorious sight
　516 Triumphant Zion, lift thy
INCREASE OF—See *Missions.*
　513 Though now the nations sit
REJOICING.
　83 Early, my God, without
　79 Great God, attend while
　536 Let Zion and her sons
SECURE.
　511 O where are kings and
　521 Zion stands by hills
TRIUMPH OF.
　536 Let Zion and her sons
　528 On the mountain's top
　516 Triumphant Zion, lift thy
　152 Watchman, tell us of the
UNITY OF.
　508 Blest be the dear, uniting
　513 Blest be the tie that binds
　509 Come, let us join our
　504 Happy the souls to Jesus
CLOSE OF SERVICE.
　518 Blest be the dear, uniting
　513 Blest be the tie that binds
　48 Dismiss us with Thy
　405, 73 Lord, dismiss us with
　19 O happy, happy place

CLOSE OF SERVICE.
　34 Part in peace, Christ's life
　59 Thy name, Almighty
　98 Thy presence, everlasting
CLOSET—See *Meditation.*
COMFORT.
　252 Child of sin and sorrow
　228 Come unto me, when
　Also see *Afflictions.*
COMING TO CHRIST—See *Sinners.*
COMMUNION:
OF SAINTS.
　513 Blest be the tie that binds
　509 Come, let us join our
　504 Happy the souls to Jesus
　27 How blest the sacred tie
　541 'Mid scenes of confusion
　30 O Lord, how joyful 'tis to
　506 Our souls, by love together
　527 Through the night of doubt
WITH GOD.
　51 Far from the world, O
　415 God, my Supporter and
　452 My God, my life, my
　441 My God, my Portion, and
　443 My God, the spring of all
　113 Our heavenly Father calls
WITH CHRIST.
　12 Far from my thoughts, vain
　345 O Love divine, how sweet
　319 O that I could so ever
　313 Sweet the moments, rich
CONFESSION OF FAITH—See *Faith.*
CONFESSION OF SIN—See *Sin.*
CONFIDENCE.
　415 Cast thy burden on the
　380 How firm a foundation
　401 In the cross of Christ
　410 My hope is built on nothing
　378 The Lord is my Shepherd
CONFORMITY TO CHRIST.
　435 O for a heart to praise
　Also see *Christ, Example of.*
CONSCIENCE.
　437 I want a principle within
　247 Not all the blood of beasts
　410 O that the Lord would
CONSECRATION
OF POSSESSIONS.
　182 When I survey the
　539 With my substance I will
OF SELF.
　294 And can I yet delay
　286 Lord, I am Thine, entirely
　74 Welcome, welcome, dear
　182 When I survey the
　485 Witness, ye men and angels
RENEWED.
　418 Come, let us to the Lord
　416 O for a closer walk
　288 Once again beside the cross
TO CHRIST.
　566 Jesus, our best beloved
　565 My gracious Lord, I own
CONSOLATION—See *Afflictions.*
CONSTANCY.
　390 A charge to keep I have
　398 Awake, my soul, stretch
　382 Fight the good fight with
　394 Go forward, Christian
　391 My soul, weigh not thy life

CONSTANCY.
　453 Our Captain leads us on
　392 Teach me, my God, my
CONTENTMENT.
　375 Fade, fade, each earthly
　464 Father, whate'er of earthly
　342 How tedious and tasteless
　458 Sometimes a light surprises
　423 Through the love of God
CONTRITION.
　18 Alas, and did my Saviour
　181 O Jesus, sweet the tears I
　276 Pass me not, O gentle
　313 Sweet the moments, rich
CONVERSION.
　396 Amazing grace, how sweet
　294 And can I yet delay
　337 Arise, my soul, arise
　257 Awaked by Sinai's awful
　294 Father, I stretch my hands
　307 Hail, my ever blessed
　304 I am coming to the cross
　305 I heard the voice of Jesus
　561 I love to tell the story
　318 I send the joys of earth
　303 I was a wandering sheep
　404 Jesus, I my cross have
　315 Jesus, my All, to Heaven
　285 Just as I am, without
　391 Let word fly minds the
　316 Lord, I was blind! I could
　231 Lord, Thou hast won, at
　308 Lord, with glowing heart
　377 Now I have found a Friend
　293 O how happy are they
　317 The Saviour smiles; upon
　448 When God revealed His
　Also see *Faith.*
CONVERTS WELCOMED.
　495 Come in, Thou blessed of
　443 Pilgrim, burdened with thy
COURAGE.
　397 Am I a soldier of the cross
　384 Awake, our souls, away
　395 Brethren, while we sojourn
　382 Fight the good fight with
　394 Go forward, Christian
　391 My soul, weigh not thy life
　341 Stand up, my soul, shake
　393 Stand up, stand up for Jesus
COVENANT, ENTERING INTO.
　365 In all my Lord's appointed
　286 Lord, I am Thine, entirely
　492 People of the living God
　494 Thine for ever, God
　485 Witness, ye men and
CROSS:
AT THE CROSS.
　304 I am coming to the cross
　275 I see the crowd in Pilate's
　271 In evil long I took delight
　286 Lord, I am Thine, entirely
　175 Lord Jesus, when we stand
　181 O come, and mourn with
　181 O Jesus, sweet the tears I
　178 O sacred Head, now
　190 Surely Christ thy griefs hath
　313 Sweet the moments, rich in
　182 When I survey the wondrous
　174 Ye that pass by, behold the
BEARING.
　400 I'm not ashamed to own
　404 Jesus, I my cross have

INDEX OF SUBJECTS.

CROSS:
399 Must Jesus bear the cross
407 My precious Lord, for Thy
514 O what, if we are Christ's
GLORYING IN.
486 At Thy command, our
401 In the cross of Christ
407 My precious Lord, for Thy
POWER OF.
499 O the sweet wonders of
248 The head that once was
SOLDIER OF.
307 Am I a soldier of the cross
393 Stand up, stand up for
CROWNS OF GLORY
337 A crown of glory bright
323 Awake, my soul, stretch
346 Sing, ye redeemed of the
331 Stand up, my soul, shake
631 Ye angels, who stand round
CRUCIFIXION—See *Christ*.
TO THE WORLD.
401 No more, my God, I boast
133 When I survey the
Also see *Forsaking all for Christ*.

DARKNESS, SPIRITUAL.
419 As pants the hart for
432 God of my life, to Thee
411 Jesus, Lover of my soul
554 Light of those whose dreary
413 Out of the deep I call
431 Out of the depths
51 Why should the children of
Also see *Dejection*.
DAY OF GRACE.
259 Behold, a stranger's at the
253 Child of sin and sorrow
236 Life is the time to serve
234 Lo, on a narrow neck of
248 Now is the accepted time
253 O where shall rest be found
239 To-day the Saviour calls
237 While life prolongs its
DEATH:
ANTICIPATED.
503 Brighter still and brighter
692 Far from my heavenly
510 Forever with the Lord
583 Forth to the Land of
22 Gently, Lord, O gently lead
591 See Thy house in order
581 Through sorrow's night and
BED OF.
534 Earth with its dark and
500 In the hour of trial
549 The hour of my departure's
583 When languor and disease
CONFIDENCE IN.
623 And let this feeble body
340 How firm a foundation
603 It is not death to die
588 Why should we start and
CONQUERED.
534 Earth with its dark and
508 No, no, it is not dying
537 Unveil thy bosom, faithful
OF INFANTS.
597 With joy I see a thousand
OF SAINTS.
585 Asleep in Jesus: blessed
596 Hear what the voice from
586 How blest the righteous

DEATH:
600 O for the death of those
601 Rest for the toiling hand
595 Why should our tears in
DECLENSION, SPIRITUAL.
417 Come, Holy Spirit, heavenly
418 Come, let us to the Lord
278 Depth of mercy, can there
446 O for a closer walk with
179 O Jesus, Thou art standing
251 Return, O wanderer
573 Saviour, visit Thy plantation
429 Sweet was the time when
DEDICATION OF CHURCH.
517 Arise, O King of grace,
519 Lord of Hosts, to Thee we
518 O Thou, whose own vast
DELAY, DANGER OF.
294 And can I yet delay?
253 Behold, a stranger's at the
223 Delay not, delay not
243 Now is the accepted time
230 O sinner, why so long
239 To-day the Saviour calls
246 To-morrow, Lord, is Thine
DEPENDENCE:
ON CHRIST.
289 My faith looks up to Thee
473 My spirit, on Thy care
See *Christ, All in All.*
ON GOD.
67 Call Jehovah thy salvation
415 Cast thy burden on the
643 Great God, how infinite art
68 Vainly through night's
ON GRACE.
306 Amazing grace, how sweet
112 Grace, 'tis a charming
DELIVERANCE.
426 Oft when the waves of
431 Out of the depths
417 Through all the changing
DEPRAVITY:
NATIVE—See *Sin, Original.*
UNIVERSAL.
569 Arise, my tenderest
146 How heavy is the night
570 Look down, O Lord, with
137 Plunged in a gulf of dark
DEPRESSION—See *Darkness.*
DESPONDENCY—See *Christian, Conflicts of.*
DISMISSIONS—See *Close of Service.*
DOUBTS AND FEARS.
474 Give to the winds thy fears
476 If, through unruffled seas
468 My God, my Father
421 When sins and fears
DOXOLOGIES.
103 From all that dwell below
8 Holy, holy, holy, Lord God
21 Praise to Thee, Thou great
5 Round the Lord in glory
59 Thy name, Almighty
Pages 227, 298
DUTIES—See *Christian.*

ETERNITY.
593 Forever with the Lord
643 Great God, how infinite art
234 Lo, on a narrow neck of
614 Lo, what a glorious sight

ETERNITY:
253 O where shall rest be found
256 When Thou, my righteous
637 While with ceaseless course
EVENING.
71 Abide with me; fast falls
61 All praise to Thee, my God
40 At even, ere the sun was
592 Brighter still and brighter
69 Father, by Thy love and
43 Father of love and power
37 For the mercies of the
66 Hear my prayer, O heavenly
70 Now from labor and from
58 Our day of praise is done
64 Saviour, breathe an evening
36 Softly now the light of day
62 Sun of my soul, Thou
65 Tarry with me, O my!
57 The day, O Lord, is spent
63 Thus far the Lord has led
59 Thy name, Almighty
68 Vainly through night's
OF LIFE—See *Death, Bed of.*
71 Abide with me; fast falls
OF LORD'S DAY—See *Lord's Day.*
EXAMPLE:
OF CHRIST—See *Christ.*
OF CHRISTIANS—See *Christians.*
EXPOSTULATION.
259 Behold, a stranger's at the
191 Heart of stone, relent
241 Sinners, turn, why will ye
234 Sinners, will you scorn
239 To-day the Saviour calls
237 While life prolongs its

FAITH:
ACT OF.
204 Father, I stretch my hands
304 I am coming to the cross
271 Jesus, the sinner's Friend
285 Just as I am, without one
292 Lord, I know Thy grace is
201 " Mercy, O Thou Son of"
284 Take me, O my Father
See *Conversion.*
ASPIRATION OF.
510 Give me the wings of faith
411 Jesus, Lover of my soul
283 My faith looks up to Thee
130 O Jesus, when I think of
416 O Lord, impart Thyself
412 Thou, O Christ, art all I
ASSURANCE OF.
312 I bless the Christ of God
300 The Saviour, O what
302 There is a fountain
See *Assurance.*
BLESSEDNESS OF.
305 I heard the voice of Jesus
293 O how happy are they
CONFESSION OF.
406 Jesus, and shall it ever be
401 Jesus, I my cross have
490 O happy day that fixed
452 People of the living God
See *Covenant.*
JUSTIFICATION BY.
401 No more, my God, I boast
297 Not all the blood of beasts
287 Rock of ages, cleft for me

INDEX OF SUBJECTS.

FAITH:
 Prayer of.
  255 O Thou, that hearest the
 Walking by.
  510 Give me the wings of faith
  385 'Tis by the faith of joys
FALL OF MAN—See *Depravity*
  and *Sin*.
FAMILY WORSHIP.
  40 At even, ere the sun was
  61 All praise to Thee, my God
  60 Awake, my soul, and with
  593 Brighter still and brighter
  67 Call Jehovah thy salvation
  63 Father, by Thy love and
  52 I love to steal awhile away
  70 Now from labor and from
  332 O God of Bethel, by whose
  64 Saviour, breathe an evening
  356 Saviour, like a shepherd
  23 Shepherd of tender youth
  34 Softly now the light of day
  62 Sun of my soul, Thou
  33 Sweet hour of prayer
  63 Thus far the Lord has led
  63 Vainly through night's
  See *Evening*, *Morning*, *Praise*,
  and *Prayer*.
FASTS.
  653 In prayer together let us
  654 While o'er our guilty land
FESTIVALS—See *Christmas*, *National*, *Thanksgiving-day*, and *Year*.
FOREFATHERS' DAY.
  657 Let children hear the
  655 My country, 'tis of thee
  658 O Lord, our fathers oft have
  658 Our God, beneath Thy
FORGIVENESS OF SIN—See *Sinner*.
FORMALITY.
  261 Broad is the road that leads
  417 Come, Holy Spirit
  94 Lord, when we bend before
FORSAKING ALL FOR CHRIST.
  271 And can I yet delay
  318 I send the joys of earth
  404 Jesus, I my cross have
  301 Let worldly minds the
  432 People of the living God
  74 Welcome, welcome, dear
  181 When I survey the
  205 Vain, delusive world, adieu
FOUNTAIN:
 Of Blood.
  232 Come to Calvary's holy
  302 There is a fountain filled
  174 Ye that pass by, behold
 Of Living Water.
  536 Glorious things of thee are
  234 Let every mortal ear attend
  140 The Saviour calls, let every
FRAILTY OF MAN—See *Life*.
FUNERAL HYMNS.
  503 Lowly and solemn be
  534 Why do we mourn departing
  547 Unveil thy bosom, faithful
FUTURE PUNISHMENT.
  258 O where shall rest be found
  237 While life prolongs its
   See *Judgment*.

GETHSEMANE—See *Christ*.
GOD:
 Adoration of.
  103 All people that on earth do
  104 Before Jehovah's awful
  122 Bless, O my soul, the living
 All in All.
  452 My God, my life, my love
  444 My God, my portion and my
 Almighty—See *Omnipotent*.
 Attributes of.
  449 My God, how wonderful
 Being of.
  117 Keep silence, all created
  149 The heavens declare Thy
 Communion with—See *Communion*.
 Compassion of.
  119 My soul, repeat His praise
  120 The pity of the Lord
 Creator.
  123 Come, O my soul, in sacred
  115 I'll praise my Maker with
  80 O come, loud anthems let
 Decrees of.
  466 God moves in a mysterious
  117 Keep silence, all created
  471 The Lord is King: lift up
  473 Wait, O my soul, thy
 Eternal.
  642 Great God, how infinite art
  641 Our God, our help in ages
 Faithfulness of.
  415 Cast thy burden on the
  380 How firm a foundation
  447 Through all the changing
 Father.
  454 Behold what wondrous
  403 I would love Thee, God and
  101 The Lord Jehovah reigns
 Forbearance of—See *Long-suffering of*.
 Glory of.
  123 Come, O my soul, in sacred
  20 Father, Thine elect, who
  5 Round the Lord, in glory
  122 The heavens declare Thy
 Goodness of.
  122 Bless, O my soul, the living
  115 I'll praise my Maker with
  125 Since all the varying scenes
 Grace of.
  122 Bless, O my soul, the living
  121 High in the heavens
  308 Lord, with glowing heart
 Guide.
  354 Guide me, O Thou great
  350 He leadeth me; O blessed
  357 Lead us, Heavenly Father
 Helper.
  477 Fear not, O little flock, the
  445 God, my Supporter and
  641 Our God, our help in ages
 Holiness of.
  99 Exalt the Lord our God
  111 Holy, holy, holy, Lord
  8 Holy, holy, holy, Lord God
  2 Holy, holy, holy, Lord God of
  84 Lord, in the morning Thou
  5 Round the Lord in glory
 Immutable—See *Unchangeable*.
 Incomprehensible.
  474 Give to the winds thy

 466 God moves in a mysterious
  473 Wait, O my soul, thy
 Infinite—See *Eternal*.
 Jehovah.
  114 Father of Heaven, whose
  101 The Lord Jehovah reigns
 Judge—See *Christ*.
 Long-suffering of.
  273 Depth of mercy, can there
  269 God calling yet! shall I not
 Love of.
  402 God is love; His mercy
  449 My God, how wonderful
  452 My God, my Life, my Love
  7 To Him that chose us first
 Majesty of.
  108 O worship the King, all
  116 The Lord our God is full of
 Mercy of.
  111 Holy, holy, holy Lord
  119 My soul, repeat His praise
  144 Sweet is Thy mercy, Lord
 Mercies of.
  649 Eternal source of every joy
  85 Let us, with a gladsome
  461 O bless the Lord, my soul
  643 When all Thy mercies, O
 Omnipotent.
  644 How are Thy servants
  116 The Lord our God is full of
 Omnipresent.
  463 Beyond, beyond the
  124 Jehovah, God, Thy gracious
 Omniscience.
  121 Jehovah, God, Thy gracious
 Pity of—See *Compassion of*.
 Portion.
  415 God, my Supporter and
  444 My God, my Portion and
  443 My God, the Spring of all
 Praise of—See *Praise*.
 Presence of.
  79 Great God, attend while
  83 Welcome, sweet day of rest
 Providence of.
  67 Call Jehovah thy salvation
  466 God moves in a mysterious
  350 He leadeth me; O blessed
  121 High in the heavens, eternal
  644 How are Thy servants
  476 If, through unruffled seas
  352 In some way or other
  124 Jehovah, God, Thy gracious
  95 Let us, with a gladsome
  125 Since all the varying scenes
  102 Upward I lift mine eyes
  643 When all Thy mercies, O
  467 While Thee I seek
 Reigning—See *Sovereign*.
 Reconciled.
  337 Arise, my soul, arise
 Refuge.
  469 God is the refuge of His
  379 Though faint, yet pursuing
  470 Up to the hills I lift mine
  102 Upward I lift mine
 Safety in.
  478 My spirit, on Thy care
  447 Through all the changing
 Shepherd—See *Christ*.
 Sovereign.
  474 Give to the wind thy fears

INDEX OF SUBJECTS.

GOD:
  471 The Lord is King: lift up
  101 The Lord Jehovah reigns
SUPREME.
  104 Before Jehovah's awful
    1 Come, Thou almighty King
  612 Great God, how infinite art
  117 Keep silence, all created
TRUTH OF.
  121 High in the heavens
  115 I'll praise my Maker with
  59 Thy name, Almighty Lord
UNCHANGEABLE.
  612 Great God, how infinite art
  611 Our God, our help in ages
    4 Praise the Lord, ye heavens
WATCHFUL CARE OF.
  104 Before Jehovah's awful
  474 Give to the wind thy fears
  417 How gentle God's
  478 My spirit, on Thy care
  470 Up to the hills I lift
  See *Providence of*.
WILL OF.
  465 I worship Thee, sweet Will
  473 Wait, O my soul, thy
WISDOM OF.
  121 Come, O my soul, in sacred
  402 God is love; His mercy
  471 The Lord is King: lift up
  89 To God, the only wise
  473 Wait, O my soul, thy
WORKS OF.
  123 Come, O my soul, in sacred
  103 O worship the King, all
  129 The heavens declare Thy
GOOD WORKS.
  640 Come, let us anew
  491 No more, my God, I boast
  568 So let our lips and lives
GOSPEL:
BANNER.
  510 Now be the gospel banner
EXCELLENCY OF.
  54 Behold the morning sun
  139 God, in the gospel of His
  516 How beauteous are their
  25 Let everlasting glories
  55 We lift our hearts to Thee
FEAST.
  235 Come, sinners, to the gospel
  243 Come, ye disconsolate
  242 From the cross uplifted
  234 Let every mortal ear
  239 Sinners, obey the gospel
FREENESS OF
  221 Blow ye the trumpet
  261 Life is the time to serve
  244 The Spirit, in our hearts
  226 The voice of free grace
FULLNESS OF.
  233 Come, ye disconsolate
  136 Salvation, O the joyful
  226 The voice of free grace
INVITATIONS OF.
  252 Ch'l'l of sin and sorrow
  240 Come, said Jesus' sacred
  235 Come, sinners, to the gospel
  232 Come, ye sinners, poor and
  243 Now is the accepted time
  140 The Saviour calls, let every
  243 Ye that in His courts are

GOSPEL:
MESSAGE.
  561 I love to tell the story
  234 Sinners, will you scorn the
  564 Tell me the old, old story
RECEPTION OF—See *Conversion*.
REJECTION OF.
  241 Sinners, turn, why will ye
  237 While life prolongs its
SPREAD OF.
  578 Lord of all power and might
  579 Sound, sound the truth
  563 Uplift the blood-red
  See *Missions*.
TRIUMPH OF.
  553 Hasten, Lord, the glorious
  129 The heavens declare Thy
  530 The morning light is
  See *Kingdom of Christ*.
TRUMPET.
  221 Blow ye the trumpet
  247 Ye trembling captives, hear
GRACE:
ASPIRATIONS FOR DIVINE — See
  Aspirations.
CONVERTING.
  25 Come, blessed Spirit,
  311 Come, Thou Fount of every
  46 Gracious Spirit, Dove
  47 Holy Ghost, with light
  344 I hear the Saviour say
  303 Lord, with glowing heart
FREE.
  221 Blow ye the trumpet
  235 Come, sinners, to the gospel
  243 Now is the accepted time
  227 O come to the merciful
  234 Sinners, will you scorn the
  244 The Spirit in our hearts
  226 The voice of free grace cries
FRUITS OF.
  568 So let our lips and lives
FULLNESS OF.
  240 Come, said Jesus' sacred
  245 Come to the land of
  229 Come unto me, when
  233 Come, ye disconsolate
  232 Come, ye sinners, poor and
  234 Let every mortal ear attend
  140 The Saviour calls, let every
  243 Ye that in His courts are
JUSTIFYING.
  257 Awaked by Sinai's awful
  401 No more, my God, I boast
  287 Rock of ages, cleft for me
MIRACLE OF.
  307 Hail, my ever blessèd Jesus
QUICKENING.
  32 Come, Holy Spirit, calm
  417 Come, Holy Spirit, heavenly
RENEWING.
  16 Come, Holy Spirit, come
  534 Spirit of power and might
  448 When God revealed His
REVIVING.
  16 Come, Holy Spirit, come
  571 Come, sacred Spirit, from
  15 Lord God, the Holy Ghost
  343 We praise Thee, O God
SANCTIFYING
  24 Come, Holy Spirit, heavenly
  47 Holy Ghost, with light
  146 How heavy is the night

GRACE:
SOVEREIGN.
  306 Amazing grace, how sweet
  142 Grace, 'tis a charming
  146 How heavy is the night
  424 To God I cried when
GRACES, CHRISTIAN—See *Christians, Faith, Hope,* and *Love*.
GRATITUDE.
  311 Come, Thou Fount of every
  322 I bless the Christ of God
  344 I hear the Saviour say
  310 I will love Thee, all
  303 I was a wandering sheep
  315 Jesus, my All, to Heaven is
  323 Jesus, my Lord, my God
  320 Jesus, this heart within me
  312 Praise, my soul, the King
  340 Sing of Jesus, sing for ever
GRAVE—See *Death* and *Funeral Hymns*.
GRIEVING THE SPIRIT — See
  Holy Spirit.
GROWTH IN GRACE.
  167 Behold, where in a mortal
  430 Jesus, my strength, my
  438 Jesus, Thine all-victorious
  168 My dear Redeemer, and my
  495 O for a heart to praise my
  439 O that the Lord would
  409 O Thou, to whose
  358 Rise, my soul, and stretch
  568 So let our lips and lives
GUIDANCE.
  456 In heavenly love abiding
  378 The Lord is my Shepherd
  400 The Lord my Shepherd is
SOUGHT.
  24 Come, Holy Spirit, heavenly
  22 Gently, Lord, O gently lead
  354 Guide me, O Thou great
  300 Jesus, still lead on
  357 Lead us, heavenly Father
  362 O God of Bethel, by whose
  356 Saviour, like a shepherd
  275 Saviour, though the desert
  361 The way is dark; I cannot
  494 Thine for ever!—God of
GUILT—See *Sin*.

HAPPINESS—See *Joy*.
HEART:
CHANGE OF—See *Regeneration*.
CLEAN.
  16 Come, Holy Spirit, come
  435 O for a heart to praise
CONTRITE.
  268 A broken heart, my God
  272 With broken heart and
SURRENDER OF.
  298 And can I yet delay
  269 God calling yet; shall I not
  231 Lord, Thou hast won, at
  74 Welcome, welcome, dear
VILE—See *Sin*.
HEATHEN.
  569 Arise, my tenderest
  547 From Greenland's icy
  557 Hark, what mean those
  570 Look down, O Lord, with
  543 Though now the nations

INDEX OF SUBJECTS.

HEAVEN:
ANTICIPATED.
 612 And let this feeble body fail
 351 As when the weary traveller
 437 I know no life divided
 353 I'm a pilgrim, and I'm
 373 My heavenly home is bright
 612 On Jordan's rugged banks I
 634 We are on our journey
 346 We've no abiding city here
 613 When I can read my title
BLESSEDNESS OF.
 625 I long to behold Him
 611 Lo, what a glorious sight
 507 My Lord, my Love, was
 612 On Jordan's rugged banks I
 353 Our journey is a thorny
 633 Shall we gather at the river
 615 There is a land of pure
HOME.
 599 Forever with the Lord
 617 For thee, O dear, dear
 631 In the Christian's home in
 623 Jerusalem, my happy home
 618 Jerusalem the glorious
 616 Jerusalem the golden
 636 Joyfully, joyfully, onward I
 511 'Mid scenes of confusion
 373 My heavenly home is bright
 371 Out on an ocean all
 635 Safe Home, safe Home in
 604 The world is very evil
 631 We are on our journey home
 435 We have a house above
LONGED FOR—See Aspirations.
NEARNESS TO.
 367 A crown of glory bright
 372 My days are gliding swiftly
 368 One sweetly solemn tho't
 369 Your harps, ye trembling
PRAISE OF.
 510 Give me the wings of faith
 8 Holy, holy, holy, Lord God
 3 See the ransomed millions
 609 Who are these like stars
 See Christ, Lamb of God.
PROSPECT OF.
 367 A crown of glory bright
 373 My heavenly home is bright
 620 My soul, there is a country
 621 O mother dear, Jerusalem
 514 O what, if we are Christ's
 441 Take, my soul, thy full
 630 We shall meet beyond the
REST OF.
 631 In the Christian's home in
 629 There is an hour of peaceful
 349 This is the day of toil
 386 We've no abiding city here
SECURITY OF.
 612 On Jordan's rugged banks I
 81 Thine earthly Sabbaths
 455 We have a house above
SOCIETY OF.
 510 Give me the wings of faith
 627 High in yonder realms of
 3 See the ransomed millions
 619 Ten thousand times ten
 626 What are these in bright
 609 Who are these like stars
SONGS OF.
 632 Hark the sound of holy
 627 High in yonder realms of

HEAVEN:
 624 Ye angels, who stand round
HEIRSHIP—See Adoption.
HELL—See Future Punishment.
HOLINESS—See God, Heaven, and
 Saints.
HOLY SCRIPTURES—See Word
 of God.
HOLY SPIRIT:
ABSENCE OF.
 418 Come, let us to the Lord
COMFORTER.
 44 Come, Holy Ghost, in love
 9 Come, O Creator Spirit
 47 Holy Ghost, with light
 50 Why should the children of
DESCENT OF.
 571 Come, Sacred Spirit, from
 48 Granted is the Saviour's
 25 Lord God, the Holy Ghost
DIVINE.
 48 Granted is the Saviour's
 47 Holy Ghost, with light
 15 Lord God, the Holy Ghost
 534 Spirit of power and might
EARNEST OF.
 46 Gracious Spirit, Dove
 53 Great Father of each perfect
 50 Why should the children of
ENLIGHTENER.
 25 Come, blessed Spirit, source
 10 Eternal Spirit, we confess
 47 Holy Ghost, with light
GRIEVED.
 232 Child of sin and sorrow
 239 Delay not, delay not, O
 230 O sinner, why so long
 273 Stay, Thou insulted Spirit
 339 To-day the Saviour calls
GUIDE.
 24 Come, Holy Spirit, heavenly
 9 Come, O Creator Spirit
INDWELLING.
 9 Come, O Creator Spirit
 441 Take, my soul, thy full
 50 Why should the children of
INFLUENCE OF.
 44 Come, Holy Ghost, in love
 32 Come, Holy Spirit, calm
 16 Come, Holy Spirit, come
 24, 417 Come, Holy Spirit, heav
 10 Eternal Spirit, we confess
 570 Look down, O Lord, with
 534 Spirit of power and might
INVOKED—See Prayer.
PRAYED FOR—See Prayer.
REGENERATING.
 16 Come, Holy Spirit, come
 570 Look down, O Lord, with
 534 Spirit of power and might
SANCTIFYING.
 32 Come, Holy Spirit, calm my
 16 Come, Holy Spirit, come
 24 Come, Holy Spirit, heavenly
 9 Come, O Creator Spirit
 47 Holy Ghost, with light
STRIVING.
 260 God calling yet, shall I
 214 The Spirit, in our hearts
WITNESS OF—See Earnest of.
HOME MISSIONS—See Missions.

HOPE:
ASPIRATIONS OF.
 454 Behold what wondrous
 445 God, my Supporter and
 472 God of my life, through all
 401 In the cross of Christ I
 411 Jesus, Lover of my soul
 428 Through the love of God
 See Heaven, Anticipated.
IN AFFLICTION—See Afflictions.
IN CHRIST.
 400 I'm not ashamed to own
 324 Now I have found the
 423 When sins and fears
IN DEATH—See Death.
IN GOD.
 469 God is the refuge of His
 431 Out of the depths of woe
 369 Your harps, ye trembling
 OF HEAVEN—See Heaven.
HUMILIATION—See Fasts.
 OF CHRIST—See Christ.
HUMILITY—See Meekness.

IMMORTALITY.
 599 Forever with the Lord
 512 Hark, hark, my soul
 603 It is not death to die
 258 O where shall rest be found
 601 Rest for the toiling hand
 581 Through sorrow's night
 435 We have a house above
 See Eternity and Heaven.
IMPORTUNITY—See Prayer.
IMPUTATION.
 190 Alas! and did my Saviour
 215 Hail, thou once despised
 444 No more, my God, I boast
 297 Not all the blood of beasts
 178 O sacred Head, now
 345 Thy tears, not mine, O
INCARNATION—See Christ.
INFANT SALVATION.
 507 With joy I see a thousand
INGRATITUDE.
 261 Is this the kind return
INSPIRATION—See Word of God.
 128 How precious is the book
INSTALLATION—See Ministry.
INTERCESSION—See Christ.
INVITATIONS—See Gospel, Grace,
 and Sinners.
INVOCATION.
 77 Another six days' work is
 42 Come, dearest Lord
 1 Come, Thou almighty King
 12 Far from my thoughts, vain
 94 Forth from the dark and
 76 Great Creator, who this day
 72 In Thy name, O Lord
 14 Jesus, where'er Thy people
 84 Lord, in the morning Thou
 34 Lord, we come before Thee
 75 Safely, through another
 99 Welcome, delightful morn
 11 Where two or three, with
 See Prayer and Praise.
ISRAEL.
 553 Daughter of Zion, from the
 536 Let Zion and her sons
 562 O that the Lord's salvation

INDEX OF SUBJECTS.

JERUSALEM, NEW.
622 Jerusalem, my happy home
618 Jerusalem the glorious
616 Jerusalem the golden
621 O mother dear, Jerusalem
634 We are on our journey
JOINING THE CHURCH—See *Faith, Confession of*, and *Converts Welcomed.*
JOY, SPIRITUAL.
338 Awake, my soul, to joyful
346 Children of the heavenly
451 Come, we that love the
375 Fade, fade each earthly joy
342 How tedious and tasteless
323 Jesus, my Lord, my God
329 Jesus, the very thought of
347 Now begin the heavenly
328 O for a thousand tongues
606 O happy band of pilgrims
615 Rejoice, rejoice, believers
222 Rejoice, the Lord is King
454 Sometimes a light surprises
317 The Saviour smiles; upon
450 To Thee, my God and
 In Hope—See *Sinners.*
JUBILEE
221 Blow ye the trumpet
553 Hark, the song of jubilee
540 Wake the song of jubilee
JUDGMENT, THE.
611 Lo, He comes with clouds
254 Lo, on a narrow neck of
610 O'er the distant mountains
604 The world is very evil
259 When Thou, my righteous
JUSTIFICATION—See *Faith, Justifying.*

KINGDOM OF CHRIST:
Prayer for.
535 Great God, the nations of
542 O Spirit of the living God
551 Saviour, sprinkle many
534 Spirit of power and might
Progress of.
577 Christ for the world we
551 Hail to the Lord's Anointed
553 Hark, the song of jubilee
553 Hasten, Lord, the glorious
545 Jesus shall reign where'er
578 Lord of all power and
519 Now be the Gospel banner
523 O'er the gloomy hills of
554 See, how great a flame
550 The morning light is
543 When shall the voice of

LAMB OF GOD—See *Christ.*
LAST HOURS—See *Death, Bed of.*
LATTER DAY.
532 Behold the Mountain of
534 Spirit of power and might
540 Wake the song of jubilee
543 When shall the voice of
LAW OF GOD—See *Word of God.*
LIFE:
Brevity of.
647 A few more years shall roll
648 How swift the torrent rolls
339 Time is winging us away
637 While with ceaseless course

LIFE:
Object of.
266 Life is the time to serve the
391 My soul, weigh not thy life
258 O where shall rest be found
358 Rise, my soul, and stretch
Solemnity of.
393 A charge to keep I have
254 Lo, on a narrow neck of
Uncertainty of.
368 One sweetly solemn thought
65 Tarry with me, O my
246 To-morrow. Lord, is Thine
267 While life prolongs its
Vanity of.
642 Great God, how infinite art
641 Our God, our help in ages
LONGINGS—See *Aspirations.*
LOOKING TO JESUS.
282 Jesus, Thou art the sinner's
249 My faith looks up to Thee
270 With tearful eyes I look
LORD'S DAY AND WORSHIP:
Delight in.
91 Again our earthly cares we
101 All people that on earth do
83 Early, my God, without
12 Far from my thoughts, vain
94 Forth from the dark and
79 Great God, attend while
88 How charming is the place
82 How did my heart rejoice
106 How pleased and blest
72 In Thy name, O Lord
95 Let us with a gladsome
100 Lord of the worlds above
56 Sweet is the work, O Lord
81 Thine earthly Sabbaths,
107 'Tis Heaven begun below
96 To Thy temple I repair
Evening
71 Abide with me: fast falls
70 Now from labor and from
54 Our day of praise is done
57 The day, O Lord, is spent
Morning.
93 Again the Lord of life and
77 Another six days' work is
76 Great Creator, who this day
84 Lord, in the morning Thou
75 Safely thro' another week:
78 Sweet is the work, my God
99 Welcome, delightful morn
Welcomed.
97 O day of rest and gladness
98 The day of resurrection
85 This is the day the Lord
86 Welcome, sweet day of rest
 See *Invocation* and *Close of Service.*
LORD'S SUPPER:
502 According to Thy gracious
496 At Thy command our
503 How sweet and awful is the
501 If human kindness meets
498 Jesus, thou Joy of loving
497 My God, and is Thy table
313 Sweet the moments, rich in
 See *Cross.*
LOVE:
Of Christ—See *Christ.*
Of God—See *God.*

LOVE:
For Christ.
330 Do not I love Thee, O my
307 Hail, my ever blessed Jesus
322 How sweet the Name of
561 I love to tell the story
310 I will love Thee, all my
323 Jesus, I love Thy charming
321 Jesus, my Lord, my God
331 Jesus, these eyes have
329 Jesus, this heart within me
308 Lord, with glowing heart
376 More love to Thee, O
333 My God, I love Thee; not
311 O could I speak the
315 O Love divine, how sweet
414 Saviour, teach me, day by
364 Thou dear Redeemer, dying
For God.
403 I would love Thee, God and
452 My God, my Life, my Love
444 My God, my Portion, and
413 My God, the spring of all
For Saints.
508 Blest be the dear, uniting
513 Blest be the tie that binds
504 Happy the souls to Jesus
506 Our souls, by love together
527 Through the night of doubt
For the Church.
515 I love Thy kingdom, Lord

MAN, FALL OF—See *Depravity.*
MARTYRS.
627 High in yonder realms of
626 What are these in bright
MEDITATION.
51 Far from the world, O Lord
52 I love to steal awhile away
31 My God, permit me not to
319 O that I could for ever
313 Sweet the moments, rich in
583 When languor and disease
MEEKNESS.
167 Behold, where in a mortal
171 How beauteous were the
168 My dear Redeemer and my
MERCY:
Of God—See *God.*
Sought—See *Sinners.*
MERCY-SEAT.
198 Done is the work that saves
29 From every sto'my wind
88 How charming is the place
14 Jesus, where'er Thy people
41 What various hindrances
MILLENNIUM—See *Latter Day.*
MINISTRY.
544 Assembled at Thy great
552 Go, ye messengers of God
516 How beauteous are their
542 O Spirit of the living God
579 Sound, sound the truth
563 Uplift the blood-red banner
541 Ye Christian heralds, go
MIRACLES—See *Christ.*
MISSIONS—See *Kingdom of Christ.*
Home.
556 Hark, the voice of Jesus
597 On Zion and on Lebanon
Foreign.
500 Arise, my tenderest
544 Assembled at Thy great

INDEX OF SUBJECTS.

335

MISSIONS:
427 Fear not, O little flock, the
547 From Greenland's icy
535 Great God, the nations of
557 Hark, what mean those
516 How beauteous are their
570 Look down, O Lord, with
530 O city of the Lord, begin
529 O'er the gloomy hills of
538 Spread, O spread, Thou
540 Thou, whose Almighty
543 Though now the nations sit
152 Watchman, tell us of the
548 When shall the voice of
539 With my substance I will

MISSIONARIES.
552 Go, ye messengers of God
563 Uplift the blood-red banner

WORKS, CALLS TO.
537 Hark, what mean those
500 He that goeth forth with
579 Sound, sound the truth
558 We are living, we are

MORNING.
60 Awake, my soul, and with
54 Behold the morning sun
83 Early, my God, without
56 Sweet is the work, O Lord
430 To Thee, my God and
13 While now the daylight

OF LORD'S DAY—See *Lord's Day.*
MORTALITY—See *Death* and *Life.*

NATIONAL.
669 God bless our native land
655 God of nations, King of
657 Let children hear the
659 My country, 'tis of thee
653 O Lord, our fathers oft have
63 Our God, beneath Thy

NATURE.
54 Behold, the morning sun
4 Praise the Lord, ye heavens
129 The heavens declare Thy

NEARNESS TO GOD.
374 Nearer, my God, to Thee
416 O for a closer walk with
62 Sun of my soul, Thou

To HEAVEN—See *Heaven.*
NEW JERUSALEM—See *Jerusalem.*
NEW YEAR—See *Year.*
NOW—See *Grace, Day of.*

OBEDIENCE:
OF CHRIST—See *Christ.*
OF THE CHRISTIAN.
565 My gracious Lord, I own
491 No more, my God, I boast
OFFERS OF GRACE—See *Grace.*
OFFICES OF CHRIST — See *Christ.*
OLD AGE.
380 How firm a foundation
65 Tarry with me, O my
OMNIPOTENCE—See *God.*
OMNIPRESENCE—See *God.*
OMNISCIENCE—See *God.*
OPENING OF SERVICE—See *Invocation.*
ORDINANCES—See *Baptism* and *Lord's Supper.*
ORDINATION—See *Ministry.*

ORIGINAL SIN—See *Sin.*

PARDON:
FOUND—See *Sinners, Rejoicing in Hope and Saved.*
OFFERED—See *Gospel, Invitations of,* and *Sinners, Invited.*
SOUGHT—See *Sinners, Seeking.*
PARTING—See *Close of Service.*
PASSOVER—See *Christ.*
PASTORS—See *Ministry.*
PATIENCE—See *Afflictions, Resignation under.*

PEACE:
CHRISTIAN.
193 He lives, the great
457 While Thee I seek
FOR THE TROUBLED.
245 Come to the land of peace
228 Come unto me when
219 Ye that in His courts are
PRAYER FOR.
450 Calm me, my God, and keep
464 Father, whate'er of earthly
431 Jesus, my Lord, attend

NATIONAL.
660 God bless our native land
651 While o'er our guilty land

PENITENTIAL.
268 A broken heart, my God
180 Alas! and did my Saviour
281 Come, humble sinner, in
278 Depth of mercy, can there
260 Did Christ o'er sinners
432 Have mercy, Lord, on me
275 I see the crowd in Pilate's
274 In evil long I took delight
261 Is this the kind return?
283 Jesus, full of all compassion
280 Jesus, full of truth and love
434 Jesus, my Lord, attend
264 Lord, I am vile, conceived
131 O Jesus, sweet the tears I
257 O that my load of sin
431 Out of the depths of woe
276 Pass me not, O gentle
245 Show pity, Lord, O Lord
279 Sovereign Ruler, Lord of
273 Stay, Thou insulted Spirit
262 Thou Lord of all above
272 With broken heart and

PENTECOST.
15 Lord God, the Holy Ghost
PERSEVERANCE—See *Saints.*
PESTILENCE.
67 Call Jehovah thy salvation
64 Saviour, breathe an evening
PILGRIMS:
BAND OF.
606 O happy band of pilgrims
527 Through the night of doubt
PRAYER OF.
22 Gently, Lord, O gently lead
354 Guide me, O Thou great
360 Jesus, still lead on
355 Saviour, through the desert
361 The way is dark; I cannot

SONG OF.
346 Children of the heavenly
372 My days are gliding swiftly
358 Rise, my soul, and stretch
360 Sing, ye redeemed of the

PILGRIMS:
SPIRIT OF.
647 A few more years may
351 As when the weary
602 Far from my heavenly
353 I'm a pilgrim, and I'm a
239 My faith looks up to Thee
369 Your harps, ye trembling
PILGRIMAGE.
583 Forth to the Land of
344 From Egypt lately come
512 Hark, hark, my soul
365 In all my Lord's appointed
319 This is the day of toil
531 Through sorrow's night
359 Time is winging us
634 We are on our journey
370 We're bound for yonder
346 We've no abiding city
PITY OF GOD—See *God, Compassion of.*
PLEASURES, WORLDLY. — See *Forsaking all for Christ.*
PRAISE.
105 From all that dwell below
472 God of my life, through all
111 Holy, holy, holy Lord
110 Songs of praise the angels
59 Thy name, almighty Lord
CALLS TO.
451 Come, we that love the
431 O bless the Lord, my soul
656 Praise the Lord, His glories
4 Praise the Lord, ye heavens
87 Stand up, and bless the
78 Sweet is the work, my God
To CHRIST.
217 All hail the power of Jesus'
143 Awake, and sing the song
338 Awake, my soul, to joyful
219 Behold the glories of the
102 Brightness of the Father's
205 Come, all ye saints of God
607 Come, every pious heart
214 Come, let us join in songs
213 Come, let us
185 Come, let us sing the song
311 Come, Thou Fount of every
223 Come, ye faithful, raise
191 Glory, glory everlasting
307 Hail, my ever blessed
215 Hail, Thou once despised
608 Hark, ten thousand harps
322 I bless the Christ of God
326 Jesus, I love Thy charming
329 Jesus, the very thought of
150 Joy to the world, the Lord
317 Now begin the heavenly
186 Now to the Lord, who
334 O could I speak the
328 O for a thousand tongues
499 O the sweet wonders of
177 Plunged in a gulf of dark
341 Saints in glory, we together
23 Shepherd of tender youth
340 Sing of Jesus, sing for ever
203 Sons of Zion, raise your
364 Thou dear Redeemer, dying
439 To Thee, my God and
216 Worship, honor, power and
109 Ye servants of God
To GOD.
103 All people that on earth

INDEX OF SUBJECTS.

PRAISE:
104 Before Jehovah's awful
123 Bless, O my soul, the living
121 Come, O my soul, in sacred
649 Eternal source of every joy
90 Exalt the Lord our God
115 I'll praise my Maker with
308 Lord, with glowing heart
119 My soul, repeat His praise
312 Praise, my soul, the King
21 Praise to Thee, Thou great
5 Round the Lord in glory
101 The Lord Jehovah reigns
89 To God, the only wise
613 When all Thy mercies, O
To THE HOLY SPIRIT.
10 Eternal Spirit, we confess
531 Spirit of power and might
To THE TRINITY.
1 Come, Thou Almighty King
111 Father of Heaven, whose
20 Father, Thine elect who
8 Holy, holy, holy, Lord God
2 Holy, holy, holy, Lord God of
6 I give immortal praise
112 Praise to Him, whose love
113 The royal banners forward
7 To Him that chose us first
313 We praise Thee, O God

PRAYER.
51 I love to steal awhile away
31 My God, permit me not to
49 Prayer is the soul's sincere
41 What various hindrances
ENCOURAGEMENT TO.
17 Behold the Throne of grace
35 Come, my soul, thy suit
493 Pilgrim, burdened with thy
HOUR OF.
39 Sweet hour of prayer
IMPORTUNITY IN.
321 Come, O Thou Traveller
34 Lord, we come before Thee
479 Our Lord, who knows full
SINCERITY IN.
92 Lord, when we bend before
To CHRIST.
169 Awhile in spirit, Lord, to
323 Jesus, my Lord, my God
175 Lord Jesus, when we stand
178 O sacred Head, now
64 Saviour, breathe an evening
62 Sun of my soul, Thou
65 Tarry with me, O my
To THE HOLY SPIRIT.
25 Come, blessed Spirit
44 Come, Holy Ghost, in love
32 Come, Holy Spirit, calm
16 Come, Holy Spirit, come
24, 417 Come, Holy Spirit, heav-
9 Come, O Creator Spirit
571 Come, sacred Spirit, from
46 Gracious Spirit, Dove
48 Granted is the Saviour's
53 Great Father of each perfect
47 Holy Ghost, with light
574 Light of those, whose
15 Lord God, the Holy Ghost
542 O Spirit of the living God
11 Where two or three, with
50 Why should the children of
To THE TRINITY.
1 Come, Thou Almighty King

PRAYER:
69 Father, by Thy love and
76 Great Creator, who this day
357 Lead us, heavenly Father
580 Thou, whose almighty
UNITED.
14 Jesus, where'er Thy people
84 Lord, we come before Thee
80 O Lord, how joyful 'tis to
18 O Lord, Thy work revive
11 Where two or three, with
PROBATION—See *Grace, Day of.*
PROCRASTINATION—See *Delay.*
PROGRESS, CHRISTIAN — See
  Growth in Grace.
OF CHRIST'S KINGDOM — See
  Kingdom of Christ.
PROMISED LAND—See *Heaven.*
PROMISES.
17 Behold, the Throne of
480 God is the refuge of His
339 How firm a foundation
115 I'll praise my Maker with
245 Just as I am, without one
26 Let everlasting glories
285 Show pity, Lord, O Lord
PROVIDENCE—See *God.*
PURE IN HEART—See *Heart.*
PURPOSES OF GOD—See *God, Decrees of.*

RACE, CHRISTIAN.
368 Awake, my soul, stretch
334 Awake, our souls, away
382 Fight the good fight with
385 Stand up, my soul, shake
385 'Tis by the faith of joys to
REDEMPTION—See *Atonement.*
REFUGE—See *Christ* and *God.*
REGENERATION:
NECESSARY.
257 Awaked by Sinai's awful
264 Lord, I am vile, conceived
SOUGHT.
571 Come, sacred Spirit, from
46 Gracious Spirit, Dove divine
47 Holy Ghost, with light
574 Light of those whose dreary
570 Look down, O Lord, with
435 O for a heart to praise my
WROUGHT.
16 Come, Holy Spirit, come
10 Eternal Spirit, we confess
50 Why should the children of
REJOICING IN GOD—See *Joy.*
REJOICING IN HOPE—See *Sinners.*
RENOUNCING ALL FOR CHRIST
  —See *Forsaking all for Christ.*
REPENTANCE—See *Penitential.*
RESIGNATION.
430 Calm me, my God, and keep
464 Father, whate'er of earthly
465 I worship Thee, sweet Will
352 In some way or other my
92 Lord, when we bend before
468 My God, my Father, blissful
480 My Jesus, as Thou wilt
125 Since all the varying scenes
481 Thy way, not mine, O
473 Wait, O my soul, Thy
583 When languor and disease
407 While Thee I seek

REST—See *Heaven* and *Weary.*
RESURRECTION:
OF CHRIST—See *Christ.*
OF BELIEVERS.
600 O for the death of those
601 Rest for the toiling hand
587 Unveil thy bosom, faithful
594 Why do we mourn
RETIREMENT—See *Meditation.*
REVELATION—See *Word of God.*
REVIVAL:
HOPING FOR.
572 While I to grief my soul
PRAYED FOR.
16 Come, Holy Spirit, come
571 Come, sacred Spirit, from
53 Great Father of each perfect
570 Look down, O Lord, with
18 O Lord, Thy work revive
573 Saviour, visit Thy plantation
REJOICING IN.
536 Let Zion and her sons
343 We praise Thee, O God
448 When God revealed His
SOUGHT.
418 Come, let us to the Lord
277 Lord, I hear of showers of
276 Pass me not, O gentle
RICHES.
354 Rise, my soul, and stretch
182 When I survey the
RIGHTEOUSNESS OF CHRIST—
  See *Christ.*
ROCK OF AGES—See *Christ.*

SABBATH—See *Lord's Day.*
SACRAMENTS—See *Baptism* and
  Lord's Supper.
SACRIFICE—See *Atonement* and
  Christ.
SAFETY OF BELIEVERS — See
  Saints.
SAILORS—See *Sea.*
SAINTS:
BLESSEDNESS OF.
33 Blessed are the sons of God
627 High in yonder realms
644 How are Thy servants blest
626 What are these in bright
COMMUNION OF—See *Love.*
DEATH OF—See *Death.*
GLORIFIED.
510 Give me the wings of faith
625 I long to behold Him
634 Ye angels, who stand round
PERSEVERANCE OF.
348 Awake, my soul, stretch
395 Brethren, while we sojourn
382 Fight the good fight with all
394 Go forward, Christian
388 My soul, be on thy guard
363 Our journey is a thorny
393 Stand up, stand up for
385 'Tis by the faith of joys to
SECURITY OF.
67 Call Jehovah thy salvation
469 God is the refuge of his
380 How firm a foundation, ye
436 In heavenly love abiding
478 My spirit, on Thy care
108 O worship the King
641 Our God, our help in ages
460 The Lord my Shepherd is

INDEX OF SUBJECTS.

SAINTS:
447 Through all the changing
470 Up to the hills I lift mine
102 Upward I lift mine eyes
UNION OF, WITH CHRIST.
457 I know no life divided
118 Our heavenly Father calls
UNION OF, WITH EACH OTHER.
508 Blest be the dear, uniting
513 Blest be the tie that binds
509 Come, let us join our friends
504 Happy the souls to Jesus
506 Our souls by love together
527 Through the night of doubt
SALVATION—See *Atonement, Gospel, Grace,* and *Sinners.*
SANCTIFICATION—See *Growth in Grace.*
SANCTUARY:
CORNER-STONE LAID.
520 Christ is made the sure
526 Glorious things of thee are
DEDICATION OF—See *Dedication.*
LOVE FOR—See *Lord's Day* and *Worship.*
SAVIOUR—See *Christ.*
SCRIPTURES, HOLY—See *Word of God.*
SEA:
AT SEA.
644 How are Thy servants blest
426 Oft when the waves of
371 Out on an ocean all
523 Rocked in the cradle of the
421 The billows swell, the
SEAMEN.
525 Eternal Father, strong to
524 Star of peace, to wanderers
522 Tossed upon life's raging
SEASONS, THE.
649 Come, let us anew
641 Eternal Source of every
633 For Thy mercy and Thy
655 God of nations, King of
650 Great God, we sing that
654 Praise to God, immortal
648 Thou, who roll'st the year
637 While with ceaseless course
645 With songs and honors
SECOND BIRTH—See *Regeneration.*
SECOND DEATH—See *Future Punishment.*
SECURITY OF SAINTS—See *Saints.*
SELF-DEDICATION—See *Consecration* and *Covenant.*
DENIAL.
307 Am I a soldier of the cross
263 Broad is the road that leads
311 Must Jesus bear the cross
491 No more, my God, I boast
131 When I survey the
RENUNCIATION—See *Forsaking all for Christ.*
SHEPHERD—See *Christ.*
SICKNESS.
40 At even, ere the sun was
425 Fountain of grace, rich, full
590 In the hour of trial
373 My heavenly home is bright
583 When languor and disease

SHOWERS OF GRACE.
277 Lord, I hear of showers of
SIN:
CONFESSION OF.
278 Depth of mercy, can there
260 Did Christ o'er sinners
432 Have mercy, Lord, on me
261 Is this the kind return?
283 Jesus, full of all compassion
277 Lord, I hear of showers of
259 My former hopes are fled
423 Out of the deep I call
276 Pass me not, O gentle
265 Show pity, Lord, O Lord
279 Sovereign Ruler, Lord of
273 Stay, Thou insulted Spirit
284 Take me, O my Father
263 Thou Lord of all above
272 With broken heart and
HATRED OF.
437 I want a principle within
175 Lord Jesus, when we stand
416 O for a closer walk with
INDWELLING—See *Holy Spirit.*
40 At even, ere the sun was
395 Brethren, while we sojourn
434 Jesus, my Lord, attend
438 Jesus, Thine all-victorious
267 O that my load of sin were
439 O that the Lord would
409 O Thou, to whose
ORIGINAL.
569 Arise, my tenderest
570 Look down, O Lord, with
264 Lord, I am vile, conceived
SINAI.
257 Awaked by Sinai's awful
SINNERS:
ANXIOUS.
253 Art thou weary, art thou
177 Lord, in this Thy mercy's
172 O where is He that trod the
256 When Thou, my righteous
AWAKENED.
257 Awaked by Sinai's awful
266 Life is the time to serve the
254 Lo, on a narrow neck of
259 My former hopes are fled
249 O cease, my wandering soul
BELIEVING.
347 Arise, my soul, arise
494 Father, I stretch my hands
344 I hear the Saviour say
318 I send the joys of earth
414 Jesus, I my cross have
323 Jesus, my Lord, my God
301 Let worldly minds the
292 Lord, I know Thy grace is
289 My faith looks up to Thee
297 Not all the blood of beasts
324 Now I have found the
436 O Lord, impart Thyself to
288 Once again beside the cross
300 The Saviour, O what endless
295 Vain, delusive world, adieu
CARELESS.
269 God calling yet I shall I not
191 Heart of stone, relent
234 Sinners, will you scorn the
246 To-morrow, Lord, is Thine
COMING TO CHRIST.
281 Come, humble sinner, in
304 I am coming to the cross

SINNERS:
280 Jesus, full of truth and
271 Jesus, the sinner's Friend
285 Just as I am, without one
CONFESSING CHRIST.
561 I love to tell the story
565 My gracious Lord, I own
491 No more, my God, I boast
492 People of the living God
485 Witness, ye men and angels
CONVICTED OF SIN.
260 Did Christ o'er sinners
275 I see the crowd in Pilate's
274 In evil long I took delight
261 Is this the kind return
262 Thou Lord of all above
DELAYING—See *Delay.*
DIRECTED.
475 Commit thou all thy griefs
493 Pilgrim, burdened with thy
190 Surely Christ thy griefs hath
243 Ye that in His courts are
174 Ye that pass by, behold the
EXPOSTULATED.
181 O come and mourn with me
227 O come to the merciful
230 O sinner, why so long
241 Sinners, turn, why will ye
239 To-day the Saviour calls
INVITED.
253 Art thou weary, art thou
250 Behold, a stranger's at the
252 Child of sin and sorrow
240 Come, said Jesus' sacred
235 Come, sinners, to the gospel
242 Come to Calvary's holy
245 Come to the land of peace
233 Come, ye sinners, poor and
242 From the cross uplifted
244 Let every mortal ear attend
248 Now is the accepted hour
145 Raise your triumphant
251 Return, O wanderer, return
236 Sinners, obey the gospel
140 The Saviour calls, let every
226 The voice of free grace cries
217 Ye trembling captives, hear
PENITENT.
189 Alas! and did my Saviour
482 I need Thee, precious
434 Jesus, my Lord, attend
264 Lord, I am vile, conceived
181 O Jesus, sweet the tears I
178 O sacred Head, now
421 Out of the depths of woe
265 Show pity, Lord, O Lord
279 Sovereign Ruler, Lord of
PLEADING FOR MERCY.
278 Depth of mercy, can there
432 Have mercy, Lord, on me
277 Lord, I hear of showers of
291 "Mercy, O Thou Son of"
433 Out of the deep I call
276 Pass me not, O gentle
273 Stay, Thou insulted Spirit
272 With broken heart and
PRAYER OF ANXIOUS.
114 Father of Heaven, whose
94 Forth from the dark and
46 Gracious Spirit, Dove
47 Holy Ghost, with light
282 Jesus, Thou art the sinner's
126 Laden with guilt, and full

INDEX OF SUBJECTS.

SINNERS:
255 O Thou that hearest the
287 Rock of ages, cleft for me
224 Take me, O my Father
REJOICING IN HOPE.
334 Awake, my soul, to joyful
349 From Egypt lately come
561 I love to tell the story
442 I once was a stranger
299 I've found the pearl of
301 I was a wandering sheep
315 Jesus, my All, to Heaven is
26 Let everlasting glories
316 Lord, I was blind! I could
377 Now I have found a Friend
293 O how happy are they
313 Sweet the moments, rich in
441 Take, my soul, thy full
317 The Saviour smiles; upon
448 When God revealed His
SEEKING.
268 A broken heart, my God
321 Come, O Thou Traveller
194 Done is the work that saves
283 Jesus, full of all compassion
267 O that my load of sin were
270 With tearful eyes I look
SONG OF PRAISE.
217 All hail the power of Jesus'
185 Come let us sing the song
141 Glory, glory everlasting
142 Grace, 'tis a charming
307 Hail, my ever blessed Jesus
322 I bless the Christ of God
316 I will love Thee, all my
304 Lord, with glowing heart
137 Plunged in a gulf of dark
312 Praise, my soul, the King
114 Praises to Him whose love
135 Salvation, O the joyful
302 There is a fountain filled
435 To Thee, my God and
WARNED.
243 Broad is the road that leads
229 Delay not, delay not; O
117 Keep silence all created
253 O where shall rest be found
115 The Lord our God is full of
235 To-day the Saviour calls
246 To-morrow, Lord, is Thine
237 While life prolongs its
YIELDING.
228 And can I yet delay?
269 God calling yet I shall I not
246 Lord, I am Thine, entirely
231 Lord, Thou hast won, at
296 Saviour, see me from above
SLAVERY.
552 Go, ye messengers of God
551 Hail to the Lord's Anointed
563 Uplift the blood-red banner
SLEEP.
61 All praise to Thee, my God
60 Awake, my soul, and with
67 Call Jehovah thy salvation
63 Father, by Thy love and
62 Sun of my soul, Thou
65 Thus far the Lord has led
68 Vainly through night's
55 We lift our hearts to Thee
SOLDIER, CHRISTIAN—See *Warfare.*
SOUL—See *Immortality.*

SONG:
NEW.
218 Come, let us join our
185 Come, let us sing the song
626 What are these in bright
OF MOSES AND THE LAMB.
143 Awake, and sing the song
OF PILGRIMS—See *Pilgrims.*
OF THE ANGELS—See *Angels.*
SORROW—See *Afflictions.*
FOR SIN—See *Penitential.*
SOWING AND REAPING.
560 He that goeth forth with
576 Sow in the morn thy seed
448 When God revealed His
STAR OF BETHLEHEM.
157 What star is this, with
156 When marshalled on the
STAR OF THE EAST.
155 As with gladness men of
159 Brightest and best of the
152 Watchman, tell us of the
STEADFASTNESS — See *Saints, Perseverance of.*
SUBMISSION—See *Afflictions* and *Resignation.*
SUPPER, LORD'S – See *Lord's Supper.*
SURRENDER—See *Sinners yielding.*
SYMPATHY OF CHRIST—See *Christ.*
OF CHRISTIANS—See *Communion.*

THANKFULNESS—See *Gratitude.*
THANKSGIVING.
643 Eternal source of every joy
639 For Thy mercy and Thy
655 God of nations, King of
657 Let children hear the
95 Let us, with a gladsome
461 O bless the Lord, my soul
653 O Lord, our fathers oft have
633 Our God, beneath Thy
656 Praise the Lord, His glories
651 Praise to God, immortal
57 Stand up, and bless the
638 Thou, who roll'st the year
643 When all Thy mercies, O
615 With songs and honors
THRONE OF GRACE—See *Mercy-seat.*
17 Behold the throne of grace
464 Father, whate'er of earthly
TIME - See *Death, Life,* and *Year.*
TO-DAY.
252 Child of sin and sorrow.
243 Now is the accepted time
239 To-day the Saviour calls
TO-MORROW.
246 To morrow, Lord, is Thine
TRIALS—See *Afflictions.*
TRIBULATIONS—See *Afflictions.*
TRINITY:
ADORATION OF.
8 Holy, holy, holy, Lord God
2 Holy, holy, holy, Lord God of
INVOKED.
1 Come, Thou Almighty King
580 Thou, whose Almighty
PRAISE TO—See *Praise.*
PRAYER TO—See *Prayer.*

TRINITY:
WORSHIP OF.
114 Father of heaven, whose
76 Great Creator, who this day
TRUST:
IN CHRIST.
425 Fountain of grace, rich, full
477 How gentle God's
304 I am coming to the cross
211 I know that my Redeemer
442 I once was a stranger to
490 I'm not ashamed to own my
436 In heavenly love abiding
336 Lord, Thou art my Rock of
480 My Jesus, as Thou wilt
416 My Saviour, my Almighty
478 My spirit, on Thy care
324 Now I have found the
139 O Jesus, when I think of
514 O what, if we are Christ's
458 Sometimes a light surprises
421 The billows swell, the
412 Thou, O Christ, art all I
428 Through the love of God
421 To God I cried when
423 When sins and fears
IN GOD
462 Father, I know that all my
427 Fear not, O little flock, the
474 Give to the winds thy
468 My God, my Father
467 While Thee I seek
IN PROVIDENCE.
475 Commit thou all thy griefs
380 How firm a foundation
613 When all Thy mercies, O

VANITY OF LIFE—See *Life.*
VICTORY OF BELIEVERS—See *Warfare.*
OF CHRIST—See *Christ.*
VOWS TO GOD.
286 Lord, I am Thine, entirely
490 O happy day that fixed my
485 Witness, ye men and angels

WARFARE, CHRISTIAN.
397 Am I a soldier of the cross
383 Awake, my soul, lift up
394 Awake, my soul, stretch
395 Brethren, while we sojourn
427 Fear not, O little flock, the
382 Fight the good fight with
394 Go forward, Christian
389 Gracious Redeemer, shake
388 My soul, be on thy guard
391 My soul, weigh not thy life
453 Our Captain leads us on
387 Soldiers of Christ, arise
381 Stand up, my soul, shake
393 Stand up, stand up for Jesus
WARNINGS—See *Sinners warned.*
WATCHFULNESS AND PRAYER.
390 A charge to keep I have
343 Awake, my soul, lift up
389 Gracious Redeemer, shake
430 Jesus, my Strength, my
251 Lo, on a narrow neck of
388 My soul, be on thy guard
605 Rejoice, rejoice, believers
601 The world is very evil
575 Ye servants of the Lord

INDEX OF SUBJECTS. 339

WATCHMEN.
516 How beauteous are their
152 Watchman, tell us of the
575 Ye servants of the Lord
WAY OF SALVATION — See *Atonement, Grace,* and *Sinners.*
WAY, TRUTH AND LIFE—See *Christ.*
WEARY, REST FOR THE.
253 Art thou weary, art thou
228 Come unto me, when
305 I heard the voice of Jesus
631 In the Christian's home in
249 O cease, my wandering soul
629 There is an hour of
WORD OF GOD.
127 A glory gilds the sacred
51 Behold, the morning sun
131 Father of mercies, in Thy
130 God, in the gospel of His
469 God is the refuge of His

WORD OF GOD.
133 Hail, sacred truth, whose
128 How precious is the book
126 Laden with guilt and full of
132 Lamp of our feet, whereby
26 Let everlasting glories
134 O Word of God Incarnate
538 Spread, O spread, thou
129 The heavens declare Thy
WORKING AND GIVING.
567 Go, labor on; spend and be
536 Hark, the voice of Jesus
539 With my substance I will
628 Work, for the night is
WORLD RENOUNCED—See *Forsaking all for Christ.*
WORSHIP—See *Family Worship, Lord's Day, Praise,* and *Prayer.*

YEAR—See *Seasons.*
BEGINNING OF.
640 Come, let us anew

YEAR:
649 Eternal Source of every joy
650 Great God, we sing that
637 While with ceaseless course
CLOSE OF.
647 A few more years shall roll
639 For Thy mercy and Thy
648 How swift the torrent rolls
OF JUBILEE.
221 Blow ye the trumpet
535 Hark, the song of Jubilee
540 Wake the song of Jubilee

ZEAL.
390 A charge to keep I have
397 Am I a soldier of the cross
398 Awake, my soul, stretch
830 Do not I love Thee, O my
385 In all my Lord's appointed
381 Stand up, my soul, shake
ZION—See *Church.*

INDEX OF FIRST LINES.

	HYMN		HYMN
A BROKEN heart, my God, my King	268	Awake, my soul, stretch every nerve	398
A charge to keep I have	390	Awake, my soul, to joyful lays	338
A crown of glory bright	367	Awake, our souls, away our fears	384
A few more years shall roll	647	Awaked by Sinai's awful sound	257
A glory gilds the sacred page	127	Awhile in spirit, Lord, to Thee	169
A little child the Saviour came	488		
Abide with me, fast falls the eventide	71	BEFORE Jehovah's awful throne	104
According to Thy gracious word	502	Behold, a stranger's at the door	250
Again our earthly cares we leave	91	Behold the glories of the Lamb	219
Again the Lord of life and light	93	Behold, the morning sun	54
Alas, and did my Saviour bleed	180	Behold, the Mountain of the Lord	532
All hail the power of Jesus' Name	217	Behold the throne of grace	17
All people that on earth do dwell	103	Behold, what wondrous grace	454
All praise to Thee, my God, this night	61	Behold, where, in a mortal form	167
Am I a soldier of the cross	397	Beyond, beyond that boundless sea	463
Amazing grace, how sweet the sound	306	Bless, O my soul, the living God	122
And can I yet delay	298	Blessed are the sons of God	33
And let this feeble body fail	622	Blest be the dear, uniting love	508
Angels, from the realms of glory	163	Blest be the tie that binds	513
Another six days' work is done	77	Blow ye the trumpet, blow	221
Arise, my soul, arise	337	Brethren, while we sojourn here	395
Arise, my tenderest thoughts, arise	569	Bright and joyful is the morn	154
Arise, O King of grace, arise	517	Brighter still and brighter	592
Art thou weary, art thou languid	253	Brightest and best of the sons of the	159
As pants the hart for cooling streams	419	Brightness of the Father's glory	162
As when the weary traveller gains	351	Broad is the road that leads to death	263
As with gladness men of old	155		
Asleep in Jesus, blessed sleep	585	CALL Jehovah thy salvation	67
Assembled at thy great command	544	Calm me, my God, and keep me calm	450
At even, ere the sun was set	40	Calm on the listening ear of night	166
At Thy command, our dearest Lord	496	Cast thy burden on the Lord	415
Awake, and sing the song	143	Child of sin and sorrow	252
Awake, my soul, and with the sun	60	Children of the Heavenly King	346
Awake, my soul, lift up thine eyes	383	Christ for the world we sing	577

INDEX OF FIRST LINES.

	HYMN
Christ is made the sure Foundation	520
Christ, the Lord, is risen again	201
Christ, the Lord, is risen to-day	200
Come, all ye saints of God	205
Come, blessed Spirit, Source of light	25
Come, dearest Lord, descend and dwell	42
Come, every pious heart	607
Come, happy souls, approach your	225
Come, Holy Ghost, in love	44
Come, Holy Spirit, calm my mind	32
Come, Holy Spirit, come	16
Come, Holy Spirit, heavenly dove, My	24
Come, Holy Spirit, heavenly dove, With	417
Come, humble sinner, in whose breast	281
Come in, thou blessed of the Lord	495
Come let us anew	640
Come, let us join in songs of praise	214
Come, let us join our cheerful songs	213
Come, let us join our friend above	509
Come, let us lift our joyful eyes	209
Come, let us sing the song of songs	185
Come, let us to the Lord, our God	418
Come, my soul, thy suit prepare	35
Come, O Creator, Spirit blest	9
Come, O my soul, in sacred lays	123
Come, O Thou Traveller unknown	321
Come, sacred Spirit, from above	571
Come, said Jesus' sacred voice	240
Come, sinners, to the gospel feast	235
Come, Thou almighty King	1
Come, Thou Fount of every blessing	311
Come, Thou long-expected Jesus	161
Come to Calvary's holy mountain	232
Come to the land of peace	245
Come unto me, when shadows darkly	228
Come, we that love the Lord	451
Come ye disconsolate, where'er ye	238
Come, ye faithful, raise the anthem	223
Come, ye sinners, poor and wretched	233
Commit thou all thy griefs	475
DAUGHTER of Zion, from the dust	533
Dear Saviour, if these lambs should	489
Dearest of all the names above	141
Delay not, delay not; O sinner draw	229
Depth of mercy, can there be	278

	HYMN
Did Christ o'er sinners weep	260
Dismiss us with Thy blessing, Lord	43
Do not I love Thee, O my Lord	330
Done is the work that saves	198
EARLY, my God, without delay	83
Earth, with its dark and dreadful ills	584
Eternal Father, strong to save	525
Eternal Source of every joy	649
Eternal Spirit, we confess	10
Exalt the Lord our God	90
FADE, fade, each earthly joy	375
Far from my heavenly home	602
Far from my thoughts, vain world	12
Far from the world, O Lord, I flee	51
Father, by Thy love and power	69
Father, I know that all my life	462
Father, I stretch my hands to Thee	294
Father of heaven, whose love profound	114
Father of love and power	45
Father of mercies, in Thy word	131
Father, Thine Elect who lovest	20
Father, whate'er of earthly bliss	464
Fear not, O little flock, the foe	427
Fight the good fight with all thy might	382
For ever with the Lord	599
For the mercies of the day	37
For thee, O dear, dear country	617
For Thy mercy and Thy grace	639
Forth from the dark and stormy sky	94
Forth to the Land of Promise bound	582
Fountain of grace, rich, full and free	425
From all that dwell below the skies	105
From Egypt lately come	348
From every stormy wind that blows	29
From Greenland's icy mountains	547
From the cross uplifted high	242
GENTLY, Lord, O gently lead us	22
Give me the wings of faith, to rise	510
Give to the wind thy fears	474
Glorious things of Thee are spoken	526
Glory, glory everlasting	189
Glory to God on high	204
Go forward, Christian soldier	394

INDEX OF FIRST LINES.

First line	HYMN
Go, labor on, spend and be spent	567
Go to dark Gethsemane	176
Go, ye messengers of God	552
God bless our native land	660
God calling yet! shall I not hear?	269
God, in the gospel of His Son	130
God is love: His mercy brightens	402
God is the refuge of His saints	469
God moves in a mysterious way	466
God, my Supporter and my Hope	445
God of my life, through all its days	472
God of my life, to Thee I call	422
God of nations, King of kings	655
Grace, 'tis a charming sound	142
Gracious Redeemer, shake	389
Gracious Spirit, Dove Divine	46
Granted is the Saviour's prayer	48
Great Creator, who this day	76
Great Father of each perfect gift	53
Great God, attend while Zion sings	79
Great God, how infinite art Thou	642
Great God, the nations of the earth	535
Great God, we sing that mighty hand	650
Guide me, O Thou great Jehovah	354
Hail, my ever blessèd Jesus	307
Hail, sacred truth, whose piercing rays	133
Hail the day that sees Him rise	202
Hail, Thou once despisèd Jesus	215
Hail, to the Lord's Anointed	551
Happy the souls to Jesus joined	504
Hark, hark, my soul; angelic songs	512
Hark, my soul, it is the Lord	413
Hark, ten thousand harps and voices	608
Hark, the glad sound, the Saviour	149
Hark, the herald angels sing	153
Hark, the song of jubilee	555
Hark, the sound of holy voices	632
Hark, the voice of Jesus calling	556
Hark, the voice of love and mercy	188
Hark! what mean those holy voices	160
Hark, what mean those lamentations	557
Hasten Lord, the glorious time	553
Have mercy, Lord, on me	432
He comes in blood-stained garments	135
He dies, the Friend of sinners dies!	192
He leadeth me; O blessed thought	350
He lives, the Great Redeemer lives	193
He that goeth forth with weeping	560
Hear my prayer, O heavenly Father	66
Hear what the voice from heaven	596
Heart of stone, relent, relent	191
High in the heavens, eternal God	121
High in yonder realms of light	627
Holy Ghost, with light divine	47
Holy, holy, holy Lord, Be Thy	111
Holy, holy, holy, Lord God Almighty	8
Holy, holy, holy, Lord God of Hosts	2
How are Thy servants blest, O Lord	644
How beauteous are their feet	516
How beauteous were the marks divine	171
How blest the righteous, when he dies	586
How blest the sacred tie that binds	27
How calm and beautiful the morn	199
How charming is the place	88
How did my heart rejoice to hear	82
How firm a foundation, ye saints of the	380
How gentle God's commands	477
How heavy is the night	146
How pleased and blest was I	106
How precious is the book divine	128
How sweet and awful is the place	503
How sweet the name of Jesus sounds	332
How swift the torrent rolls	648
How tedious and tasteless the hours	342
I am coming to the cross	304
I bless the Christ of God	322
I give immortal praise	6
I hear the Saviour say	344
I heard the voice of Jesus say	305
I know no life divided	457
I know that my Redeemer lives, And	211
I know that my Redeemer lives, What	195
I'll praise my Maker with my breath	115
I long to behold Him arrayed	625
I love Thy kingdom, Lord	515
I love to steal awhile away	52
I love to tell the story	561
I'm a pilgrim and I'm a stranger	353
I'm not ashamed to own my Lord	400
I need Thee, precious Jesus	482

INDEX OF FIRST LINES.

	HYMN
I once was a stranger to grace and to	442
I see the crowd in Pilate's hall	275
I send the joys of earth away	318
I've found the pearl of greatest price	299
I want a principle within	437
I was a wandering sheep	303
I will love Thee, all my treasure	310
I worship Thee, sweet Will of God	465
I would love Thee, God and Father	403
If human kindness meets return	501
If, through unruffled seas	476
In all my Lord's appointed ways	365
In Christ I've all my soul's desire	408
In evil long I took delight	274
In heavenly love abiding	456
In prayer together let us fall	652
In some way or other the Lord will	352
In the Christian's home in glory	631
In the cross of Christ I glory	401
In the hour of trial	590
In Thy name, O Lord, assembling	72
In token that Thou shalt not fear	487
Infinite excellence is Thine	210
Is this the kind return	261
It came upon the midnight clear	165
It is not death to die	603
Jehovah, God, Thy gracious power	124
Jerusalem, my happy home	623
Jerusalem the glorious	618
Jerusalem the golden	616
Jesus, and shall it ever be	406
Jesus came, the heavens adoring	164
Jesus, full of all compassion	283
Jesus, full of truth and love	280
Jesus, I love Thy charming name	326
Jesus, I my cross have taken	404
Jesus is the Name we treasure	309
Jesus, Lover of my soul	411
Jesus, my All, to Heaven is gone	315
Jesus, my Lord, attend	434
Jesus, my Lord, my God, my All	323
Jesus, my Strength, my Hope	430
Jesus, our best beloved Friend	566
Jesus shall reign where'er the sun	545
Jesus, still lead on	360

	HYMN
Jesus, the sinner's Friend, to Thee	271
Jesus, the very thought of Thee	329
Jesus, these eyes have never seen	331
Jesus, Thine all-victorious love	438
Jesus, this heart within me burns	320
Jesus, Thou art the sinner's Friend	282
Jesus, Thou joy of loving hearts	498
Jesus, Thy blood and righteousness	500
Jesus, Thy name I love	290
Jesus, where'er Thy people meet	14
Join all the glorious names	336
Joy to the world, the Lord is come	150
Joyfully, joyfully onward I move	636
Just as I am, without one plea	285
Keep silence, all created things	117
Laden with guilt, and full of fears	126
Lamp of our feet, whereby we trace	132
Lead us, heavenly Father, lead us	357
Let children hear the mighty deeds	657
Let everlasting glories crown	26
Let every mortal ear attend	224
Let us, with a gladsome mind	95
Let worldly minds the world pursue	301
Let Zion and her sons rejoice	530
Life is the time to serve the Lord	260
Lift up to God the voice of praise	646
Light of those whose dreary dwelling	574
Lo He comes, with clouds descending	611
Lo, on a narrow neck of land	254
Lo, what a glorious sight appears	614
Look down, O Lord, with pitying eye	570
Lord, dismiss us with Thy blessing, Bid	405
Lord, dismiss us with Thy blessing, Fill	73
Lord God, the Holy Ghost	15
Lord, I am Thine, entirely Thine	286
Lord, I am vile, conceived in sin	264
Lord, I hear of showers of blessing	277
Lord, I know Thy grace is nigh me	292
Lord, I was blind! I could not see	316
Lord, in the morning Thou shalt hear	84
Lord, in this Thy mercy's day	177
Lord Jesus, when we stand afar	175
Lord of all power and might	578
Lord of hosts, to Thee we raise	519

INDEX OF FIRST LINES.

	HYMN		HYMN
Lord of the worlds above	100	Now from labor and from care	70
Lord, Thou art my Rock of strength	396	Now I have found a Friend	377
Lord, Thou hast won, at length I yield	231	Now I have found the ground wherein	324
Lord, we come before Thee now	34	Now is the accepted time	248
Lord, when we bend before Thy throne	92	Now let our cheerful eyes survey	220
Lord, with glowing heart I'd praise Thee	308	Now to the Lord who makes us know	186
Love Divine, all love excelling	440		
Lowly and solemn be	593	O BLESS the Lord, my soul	461
		O cease, my wandering soul	249
MAJESTIC sweetness sits enthroned	325	O city of the Lord, begin	530
"Mercy, O Thou Son of David"	291	O come and mourn with me awhile	184
'Mid scenes of confusion and creature	511	O come, loud anthems let us sing	80
More love to Thee, O Christ	376	O come to the merciful Saviour that	227
Must Jesus bear the cross alone	399	O could I speak the matchless worth	334
My country, 'tis of thee	659	O day of rest and gladness	97
My days are gliding swiftly by	372	O'er the distant mountains breaking	610
My dear Redeemer, and my Lord	168	O'er the gloomy hills of darkness	529
My faith looks up to Thee	289	O for a closer walk with God	416
My former hopes are fled	259	O for a heart to praise my God	435
My God, and is Thy table spread	497	O for a thousand tongues to sing	328
My God, how wonderful Thou art	449	O for the death of those	600
My God, I love Thee: not because	333	O God, beneath Thy guiding hand	653
My God, my Father, blissful name	468	O God of Bethel, by whose hand	362
My God, my Life, my Love	452	O happy band of pilgrims	606
My God, my Portion, and my Love	444	O happy day, that fixed my choice	490
My God, permit me not to be	31	O happy, happy place	19
My God, the Spring of all my joys	443	O how happy are they	293
My gracious Lord, I own Thy right	565	O Jesus, King most wonderful	327
My heavenly home is bright and fair	373	O Jesus, sweet the tears I shed	181
My hope is built on nothing less	410	O Jesus, Thou art standing	179
My Jesus as Thou wilt	480	O Jesus, when I think of Thee	139
My Lord, my Love, was crucified	507	O Lamb of God, still keep me	483
My precious Lord, for Thy dear Name	407	O Lord, how joyful 'tis to see	30
My Saviour, my Almighty Friend	446	O Lord, impart Thyself to me	436
My soul, be on thy guard	388	O Lord, our fathers oft have told	658
My soul, repeat His praise	119	O Lord, Thy work revive	18
My soul, there is a country	620	O Love divine, how sweet Thou art!	335
My soul, weigh not thy life	391	O mean may seem this house of clay	213
My spirit, on Thy care	478	O mother dear, Jerusalem	621
		O sacred Head, now wounded	178
NEARER, my God, to Thee	374	O sinner, why so long delay	230
No more, my God, I boast no more	491	O Spirit of the living God	542
No, no, it is not dying	598	O that I could forever dwell	319
Not all the blood of beasts	297	O that my load of sin were gone!	267
Now be the Gospel banner	549	O that the Lord's salvation	562
Now begin the heavenly theme	347	O that the Lord would guide my ways	439

INDEX OF FIRST LINES.

	HYMN		HYMN
O the sweet wonders of that cross	499	Return, O wanderer, return	251
O Thou that hear'st the prayer of faith	255	Rise, glorious Conqueror, rise	206
O Thou, to whose all-searching sight	409	Rise, my soul, and stretch thy wings	358
O Thou, whose own vast temple stands	518	Rock of ages, cleft for me	287
O what, if we are Christ's	514	Rocked in the cradle of the deep	523
O where are kings and empires now	531	Round the Lord in glory seated	5
O, where is He that trod the sea	172		
O where shall rest be found	258	SAFE Home, safe Home in port	635
O Word of God incarnate	134	Safely through another week	75
O worship the King, All-glorious above	108	Saints in glory, we together	341
Oft when the waves of passion rise	426	Salvation! O the joyful sound	136
On Jordan's rugged banks I stand	612	Saviour, breathe an evening blessing	64
On the mountain's top appearing	528	Saviour, like a Shepherd lead us	356
On Zion and on Lebanon	537	Saviour, see me from above	296
Once again beside the cross	288	Saviour, sprinkle many nations	559
One sweetly solemn thought	368	Saviour, teach me, day by day	414
One there is above all others	314	Saviour, through the desert lead us	355
Our Captain leads us on	453	Saviour, visit Thy plantation	573
Our day of praise is done	58	See how great a flame aspires	554
Our God, our help in ages past	641	See, Israel's gentle Shepherd stands	486
Our heavenly Father calls	118	See the ransomed millions stand	3
Our journey is a thorny maze	363	Set thy house in order	591
Our Lord is risen from the dead	194	Shall we gather at the river	633
Our Lord, who knows full well	479	Shepherd of tender youth	23
Our souls, by love together knit	506	Show pity, Lord, O Lord, forgive	265
Out of the deep I call	433	Since all the varying scenes of time	125
Out of the depths of woe	431	Sing of Jesus, sing forever	340
Out on an ocean all-boundless we ride	371	Sing to the Lord, ye distant lands	151
		Sing, ye redeemed of the Lord	366
PART in peace, Christ's life was peace	38	Sinners, obey the gospel word	236
Pass me not, O gentle Saviour	276	Sinners, turn, why will ye die	241
People of the living God	492	Sinners, will you scorn the message	234
Pilgrim, burdened with thy sin	493	So let our lips and lives express	568
Plunged in a gulf of dark despair	137	Softly now the light of day	36
Praise, my soul, the King of Heaven	312	Soldiers of Christ, arise	387
Praise the Lord, His glories show	656	Sometimes a light surprises	458
Praise the Lord, ye heavens, adore Him	4	Songs of praise the angels sang	110
Praise to God, immortal praise	654	Sons of Zion, raise your songs	203
Praise to Thee, thou great Creator	21	Sovereign Ruler, Lord of all	279
Praises to Him, whose love has given	112	Sound, sound the truth abroad	579
Prayer is the soul's sincere desire	49	Sow in the morn thy seed	576
		Spirit of power and might, behold	534
RAISE your triumphant songs	145	Spread, O spread, Thou mighty word	538
Rejoice, rejoice, believers	605	Stand up, and bless the Lord	87
Rejoice, the Lord is King	222	Stand up, my soul, shake off thy fears	381
Rest for the toiling hand	601	Stand up, stand up for Jesus	393

INDEX OF FIRST LINES.

	HYMN
Star of peace, to wanderers weary	524
Stay, Thou insulted Spirit, stay	273
Sun of my soul, Thou Saviour dear	62
Surely Christ thy griefs hath borne	190
Sweet hour of prayer	39
Sweet is the work, my God, my King	78
Sweet is the work, O Lord	56
Sweet is Thy mercy, Lord	144
Sweet the moments, rich in blessing	313
Sweet was the time when first I felt	420
Take me, O my Father, take me	284
Take, my soul, thy full salvation	441
Tarry with me, O my Saviour	65
Teach me, my God and King	392
Tell me the old, old story	564
Ten thousand times ten thousand	619
The billows swell, the winds are high	421
The day, O Lord, is spent	57
The day of resurrection	98
The happy morn is come	197
The head that once was crowned with	208
The heavens declare Thy glory, Lord	129
The hour of my departure's come	589
The Lord is King; lift up thy voice	471
The Lord is my Shepherd, no want	378
The Lord Jehovah reigns	101
The Lord my Shepherd is	460
The Lord on high ascends	207
The Lord our God is full of might	116
The morning light is breaking	550
The pity of the Lord	120
The race that long in darkness pined	147
The royal banners forward go	113
The Saviour calls, let every ear	140
The Saviour! O what endless charms	300
The Saviour smiles; upon my soul	317
The Spirit in our hearts	244
The voice of free grace cries, Escape	226
The way is dark; I cannot see at all	361
The world is very evil	604
There is a fountain filled with blood	302
There is a land of pure delight	615
There is an hour of peaceful rest	629
There is no name so sweet on earth	339
There's a Friend above all others	429

	HYMN
Thine earthly Sabbaths, Lord, we love	81
Thine forever!—God of love	494
This is the day of toil	349
This is the day the Lord hath made	85
Thou art the Way: to Thee alone	138
Thou dear Redeemer, dying Lamb	364
Thou Lord of all above	262
Thou, O Christ, art all I want	412
Thou who roll'st the year around	638
Thou, whose almighty Word	530
Though faint, yet pursuing, we go on	379
Though now the nations sit beneath	543
Through all the changing scenes of life	447
Through sorrow's night and danger's	581
Through the love of God our Saviour	428
Through the night of doubt and sorrow	527
Thus far the Lord has led me on	63
Thy name, Almighty Lord	59
Thy presence, everlasting God	28
Thy tears, not mine, O Christ	345
Thy way, not mine, O Lord	481
Time is winging us away	359
'Tis by the faith of joys to come	385
"'Tis finished!" so the Saviour cried	183
'Tis Heaven begun below	107
'Tis midnight; and on Olive's brow	173
To-day the Saviour calls	239
To God I cried when troubles rose	424
To God, the only wise	89
To Him that chose us first	7
To-morrow, Lord, is Thine	246
To Thee, my God and Saviour	459
To Thy temple I repair	96
Tossed upon life's raging billow	522
Triumphant Zion, lift thy head	546
Unveil Thy bosom, faithful tomb	587
Up to the hills I lift mine eyes	470
Uplift the blood-red banner	563
Upward I lift mine eyes	102
Vain, delusive world, adieu	295
Vainly through night's weary hours	68
Wait, O my soul, Thy Maker's will	473
Wake the song of jubilee	540

INDEX OF FIRST LINES.

First Line	HYMN
Watchman, tell us of the night	152
We are living, we are dwelling	558
We are on our journey home	634
We have a house above	455
We lift our hearts to Thee	55
We long to move and breathe in Thee	484
We praise Thee, O God, for the Son	343
We're bound for yonder land	370
We shall meet beyond the river	630
"We've no abiding city here"	386
Welcome, delightful morn	99
Welcome, sweet day of rest	86
Welcome, welcome, dear Redeemer	74
What are these in bright array	626
What star is this, with beams so bright	157
What various hindrances we meet	41
When all Thy mercies, O my God	643
When God revealed His gracious name	448
When I can read my title clear	613
When I survey the wondrous cross	182
When Jordan hushed his waters still	153
When languor and disease invade	583
When like a stranger on our sphere	170
When marshalled on the nightly plain	156
When shall the voice of singing	543
When sins and fears prevailing rise	423
When Thou, my righteous Judge	256
Where high the heavenly temple stands	187
Where two or three, with sweet accord	11
While I to grief my soul gave way	572
While life prolongs its precious light	237
While now the daylight fills the sky	13
While o'er our guilty land, O Lord	651
While shepherds watched their flocks	148
While Thee I seek, protecting Power	467
While with ceaseless course the sun	637
Who are these like stars appearing	609
Why do we mourn departing friends	594
Why should our tears in sorrow flow	595
Why should the children of a King	50
Why should we start and fear to die	588
With broken heart and contrite sigh	272
With joy I see a thousand charms	597
With joy we meditate the grace	212
With my substance I will honor	539
With songs and honors sounding loud	645
With tearful eyes I look around	270
Witness, ye men and angels, now	485
Work, for the night is coming	628
Worship, honor, power and blessing	216
"Worthy the Lamb for sinners slain"	505
Ye angels, who stand round the throne	624
Ye Christian heralds, go, proclaim	541
Ye servants of God	109
Ye servants of the Lord	575
Ye that in His courts are found	243
Ye that pass by, behold the Man	174
Ye trembling captives, hear	247
Yes, the Redeemer rose	196
Your harps, ye trembling saints	369
Zion stands by hills surrounded	521

INDEX TO CHANTS.

	PAGE		PAGE
AND there were in the same country	308	LORD, have mercy upon us	299
BLESSED be the Lord God of Israel	307	MAKE a joyful noise unto the Lord	304
Blessed is the man that walketh not	300	My soul doth magnify the Lord	308
CHRIST our Passover is sacrificed	314	O COME, let us sing unto the Lord	302
Come unto Me all ye that labor	309	O sing unto the Lord a new song	303
		Our Father, who art in heaven	309
FROM the recesses of a lowly spirit	315		
		PRAISE the Lord, O my soul	304
GLORY be to God on high	310	Praise ye the Lord	306
Glory be to the Father, and to the Son	301		
Glory be to the Father, and to the Son	311	SHOUT the glad tidings, exultingly sing	316
Glory be to the Father, and to the Son	312	Sound the loud timbrel o'er Egypt's dark	317
God be merciful unto us, and bless us	301	Suffer little children	313
HE was despised and rejected of men	306	THE Lord is my Shepherd; I shall not	300
How amiable are Thy tabernacles	302	The mercy of the Lord is from	313
How beautiful upon the mountains	307	Then will I sprinkle clean water	313
		Thy will be done	316
I HEARD a voice from heaven	314		
I was glad when they said unto me	305	WE praise Thee, O God	311
I will lift up mine eyes	305		

INDEX OF AUTHORS.

The figures refer to the numbers of the hymns.

ADAMS, MRS. Sarah Flower. (1805—1848.) 39, 374.
ADDISON, Joseph. (1672—1719.) 643, 644.
ALEXANDER, Rev. James Waddell. (1804—1859.) 178.
ALFORD, Rev. Henry. (1810—1871.) 487, 582, 591, 619.
ALLEN, G. N. 399.
ALLEN, Rev. James. (1734—1804.) 204, 313.
ALLEN, Rev. Jonathan. 234.
AMBROSE of Milan. (340—397.) 13, 207.
ANSTICE, Prof. Joseph. (1808—1836.) 69.
ATKINSON, Rev. John. 630.
AUBER, Miss Harriet. (1773—1862.) 56, 68, 553.

BACON, Rev. Leonard. (1802—) 540, 543, 653.
BAHNMAIER, Rev. Jonathan Frederic. (1774—1841.) 538.
BAKER, Rev. Francis. 621.
BAKER, Rev. Sir Henry Williams. (1821—) 312, 433, 514, 652.
BAKEWELL, Rev. John. (1721—1819.) 215, 216.
BANCROFT, Mrs. Charitie Lees. (1841—) 135.
BARBAULD, Mrs. Anna Lætitia. (1743—1825.) 27, 93, 240, 383, 586, 654.
BARTON, Bernard. (1784—1849.) 132.
BEECHER, Rev. Charles. (1819—) 634.
BEDDOME, Rev. Benjamin. (1717—1795.) 25, 130, 260, 262, 473, 483.
BERNARD of Clairvaux. (1091—1153.) 178, 327, 329, 493.
BERNARD of Cluny. (1145—) 604, 616, 617, 618.
BETHUNE, Rev. George Washington. (1805—1862.) 139, 333, 532, 633.
BLACKLOCK, Rev. Thomas. (1721—1791.) 128.
BODEN, Rev. James. (1757—1841.) 205.
BONAR, Rev. Horatius. (1808—) 112, 198, 275, 322, 303, 305, 345, 349, 459, 481, 507, 601, 647.
BONAR, Mrs. Horatius. 375.
BURTHWICK, Miss Jane. 269, 310, 360, 480, 605.
BOWRING, Sir John. (1792—1872.) 152, 401, 402.
BOYCE, Samuel. 247.
BRIDGES, Matthew. (1800—) 206.
BRIGGS' Collection. 245.
BROWN, Mrs. Phœbe Hinsdale. (1783—1861.) 18, 52.
BROWNE, Rev. Simon. (1680—1732.) 24.
BRUCE, Michael. (1746—1767.) 187, 362, 530, 532, 589.
BRYANT, William Cullen. (1794—) 513.
BURDER, Rev. Henry Forster. 32.
BURDSALL, Rev. Richard. (1735—1824.) 227.
BURNHAM, Rev. Richard. (1749—1810.) 282.
BURTON, John. (1773—1822.) 359.
BUTTRESS, John. 133.

CAMPBELL, Thomas. (1777—1844.) 158.
CARLYLE, Rev. Joseph Dacre. (1759—1804.) 92.
CARY, Miss Alice. (1820—1871.) 584.
CARY, Miss Phœbe. (1825—1871.) 368.

CASWALL, Rev. Edward. (1814—) 9, 327, 329, 233.
CAWOOD, Rev. John. (1775—1852.) 160, 537.
CENNICK, Rev. John. (1717—1755.) 315, 346, 364.
CHANDLER, Rev. John. (1806—) 30, 157.
CLEMENT of Alexandria. (—220.) 23.
CODNER, Mrs. Elizabeth. 277.
COFFIN, Prof. Charles. (1676—1749.) 157.
COLLINS, Rev. Henry. 323.
COLLYER, Rev. William Bengo. (1782—1854.) 251, 544.
CONDER, Josiah. (1789—1855.) 3, 463, 471.
COOK, Mrs. Martha Walker. (1807—1874.) 352.
COOPER, John. 114.
CORWIN, Rev. Eli. (1824—) 230.
COTTERILL, Rev. Thomas. (1779—1823.) 190.
COWPER, William. (1731—1800.) 14, 41, 51, 127, 259, 302, 413, 416, 421, 422, 458, 466.
COX, Miss Frances Elizabeth. 609.
COXE, Bp. Arthur Cleveland. (1818—) 171, 531, 558, 539.
CRABBE, Rev. George. (1754—1832.) 493.

DANA, Mrs. Mary S. B. (1810—) 353.
DAVIES, Rev. Samuel. (1724—1761.) 286, 651.
DE FLEURY, Miss Maria. 624.
DECK, James George. 290, 483.
DENHAM, Rev. David. 511.
DEXTER, Rev. Henry Martyn. (1821—) 23.
DICKSON, Rev. David. (1583—1663.) 621.
DIX, William Chatterton. (1837—) 155.
DOANE, Bp. George Washington. (1799—1859.) 36, 138.
DOBELL, John. (1757—1840.) 99, 248, 408.
DODDRIDGE, Rev. Philip. (1702—1751.) 28, 53, 81, 118, 142, 149, 196, 220, 246, 326, 330, 362, 366, 398, 472, 477, 490, 497, 546, 565, 569, 570, 571, 575, 597, 648, 649, 650.
DOWNTON, Rev. Henry. (1818—) 630.
DUFFIELD, Rev. George. (1818—) 288, 393.
DUNN, Prof. Robinson Potter. (1825—1867.) 598.
DWIGHT, Rev. John Sullivan. (1812—) 660.
DWIGHT, Rev. Timothy. (1752—1817.) 237, 515.
DYER, Rev. Sidney. 628.

EDMESTON, James. (1791—1867.) 64, 357, 425, 548.
ELLERTON, Rev. John. (1826—) 58.
ELLIOTT, Miss Charlotte. (1789—1871.) 270, 285.
ELLIOTT, Mrs. Julia Anne. (—1841.) 76.
ELVEN, Rev. Cornelius. (1797—) 272.
ENFIELD, Prof. William. (1741—1797.) 167.
EVANS, Rev. Jonathan. (1749—1809.) 188.

FABER, Rev. Frederick William. (1814—1863.) 184, 227, 449, 465, 512.
FABRICIUS, Rev. Jacob. (1593—1654.) 427.
FAWCETT, Rev. John. (1739—1817.) 21, 128, 210, 513.

INDEX OF AUTHORS.

FORTUNATUS, Venantius. (530—609.) 113.
FRANCIS, Rev. Benjamin. (1734—1799.) 406, 539.
FRANKE, Rev. August Hermann. (1663—1727.) 396.

GAMBE, Rev. Hervey Doddridge. (1822—) 292.
GERHARDT, Rev. Paul. (1606—1676). 178, 474, 475.
GIBBONS, Rev. Thomas. (1720—1785.) 535.
GILL, Thomas Hornblower. (1819—) 20, 213.
GILMORE, Rev. Joseph H. 350.
GOUGH, Benjamin. (1805—) 563.
GOULD, Rev. Sabine Baring. (1834—) 527.
GRANT, Sir Robert. (1785—1838.) 108.
GRIGG, Rev. Joseph. (—1768.) 250, 406.
GUSTAVUS ADOLPHUS. (1594—1632.) 427.
GUYON, Madame Jeanne M. B. de la M. (1648—1717.) 403.

HALL, Mrs. E. M. 344.
HAMMOND, Rev. William. (—1783.) 34, 143.
HANKEY, Miss Kate. 561, 564.
HARBAUGH, Rev. Henry. (1818—1867.) 655.
HARMER, Rev. Samuel Young. (1809—) 631.
HART, Rev. Joseph. (1712—1768.) 16, 43, 223.
HASTINGS, Thomas. (1784—1872.) 22, 70, 199, 229, 238, 239, 252, 549, 560.
HAWEIS, Rev. Thomas. (1732—1820.) 197, 242, 459.
HEATH, George. 388.
HEBER, Bp. Reginald. (1783—1826.) 8, 94, 159, 547.
HEMANS, Mrs. Felicia Dorothea. (1794—1835.) 593.
HERBERT, Rev. George. (1593—1632.) 302.
HERVEY, Rev. James. (1714—1758.) 125.
HILL, Rev. Rowland. (1744—1833.) 243, 415.
HILLHOUSE, Abraham Lucas. (1792—1859.) 317.
HOPE, Henry Joy McCracken. (1809—1872.) 877.
How. Rev. William Walsham. (1823—) 134, 175, 179.
HUMPHREYS, Rev. Joseph. (1720—) 33.
HUNTER, Rev. William. (1811—) 373, 636.
HUPTON, Rev. Job. (1762—1849.) 223.
HYDE, Mrs. Ann Bradley. (—1872.) 489.

INGEMANN, Bernhardt Severin. (1789—1862.) 527.

JOHN of Damascus. (About 750.) 98.
JONES, Rev. Edmund. (1732—1765,) 281.
JOSEPH of the Studium. (—883.) 606, 635.

KEBLE, Rev. John. (1792—1866.) 62.
KEITH, George. 380.
KELLY, Rev. Thomas. (1769—1855.) 72, 189, 203, 208, 340, 348, 355, 370, 386, 495, 521, 528, 579, 608.
KEMPTHORNE, Rev. John. (1775—1838.) 4.
KEN, Bp. Thomas. (1637—1711.) 43, 60, 61.
KETHE, Rev. William. 103.
KEY, Francis Scott. (1799—1843.) 308.

LAURENTIUS, Laurenti. (1660—1722.) 605.
LOWRY, Rev. Robert. 633.
LYNCH, Rev. Thomas Toke. (1818—1871.) 172.
LYTE, Rev. Henry Francis. (1793—1847.) 71, 312, 404, 419, 441, 478, 562, 602, 656.

MACKAY, Mrs. Margaret. 585.
MACKAY, Rev. W. P. 312.
MADAN, Rev. Martin. (1726—1790.) 143, 347, 611.
MAHMIED, S. P. 341.
MALAN, Rev. Cæsar Henri Abraham. (1787—1864.) 598, 603.
MANT, Bp. Richard. (1776—1848.) 5.
MARCH, Rev. Daniel. (1816—) 536.
MARRIOTT, Rev. John. (1780—1825.) 580.
MARSDEN, Rev. Joshua. 552.
MASON, Rev. John. (—1694.) 239, 507.

MASON, Rev. William. (1725—1797.) 74.
MASSIE, Richard. 457.
MATSON, Rev. William Tidd. 316.
MAUDE, Mrs. Mary Fawler. 494.
MCCHEYNE, Rev. Robert Murray. (1813—1843.) 442.
MCDONALD, Rev. William. (1820—) 304.
MEDLEY, Rev. Samuel. (1738—1799.) 195, 334, 338.
MILLER, Rev. William Edward. (1766—1839.) 506.
MILTON, John. (1608—1674.) 95.
MONSELL, Rev. John Samuel Bewley. (1811—) 144, 382, 610.
MONTGOMERY, James. (1771—1854.) 2, 15, 49, 67, 87, 96, 110, 154, 163, 170, 176, 185, 232, 278, 378, 431, 492, 502, 505, 519, 533, 534, 542, 551, 555, 566, 576, 590, 599, 626.
MOORE, Thomas. (1779—1852.) 238.
MORAVIAN COLLECTION. 407.
MORRISON, Rev. John. (1749—1798.) 147, 418.
MOTE, Rev. Edward, 410.
MUHLENBURG, Rev. William Augustus. (1796—) 249.

NEALE, Rev. John Mason. (1818—1866.) 13, 57, 98, 113, 223, 253, 309, 520, 604, 606, 616, 617, 618, 635, 652.
NELSON, Rev. David. (1793—1844.) 372.
NETTLETON, Rev. Asahel. (1783—1844.) 257.
NEWTON, John. (1725—1807.) 17, 85, 75, 91, 231, 274, 291, 301, 306, 314, 332, 342, 351, 420, 429, 479, 526, 572, 573, 637.
NOEL, Hon. and Rev. Gerard Thomas. (1782—1851.) 501.
NOEL, Rev. Baptist Wriothesley. 37.
NUNN, Miss Marianne. (1779—1847.) 429.

OCCUM, Rev. Sampson. (1723—1792.) 257.
ONDERDONK, Bp. Henry Ustick. (1789—1858.) 244, 537.
OSLER, Edward. (1798—1863.) 4.

PALMER, Rev. Ray. (1808—) 44, 181, 284, 289, 320, 331, 498, 638.
PARR, Miss Harriet. 66.
PERRONET, Rev. Edward. (—1792.) 217.
PETERS, Mrs. Mary Bowly. (—1856.) 428.
PIRIE, Rev. Alexander. (—1804.) 214.
PRENTISS, Mrs. Elizabeth Payson. (1819—) 376.

RAFFLES, Rev. Thomas. (1788—1863.) 279, 627.
RAWSON, George. (1807—). 45, 415.
REED, Rev. Andrew. (1787—1862.) 47, 319.
RIPPON, Rev. John. (1751—1836.) 595.
ROBERT II, King of France. (972—1021.) 44.
ROBERTSON, Rev. William. (—1743.) 488.
ROBINSON, Rev. Robert. (1735—1790.) 162, 311.
ROTHE, Rev. John Andrew. (1688—1758.) 324.
RYLAND, Rev. John. (1753—1825.) 365.

SCHENK, Rev. Heinrich Theodor. (—1727.) 609.
SCHMOLKE, Rev. Benjamin. (1672—1737.) 480.
SEAGRAVE, Rev. Robert. (1693—) 358.
SEARS, Rev. Edmund Hamilton. (1810—) 165, 166.
SELINA, Countess of Huntingdon. (1707—1791.) 256.
SHIRLEY, Hon. and Rev. Walter. (1725—1786.) 73, 313.
SILESIUS, Johann Angelus. (1624—1677.) 310.
SIMPSON, Mrs. Jane Bell Cross. 524.
SINGLETON, Robert Corbet. 207.
SMITH, Mrs. Caroline Sprague. 65.
SMITH, Rev. Samuel Francis. (1808—) 239, 550, 600, 639.
SPITTA, Rev. Carl Johann Philipp. (1801—1859.) 457.
STEELE, Miss Anne. (1717—1778.) 131, 140, 193, 300, 423, 464, 468.
STENNETT, Rev. Joseph. (1663—1713.) 77.

INDEX OF AUTHORS.

STENNETT, Rev. Samuel. (1727—1795.) 11, 88, 183, 325, 607, 612.
STEPHEN of St. Sabas. (725—794.) 253.
STOCKER, John. 46.
STOWELL, Rev. Hugh. (1799—1865.) 29. 578.
SWAIN, Rev. Joseph. (1761—1796.) 107, 395.

TAPPAN, Rev. William Bingham. (1794—1849.) 173, 629.
TATE & BRADY. 80, 148, 419, 432, 447, 658.
TERSTEEGEN, Gerhardt. (1697—1769.) 269, 409.
THOMSON, Rev. John. (1782—1818.) 124.
TURING, Rev. Godfrey. (1823—) 164, 592.
THRUPP, Miss Dorothy Ann. (1779—1847.) 356.
THRUPP, Rev. Joseph Francis. 169.
TOPLADY, Rev. Augustus Montague. (1740—1778.) 190, 215, 216, 255, 287, 369, 476, 583.
TURNER, Rev. Daniel. (1710—1798.) 283.
TUTTIETT, Rev. Lawrence. (1825—) 594.
TWELLS, Rev. Henry. (1823—) 40.

UPHAM, James. 361.

VAN ALSTYNE, Mrs. Fanny Jane Crosby. (1823—). 276.
VAUGHAN, Henry. (1621—1695.) 620.
VICTORINUS SANTOLIUS. (1630—1697.) 30.
VOKE, Mrs. 541.

WALFORD, Rev. W. W. 39.
WARDLAW, Rev. Ralph. (1779—1853.) 646.
WARING, Miss Anna Lætitia. 456, 462.
WATTS, Rev. Isaac. (1674—1748.) 6, 7, 10, 12, 26, 31, 42, 54, 50, 63, 78, 79, 82, 83, 84, 85, 86, 89, 90, 100, 101, 102, 104, 105, 106, 115, 117, 119, 120, 121, 122, 126, 129, 136, 137, 141, 145, 146, 150, 151, 168, 180,

182, 186, 192, 209, 212, 218, 219, 224, 225, 261, 263, 264, 265, 266, 268, 297, 318, 336, 363, 381, 384, 385, 397, 400, 417, 424, 439, 443, 444, 445, 446, 448, 451, 452, 454, 460, 461, 469, 470, 491, 496, 499, 503, 510, 516, 517, 536, 545, 568, 587, 588, 594, 596, 613, 614, 615, 611, 642, 645, 657.
WEISSE, Rev. Michael. (—1540.) 201.
WESLEY, Rev. Charles. (1708—1788.) 1, 19, 48, 109, 153, 161, 174, 131, 194, 200, 202, 211, 221, 232, 235, 236, 241, 254, 267, 271, 273, 278, 280, 293, 294, 295, 296, 298, 321, 328, 335, 337, 387, 389, 390, 411, 412, 426, 430, 434, 435, 436, 437, 438, 440, 453, 455, 504, 508, 509, 554, 574, 611, 622, 625, 640.
WESLEY, Rev. John. (1703—1791.) 55, 104, 192, 280, 321, 409, 474, 475, 500.
WHITE, Henry Kirke. (1785—1806.) 116, 156, 581.
WHITFIELD, Rev. Frederick. (1829—) 432.
WHITING, William. (1825—) 525.
WILLARD, Mrs. Emma C. (1787—1870.) 523.
WILLIAMS, Miss Helen Maria. (1762—1827.) 467.
WILLIAMS AND BODEN'S COLLECTION. 623.
WILLIAMS, Rev. Benjamin. 111.
WILLIAMS, Rev. Isaac. (1802—1865.) 177.
WILLIAMS, Rev. Peter. (1719—1796.) 354.
WILLIAMS, Rev. William. (1717—1791.) 354, 529.
WINGROVE, John. 307.
WINKWORTH, Miss Catharine. (1829—) 201, 396, 427, 538.
WOLCOTT, Rev. Samuel. (1813—) 577.
WORDSWORTH, Rev. Christopher. (1807—) 97, 632.

XAVIER, Francis. (1506—1552.) 333.

ZINZENDORF, Nicolaus Ludwig. (1700—1760.) 360, 500.

INDEX OF COMPOSERS.

The figures refer to the numbers of the pages.

ADAMS' CHURCH PASTORALS. 153.
AHLE, Johann Rudolph. (1625—1673.) 156, 294.
AMERICAN MELODY. 131, 135, 144, 163.
ARNE, Thomas Augustine. (1710—1778.) 218, 239.
AVISON, Charles. (1710—1770.) 316.

BACH, Johann Sebastian. (1685—1750.) 83.
BAILLOT, Pierre-Marie-Françoise de Sales. (1771—1842.) 169.
BEETHOVEN, Ludwig von. (1770—1827.) 111, 266.
BISHOP, Sir Henry Rowley. (1780—1855.) 248.
BOST, Ami. 191.
BOYD, Robert. 123.
BRADBURY, William Batchelder. (1816—1868.) 16, 18, 76, 94, 112, 116, 120, 123, 124, 128, 144, 152, 158, 161, 185, 208, 215, 245, 260.
BRISTOL COLLECTION. 241.
BULL, John (?). (1513—1628.) 296.
BURGMUELLER, Friedrich. (1804—) 277.
BURNAP, Uzziah C. (1834—) 265.
BURNEY, Charles. (1726—1814.) 54.

CAREY, Henry. (1683—1743.) 290.
CHANDLER, S. 115.
CHAPIN, Aaron. 19, 181, 226.
CHERUBINI, Maria Luigi. (1760—1842.) 21.
CHRISTIAN LYRE. 152.
CLARK, Thomas. 98, 209.
CLARKE, John. (1770—1818.) 101.
CONKEY, Ithamar. (1815—1867.) 182.
CRANE, ———. 192.
CROFT, William. (1677—1727.) 298.
CROTCH, William. (1775—1847.) 311.

DARWELL, Rev. John. 4.
DAVISSON, Ananias. 117, 195.
DAY'S (John) PSALTER. 255.
DEVEREAUX, ———. 148.
DIXON, William. 36.
DOANE, William Howard. (1832—) 123, 163, 251.
DUPUIS, Thomas Saunders. (1733—1796.) 302, 307.
DUTTON, jr., Deodatus. 23.
DYKES, Rev. John Bacchus. 5, 97, 128, 239, 262.

EBERWEIN, Traugott Maximilian. (1775—1831.) 61.
EDSON, Jonathan. 96, 154, 278.
EMERSON, Luther Orlando. (1820—) 106, 138, 190, 249.
ENGLISH MELODY. 86, 100, 154, 236, 254, 284.
EVANS, John M. 166.
EWING, Bp. Alexander. (—1873.) 200, 274.

FISCHER, William Gustavus. (1835—) 136, 250.
FLINTOFF, ———. 306.

FLOTOW, Friedrich von. (1812—) 29.
FRANCKE, Guillaume. 46, 201, 288.

GARDINER, William. (1770—1853.) 147.
GERMAN AIR. 67, 174.
GERMAN MELODY. 43. 104. 153, 159, 172. 231.
GIARDINI, Felice. (1716—1796.) 1, 11, 137, 257.
GIORNOVICHI, Jean Maria. (1745—1804.) 276.
GLAESER, Carl Gotthilf. (1784—1829.) 196.
GOULD, John Edgar. (1822—) 24, 219.
GOULD, Nathaniel D. (1781—1864.) 125, 280.
GRAPE, John T. 155.
GREATOREX, Henry Wellington. (1816—1857.) 39, 40.
GREEK MELODY. 78.

HANDEL, George Frederick. (1685—1759.) 53. 65, 93. 180, 205, 227.
HARRINGTON, Calvin Sears. 159, 168.
HARRISON, Rev. Ralph. (1748—1810.) 197, 204.
HASTINGS, Thomas. (1784—1872.) 14, 20, 22, 87, 113, 128, 146, 191, 237.
HATTON, John. 57, 243.
HAVERGAL, Rev. William Henry. (1793—1870.) 49.
HAWEIS, Rev. Thomas. (1782—1820.) 58.
HAYDN, Francis Joseph. (1732—1809.) 12, 27, 30, 41, 48.
HAYES, Philip. (1739—1797.) 309.
HAYES, William. (1708—1779.) 314.
HEROLD, Louis Joseph Ferdinand. (1791—1833.) 2, 186, 221.
HERRMAN, Nicholaus. (—1561.) 290.
HOLDEN, Oliver. (1756—1831.) 96.
HOPKINS, Rev. Josiah. (1786—1862.) 102.
HUMMEL, Johann Nepomuk. (1778—1837.) 25.

INGALLS, Jeremiah. (1764—1838.) 104, 145, 177, 273.
IRISH MELODY. 279.
IVES, jr., Elam. (1802—1864.) 279.

JENKS, Stephen. (—1856.) 130.
JOCELYN'S CHORISTER'S COMPANION. 192.
JONES, Rev. Darius Eliot. (1815—) 28.
JONES, Rev. William. (1726—1800.) 202.

KATHOLISCHES GESANGBUCH. 268.
KINGSLEY, George. (1811—) 2, 61, 119, 143, 165, 186, 188, 203, 221, 224, 224, 272.
KREUTZER, Rudolf. (1766—1831.) 68.

LAMPE, Johann Friedrich. (—1750.) 292.
LANGDON, Richard. (—1798.) 301.
LOCKHART, Charles. (—1816.) 271.
LOWRY, Rev. Robert. (1826—) 283.

INDEX OF COMPOSERS.

MAIN, Hubert Platt. (1839—) 281.
MALAN, Rev. Cæsar Henri Abraham. (1787—1864.) 15, 42, 109, 187.
MARECHIO, ———. 10, 95, 198.
MARSH, Simeon Butler. (1798—) 109, 186.
MASON, Lowell. (1792—1872.) 3, 6, 7, 8, 9, 13, 32, 33, 34, 35, 43, 45, 51, 55, 56, 64, 65, 66, 74, 82, 85, 86, 90, 99, 100, 102, 103, 107, 110, 114, 122, 129, 133, 134, 142, 149, 150, 151, 160, 167, 170, 171, 174, 176, 184, 189, 193, 196, 207, 210, 212, 222, 223, 225, 230, 244, 256, 263, 270, 280, 289, 291, 316.
McDONALD, Rev. William. (1820—) 282.
MEHUL, Etienne Henri. (1763—1817.) 213.
MENDELSSOHN-BARTHOLDY, Felix. (1809—1847.) 80, 185, 246.
MERRILL, Rev. Abraham Dow. (1796—) 285.
MILLER, William. (1810—) 160.
MITCHELL, Nahum. (1770—1853.) 211.
MONK, William Henry. 12, 27, 31, 113.
MORNINGTON, Lord Garret Wellesley. (1720—1781.) 9.
MOZART, Johann C. W. A. (1756—1791.) 59, 69, 88, 141, 130, 183.

NAEGELI, Hans Georg. (1773—1836.) 208, 210, 215.
NARES, James. (1715—1783.) 102.
NETTLETON, Rev. Asahel. (1783—1844.) 140.
NEUKOMM, Sigismund. (1778—1858.) 35.
NORRIS, Charles. (1740—1790.) 304.

OAKLEY, William Henry. (1808—) 132.
OLIVER, Henry Kemble. (1800—) 80, 293.

PARKER, Rev. Edwin Pond. (1836—) 166.
PLEYEL, Ignace. (1757—1831.) 17, 211.
POND, Sylvanus Billings. (1815—1871.) 60, 214.
PURCELL, Henry. (1658—1695.) 301.

READ, Daniel. (1757—1836.) 38, 118.
READING, John. (1690—1766.) 173.
REDHEAD, Richard. 77.
RIMBAULT, Edward Francis. (1816—) 220.
RINK, Johann C. H. (1770—1846.) 75, 209.

ROOT, George Frederick. (1820—) 75, 168, 209, 261.
ROSSINI, Gioacchino. (1792—1868.) 73, 119.
ROUSSEAU, Jean Jacques. (1712—1778.) 105.

SCHNEIDER, Friedrich. (1786—1853.) 44, 284.
SCHULZ, Johann Abraham Peter. (1747—1800.) 34.
SCOTCH MELODY. 56, 149, 164, 212, 225.
SURUBSOLE, Rev. William. (1729—1797.) 97.
SICILIAN MELODY. 233.
SMITH, Isaac. 62, 157.
SPANISH MELODY. 10, 95, 179, 198.
SPOHR, Ludwig. (1784—1859.) 311.
SWAN, Timothy. (1758—1842.) 264.
SWEETSER, Joseph E. (1825—) 267.

TALLIS, Thomas. (1529—1585.) 26, 300, 312.
TANSUR, William. (1699—1774.) 63, 232, 295.
TAYLOR, Virgil Corydon. (1817—) 121, 252.
TUCKERMAN, Samuel Parkman. (1818—) 258.

VAN ARSDALE, Philip P. (1816—) 248.
VENUA, Frederick Marc Antoine. (1788—) 84.

WARTENSEE, Xavier Schnyder von. (1786—) 108.
WEBB, George James. (1803—) 178, 245.
WEBBE, Samuel. (1740—1816.) 107, 247, 286, 287.
WEBER, Carl Maria von. (1786—1826.) 70, 71, 216.
WELSH AIR. 37.
WESLEY, Rev. Samuel. (1662—1735.) 308.
WESLEY, Samuel Sebastian. 217.
WHITE, Edward L. (—1851.) 199.
WILLCOX, John Henry. (1827—) 139.
WILLIAMS, Aaron. (1731—1776.) 37, 47, 235.
WILLIS, Richard Storrs. (1819—) 72.
WILSON, Hugh. 56, 79, 149, 225, 259.
WOODBURY, Isaac Beverly. (1819—1858.) 94, 126.
WOODMAN, Jonathan C. 194.

ZEUNER, Charles. (1795—1857.) 50, 52, 91, 175, 200, 240, 242.
ZUNDEL, John. (1815—) 136.

By the Same Editors.

HYMNS AND SONGS OF PRAISE,
FOR
PUBLIC AND SOCIAL WORSHIP,
EDITED BY
ROSWELL D. HITCHCOCK, ZACHARY EDDY,
PHILIP SCHAFF.

Musical Editors: J. K. PAINE, U. C. BURNAP.

CONTAINING

600 Pages, over 1,400 Hymns, with 450 Tunes and
Chants. Large 8vo. Price, - - - - - $2.50
Without Music, - - - - - - - - 1 75

ANSON D. F. RANDOLPH & CO.,

770 Broadway, New York.

www.ingramcontent.com/pod-product-compliance
Lightning Source LLC
Chambersburg PA
CBHW020232240426
43672CB00006B/498